Modernization, Tradition and Identity

ICAS Publications Series

The *ICAS Publications Series* consists of Monographs and Edited Volumes. The Series takes a multidisciplinary approach to issues of interregional and multilateral importance for Asia in a global context. The Series aims to stimulate dialogue amongst scholars and civil society groups at the local, regional and international levels.

The International Convention of Asia Scholars (ICAS) was founded in 1997. Its main goals are to transcend the boundaries between disciplines, between nations studied, and between the geographic origins of the Asia scholars involved. ICAS has grown into the largest biennial Asia studies event covering all subjects of Asia studies. So far six editions of ICAS have been held respectively in Leiden (1998), Berlin (2001), Singapore (2003), Shanghai (2005), Kuala Lumpur (2007) and Daejeon, South Korea (2009). ICAS 7 will be held in Honolulu from 30 March-3 April 2011.

In 2001 the ICAS secretariat was founded which guarantees the continuity of the ICAS process. In 2004 the *ICAS Book Prize* (IBP) was established in order to create by way of a global competition both an international focus for publications on Asia while at the same time increasing their visibility worldwide. Also in 2005 the *ICAS Publications Series* were established.

For more information: www.icassecretariat.org

Modernization, Tradition and Identity

The Kompilasi Hukum Islam and Legal Practice in the Indonesian Religious Courts

Euis Nurlaelawati

Amsterdam University Press

ICAS Publications Series

Monographs 4

Cover design: JB&A raster grafisch ontwerp, Delft
Layout: The DocWorkers, Almere

ISBN 978 90 8964 088 8
e-ISBN 978 90 4850 814 3
NUR 820 / 717

Table of Contents

List of Tables

Notes on Transliteration and Translations

Throughout the text I use the system of Arabic transliteration adopted by many institutions and journals in the English-speaking world. Names of personalities, organizations, and foundations, as well as the titles of books, journals and articles are rendered as they are locally spelled and transliterated, except in cases such as *baḥth al-masāil* and *majlis tarjīh*. The plural of Arabic words is written simply by adding 's' to their more familiar singular writings: thus, *fatwās* instead of *fatāwā* or *ḥadīth*s instead of *aḥādīth*. The translation of the Qur'ān follows Yusuf Ali's translation (Ali, *The Holy Qur'ān*, Washington DC: Amanah Corporation, 1989). Translations of *ḥādīth* and *fiqh* doctrines are my own where no other English translation is cited.

Acknowledgements

I am deeply indebted to a large number of people and institutions for help in conceiving and writing this book, which was originally the Ph.D. dissertation I defended at Utrecht University in December 2007. I am particularly grateful to Prof. Léon Buskens and Dr. Nico Kaptein, my supervisor and co-supervisor, whose innovative and inspiring comments and suggestions have guided my thinking, and who have helped me in numerous other ways. I would like also to convey my gratitude to Prof. Wim Stokhof, the director of the Indonesian-Netherlands Cooperation for Islamic Studies (INIS), for his help and kindness during my four years of research in Leiden. My special appreciation goes also to Dr. Dick van der Meij, Drs. Rinske Boersma, Drs. Amis Boersma, and Marise van Amersfoort for their assistance and the facilities rendered to me during my research.

Some scholars who have been involved in discussing certain parts of my research and offering their wisdom and advice and sharpening my analytical framework deserve also my sincere thanks. These include Prof. Nasr Hamid Abu Zayd, Prof. Martin van Bruinessen, Dr. Johan H. Meuleuman, Prof. Saleh Yaapar, Prof. Azyumardi Azra, Prof. Bustanul Arifin, Dr. Michael Feener and Dr. Michael Laffan. My special thanks also go to all my colleagues at the Indonesian-Netherlands Cooperation for Islamic Studies (INIS) and the International Institute for Asian Studies (IIAS). I would like also to give my thanks to all the parties who have helped me in different ways during one and half years of fieldwork in Indonesia, particularly judges at the religious courts of South and East Jakarta, Cianjur, Rangkasbitung, Bogor and Tasikmalaya, KUA officials of Cianjur and Rangkasbitung and the staffs of the Directorate of Islamic Justice of the Department of Religious Affairs. *Ibu* Rosemary Robson, who has patiently corrected and edited my English, deserves my special appreciation. My gratitude goes also to *Ibu* Wurian, who helped me translate the English summary of this dissertation into Dutch. They not only helped me solve the problems of the two languages, but also sincerely offered their motherly love during my stay in Leiden.

I am indebted to the State Islamic University Syarif Hidayatullah, Jakarta as well as the Department of Religious Affairs of the Republic of Indonesia, which gave me permission to leave my academic tasks in

Indonesia for about five years in order to study in the Netherlands and finish my research. I am also grateful to the Dutch government for providing financial support through IIAS and INIS so that I could complete this book. My thanks also to several staff members at the KITLV Library, University Library, and Van Vollenhoven Institute Library, and a number of libraries in Indonesia who have assisted me in numerous ways and made research pleasant and fruitful.

I dedicate this book to my family as an eternal source of spirit and inspiration. My father, Mansur Suherman, and my mother, Yoyoh, as well as my late-father in-law and my mother in-law have always offered their support and prayers for the success of my study. My brother and sisters, especially *Oi*, have also helped me in many ways conceive the writing of this book. My husband, Noorhaidi Hasan, has always shared his time with me in caring for our daughter and son and household, while he himself was also busy completing his study. My children, Afrouza S. Paramasita and Gema Andhika Hasan, have enriched my life. I thank all of them for having always been there for me with devotion and love.

Preface

The practice of Islamic law in Indonesia is an issue that has interested me since I was a student of the Faculty of Islamic Law at the State Institute in Islamic Studies (IAIN) in Jakarta. Although Indonesia has the largest Muslim population of any country in the world with more than 80 per cent, it is a constitutionally secular state. As a consequence of the state ambivalence toward the position of religion in the state system, demands to institutionalize Islam in politics, education, the justice system and other fields of public life have abounded. Tensions between the state and revelation implicit in Islam are thus inevitable and have had a profound impact on the development of Islamic law in Indonesia.

The resulting debate and fragmentation which have evolved from the tension are inexorably associated with the political dynamics of the state. In tandem with its attempts to establish its political control over Indonesian society, the secular Suharto's New Order regime sponsored the proposal for the ratification of an Islam-based marriage law in the early 1970s. This bill represented an attempt to reach a unification of those laws relating to the act of marriage itself and other related fields conforming to the various customary *(adat)* and religious laws. It was also a response to Indonesian women's questions about their legal position in the event of polygyny and divorce. Despite this apparently progressive gesture, Muslims perceived this proposal as being informed by political interest, as through adducing this proposal it seemed the New Order was apparently seeking to reduce the role of Islamic institutions which were beyond state control, and at the same time, strengthen the role of civil administration.

Towards the late 1980s, the attitude of the state toward Islam shifted toward accommodating Muslim interests in the legislature. One move related to the development of the religious courts was the enactment of the Islamic Judicature Act (*Undang-Undang Peradilan Agama No.1. Th 1989*), dealing with the legal procedures to be applied in the religious courts, whose process of legislation very clearly reveals the extensive role of the State, following the trend toward codification of Islamic family law attempted by the Muslim world. It must be mentioned that the attempt at codification in Indonesia has been ongoing since 1946, when the government issued the regulation of the registration of marriage, divorce, and reconciliation (*rujuk*). The early 1970s marked the development of the institution of Islamic justice in Indonesia, particularly in 1974, when it issued the Law of Marriage No. 1/1974. Although not covering all the rules on those issues under the jurisdiction of the religious court, the Law provided substantive laws on marital issues.

The further attempt at codification was seen in the issuance of the Presidential Instruction No. 1 of 1991 on the *Kompilasi Hukum Islam di Indonesia* (Compilation of Islamic Law in Indonesia), compiling Islamic rules on three familial areas of law, including marriage, inheritance and endowment, from diverse numbers of classical *fiqh* texts. This further enhanced my interest in the issue. The *kompilasi* takes the form of a modern legal text in the Indonesian language, whose creation involved not only legal experts but also religious scholars and leaders from different Islamic organizations. It is therefore considered to be the product of the State's nationalizing Islamic law and, at the same time, the consensus of Indonesian *'ulam^a^*. It was issued to administer the Islamic familial problems and unify the legal reference of the religious court judges. Introducing a number of reform ideas reflecting the accommodation of local customs, state policy and the current demands, the *kompilasi* has contributed to the discursive changes in the courts as well as society.

The experience of lecturing on a number of subjects related to the issue of Islamic family law, which I began doing in 2000, has made me better acquainted with the issue and granted me deep understanding of the problematic application of the law and the ambiguous attitude of the society, as well as the state apparatus, toward the law. I learned that the very existence of the *kompilasi* as well as the Law of Marriage No. 1/1974 is still debated. The debates ensue in numerous socio-religious spaces, from mosques to court rooms, and influence the way judges issue verdicts on the cases brought before them. Such a phenomenon has been clearly expressed and illustrated in public discourse, debate, and general attitudes within the society I have witnessed and heard.

I understood that such a phenomenon is based on the domination of Islamic legal doctrines found in the classical texts, and that there are several relevant factors. I started this research project in 2002 with the intention of contributing to the development of the socio-legal studies in Indonesia by using the theory of legal sociology developed by some modern scholars.

Based on extensive fieldwork, document analysis, and numerous interviews, in this study I shall observe the attitude of the religious courts' judges toward the *kompilasi* when resolving familial cases brought before them. While demonstrating that they have referred to the *kompilasi*, I also find that a number of judgments are still grounded on the *fiqh* texts, the legal texts to which the judges were recommended to refer, before the issuance of the *kompilasi*. There are multiple reasons why the *fiqh* texts remain central in the domain of the religious court. The judges claim that referring to the classical *fiqh* texts is still necessary in many cases, especially in order to maintain their public utility and avoid decisions deviating from the classical Islamic legal rules prescribed in the *fiqh* texts. Behind these reasons, the dominant position of the *fiqh* texts cannot be dissociated with the hesitation of the religious court to dispel its traditional peculiarities, especially the tradition of its judges to quote open *fiqh* texts based on their preferences. In addition, in the eyes of the judges the *kompilasi* is not binding enough as it is issued only in the form of presidential instruction.

Reviewing hundreds of documents containing verdicts issued by the religious court, I discover that while in a number of cases judges have reached uniformity in making judgments, in other cases, particularly inheritance, they still often produced divergent decisions. This is because in those cases on which the *kompilasi* stands differently from the *fiqh* texts, judges are not inclined to refer to the *kompilasi*. In fact, there is some reluctance among them to fully accept the *kompilasi,* and this has resulted in uncertainty of the legal transaction among justice seekers in the religious court.

I find that the reluctance of the judges to rely on the *kompilasi* reflects the legal awareness of Indonesian Muslims and their discursive formation. They consider the opinions of the *'ulamā'* to be frequently more acceptable and suitable to real conditions and problems facing the society. Therefore, many of the disputants, particularly those involved in divorce cases, come to the court merely to legalize their actions formally. Disputes on diverse Islamic legal issues inevitably occur among Indonesian Muslims, as reflected in the words like "this (action) is lawful according to Islamic law, but it is illegal according to the state law." These facts confirm that the State project to nationalize Islamic law has not necessarily resulted in modernizing the legal framework of Muslim society.

Introduction

The twentieth-century Muslim world witnessed a phenomenal development in the codification of Islamic family law. Initiated by the Turkish Government which issued the Ottoman Law of Family Rights (*Qānūn Qarār al-Ḥuqūq al-'Ā'ilah al-Uthmāniyya*) in 1917, the trend towards codification was soon adopted by other Muslim countries. In 1920 Egypt ratified Law No. 25, which was followed by Law No. 25 of 1929. The ratification of these two laws introduced some fundamental reforms in various aspects of Islamic family law, particularly divorce[1]. Iran followed Egypt by issuing the Marriage Law codifying rules of marriage and divorce in 1931, which was later replaced by the Family Protection Act in 1967 (*Qānūn al-Himayat al-Khaniwad*). This act was abrogated by the Protection of Family Rights of 1975, which was banned following the Iranian Revolution in 1979.[2] In 1957, Tunisia also applied the Code of Personal Status No. 66 of 1956 (*Majallat al-Aḥwāl al-Shakhṣiyya*), which underwent several amendments in Law No. 70 of 1958, Law No. 77 of 1959, Law No. 61 of 1961, Law No. 17 of 1964, Law No. 49 of 1966 and Law No. 7 of 1980.[3] Likewise, after the declaration of independence in 1957, Morocco issued the so-called *Mudawwana al-Aḥwāl al-Shakhṣiyya*, which was formally applied in 1958.[4]

The same phenomenon occurred in other parts of the Muslim world. The new Muslim nation of Pakistan, for an example, followed the trend through its Marriage and Family Laws issued in June 1956, which was then modified through the ratification of the Muslim Family Law Ordinance of 1961.[5] In Southeast Asia, the attempt at codification was initiated by Malaysia with the introduction of the Muhammedan Marriage Ordinance No. 5 of 1880, followed by other enactments such as the Registration of Muhammadan Marriages and Divorce Enactment in 1885, in force in the United Malay States; Perak, Selangor, Negeri Sembilan, and Pahang, and the Divorce Regulation of 1907, applied to the Non-United Malay States, and then the Islamic Family Act (*Undang-Undang Keluarga Islam*) in 1983.[5]

Indonesia is another Southeast Asian country which has attempted to codify rules in Islamic family law. Soon after independence in 1945, Indonesia introduced Act (*Undang-Undang*) No. 22 of 1946 on Pendaftaran *Nikah, Talak,* and *Rujuk* (the registration of marriage, divorce, and reconciliation) which was applied throughout Java. Under Law No. 32 of 1954, its enforcement was expanded to include all parts of the country. A significant development occurred when the Government introduced what has been termed the Marriage Law in 1974, in which reform ideas were more widely accommodated. Given that this law deals with only marriage, divorce, and reconciliation issues, Indonesia felt a necessity to enact a new code to cover other domains of Islamic family law. In 1991, the Government issued a Presidential Instruction (*Inpres*) on the Socialization of the Compilation of Islamic Law in Indonesia (*Kompilasi Hukum Islam di Indonesia*), henceforth referred to as the *kompilasi,* which covers the administration of the issues of marriage, inheritance, and endowment. The issuing of this instruction ushered in a new phase in the history of Islamic law in modern Indonesia.

I From *Fiqh* Texts to a Systematized Legal Code

There is no doubt that the trend towards codification in the Muslim world has been accompanied by an increasing process of secularization, which demanded a reformulation of the concept of the application of Islamic family law.[6] In this context, some countries have seen codification as a must to answer contemporary challenges, especially because of the advantages it offers in providing uniformity, systematization, and accessibility to their legal system. Therefore the primary aim of codification is to unify rules in Islamic family law or create the sole frame of reference which will allow familial issues to be entered into the process of judicial decision.[7] At the same time, it is intended to systematize Islamic rules in a modern legal form and national (vernacular) languages, to make them easily accessible to judges, lawyers, other interested individuals, and the general public. Some other countries have seen codification as an essential response to the growing demand for certainty in the legal status of women in particular, and the assumption that the classical books of *fiqh* could no longer anticipate the sorts of legal questions likely to arise in present-day society.[8] Consequently, the codification was intended to introduce some changes in the application of Islamic family law. Through the codification, for instance, polygamy has been limited, a husband's right to unilateral divorce has been limited, and the notion of obligatory bequest has been introduced into the law of inheritance.

One remarkable example of this trend is the *kompilasi*, which was issued by the Indonesian Government in an attempt both to achieve the uniformity in the application of Islamic family law among Indonesian Muslims and to cope with the legal needs and challenges of the present time. In spite of the debate on the use of the word "*kompilasi*" and the legal status under which it is enforced, which I shall discuss in detail later, all judges in Indonesian religious courts have been without exception requested to refer to the *kompilasi* when solving the familial cases brought before them. As functionaries of the law, they have authority and are responsible for its application, so that unification of laws and thereby certainty in legal transactions among Indonesian Muslims can be achieved.

The issuing of the *kompilasi* complemented the reform of the religious judicial system in Indonesia, which had previously witnessed the ratification of the Religious Judicature Act in 1989. This Act not only reinforced the position of the Indonesian religious courts but also unified their jurisdiction. Besides setting out legal procedures to be followed uniformly by the religious court judges, the Act stipulates that the religious courts have jurisdiction over the issues of marriage, inheritance, and endowment. With the broadening of their jurisdiction, judges of the religious courts need a substantive law as a reference tool when making judgments.

It is worth noting that before the issuing of the *kompilasi*, judges in the Indonesian religious courts decided legal cases brought before them largely on the basis of "classical *fiqh* texts" (authoritative manuals). It is true that since 1974 there has been a law of marriage to which judges can refer in resolving marital cases. Since it deals only with marital issues and still leaves several of these unanswered; *fiqh* doctrines, however, remained significant references. The Islamic legal thought reflected in such texts was usually identified as "jurist law" and was characterized by its focus on the casuistic method. On the one hand, as a jurist law, the *fiqh* texts were largely hypothetical rather than reality-oriented. On the other hand, the casuistry of *fiqh* texts is closely related to the structure of legal concepts, which was the outcome of an analogical way of thinking. As a consequence, there was no distinct structure of law which could guarantee certainty in legal transactions in society.[9] Therefore, in making their decisions the judges remained heavily influenced by *madhhab* affiliations, in which subjective preferences significantly determined what they considered the truth. This situation resulted in ambiguity.[10]

The phenomenon of the lack of "positive law" has also had a consequence on the discursive formation of Indonesian Muslims, whose socio-political world was often fragmented into *madhhab* and other equivalent groupings. Disputes arising from *madhhab* differences therefore constitute a striking element in their discourse. The ratification of Law No. 22 of 1946 and Law No. 32 of 1954 on Pendaftaran *Nikah, Talak,* and *Rujuk* (the registration of marriage, divorce, and reconciliation), as well as the Law on Marriage of 1974, which had adopted a number of Islamic doctrines on marital issues, did not eliminate such a fragmentation. Ambivalence in ways of viewing Islamic law is still apparent from time to time in society. People consider Islamic law an entity which should be separated from positive law. Addressing a case, they repeatedly argue, for instance, "*Ini sah menurut hukum Islam tapi tidak sah menurut pandangan negara* (This case is legal according to Islamic law, but illegal in the view of positive law)" or vice-versa. In this respect, they consider Islamic law the sole determinant of the validity of their legal acts and the State law merely as the administrative justification. Consequently, uncertainty is virtually unavoidable.

The situation was exacerbated by the fact that the procedure in the Islamic courts still followed the traditional requirements which, even in the early 1920s, according to C. Snouck Hurgronje, were no longer suitable to the needs of a modern society.[11] Accordingly, as Daniel S. Lev put it, it appeared to be haphazard in the sense that judges often established facts in whatever reasonable way they could find.[12] Witnesses were brought by the litigants themselves and tended to reaffirm their statements. The cases were moreover rarely examined carefully by the judges. If litigants failed to bring enough witnesses or evidence, personal oaths were accorded profound authority. Documentary material had not commonly been required to be put forward as evidence. Although some changes, especially the adoption of documentary material as evidence, had crept in over time, any such adaptations were characteristically casual. In this respect, as Lev has observed, there were often arguments between judges or judges and clerks about what kind of proof the court should accept. While judges or clerks who had been influenced by civil judicial example often wanted to examine a testimony and to check it against the documents and other material, those who were still strongly tied to the traditional process of legal transaction accepted as true whatever the litigants and witnesses said.[13]

This paradigm calls to mind what Weber identified as the law traditions of patrimonial societies, characterized by "arbitrary, *ad hoc* lawmaking" and the "uncertainty of legal rights."[14] Weber explained that the arbitrary, *ad hoc* lawmaking situation was related to the patrimonial context of legal administration, in which lies the locus of "*Qadi*-justice," whose jurisdiction is bound to sacred tradition and is often a highly formalistic interpretation.[15] As Weber saw it, *Qadi*-justice was conducted in terms of subjective decisions rather than in terms of rules. This was typical of all patrimonial systems and genuinely related to charismatic justice.

Weber observed that a radical change occurred during the Enlightenment era, which stimulated a transfer from the patrimonial tradition of law to a systematic, rational, and abstract legal code, characterized by the "reasons for reliability of the law and freedom of the individual."[16] The relevance of the *kompilasi* to Weber's discussions of the different principles of rationalization at work when history was undergoing a so-called rupture lies in the attempt of the former to "rationalize" Islamic law more attuned to the structured, rational, modern form of law. In fact, the *kompilasi* presented a codified system of substantive Islamic family laws and legal procedures in the courts, which had previously been scattered throughout various classical texts and were expressed in the Arabic language, in a more systematic and structured way using the Indonesian language. With the application of the *kompilasi*, Indonesian Muslims are hoping to understand the laws pertaining to familial cases which arise and the procedures to resolve the cases. At the same time, judges can systematically explore the legal basis of their judicial practices and decisions on the cases put before them.

II The Focus of the Study

This study concentrates on the judicial practices and judgments of judges in the Indonesian religious courts since the *kompilasi*, which when issued indubitably introduced a new type of authoritative text, the legislated code. It emerged as a substantive law systematizing and compiling in one volume the Islamic legal rules, particularly family law, derived from various *fiqh* texts. The *kompilasi* is not legislation, however. It can be called a codification, or *fiqh* in the form of legislation.[17] The *kompilasi* is divided into three books. Book One addresses marriage and divorce law. Book Two covers inheritance. Book Three is about endowment (*waqf*). The material is subdivided by topic into books, chapters, and articles, beginning with a chapter addressing general provisions, followed by chapters treating specific subject areas in each book.

This study examines how judges in the Indonesian Islamic courts accept, treat, and debate the *kompilasi* by looking particularly at the ways they decide the legal cases put before them. This study also links the levels of acceptance of the *kompilasi* among the judges with broader debates on Islamic law among Islamic legal observers, academics, activists, *'ulamā'*, and society at large. Next, this study explores the factors which contribute to the acceptance of the *kompilasi*. By doing so, it sets out both to explain important dynamics in the history of Islamic justice in Indonesia, and to portray the shifts in the legal awareness among Muslims in the country.

This study, therefore, places an emphasis on the rupture in the history of the Islamic legal practices of Indonesian Muslims after the issuing of the *kompilasi*. As I shall discuss in more detail later, the *kompilasi* is the most important document on the *shari'a* promulgated in modern Indonesia. In contrast to the Indonesian Marriage Law No. 1 of 1974, applicable to all Indonesians, regardless of their religion, and thus national in character, the *kompilasi* constitutes a specific "Muslim Code" which serves as a substantive law for judges within the jurisdiction of the institutions of religious court in solving the cases submitted to them. It is an example of how the rules of *fiqh* have been translated into bureaucratic formulae. Its character as a substantive law makes it distinguishable from the Religious Judicature Act No. 7 of 1989. The latter is a formal law regulating the position of the religious court within the national legal system, plus the composition and jurisdiction of the court and the law on applicable court procedure. In other words, the *kompilasi* is a product of the rationalization of law, which signified a shift from an open and arbitrary to a codified and legislated form of law, a guide to the actual practices and judgments of judges in the Indonesian religious courts. By examining the actual practices and judgments of the judges, this study endeavors to trace the process of the rationalization of the law taking place in the Indonesian religious courts. Focusing on such documents as the judgments of judges in the Islamic courts is of importance, as Durkheim noted, since a legal document "represents a bringing together of socially constituted and enduring legal principles with individually constituted and *ad hoc* negotiated terms."[19] A document text plays an important role in the system of the reproduction of law. Through the document text, the law was incorporated into the world.

When I began my research, a judge to whom I first spoke told me that the *kompilasi* is not a law. He complained that the secular features of the *kompilasi*, as shown in its adoption of *adat* law for instance, are much more dominant than its Islamic element. He went on to state that as a judge he should be very critical of the *kompilasi* and that *fiqh* texts possibly remain the most authoritative sources to which to refer. Another judge took the same line of argument in discussing the *kompilasi*, particularly its position in relation to the classical *fiqh* doctrine of marriage and divorce. In his opinion, the *kompilasi* is a set of State rules which cannot be given the same footing as the classical *fiqh* texts.

Notwithstanding the diversity of opinions which may be found among judges, what they have to say is both crucial and relevant to my research findings. When I read and scrutinized their judgments and identified the legal bases of their decisions, I found that although they normally refer to the rules in the *kompilasi*, the position of the *fiqh* texts remains fairly unchallenged. It is apparent that the *kompilasi* has failed to dislodge the central position of the *fiqh* texts in the eyes of judges in the Indonesian religious courts. They are trapped in what can be referred to as a problem of dual-validity, which demands they provide both a religious legitimacy and a national, legal basis when passing judgments on the cases brought before them. Adopting a modern legal form and system, it is hoped the *kompilasi* will eliminate such a dual validity in the legal transactions in Muslim society, members of which often consider that the State is merely relevant to dealing with administrative affairs. In this context many *'ulamā'* do not yet see the *kompilasi* as the final definer of the legality of the legal transactions among Indonesian Muslims. This is quite problematic, as the *'ulamā'* remain the *avant-garde* religious authority in the eyes of the society, whereas the judges are considered State employees appointed to deal with Muslim familial issues brought to judicial decision before the court. In other words, the *'ulamā'* are privileged as the guardians of Islamic law in society. It is not surprising that many people are inclined to listen to and trust the legal doctrines uttered by the *'ulamā'*, which can frequently be adapted to the real situations confronting society.

In detail, major questions to be answered in this study are:

1. Has the *kompilasi* been effectively taken as a reference by the judges, and what is the position of the classical *fiqh* texts in their judgments?
2. Is the *kompilasi* effective in providing a solid legal basis for the judges in rendering decisions, by supplementing or replacing citations from classical *fiqh* texts?
3. To what extent is Islamic law interpreted by the State grounded among and accepted by judges of religious courts?
4. Has application of the *kompilasi* caused actual practices and legal decisions of the judges to become "certain" and "structured"?
5. Does the State often play a crucial role in defining the directions of its societal discourses, and how does the society respond to State policies, particularly in terms of Islamic law?

Using the case of the Indonesian religious court, this study seeks to contribute to the scholarly discussion on Islamic legal practices in Indonesia. The decisive move from "*Qadi*-justice" to legislated code, from open to closed Islamic law texts, represents both the key instance of discursive transformation and an important backdrop to the changes which have occurred. A transformation in society, which consequently changes its collective representation, can be seen in the changes in the legal administration and judgments. Shifts in the construct of legal judgments, for instance, spell out not only parallel developments in bureaucratic administration but also alterations in physical space and changes in the space of knowledge. Focusing on the legal judgments and practices, the hope of this study is to provide an empirically rich analysis revealing the extent of the religious court judges' acceptance of Islamic law interpreted by the State in *kompilasi*.

So far there has been no study focusing on the actual practices and judgments of judges in the Indonesian religious courts. A number of the studies which do exist are simply concerned with the historical background and the contents of the *kompilasi*. At most, the studies attempt to examine political aspects behind the issuing of this Presidential Instruction. These include, for instance, Juhaya S. Praja (1991), *Hukum Islam di*

Indonesia: Perkembangan dan Pembentukan (Islamic Law in Indonesia: Development and Formation); Abdurrahman (1992), *Kompilasi Hukum Islam di Indonesia (The Compilation of Islamic Law in Indonesia)*; Mohammad Mahfud (eds) (1993), *Peradilan Agama dan Kompilasi Hukum Islam dalam Tata Hukum Indonesia (Islamic Judicature and the Compilation of Islamic Law in the Indonesian Law Order)*; Busthanul Arifin (1996), *Pelembagaan Hukum Islam di Indonesia: Akar Sejarah, Hambatan, dan Prospeknya (Institutionalization of Islamic Law in Indonesia: Its Historical Roots, Hindrances, and Prospects)*; Marzuki Wahid (2001), *Fiqh Mazhab Negara: Kritik atas Politik Hukum Islam di Indonesia (The State Fiqh: Critique of the Policy of Islamic Law in Indonesia)*; and Ahmad Imam Mawardi's chapter entitled "The Political Backdrop of the Enactment of the Compilation of Islamic Laws in Indonesia," in Arskal Salim and Azyumardi Azra (eds) (2003), *Shari'a and Politics in Modern Indonesia*, 125-47.

In addition to these, there are a number of works touching upon the issue of the *kompilasi* on the broader context of Islamic legal development in Indonesia. Notable examples are John R. Bowen (1998), "You May Not Give It Away: How Social Norms Shape Islamic Law in Contemporary Indonesian Jurisprudence," *Islamic Law and Society* 5, 3: 382-408. M.B. Hooker (1999), "The State and *Syariah* in Indonesia 1945-1995," in Timothy Lindsey (ed), *Indonesia, Law and Society*, 97-110; and Mark Cammack (1999), "Inching towards Equality: Recent Developments in Indonesian Inheritance Law," Dossier 22: 1-18. Recently Bowen (2003) published a lengthy monograph, *Islam, Law and Equality in Indonesia*, examining the tension between local practice and universal faith, the relationship between the state and religion, and gender and equality in the Islamic legal discourse and practice in Indonesia. In his discussion on the *kompilasi*, Bowen demonstrates that, despite the fact that the *kompilasi* constitutes the product of the *ijmā`* of the Indonesian *'ulamā'*, it is still contested.[20] In spite of these valuable discussions, he does not touch upon the issue of the attitude of judges in giving legal bases for their judgments and on their viewpoints on the classical texts to which they are attached.

Consequently it is obvious that there is a gaping hole in the study of Islamic law in Indonesia, because an observation and analysis of the Islamic legal practice and discourse have not been undertaken adequately. This hole needs to be filled, and this kind of study contributes not only to the sociology of Muslim society, but also to the way State policies and law should be observed and evaluated.

III Methods

This research involves both bibliographical and empirical investigations. The bibliographical research has been tackled by surveying a number of relevant libraries and research institutes, and consulting books, articles, academic theses, journals, statistic data, and research reports.

The second part of this study contains empirical research conducted during a period of approximately one-and-a-half years of fieldwork in Indonesia. The research was undertaken in two periods. The first period lasted one year, from September 2002 to August 2003, and the second only three-and-a-half months, from February to April 2005, as a supplement to confirm the data gained during the initial fieldwork. The research was undertaken in various districts in Jakarta and West Java, including Cianjur, Lebak (Rangkasbitung), Bogor, Tasikmalaya, and Cibinong.

During these fieldwork periods, I interviewed several dozen judges and relevant officials of the religious courts I visited. These interviews were designed to gain an understanding of how they have responded to the application of the *kompilasi*, its legal status, and enforcement. These interviews were also intended to discover their opinions of the contents and reforms in the *kompilasi*. A number of prominent Muslim scholars in Indonesia and officials in the Ministry of Religious Affairs, particularly those employed in the Directorate of Religious Justice, were also interviewed. Besides being an aid to comprehending their opinion on the application of the *kompilasi*, the purpose of these interviews was also to elicit their responses to the judicial attitudes of the judges.

Moreover, during the fieldwork periods, I collected 118 judgments chosen randomly from the religious courts of Rangkasbitung, Cianjur, Bogor, Tasikmalaya, and South and East Jakarta, mostly issued between 2001 and 2002. The judgments were read and checked carefully to explore what kind of legal reference had been used. Through the material provided by the judgements, the character and condition of cases plus the substance of the decisions have also been examined, so as to find out whether or not the legal bases taken by judges are relevant. Examining the judgments makes it possible to discover whether or not the judges still retain their personal legal preferences in pronouncing decisions on the cases brought before them.

In addition, I attended more than thirty hearings at the courts. After hearings I discussed the details of cases with the judges concerned and members of their staff. Most of the cases concerned matters relating to marriage and divorce. By sitting in on formal court sessions, I was able to acquire important insights into the discretion exercised by religious courts judges in solving cases and also into the litigants' understanding of the Islamic legal system. In other words, undertaking this activity helped me comprehend the legal tendency as well as judicial discretion of the judges in solving cases much better and to gain a better understanding of to what extent society, particularly the litigants, knows the law, and the real problems which led them to go to court in the first place. These activities especially helped me to recognize the conflict and contradictions between the judges and litigants in understanding the Islamic legal rules as prescribed in the *kompilasi*. I was then repeatedly struck by the conspicuous nature of some litigants' lack of knowledge of the judicial system, particularly those from remote villages. At the same time they also shed light on how in some cases the judges decided to take an approach other than what is set in the *kompilasi* in solving cases, and how this determined that cultural understanding and the idea of the public good are relevant to it.

Such data is then complemented by the information gained from the interviews with a number of litigants. Some twenty-three litigants in all were interviewed. It is interesting that the litigants, particularly women, felt no inhibitions in airing their problems to me, although I mentioned that I had come to sit in for research purposes. Instead, they appeared to be happy that there are persons who are ready to listen to their complaints and to whom they can express their feelings about both their opponents' attitudes and the judicial process. Therefore, while I was sitting waiting for judges and/or for the court sessions, I could talk informally to both litigants and the family members accompanying them. In relation to the modern concept of gender and reformed rules on issues like polygamy, these interviews illustrate that women, particularly villagers, do not speak with the same voice as the feminists who struggle for equality. They also demonstrate that both men and women have their own strategies with which to handle their cases in the courts. Finally, they also gave me an understanding that several litigants' decisions to bring cases to the courts were not necessarily motivated by the implementation of the Islamic law, but by the need for the legitimacy of the State to endorse their legal acts.

Data obtained from observation of court sessions and from discussions with judges about the written records and legal awareness in society in solving such familial issues as divorce, marriage, and inheritance were supplemented by interviews with a number of officials at the offices of Religious Affairs and prominent people in the society. I visited various offices of Religious Affairs at district level (KUA) in South Jakarta, Cianjur and Rangkasbitung, during which I succeeded in interviewing their directors and a number of their officials. From these visits, I was able to understand how the officials of the offices handled marriage issues and confirm what the judges had said about the legal awareness in society and people's attitudes to solving the familial problems they face. I was also able to witness directly how the officials treated marriage affairs flexibly. One of the objectives of this activity was to try to determine the extent to which the officials follow the rules of the State. I was especially interested in ascertaining whether or not KUA officials have co-operated with judges in solving cases or if they tend to turn to the local *'ulamā'* or village leaders.

With the help of a female teacher whom I also interviewed, I had the opportunity to interview a number of persons who admitted to not having solved problems according to the State laws, but had sought recourse to the *sharī'a*. These problems included having not divorced in the court and remarried only before an *'ulamā'*. This enriched and confirmed the data I obtained from both the judges and officials of the KUA on the issue of legal awareness in the society.

IV The Structure of the Book

This book, which consists of six chapters and is divided into two parts, starts with an introduction which explains the background, research focus, aims, methodology, and structure of the study. An overview of the trend towards codification in Muslim countries is provided, to shed some light on the application of Islamic family law in the modern period. The reason adduced for undertaking the work of the *kompilasi* and then the position of judicial practice in Indonesian religious courts before the *kompilasi* was issued are also highlighted to determine the continuity and change in the application of Islamic family law.

Chapter One discusses the formation and development of the religious courts in Indonesia. Attention is devoted to their institutional development and judicial progress, marked by the issuing of acts regulating legal procedure and references for deciding cases put to it. Details of development in its jurisdiction, legal position within the national legal system, and the character and profiles of its employees are surveyed here. The overview provides a guide with pointers for considering the shift in judicial practice among judges in the Indonesian religious courts.

Chapter Two is concerned with the creation of the *kompilasi*. This chapter attempts to reveal the political background and the historical ideas which led to the formation of this Presidential Instruction. Subsequently, this chapter discusses the process of its creation. The initial attempt and steps are then explored. This is to show how some elements have contributed to the body of the *kompilasi*. Finally, this chapter analyses the nature of the *kompilasi* in relation to the project of Islamization and legal development in Indonesia. The political interest of the State is also examined.

Chapter Three explores debates on the reforms introduced into the Islamic legal discourse in Indonesia by the *kompilasi*. This chapter first surveys those issues which rules have been reformed, and their assessment in the classical *fiqh* texts. Exploring the debates, this chapter examines the method and the character of the reform on Islamic family law in Indonesia. The arguments behind the debates are presented in order to know the tendency in the legal thinking among the Indonesian Muslim scholars. In order to make the discussion of the debate representative, the existing polarization of modernist and traditionalist Muslims is used as the standard of the debate in terms of the method of the deduction of Islamic law. The growing influence of feminism and its legal point of view are also studied so as to examine the extent of the reform on Islamic family law.

Chapter Four analyses the judgments issued by judges in the Indonesian religious courts. This chapter examines how they treat the *kompilasi* in searching for the legal foundations for their judgments. This is of importance in revealing to what extent the judges have accepted the existence of the *kompilasi* and in looking closely at the change and continuity in their judicial practice. What seems intriguing is the fact that the judges still have a marked tendency to cite the classical *fiqh* texts, while they also mention the *kompilasi* in their judgments. Some of them even dare to deviate from the provisions of the *kompilasi* when they feel that they have sufficient legal grounds from the classical *fiqh* texts, and that doctrines from the *fiqh* texts are more suitable to the public utility.

Chapter Five discusses the central position of the *fiqh* texts in the Indonesian religious courts. This chapter analyses various fundamental reasons behind the reluctance of judges to leave the *fiqh* texts behind and adopt the provisions of the *kompilasi*. In this context, judges' socio-religious background and the system of their recruitment are explored. In addition, this chapter will scrutinize how, through the quotation of the *fiqh* texts, identity and authority are maintained and negotiated by the judges. Finally, this chapter looks at how the judges creatively give a meaning to the concept of *ijtihād* in their attempts to maintain their identity and authority.

Chapter Six examines the problems facing the judges in positioning themselves in society and the complicated relationships between the judges and *'ulamā'*. In addition, this chapter analyses how Muslims have still tried to solve their familial problems by themselves, even after the issuing of the *kompilasi,* and how their attitudes affect the judicial records and practices of the religious courts. At the same time, this chapter explores to what extent the *kompilasi* has succeeded in influencing the societal legal perceptions and practices by looking at the case of divorce.

At the end this book presents a conclusion summarizing the findings of the study.

I The Indonesian Religious Courts: Institutional and Judicial Developments

The enactment of the *kompilasi* cannot be dissociated from the very existence of the religious courts in Indonesia. There are currently 331 first instance and twenty-five appellate religious courts across the country. The former have been established at regency level, and the latter at provincial level. Administratively, these courts used to fall under the Ministry of Religious Affairs, but were judicially the responsibility of the Supreme Court. Since 30 June 2004, they have fallen both administratively and judicially under the control of the Supreme Court. Their competency covers such familial issues as marriage, inheritance, and endowment. This relatively wide competence was not granted instantaneously, but achieved through political struggle and dynamics over a long period of time. Initially, the courts barely existed in recognizable form and were subject to distinct limitations. Over time, they continued to evolve, keeping pace with the developments taking place in the Indonesian legal system. The peak of this process was reached when the Indonesian government promulgated the Islamic Judicature Act (*Undang-Undang Peradilan Agama* No. 1/1989) in 1989.

The aim of this chapter is to analyze the historical dynamics of the religious courts, which are particularly important in any attempt to provide a background to an analysis of the *kompilasi*, the major theme of this study. This chapter will begin with a general overview of the religious courts.

I A Portrait of the Religious Court

The promulgation of the Islamic Judicature Act, which was followed by the issuance of the Presidential Instruction on the socialization of the *kompilasi* in 1991, might have been expected to strengthen the position of religious courts in the judicial system of Indonesia. At first glance, this does seem to have been the case, because the two regulations provide a guarantee to allow the religious court to emerge as an independent court on the same footing as the other courts – including general, military, and administrative courts. The fly in the ointment is that the issuance of these two laws has not been complemented by a systematic attempt to construct the institution of the religious courts, to the extent that they can be regarded as equal to the other courts. As far as my investigation is concerned, the attention spared by the government has not been sufficient to improve their real conditions, which are marginal and poor. The premises of a first-instance religious court are usually built on an area of about 250 m^2, and those of their appellate counterparts on area of no more than 500 m^2. Not all the Islamic courts even have their own buildings. In fact, there are twenty-seven occupying rented space. Not only are their premises cramped, not all the religious courts have been supplied with adequate office equipment. Even more damaging is that no religious court has a library. In 2001 Wahyu Widiana, the Head of the Directorate of Religious Justice in the Ministry of Religious Affairs, reported that 50 percent of the religious courts did not have computers, and 60 percent of them did not have cars[1].

The unpleasant conditions under which the religious courts have to work can be clearly seen in the examples of the religious courts where I conducted my field research. These include the religious courts in South Jakarta, East Jakarta, Central Jakarta, Bogor, Cianjur, Tasikmalaya, Cibinong, and Rangkasbitung. Generally speaking, the locations of these courts are hidden away from the public gaze. Unlike the civil courts, which can be reached easily because they are almost invariably located in the main streets, the offices of the religious courts are located in out-of-the-way places. The religious court of South Jakarta is situated far from the main street. The court of East Jakarta is located in a residential area, among houses, so that it is not properly visible from the main street. Precisely the same can be said of the religious court of Central Jakarta.

Despite the fact that, as a rule, the religious courts outside Jakarta are located in the main streets, their appearance is usually far more dilapidated than that of those in Jakarta. The religious court of Bogor is a prime example of this sad state of affairs. The religious court of Rangkasbitung is in the same or an even worse state. The director of the court, whose family happens to live in another city, namely Bandung, has to spend nights in Rangkasbitung with no bed or other facilities in a room attached to the courtroom, which also functions as a mosque. This court does indeed have a car, but it is old and was bought from a collective contribution by its judges. Complaining about the physical situation of the court and its facilities, the chairman confided to me that it would be much more pleasant to serve as a judge in Bandung or another larger city than to be chairman of the court of Rangkasbitung.[2]

The offices of the religious courts of Cianjur and Tasikmalaya present a more pleasant appearance, revealed by their well-equipped directors' offices, complete with at least a good set of chairs. Nonetheless, other facilities are poor. The religious court of Cianjur has a car, but again it is a very old one. Regrettably, none of these courts has a library. The vice-chairman of Cianjur showed me the court's book collection, but said that it could not be construed as a library, as it holds only a small number, about two hundred, of *fiqh* books and journals published by the Ministry of Religious Affairs, and is not accommodated in a separate building, but in a corridor between the judge's chamber and that of the vice-chairman of the court.

The courtrooms of every court I visited were small and plain, furnished with a long table and four seats on quite a high platform where three judges and a clerk sit when hearing cases. The table is covered with a green cloth, a color connoting peace, embellished with the logo of the Ministry of Religious Affairs. In the front of the table stand several chairs, arranged with two in the first row where plaintiff and defendant sit, or plaintiff or defendant and the witness he or she brings, and some others in rows behind. While the waiting rooms, usually situated just outside the courtroom, of the religious court of Jakarta are always busy, those of Rangkasbitung, Bogor, and Cianjur are relatively quiet. It is therefore understandable that, while the waiting rooms of the courts of Jakarta are full of chairs, those of the courts of Rangkasbitung, Bogor, and Cianjur are no more than a passageway, with one row of a few chairs.

Every court consists of a chairman, a vice-chairman, and six to eight judges, a clerk, and other administrative staff. Because of problems which will be further elaborated later, the courts are usually short of administrative personnel and even judges. Although archives exist and the administration has developed to some extent, funds for more improvement and management are still scarce. Besides the lack of financial wherewithal to make improvement, the staff dealing with cases is still largely unfamiliar with such instruments of modern technology as computers.

Almost all the judges of the courts of Cianjur and Rangkasbitung are young men and women aged between thirty and thirty-eight. The majority of the judges of the courts of South and East Jakarta are older than forty-five. This general picture is not mirrored in the age pattern of the chairmen of the courts and their vices. The chairmen of the courts of Cianjur and Rangkasbitung appear to be older than fifty. Likewise, the chairman of the religious courts of South and East Jakarta are senior judges who have had long judicial careers.[3] The fact that most of the judges in the Islamic courts in Jakarta had generally been appointed to a judicial capacity in areas outside Jakarta when they were younger, before being transferred to Jakarta or other large cities to take up positions as senior judges, is relevant to this age categorization.

The number of judges in each court in which I conducted my fieldwork fluctuates between nine and ten, including the chairman and the vice-chairman. This is the optimal situation. Judges in the religious courts outside Jakarta are always fewer in number, and in certain periods considerably even fewer than their fellow judges in Jakarta. This disproportion in the number of judges outside Jakarta is largely attributable to the fact that the cases to be tried outside the capital are fewer than in it. The fact that it is sometimes far fewer is closely related to the practice of mutation. One year earlier, I stumbled upon the fact that the court of Cianjur employs nine judges, the court of Rangkasbitung nine, the court of South Jakarta ten and the court of East Jakarta also ten. On re-checking these figures recently, I found that although the number of judges in the Islamic courts in both southern and eastern parts of Jakarta had remained the same, the number of those in Rangkasbitung and Cianjur had dropped. After three of them had been posted to other regions, no new judge had been sent to replace them. The judges of the court of Rangkasbitung now number six. The number of judges at the court of Cianjur has now dropped to only seven after two were posted to other regions.

The majority of the judges in every court is male; to wit, seven or even eight out of nine or ten judges. The religious court of Cianjur, for an example, has two female judges and Rangkasbitung has only one. The religious court of South Jakarta, as in East Jakarta, has only two female judges. This small number of women judges can be considered acceptable as it was only after 1985 that women could be appointed judges to the religious courts. Of the almost 2,700 judges spread across both the first-instance and appellate religious courts, there are only 500 female judges. Considering that first-instance and high Islamic courts account for 356 (I refer to the year 2000), it is assumed that not all the religious courts employ female judges.

II Judicial Practices in the Religious Courts

Judges in the Islamic courts deal with a variety of cases brought before the court by seekers of justice. When hearing the cases, they usually form panels, each of which consists of one chief judge and two associates. The members of this panel take their seats at a table facing the courtroom with a clerk invariably sitting to their right. They are dressed in a special uniform of a *jellaba*, colored black and green with a special white tie. When they are ready, the clerk calls litigants to enter the courtroom.

Regardless of the kind of case or the details contained in the petition and the session of the hearing, the judges, usually the chief judge but sometimes confirmed by his or her associates, always begin by ascertaining identities through asking for name, address, parent, age, and job, and how the parties are connected to each other. They are generally careful to ask how litigants or people are related to each other when marital or inheritance matters are involved, and to decide if the parties are speaking on behalf of themselves or through a spokesman. Their first substantive question usually constitutes the signal for the argument to begin. Everyone is eager to tell his or her side of the story and does not have the patience to sit quietly while an adversary has the word. They keep interrupting each other, desperate to correct the story told by their opponent with their own version, although the judges continuously remind them that they want only to hear answers from party whom they are interrogating. The judges listen, nod, question, confirm, sometimes get angry, and try to quiet people by holding their hands down, while the litigants talk, shout, and cry. While those in the religious courts of Jakarta use the national language, Indonesian, those outside Jakarta use the local language with the national language sometimes being used, particularly by those who are imperfectly acquainted with the local language. The clerk rushes in his efforts to finish writing down all he hears. When the hearing of a case is considered to have finished with or without a possibility of being heard again on another day, the clerk locates the correct file for the next case. He then dismisses the people, who shake the judges' hands and leave the courtroom. The clerk then calls the litigants in the next case. Postponement of a hearing is usual if the relevant documents or copies of documents are lacking.

While the procedure for a hearing is generally standard in every court, differences in judicial practice appeared in the religious courts in which I conducted my fieldwork. Take, for example, the crucial issue of witnesses. The judges are particularly eager to hear the testimony of any witness to the event at stake or to receive indications from the witnesses' statements. In assessing the truth of their utterances, the judges usually employ a number of strategies. One of these is oath-taking. The witnesses of litigants are summoned forward to stand exactly before the judges without first being asked whether or not he or she is prepared to take the oath. After he has cautioned the witness to repeat what he or she will say, the chief judge then repeats the formula of the oath: '*Demi Allah saya akan menyampaikan apa yang benar dan tiada kebenaran kecuali kebenaran itu sendiri* (I swear that I shall tell only the truth and nothing but the truth).' While the formula uttered is generally the same, the procedure of oath-taking may be quite divergent. The religious court of Rangkasbitung, for example, always uses the Qur'ān held upon the head of the witnesses when the oath formula is being uttered. Cianjur is not nearly so strict. I also found that, although at hearings in other courts, plaintiffs always sit on the right side of the judges and the defendants on the left, in Cianjur the seating pattern is reversed, plaintiffs on the left and defendants on the right.

There are also differences in the process of investigation. The judges in the religious courts have to deal with diverse familial cases brought before them by disputants every day. The number of cases accepted by those outside Jakarta are relatively few, and this provides the opportunity for the judges to hear the cases more seriously. This holds particularly true for the religious courts of Bogor, Rangkasbitung, and Cianjur. In this regard it must be noted that there is a hierarchy in the judicial institution, and that while those in Jakarta are grouped as class IA, those outside Jakarta, including Rangkasbitung, Cianjur and Bogor, are grouped either as class IB or II. It is the number of the cases brought before certain courts which affects the way these courts are classified, and not vice versa. Therefore, here I intend to discover why certain courts such as Rangkasbitung, Bogor, and Cianjur accept petty cases so that they are classified as class IB or II. This is puzzling, as the populations of these regions are as dense as those of Jakarta and other big cities,[4] and familial problems in these regions are believed to be just as significant as those in the latter

Coming back to the court of Rangkasbitung, I noted that in this court a judicial hearing often takes a long time, as only a small number of cases are heard, two or even only one in a day. The judges in this court claimed that the ample time they had at their disposal could be utilized to conduct hearings seriously. "We are able to review and consider cases more calmly and seriously which allows more consideration, meaning we are not as harsh in finding solutions to the cases put before us," said the vice-chairman of the court.[5] Through several hearings I attended, I observed that the judges asked the litigants and witnesses specific questions. All the judges in the session had the opportunity to address questions to both the disputants and the witnesses. They attempted to collect detailed information and confirmed the information meticulously. Accordingly, they showed no reluctance to postpone the decision to another day, giving the plaintiff time to think things over and at the same time the defendant another opportunity to come again.

The limited number of cases heard every day also made the judges of these courts more flexible and tolerant with those coming to the court late. They not only recalled them within the hearing, but also heard them, even though the whole hearing for the day had been formally closed. In the religious court of Cianjur, I witnessed a litigant who had been summoned to the courtroom but did not show up until the hearing for the day had been adjourned. The judges were rushing to leave the courtroom, and the clerk had gone to his office, when a woman suddenly appeared at the door of the courtroom saying that she had just arrived and had a hearing scheduled for the day. The judges quickly recognized that the woman was someone whose name had been called earlier; they looked at each other and then returned to their seats and donned their uniforms again. After they had called the clerk to come back to the courtroom, they gave him a sign to call the woman, who quickly came into the courtroom. Before this, they said to me that the woman had come from a distant district and spent a great deal of money, and that her effort in coming and in spending so much money would be useless, should her case not be heard.

In all the religious courts, the hearings are conducted only on four days, even though the official working days are basically six, Monday to Saturday. For the judges, actual working days are automatically reduced to only four days, from Monday to Thursday. Friday is a half-day. On this day, some of the judges do still come to their offices but others usually do not. When I wanted to stay until Friday to continue my interviews with the judges of the court of Rangkasbitung, the director of the court suggested I leave, as he wondered if I would be able to find any judge to be interviewed, because the majority of them usually do not come in to the office. The reason for their absence was that they would preach sermons in or become *imām* at Friday worship in mosques.[6] Some of them might come to the office, he added, but they usually have to leave before Friday prayers began. Nevertheless, I saw for myself that the major reason for their absence on that day was in fact the lack of cases brought before them, which resulted in lack of judicial activities. On Saturday, some of them do come to the office, but they usually have their own activities like playing tennis, and they could hardly be interrupted.

During their working days, judges in the court of Rangkasbitung have more time to perform activities outside of their judicial responsibilities. Often when I visited this court, I saw that some of judges who admitted to having finished hearing cases, usually only one or two, enjoyed playing chess or simply chatting while others sat in the judge's chambers discussing the cases they had just heard. The same situation can be found in the religious courts in Bogor and Cianjur. The judges of the court of Bogor, ten including the chairman of the court, said that, though they always hear one or two cases a day, they have plenty of spare time. They usually spend such time discussing heated national issues or simply chatting. When I visited the court for the second time, I noted that almost all the judges, including the chairman of the court, had gathered in the judge's office talking about the fame of a young (Muslim) religious preacher, A.A. Gym, whose method of preaching (*da'wa*), stressing ways of managing the heart, is considered highly appropriate to be practiced among the Indonesian Muslims.

This situation was actually very helpful to my research. It meant that when I came to this court for the first time, I could interview its judges directly, as they did not have very many pressing judicial duties. They had no important excuse to refuse or to postpone the time of their interview to another day. However, this only prevails on their working days, from Monday to Thursday. Just as with the Muslim judges in the religious court of Rangkasbitung, those in Bogor usually do not come to the office on Friday. The reasons given are the same, namely, that they, particularly male judges, would don the role of preachers or even leaders of the weekly Friday prayer. The judges of the religious court of Cianjur do likewise. They said that on Friday there are no court lists of hearings. The chairman of the court whose family lives in Jakarta told me that he often leaves Cianjur for Jakarta on Thursday evening and comes back to Cianjur on Monday morning.[7]

In contrast to the judges in the religious courts in Rangkasbitung, Bogor, and Cianjur, each of whom presides over hearings in sessions twice a week or is sometimes scheduled to sit three times a week, yet with minor cases to be heard in every session, most of the judges of the religious courts in Jakarta take their turn hearing cases. Every day there is a session, thus four times. When I visited the court of South Jakarta on the days of judicial hearings to interview its judges, they suggested I come again on Friday, when they would be available for interviews. Although there is no court list on Friday, most of the judges of the religious courts of Jakarta still come to their offices. The abundance of cases brought before them ensures that the judges of the Islamic courts of South Jakarta are kept busy with judicial matters, even on Friday. On this day, they usually prepare for hearings to be held on Sunday. Besides making preparations for hearings the next day, they are sometimes engaged in discussing some other matters related to the development of the court with the chairman of the courts. Nonetheless, though busy with such matters, they felt that it would be possible for them to deal with other activities like interviews on Friday, rather than on other (hearing) days. Moreover, as Friday prayer is commonly held around the court, most of the judges return again to their offices.

Because of a plethora of cases brought before them, judges in the religious courts in Jakarta are inclined to complete hearings quickly. I once attended twelve hearings carried out by one panel of judges in the Islamic court of South Jakarta. I observed that the chief judge of the panel addressed only brief sentences to the disputants and the other two judges said nothing. They appeared to have to finish the twelve hearings in two and half hours. When I entered the courtroom at 11:00, they said they should finish all the hearings at 13:30, including calling the disputants and the waiting time for those who did not come directly. With this schedule, they told me that they would have to *ngebut* (rush). In contrast to the religious courts outside Jakarta, flexibility and tolerance for those who turned up after the court had risen were not very evident. Though attempts at reconciliation are also made, the speeches addressed to the litigants by the (chief) judge of this busy court are not as lengthy as those given by far less busy courts such as Cianjur and Rangkasbitung.

The difference in the number of cases brought before the religious courts of Jakarta and other areas outside Jakarta also influences the length of the process of reaching a decision. In the religious courts of Jakarta, the process of deciding divorce cases, for example, can take several months, three to five or even longer. The process of deciding cases can take a fortnight for each session – from the registration of a case to the first session, to the second, and to third session in which the decision is made and the pronouncement. In the case of *ṭalāq* divorce, the time required may be longer, as after the decision to permit a husband to divorce his wife has been made, the husband needs to proclaim a formula of the *ṭalāq* before the court formally. This can take more than two weeks, from making the decision to formal utterance of the *ṭalāq* and about the same time from the utterance of the *ṭalāq* to granting a divorce decree. In the religious courts outside Jakarta, though, as admitted by their judges, a hearing could take a long time, the interval of time needed from the first session to the second and third sessions is generally only one week, as they are not overwhelmed by cases.

Examples of judgments from my collection certainly confirm this. Most of the judgments in the courts of Jakarta reveal that the pronouncement of decisions often took three or four months after the cases had just been registered. This long period can be the outcome of factors like the complexity of the cases and the absence of one of the contending parties. I noticed that although most cases are handled with considerable rapidity according to the inherent complexities and number of cases to be heard in every court, sometimes one of the principals will fail to show up, or an essential document will be missing, or the litigants will fail to present some witnesses, so that cases are not heard in their entirety or will continue over a number of months or even years. As the majority of the cases brought before the religious courts of Jakarta had to wait longer for a decision than those brought to similar courts outside Jakarta, there is no doubt that the main reason for this is not complexity of the cases or the absence of one of the parties at the scheduled time of hearing, but rather the bulk of cases to be heard by these courts. The judgment of the religious court of South Jakarta no. 585/Pdt.G/1996/PAJS, for example, records that this case was registered on 28 June 1996, and only resolved on 22 January 1997.[8] When I studied the case illustrated in the judgment mentioned above, I thought that the case was not particularly complicated. In contrast to this, most of the judgments of the courts of Rangkasbitung and Cianjur demonstrated that the issuing of decisions takes only one to one-and-half months after the time of registration. The judgments of Rangkasbitung No. 135/ Pdt.G/2002/ PA.RKS and No. 144/Pdt.G/2002/PA. RKS record that the decisions were handed down in the cases only one month after they had been registered.

Despite all these shortcomings, the religious courts continue to develop and their present conditions are in fact much better than they were. Describing the condition of the religious courts in 1960s, in his classic book published in 1972, Lev reported that people had to hunt for the religious courts, which were usually situated near the city mosque or in the *kauman*, the devoutly Islamic quarter of a city. Using a small table as their bench, religious court judges heard cases put before them. The judges sat on the floor at the front of the table. In a crowded room or even a corridor, the administrative staff received and registered people.[9] However, although better than before, the present situation is still ironic when we remember that the religious courts had formally been established many years ago.

III The Origins of the Religious Courts

The origins of the religious courts can be traced back to the period when Islam began to take root in the Indonesian archipelago, around the thirteenth century. It was brought by Gujarati and Middle Eastern merchants and *sufi* Muslims, who interacted with local communities. The process of Islamization occurred primarily through the commercial and marriage contacts the newcomers made with members of the local communities.[10] As a result, coastal towns with a majority Muslim population were gradually established. Concomitant with the establishment of Muslim towns, Islamic doctrines were accepted in varying degrees. Each region underwent a different process of assimilation of the pre-Islamic and the new Islamic norms. In some areas which had been least influenced by Hindu civilization, such as Aceh, Minangkabau, and Banten, the process of assimilation seems to have impinged more deeply upon people's consciousness. Benda argues that in these regions, Islam affected the religious, social, and political consciousness of its new adherents and manifested itself in a purer form.[11] In other areas, such as eastern and central Java, the process of interaction between the two norms had often created tension, as it was accelerated by a contestation of power and political interests. Pertinently, in the greater part of Java, the Hindu-Buddhist tradition was very dominant before the arrival of Islam. There, Islam inexorably met the centuries-old traditions and was compelled to adapt itself to this situation. This fact unsurprisingly resulted in the presence of nominal Muslims, who retained *adat* or popular customs to a large extent.[12]

Generally speaking, it can be said that the local traditions or *adat* which were deeply entrenched in the society were digesting the new

Islamic doctrines, a fact that led a number of Muslim scholars to state that Islam has developed only in the form of a quasi-Islamic religious tradition.[13] Its doctrines, as mentioned before, were being gradually absorbed and adopted by new converts in different regions to deal with the various problems they faced in their daily lives. In the process of adaptation, some local elements of culture were retained in the new belief system. This fact, according to Clifford Geertz, has generated a division between Indonesian Muslims into two categories: namely *santri* and *abangan*. The *santri* sought to understand and conform their lives to religious teachings and in doing so generally followed the ritual obligations of Islam, like praying five times a day and fasting in Ramadan. Whereas *abangan* are identified as those who, although they claimed they were Muslims, did not follow the principal tenets of Islam, or the so-called *Arkān al-Islām* strictly. They adhered to a syncretistic Islam blended with Hinduism, Buddhism, and indigenous animistic beliefs, associated with rituals such as supplication for the assistance of deceased, venerated ancestors. They seldom or perhaps even never observe their Islamic obligations as *santri*. The *santri* themselves are still divided into two groups: modernists, who are generally affiliated with the Muhammadiyah, and traditionalists, those who are included in the Nahdlatul Ulama (NU). Over the course of time, this polarized distinction appears to have become blurred. Indeed, according to a recent study carried out by the Center for Islamic and Community Studies of the State Islamic University in Jakarta, most Indonesian Muslims today are *santri* with a small number still clinging to *abangan* belief.[14]Despite this, the very existence of the two groups may suggest how to explain the process of the inter-relationship between the local traditions and the incoming Islamic values.

Keeping pace with the growth of the influence of Islam in the archipelago, the first forms of the religious court came into being. What is known as *taḥkīm* is assumed to have existed shortly after Islam began to be propagated.[16] The *taḥkīm* was an informal institution by which the persons wrestling with a problem appointed and entrusted a person to solve their difficulty, and they agreed to abide by the decision made by that person. By resorting to this institution, the early Muslim communities in the archipelago settled various conflicts and affairs concerning marriage, donations, charity, and inheritance which flared up among them.[17]

The *taḥkīm* tradition then transformed into the form of delegating authority to authoritative 'ulamā' or *tawliya ahl al-ḥalli wa'l-'aqdi*, who was given the authority to appoint a *qāḍī*, one of whose tasks was to solve familial problems among Muslims. It was prevalent among the communities which were not ruled by a king or sultan.[18] Aceh is most often cited as an example of an area which implemented this system. When

Marco Polo, the Venetian traveler, arrived at Perlak in 1292, he found that Aceh was a Muslim country. However, there was no report that Aceh had had a ruler.[19] In a society which was already ruled by a king or a sultan, a *qāḍī* was usually appointed directly by the king or the sultan, known in *fiqh* as *tawliya* by *imām* or ruler.[20] Samudera Pasai, the first Muslim kingdom in the archipelago, is often mentioned and reported to have been the first to apply this kind of *tawliya*.[21] At that time, Samudera Pasai was ruled by Sultan Mālik al- Ṣāliḥ (d. 1298 M).

The earliest forms of an religious court in Indonesia were also found in a number of sultanates in Java. The Mataram Sultanate (1613-1645), the most influential Islamic Sultanate in Central Java, for instance, had an institution named *Peradilan Surambi*. The *Peradilan Surambi* was actually an Islamic version of the *Peradilan Pradata*. Before the Mataram Kingdom converted to Islam, there had been two court systems: the *Peradilan Pradata* and the *Peradilan Padu*. The *Peradilan Pradata* dealt with affairs (problems) which fell under the authority of the king, and was based on Hindu law; the *Peradilan Padu* dealt with problems that did not pertain to the authority of the king, and was based on unwritten law or *adat*. When the Mataram kingdom converted to Islam and became a Mataram Sultanate, precisely when Sultan Agung came to power as ruler of this Sultanate in 1613,[22] the court was reformed by placing Muslims in the *Peradilan Pradata*. However, the Sultan did not abolish the system entirely, but instead adopted the institutional structure and inculcated Islamic values into it. In the process of its development, the *Peradilan Pradata* became the *Peradilan Surambi* which dealt with issues on the basis of Islamic law. Its name was derived from the fact that instead of hearing cases in the palace, the Sultan changed the venue of the court to the front of the mosque or *Surambi* (verandah). The head of the *Peradilan Surambi* was the sultan himself, but the proceedings were run by the *Penghulu* with the assistance of some *'ulamā'*.[23] Besides his function as a judge of the *Peradilan Surambi*, the *penghulu* assumed the responsibility of being the spiritual advisor to the ruler. This gave the clear message that the legal sovereignty still remained in the hands of the ruler: the *penghulu* was acting on the ruler's behalf. This may have been the theory, but it is reported that the Sultan almost never made decisions which contradicted that of the *penghulu*. In time, arising from a conflict in his reign, the *Peradilan Pradata* was revived by Amangkurat I, but *Peradilan Surambi* remained in existence, as it was still maintained by the local kingdoms, which were not ruled directly by the central Mataram Kingdom.[24] Observing the fact that the kings by dint of their power could in turn transform the structure of the legal system in the community, there can be no doubt that at that time the ruler was the source of legitimacy. This, in effect, also discloses an inter-relationship between the various norms in the legal system.

Such a dynamic is also reflected in the history of the religious court in Cirebon. Mason C. Hoadley has reported that the Muslim jurists in Cirebon retained the use of the *sijjil*, a form of written judgment, containing the same general information on the character of cases as the Javanized *Jayapattra*.[25] On this basis of this evidence, he concludes that the Muslim jurists in Cirebon did not adopt the Islamic form of the document. Nevertheless, he goes on to maintain that the continuity of the pre-Islamic judicial practice does not mean that Cirebon was not properly converted, and that its standing as one of the strongholds of the Islamic faith on Java was a pretense. It is no more than a sign that Cirebon, like many other kingdoms, was fairly slow to adopt new concepts and people felt loathe to abandon traditional customs. Hence he does not see this fact as being related to the choice between Islamic and Hindu-Javanese tradition, or between Islam and Hindu, but rather simply as a choice between old and new institutions.[26]

A religious court was also established in Priangan, West Java. This institution was called *Pengadilan Agama* and it coexisted with two other courts, namely the *Pengadilan Drigama* and the *Pengadilan Cilaga*. It was reported that the jurisdiction of the *Pengadilan Agama* not only covered matrimonial issues and inheritance, but also criminal matters.[27] The most prominent example of the existence of a religious court during the period of the Islamic sultanates in West Java is Banten.[28] In the Banten Sultanate, there was a religious court which had a stronger position than did its counterparts in other sultanates. Even though the primary duty of the *qāḍī* in charge in the religious court was to handle the administration of the law in the Sultanate, the *qāḍī* was also allotted a significant political role. This may be a reason of why the Fakih Najmuddin, the formal title of *qāḍī* at that time, occupied such a strong position and was highly influential in the Sultanate. The competence of the Islamic court in Banten covered civil cases and, to some extent, criminal matters (*ḥudūd*). However, as in many other Islamic kingdoms, corporal punishments like *ḥudūd* and *qiṣās* were often replaced with fines.[29] In effect, here Islamic law was applied more comprehensively. The payment of *zakāt*, for an example, was managed and it functioned to support the independent *'ulamā'*.[30]

Besides these Islamic kingdoms already mentioned, a number of Islamic sultanates in Sulawesi and Sumatra, including Deli, Asahan, Langkat, and Indragiri, established *Mahkamah Syar'iyyah*, an Islamic court whose authority resembled that of the similar institutions in other areas in the archipelago. Likewise, the Banjar and Pontianak Sultanates in Kalimantan set up *Peradilan Qadi*. All these places indicate that during the period of Islamic Sultanates, Islamic law had gradually been adopted as an integral part of their social practice through the institutionalization of the religious courts.

The emergence of these earliest forms of religious courts was ineluctably linked to the efforts of some Muslim scholars in the archipelago to compose *fiqh* books or, at least to adjust the standard manual *fiqh* books, particularly from the Shāfi'īte school of law, translating from Arabic into Malay, the *lingua franca* of Indonesian Muslims. Most of these men had educational experience in the Middle East, and they not only translated the *fiqh* books, but were also qualified to give commentaries on them, keeping in mind the socio-religious conditions in the archipelago. The *Ṣirāṭ al-Mustaqīm,* written by Nuruddin ar-Raniri in 1628, was said to have been the first book of Islamic jurisprudence in the vernacular language to be spread throughout the archipelago. This pioneering effort was continued by M. Arsyad al-Banjari, who wrote *Sabīl al-Muhtadīn*. This book was especially useful in resolving Islamic issues in the Banjar Sultanate. Abdul Ṣamad al-Palimbani from Palembang also wrote numerous works, one of which was his *Sayr al-Sālikīn* used in the Palembang Sultanate as its authoritative source in dealing with Muslim affairs.[31] Of course there were many other works by classical Muslim scholars in the Middle East, which were not only taken as the authoritative sources in the juridical practices among Indonesian Muslims, but, although not widely acknowledged, are also generally popular in the *pesantren* scattered throughout the archipelago. Martin van Bruinessen has recorded books of this kind, which, in his analysis, reflect a purely orthodox tradition of Shāfi'īte *fiqh*, Ash'arīte doctrine, and Ghazzalian ethics.[32] All the above-mentioned books were selected as references for the judgments of the religious courts in independent Indonesia, and it is also from these earlier works that the later development of the substantive laws in the Islamic courts has been formulated.

IV Religious Courts during the Dutch Colonial Administration

As described above, after Islam came to the archipelago, Islamic law had been adopted by Muslim communities as a law to be applied alongside *adat* law. At the beginning of its history, the Dutch East India Company (*Verenigde Oost Indische Compagnie,* VOC), which began to solidify its power at the beginning of the seventeenth century, did not interfere in the application of Islamic law by native Muslim communities. It was said that the VOC initially intended to introduce Western law, but the Muslim communities which had adopted Islamic rules on marriage, inheritance, gift-giving (*hibah)*, and endowment (*waqf*), rejected such a policy. Confronted by this refusal, in 1642 the Dutch issued the *Statuta Batavia*, which formally accredited the application of the Islamic law by the Muslim communities. It allowed existing institutions, including

Islamic courts, to continue to function. It was believed among the Dutch officials that this policy should be implemented in order to prevent any resistance from the Muslim communities.[33]

At the same time, the Dutch made a further concession to the religious courts by promoting a sort of the compilation of Islamic law. As a follow-up to the *Statuta Batavia 1642*, they endorsed the efforts of the Dutch legal scholars to compile books on Islamic law which were to serve as a guideline for the *qāḍī* or *penghulu* in making judgments on Muslim familial issues. A prototypical compilation of Islamic law was then assembled by a number of the Dutch officials. The *Compendium van Clookwijck*, which was produced by the efforts of Clookwijck, the Governor of Sulawesi during 1752-1755, was the popular compendium, along with *Compendium Freijer*. The work of compiling the *Compendium Freijer* began at the instigation of Governor-General Jacob Mossel in 1754 and was produced by Freijer in 1760,[34] after he had consulted *penghulu*, *'ulamā'*, and native leaders.[35] In 1750 a compendium was also made in Semarang. This compendium was called the *Mogharraer*, a title which was undoubtedly claimed as originating from *'al-Muḥarrar*, the title of the *fiqh* book written by Abū al-Qāsim 'Abd al-Karīm bin Muḥammad al-Rāfi'ī who died in 623 H. With such a title there could be no doubt that it was based on the *fiqh* book *al-Muḥarrar*. While there is no information available until the point at which the compendiums of *Mogharraer* and *Clookwijck* were in use, it is said that the *Compendium Freijer* was abrogated in 1804, since it was no longer functioning effectively.[36]

After this abrogation, there is no further information about what kind of substantive laws were used in the religious courts functioning under the Dutch authority. Scattered scraps of information, however, imply that a number of *fiqh* texts were taken as grounds for the judgments handed down by the judges of religious courts. The fact that the process of recruitment of the judges in a number of religious courts incorporated an exam, whose subjects included the reading of the *fiqh* book of al-Malībārī's *Fatḥ al-Mu'īn*, is a clue that this *fiqh* text was used as one of their references in resolving cases.[37] In his book published in 1934, Pijper also recorded that judgments of the religious courts on divorce were based on a number of *fiqh* texts such as al-Nawāwī's *Minḥāj al-Ṭālibīn* and Sayyid Uthmān's *al-Qawānīn al-Shar'iyya*.

The Dutch colonial administration, established at the beginning of the nineteenth century, continued to pursue the same policy. Observing the fact that in family cases, Muslims acknowledged the jurisdiction of Islamic law, the Dutch held a view that the applied or living law of the indigenous people derived from the religion they embraced. In 1855, this opinion was accredited by Dutch governmental regulation in *Staatsblad 1855 No. 2* (75 and 78), which, as I shall demonstrate below, because of the change of the name of the constitution of the Dutch from *Regeerings*

Reglement (RR) to *Indischestaatsregeling* (IS) in 1919, was later changed and became Article 134 (2) IS.[38] Article 75 of the *Regeerings Reglement* states that the government should uphold the Islamic rules, customs, and usages to be applied in lawsuits between members of the indigenous population, in as far as the legal rules of Islam and its customs and usages did not contradict the common principles of fairness and justice.

L.W.C. van den Berg (1845-1927), the Advisor for Eastern Languages and Mohammedan Law, was the main supporter of this opinion. He proposed what became known as the theory of *receptio in complexu*, highlighting that Islamic law should remain the law applied to the Muslim people.[39] Furthermore, Van den Berg perceived the necessity of maintaining the religious court as an institution in which the Muslim community could solve their family problems. On the basis of the missive and proposal of the Minister of Colonies, on 1 August 1882 the Islamic courts, called *priesterraad* (Priest's court)[40] or *Raad Agama* in Java and Madura, were formally and legally established. This establishment was ratified by the Royal Decree of King Willem III dated 19 January 1882 (*Staatsblad 1882 No. 152*).[41]

This royal decree stated that a *priesterraad* (Islamic court), with specific competence over marriage, divorce, inheritance and other issues such as *hibah* (grants) and *waqf* (endowment), should be established in every regency (*kabupaten*) in Java and Madura, in which a *landraad* (general court) had been established. It was decreed that the structure of the religious court should consist of one *penghulu* as a leader, assisted by at least three and at most eight Islamic experts as members, who would be appointed by the Governor-General. The religious court could only issue judgments if the trial was attended by at least three members, with the condition that the *penghulu* should preside as the leader.[42]

Despite this legal position and its wide-ranging competence, it must be noted that the *priesterraad* (the religious court) was under the authority of *landraad* (the general court), on which the former depended for executorial authority. With the exception of *penghulu,* the officials of the religious court did not receive a salary. The *penghulu* received remuneration as an advisor to the *landraad*. In carrying out their duties, the *penghulu* were subordinate to the regents (*bupati*). They were in fact assistants to the *bupati* with the specific task of managing religious practices.[43] Therefore, in the performance of their duties, the autonomy of the *penghulu* could be infringed upon by the superior position of the *bupati*.[44] Leaving these difficulties aside, the establishment of the *priesterraad* as an official religious court signified that the Dutch government had officially recognized and strengthened the long-time existence of the religious court.

The Dutch policy of accommodating the very existence of such religious courts as *priesterraad* provoked criticism and protest among some

Dutch scholars. Christiaan Snouck Hurgronje (1857-1936), a famous Dutch scholar and a formal advisor to the Dutch government, was one of its most vocal critics. He condemned the use of the term of *priester*, as well as the formation and the administration of the institutions.[45] Snouck's criticism of the re-organization of the religious court had, as Lev noted, some influence in official spheres. In fact, also spurred into action by the criticism among the nationalist Muslims, in 1922 the Dutch government established a commission led by Ter Haar,[46] to review the organization of the *priesterraad*. Adopting most of Snouck Hurgronje's proposals, the commission issued *Staatsblad 1931 No. 35*. This regulation contained three policies, including the change of the name of religious courts from *Priesterraad* to *Penghoeloegerecht*, the establishment of an Islamic appeal court, and the formation of the *penghoeloegerecht* which was to consist of a judge assisted by no more two assistants and one clerk.[47]

As an outcome of his investigation into Aceh in 1893, C. Snouck Hurgronje concluded that the effective law applied in this society was not the law of Islam but *adat* and therefore he proposed a new concept of Islamic law, which contradicted that of Van den Berg. His concept was called the theory of *receptie*. This theory argued that the law applied in Indonesia was actually the *adat* law. Islamic laws could be implemented only if they did not contradict the local *adat*. Furthermore, according to the structure of this theory, Islamic law which had been adapted or accepted by the *adat* law was no longer Islamic law, but had become *adat* law.[48] On the basis of this theory, Article 2 (75 and 78) RR of *Staatsblad* 1855 which recognized that the application of Islamic law was replaced by Article 134 (2) I.S of 1919, stating that "... should some private cases arise among Muslims, they are to be heard by religious courts according to Islamic law in so far as *adat* law agrees or if there are no any other laws on the cases".[49]

Basically taking a stand against C. Snouck Hurgronje and his colleagues, who used their authority to have *adat* law applied, another group recommended Dutch law should be the legal system in the Indies. Nevertheless, the weight of C. Snouck Hurgronje's arguments, not to mention his authoritative standing, ensured that the Dutch government finally endorsed *adat* law. In government circles, it was felt that were the Dutch law to be enforced, it would cause a wave of Muslim resentment, as this law was based on Christian teachings. This group believed that the enforcement of *adat* law would not provoke any reaction in Muslim society as its members were already well acquainted and attached to it.[50] C. Snouck Hurgronje and his colleagues won the debate. Regardless of what kind of law proposed was selected to be applied to the indigenous people, a number of Indonesian Muslim scholars were convinced that both groups had the same intention: to weaken the position of Islamic law in the archipelago.

Espoused by Van Vollenhoven and systematically developed by some of his students such as Ter Haar, the theory of *receptie* or the *adat* law policy increasingly attracted attention because of the failure to enforce *Staatsblad 1931/35*. With the intention of implementing *Staatsblad 1931/ 35* on the one hand and their *adat* law policy as well, they urged the Dutch government to issue another regulation, in which the jurisdiction of the religious courts in Java and Madura was to be limited to matrimonial issues only, excluding inheritance. In issuing *Staatsblad 1937 No. 116,* the government acquiesced to the demand and henceforth put inheritance under the jurisdiction of the general court (*landraad*).[51]

The removal of inheritance from the jurisdiction of the religious court was a major turning-point for both religious court judges and Muslim leaders.[52] It was not long before this policy provoked a storm of criticism and dismayed reactions among different elements in Indonesian Muslim society.[53] They felt that the Dutch colonial administration had treated them unfairly. They questioned whether or not the Christian law applied to the Christians had been received and adapted by the *adat* law. They contended that if the Dutch colonial government wanted to apply the *adat* law fully and legally, it should cover all the groups in the Indonesian community,[54] and not only apply to Muslim groups. They regarded the policy as a sign of the ambiguity and unfairness of the Dutch government and suspected the covert Dutch intention was to destroy the established position of Islamic law in the Muslim community.[55] Hazairin, a well-known Indonesian scholar of *adat* and Islamic law in the 1950s, and his supporters asserted that *Staatsblad 1937 No. 116* was a significant threat to the development of the Islamic law. They condemned the theory of *receptie,* which had generated this law, as "a theory of the devil which insults the faith of Muslims, God, the Qur'an, and the Traditions of the Prophet".[56] An adamant reaction to *Staatsblad 1937 No. 116* was also elicited among the *qāḍīs*. They rejected the application of the *Staatsblad 1937 No. 116*. To mobilize support, they set up an organization called *Perhimpoenan Pengoeloe dan Pegawainja* (PPDP) in Solo on 12 May 1937.[57] The *Majlis Islam A'la Indonesia* (MIAI) was another group which squared off determinedly against the exclusion of inheritance from the jurisdiction of the religious courts, and demanded the Dutch abolish the law by addressing some cogent reasons to support their behest.[58] In spite of these reactions, the Dutch refused to budge.[59]

The Dutch scholars made equally determined efforts to support the policy, by pointing out that in actual practice in relation to inheritance, the Javanese followed their *adat* rules. At the same time, they criticized rules of inheritance in Islam, by which adopted children and alas adoptive parents are excluded from shares of inheritance, as being in contradiction to Javanese local tradition or *adat,* in which both adopted children and adoptive parents have a right to a share of the estate. Having originated in the Arab countries, Islamic law, of inheritance in particular, was suspected by the Dutch of being irrelevant to the family life of Indonesians and far removed from the sense of justice prevailing in Indonesian societies. A number of Indonesians from the Javanese *Priyayi* class supported the implementation of *adat* law, and in their eyes, the publication of *Staatsblad 1937 No. 116* was a great achievement. Professor Soepomo (d. 1958) and his colleagues, for instance, were the most in favor of the regulation, which excludes inheritance from the jurisdiction of religious courts.[60]

This policy was seen as not merely being motivated by a religious legal aspect. Hooker has argued that the exclusion of inheritance from the jurisdiction of the religious courts represented the general policy of the Dutch colonial administration towards Islam at that time. It has been perceived as the Dutch response to an increasing anti-Colonial agitation among Muslims, which peaked in the 1920s and 1930s. Hooker's view on this issue is of relevance to what he has said about the integration between religion and politics, in which he contended that religion was closely related to politics. He maintained that, "... since the law was an integral part of religion, its substance and application were equally political in nature."[61] Noting this, Hooker suggests that the exclusion of inheritance from the jurisdiction of religious courts, regulated in *Staatsblad* 1937 No. 116, includes a political substance which implies that the legislation of that law can be understood only from the perspective of power relations.

In order to exercise further control over the workings of the religious court, the Dutch government issued *Staatsblad 1937 No. 610* on the establishment of *Mahkamah Islam Tinggi* (the Islamic Appeal Court) in Java and Madura, and *Staatsblad 1937 No. 638 and 639* on the establishment of the religious court in South Kalimantan, called *Kerapatan Qadi,* and an Islamic Appeal Court, called *Kerapatan Qadi Besar.* As did the religious courts in Java and Madura, the *Kerapatan Qadi* had a structure which consisted of one leader and three members, with the assistance of one clerk, all of whom were appointed as civil servants. The primary task of these appellate courts was to treat appeals from the religious court in the first instance and to give advice on the Islamic issues as required by the Governor General.[62]

During the Japanese occupation of the islands in World War II, the fate of Islamic law underwent no significant changes. Receiving the laws and regulations concerning the religious courts, including their competence, the Japanese government proclaimed it would continue what had been established by the Dutch colonial administration. Changes did occur but only in the terms or names used for the religious courts.[63] The name of the religious court for the first instance was, for example, changed to *Sooryoo Hooin* and the name of the religious appeal court was changed to *Kaikyoo Kootoo*.[64] The fact that this was merely a cosmetic change and that the basic structure was unaltered can possibly be attributed to the fact that the Japanese occupation of Indonesia was only for a very brief period. They had neither the time nor the opportunity to reformulate the policy of the Dutch colonial administration on Islamic law and, when push came to shove, had more or less the same interests in maintaining the status quo as the Dutch colonial administration. Benda notes that "... like their predecessors, the Japanese always kept close control over Muslim institutions."[65]

Despite a failure to introduce drastic change, it should be noted here that the Japanese government had made consistent and invariable efforts to win the support and the sympathy of the Indonesian Muslim communities in its attempt to form an "independent Great East Asia" under Japanese rule. This resolve was manifested in the establishment of an Office of Religious Affairs in March 1943. This office, which later became the Ministry of Religious Affairs, was called the *Shumubu*.[66] It is possible that the founding of this office by the Japanese government is what led Lev to conclude that Muslims had gained at least a little more advantage from the Japanese than they had from the Dutch.[67]

V The Religious Courts during Independent Indonesia

V.1 The Ministry of Religious Affairs and the Growth of the Religious Courts

After Indonesia gained its independence in 1945, significant changes in the process of the institutionalization of the Islamic courts began to occur – albeit rather slowly. The formation of what was designated the Ministry of Religious Affairs contributed greatly to this process.[68] In fact, the first policy issued by the independent Indonesian Government was concerned with authority over the religious courts. On the basis of an idea proposed by the Minister of Religious Affairs with the approval of the Minister of Justice, authority over the religious courts was transferred from the Ministry of Justice to the Ministry of Religious Affairs under regulation No. 5/1946.[69]

The impact of this transfer touched upon the issue of the administration of marriage (*nikāḥ*), divorce (*ṭalāq*), and reconciliation (*rujūʿ*). Replacing the *Huwelijks Ordonnantie S. 1929 No. 348 jo s. 1931* No. 467 and *Vorstenlandsche Huwelijks Ordonnantie Buitengewesten S. 1932* No. 482, issued on 21 November 1946, Law No. 22 of 1946 promised the unification of the administration of these three issues and provided that all Muslim marriages, divorces, and reconciliations would be dealt with by registrars (*Pegawai Pencatat Nikah Talak dan Rujuk*/PPNTR) appointed by the Minister of Religious Affairs. By introducing this law, the ministry intended to create legal certainty and stability in Islamic marriage initially, by requiring registration. Yet the law was applied only in Java and Madura, and the ministry officials acknowledged that it would take years to make the law effective in all parts of Indonesia.[70] In fact, outside Java and Madura, this law only came into effect on 26 October 1954, after the Federal State of the Republic of Indonesia (RIS) had collapsed. The law was designated Law No. 32/1954.[71]

The office of the PPNTR would be determined by local religious offices (*Jawatan Agama Daerah*, later *Kantor Urusan Agama*/KUA), which were directly under the control of the Ministry of Religious Affairs. In this context, it is pertinent to note that over time there was an increase in the number of cases registered at the religious courts in both Java and Madura. Aware of this increase, the Ministry of Religious Affairs made a division in the functions of judges as the Chief of Marriage Registrars and other religious observances, and as head of the Islamic court. Later, there were to be two separate religious institutions, namely 'Kantor Urusan Agama/KUA' and 'Pengadilan Agama' (religious court).

These changes did not take place without adverse commentary. They were challenged by a number of nationalist leaders who were inclined to press for the abolition of the Islamic courts. We have already seen that some secular nationalist leaders like Soepomo, an *adat* scholar, supported the idea of the removal of inheritance from the jurisdiction of the religious court and had indeed even suggested the abolition of the religious courts. Their effort finally produced Law No. 19/1948.[72] Although there was actually no clear regulation pertaining to abrogation of religious courts in this law, it did acknowledge only three domains of court, namely the General Court, the Administrative Court, and the Military Court in the judicial system in Indonesia. Article 35 (2) states that Muslim-law private cases, which were usually heard before the religious court, now fell under the jurisdiction of the general court. The hearing of such cases in the general courts would be handled by a panel, consisting of one Muslim judge as a president and two judges with an adequate knowledge of Islamic law as members.[73] However, the fact that the law made no mention at all of a distinct sphere for a religious court implied its imminent demise. Criticism and reaction against this new statute poured in from many parties. Muslim scholars from Aceh and West and South Sumatra rejected this law and demanded that the existing *Mahkamah Syar'iyyah* (religious courts) be reinstated and be placed under the aegis of the Ministry of Religious Affairs. Undermined by some criticism and adverse reactions from Muslim parties, which were aggravated by events during the revolution, in particular the Dutch capture of Yogyakarta,[74] the law was never enforced and the religious courts retained their previous function.[75]

So, instead of being abolished, the institution of the religious court developed and expanded into other areas. Several religious courts were established in major islands outside of Java and Madura. At the demand of its community, *Mahkamah Syar'iyyah* was established in Aceh in 1957, with the prerogative to hear and adjudicate family issues among Muslims.[76] This move was based on Regulation No. 29/1957, which was followed by Regulation No. 45/1957 on the establishment of religious courts outside Java and Madura. This regulation was put into effect in all the outer islands where civil courts already existed, with the exception of one part of South Kalimantan, Banjarmasin.[77] As a follow-up to this regulation, on 13 November 1957 the Minister of Religious Affairs issued the Decree No. 58/1957 on the establishment of religious courts in Sumatra, including Aceh. This decree automatically annulled Regulation No. 29/1957. On the grounds of the same statute, the Minister of Religious Affairs issued another decree, Degree No. 4/1958 on 6 March 1958, on the establishment of religious courts in Kalimantan. On the same date, the Minister of Religious Affairs issued Decree No. 5/1958 on the establishment of the Islamic court in Sulawesi, Nusa Tenggara, Maluku and Irian Barat.[78] Besides paying attention to the more established areas, the Ministry of Religious Affairs issued several regulations on the introduction of the branches of the religious courts in newly established provinces and districts.[79] Alongside the first instance religious courts, new appellate religious courts were also established in the outer islands.

Nevertheless, the establishment of the religious courts in Java and Madura and the other islands still left a major problem, which pertinently concerned the formal competence of these courts. While religious courts in Java and Madura shared competence in matters of matrimonial law, the new religious courts established in outer islands were given jurisdiction not only over matrimonial issues, but also over inheritance issues, thereby having a wider competence than those in Java and Madura.[80] This glaring difference disturbed Muslim judges in Java, who demanded the transfer of competence over inheritance back to the Islamic courts on the grounds of uniformity. Despite this opposition, the Ministry of Religious Affairs did not accede to the demands and was content to allow the discrepancy in the formal competence of the Islamic courts of Java and outside of Java to remain. The tendency of the Ministry to prefer divergence to uniformity stemmed from the supposition that opposition to transferring inheritance back to the religious courts in Java from the supporters of the *adat* law would be too great, and also from the reluctance of the Ministry to capitulate on the wider jurisdiction of outer-islands religious courts.[81]

The progress made in the institutional aspects of the religious courts was not followed by any substantial changes in their judicial sphere. The *fiqh* texts were still the main sources of the judgments issued by Muslim judges. It is important to recall that when the Ministry of Religious Affairs had a full control over the religious courts, it sought to unify the administration of marriage, divorces, and reconciliations, stating that these legal affairs should be handled by registrars appointed by the Ministry of Religious Affairs. Nonetheless, nothing was said in the law regulating those matters about changing the substantive law on matrimonial issues.[82] At that time, Muslim judges, who were recruited mostly from among local *'ulamā'*, were free to use and select the available various Islamic legal texts studied in *pesantren*. Only in 1958, when it issued a letter, identified as No.B/1/735/1958, did the Ministry of Religious Affairs attempt for the first time to define the sources to be referred to by judges. Point B in this circular stated that the judges in the religious courts were recommended to refer to thirteen *fiqh* books[83]: namely *Ḥāshīyat Kifāyat al-Akhyār* by Ibrahīm ibn Muḥammad al-Bājūrī (d. 1860 AD); *Fatḥ al Mu'īn* by Zayn al-Dīn al-Malībārī (ca. 975 AH); *Ḥāshiya 'alā al-Taḥrīr* by 'Alī ibn Ḥijazī ibn Ibrahīm al-Sharqāwī (d. 1737 AD); *Sharḥ Kanz al-Rāghibīn* by al-Qalyubī (d. 1659 AD); *Fatḥ al-Wahhāb* by Abū Yaḥya Zakariyya al-Anṣārī (d. 1520 AD); *Tuḥfat al-Muḥtāj* by Shihāb al-Dīn Aḥmad Ibn Ḥajar al-Haytāmī (1665-6 AD); *Targhīb al-Mushtaqq* by Shihāb al-Dīn Aḥmad Ibn Hajar al-Haytāmī; *al-Qawānīn al-Shar'iyya li'Ahl al-Majālis al-Ḥukumiyyāt wa al-Iftā'iyyāt* by Sayyid Uthmān ibn Yaḥya (1822-1914 AD); *al-Qawānīn al-Shar'iyya* by Sayyid 'Abd Allah ibn Ṣadaqah San'an Daḥlān; *Al-Farā'id* by Shamsurī; *Bughyat al-Mustarshidīn* by Ḥusayn al-Bā'alawī; *Al-Fiqh 'alā al-Madhāhib al-'Arba'a* by 'Abd al-Raḥmān al-Jazīrī (1882-1941 AD); and *Mughnī al-Muḥtāj* by Muḥammad al-Sharbinī (d. 1569 AD).

All of these books are the *fiqh* texts in the legal library of the Shāfi'īte school, with one exception, namely *Kitāb al-Fiqh 'ala al-Madhāhib al-Arba'a*. The selection of the books was said to be related to the fact that the Ministry of Religious Affairs was at the time dominated by NU circles and compounded by the fact that these were said to be *fiqh* texts commonly read by *'ulamā'*. Looking at the names of these *fiqh* texts it may be asked why no one single *fiqh* text by al-Shāfi'ī was included in the group. Leaving this query aside, while the selection of these texts was clearly designed to prevent proliferation of divergent judgments on a number of issues of the same nature, the matter of modern issues and the legal status of women, particularly relating to the issue of polygyny and divorce, had not been yet solved.

V.2 The Position of the Religious Courts After 1970

Significant changes in the institutional and judicial aspects of the religious courts began to be introduced in the early 1970s. In order to fulfill the regulation enshrined in the Article 24 of the *Undang-Undang Dasar 1945* (Indonesian Constitution of 1945), which stipulates that judicial powers shall be exercised by the Supreme Court and other courts in accordance with the statute promulgated, the government issued Law No. 14/1970 on the basic regulation of the judicial authority, under which religious courts were assured of their certain legal position. Article 10 governs the very existence of four different domains of courts: namely General, Religious, Military, and Administrative.[84]

Inevitably, the government's decision to assign the religious court an independent domain in the Indonesian court system provoked heated debates. Objections and comments on this issue were raised by different parts of society, represented by political parties. The Roman Catholic Party rejected the position of a religious court as an independent court and proposed a unification of the religious court within the domain of the public court. However, emphasizing the necessity of having independent religious courts, the then Minister of Justice, Oemar Senoadji, sought to convince all the parties to accept the religious courts.[85]

The very existence of the religious courts was strengthened by the promulgation of a Marriage Law in 1974, which was designated Law No. 1/1974. This law is applicable to all Indonesian citizens regardless of their religion, but it also gave religious courts the formal authority to deal with Muslim family issues. Under this law, religious courts across Indonesia have had the same jurisdiction over the matrimonial issues and the substantive grounds of their settlements since 1 October 1975.[86] The extension of jurisdiction of the religious courts as laid down in the Marriage Law of 1974 includes the following issues:

1. Permission to have more than one wife;
2. Permission to conclude a marriage for those who are under 21 (twenty-one) years of age, when the parents or guardians or relatives in a direct line of succession have different opinions;
3. Marriage dispensation;
4. Marriage prevention;
5. Refusal of a Marriage Registrar to register a marriage;
6. Marriage cancellation;
7. Suit for negligence of responsibility by spouse;
8. Divorce by repudiation;
9. Divorce suit;
10. Settlement of common property;
11. Child custody and alimony;

12. Child custody and alimony when the father fails to honor his responsibility;
13. Maintenance support for the ex-wife and determination of the responsibility of the ex-wife;
14. Legal status of a child;
15. Termination of parental custody;
16. Termination of guardianship;
17. Appointment of non-relatives as legal guardians in cases in which relative guardians fail to fulfill the responsibility;
18. Appointment of a guardian when a minor is abandoned by parents;
19. Financial compensation punishment of a guardian who has caused a loss of the property of the child under his guardianship;
20. Determination of the origin of a child;
21. Determination of a refusal to conclude mixed marriages;
22. Determination on the validity of marriages concluded before the promulgation of Law No. I/1974 and which were carried out in accordance with other regulations.[87]

However, despite the fact that their competence was extended, the role of the religious courts was not fully recognized. In fact, one of the articles of this law, namely Article 63, requires religious courts to submit their decisions to the civil courts for confirmation.[88] Though not publicly debated, the rule was considered by Muslim leaders and judges of the religious court to be an indication of the subordination of the religious court to the general court.

Despite such obstacles, the Law on Marriage of 1974, which has partly reinforced the position of the religious courts in the Indonesian national legal system, has to be considered a milestone in substantive changes in the application of Islamic law in Indonesia. As mentioned above, under this law, a new set of Islamic rules was established. By referring to this law, Muslim judges could approve or disapprove a petition for divorce and a request for permission to enter a polygamous marriage made by a husband. Admittedly, although a number of reforms had been made, this law still did not answer other various marital problems. Marriage during pregnancy was, for example, still debatable and was not covered by a legal rule. Above all, as its name suggests, this law said nothing about inheritance issues. Consequently, judges of the religious courts had to continue to base their judgments on inheritance, as well as those on marriage issues not yet dealt with in the Law of Marriage, on legal doctrines laid down by earlier scholars of Islamic law in various *fiqh* books.

Besides the issue of the dependence of the religious court on the general courts, the law has also indirectly resulted in a contestation of authority between the Ministry of Religious Affairs and the Supreme

Court. This began when the extension of the jurisdiction of the religious courts enshrined in the promulgation of the Law of Marriage caused an increase in the cases brought before the religious courts, which led some disputants to demand their cases be taken as high as the Supreme Court. Faced with this situation in 1977, the Supreme Court issued a regulation to organize the procedures in the examination of and decision in appeal cases from the religious courts more efficiently. However, though the Law No. 14/1970 implicitly stipulated that cases of the religious courts may be brought before the Supreme Court in appeal, the Ministry of Religious Affairs still maintained the existing law, which stated that the appeal decisions of the appellate religious courts were final.[89] This dualism gave legal scholars a field day. The debate ended when mutual cooperation was established between the two institutions. This mutual cooperation was manifested in 1979 with the establishment of a special chamber to hear cases brought from appellate religious courts, and in the appointment of six Muslim Supreme Court judges to the chamber, one of whom functioned as a chairman. These six appointed judges were to hear cases brought to the chamber.[90]

Another aspect in the development of the religious courts was related to the issue of nomenclature, which particularly concerned the Ministry of Religious Affairs. As mentioned above, since 1947 the religious courts in Java and Madura were called '*Pengadilan Agama*', but those in South Kalimantan were known as '*Kerapatan Qadi*', and those outside Java and Madura, with the exception of South Kalimantan, were designated '*Mahkamah Syar'iyyah*' or '*Pengadilan Agama*'. This confusing difference in denomination had officially ended in 1980, when the Minister of Religious Affairs issued a decree on the standardization of the name of the religious courts. The decree was ratified as regulation No. 6/1980. This regulation brought uniformity to the nomenclature of the religious courts, namely that from now on they would be '*Pengadilan Agama*' for the first-instance religious court and '*Pengadilan Tinggi Agama*' for the appellate religious court.[91] It is impossible to dissociate this law from the attempt by the Ministry of Religious Affairs to highlight the national identity of the Indonesian religious courts.

V.3 The Promulgation of the 1989 Islamic Judicature Act

As the foregoing discussion has shown, attempts to unify the competence of the religious courts in Indonesia have been made at various intervals since the founding of the independent Indonesia. It was, however, only in 1989 that the attempt was successful, namely when the Islamic Judicature Act (Act No. 7/1989) was passed. The passing of this Act was welcomed with enthusiasm by different elements in Indonesian Muslim community. It was seen as the outcome of a long struggle by

Muslims, who had been demanding the accommodation of Islamic law by the state. In fact, the Act puts the religious courts in the same position as the other courts. In the context of its substance, the Act is also perceived as marking significant progress in the application of Islamic law, as it is one of the legal spheres constituting the national legal system.

By the promulgation of the Act of 1989, all the regulations previously applied in the religious courts were abrogated. Article 107 states:

> By the time this Act is in effect: a. the regulation on the religious courts in Java and Madura (*Staatsblad* of the year 1882 No. 152 and *Staatsblad* of the year 1937 No. 116 and No. 610); the regulation on the *Qadi* Deliberation (*Kerapatan Qadi*) and the Great *Qadi* Deliberation (*Kerapatan Qadi Besar*) for the part of South and East Kalimantan regency (*Staatsblad* of the year 1937 No. 638 and No. 639; c. the Government Regulation No. 45 of the year 1957 on the establishment of the religious courts/*Sharīʻa* courts outer Java and Madura, and d. regulations as stated in Article 63 (2) of Law No. 1 of the year 1974 on Marriage (State Declaration of the year 1974 No. 1), are declared ineffective.[92]

The article clearly implies that the regulations, which were set out individually as points a, b, and c, and which actually govern only the structure and competence of the religious courts, were annulled by the passage of the Act. The abrogation of the regulations has finally brought about the unification of the competence and structure of the religious courts.

Article 49 (1) clearly states that religious courts have the responsibility and authority to process, hear and resolve issues arising among Muslims, including matters pertaining to marriage, inheritance, wills, *hibahs* (grant) which are effectuated under such Islamic stipulations of *waqf* and *ṣadaqa*.[93]

The organization of the religious courts is specifically governed in Chapter II. Article 6 states that the religious court system consists of an Islamic court as the first-instance court, and a higher religious court as the appellate religious court. Article 9 governs their structure, and states that the first-instance court consists of a presiding judge, member judges, a clerk, a secretary, and a confiscation officer, and the Islamic appeal court consists of president, member judges, a clerk, and a secretary.[94]

The issuance of the Act had a significant effect on the independence of the Islamic courts. Besides the regulations mentioned in Points a, b, and c quoted above, the Act gave clear notification that Article 63 of the Law of Marriage No. 1/1974 had been rescinded.[95] As mentioned before, this was the article which required a religious court to submit its decisions to the general court in order to have them confirmed.[96] Through this annulment, this confirmation is no longer required.

In short, by the issuance of the Act, the competence, structure, and legal procedures of the religious courts across Indonesia have been formally unified. Even executive force has been fully embraced by the Islamic courts, indicating their independence in making judgments as well as in enforcing them. No less important is the fact that the disparity of regulations, about which Muslim leaders had complained, identified the religious courts as 'quasi-courts', has also been eliminated.[97] To create a unified interpretation of the application of the Act among the judges of the religious courts and their brethrens in the general courts, the Supreme Court, as the highest court subordinating the domains of all the other courts, issued Regulation No. 2/1990 on the guidelines for the application of the Act. This circular letter includes information on the removal of inheritance from the jurisdiction of the general court to that of the religious courts.

V.4 The Renewal of the Recruitment System

The Islamic Judicature Act of 1989 not only affected the competence, structure, and executorial independence of the religious courts, it also established a new system for the recruitment of judges for the religious courts. It was a known fact that in the early independent Indonesia, the judges of the religious courts were recruited from among the local *'ulamā'*. They had generally been trained informally in the traditional Islamic schools. At the beginning of the 1960s, judges in the religious courts began to be recruited from graduates of special formal schools for Islamic judges. To provide an adequate supply of the would-be judges, the Ministry of Religious Affairs set up a secondary level training school, SGHA (Sekolah Guru dan Hakim Agama/ Religious Teachers and Judges School) in 1957. This school produced some graduates who had the technical ability and legal insights to qualify them to become judges in the religious courts. Later, this school was divided into PGA (Pendidikan Guru Agama/Religious Teachers Education) and PHIN (Pedidikan Hakim Islam Negeri/Islamic Judges Education).[98] The graduates of the "official school" were also sent to PTAIN (Perguruan Tinggi Agama Islam Negeri/State Islamic Higher Learning) and ADIA (Akademi Dinas Ilmu Agama/Government Academy for Religious Officials), which were later transformed into IAIN (Institut Agama Islam Negeri/State Institute for Islamic Studies). All IAINs have faculties of *sharī'a* with graduates who are qualified to be, among other positions, judges in the religious courts. To achieve this goal, students of the faculty inculcated with an in-depth understanding and comprehension of Islamic law, a good grasp of theory, and practical guidance to assist them to fulfill the task of being judges in the Islamic courts.

Since the promulgation of the Islamic Judicature Act in 1989, which was basically intended to eliminate the subordinate position previously assigned to the religious courts in the structure of the national judicial systems, and to broaden their jurisdiction over familial cases, all judges in the religious courts are without exception to be recruited from university graduates. This Act stipulates a number of requirements for a candidate recruited to be a judge in the religious courts; he or she should be Muslim, adult (twenty five is the minimum age), observant, competent, honest, just, well-behaved, and well-versed in Islamic law, loyal to *Pancasila* and the 1945 Constitution, and never have been a member of or involved in banned organizations.[99] Expanding upon the requirement of being well-versed in Islamic law, the Act defines those who are qualified as such in Islamic law to be graduates from an Islamic law or civil law school or faculty.

The Act legalized the practice of recruitment of female judges for the religious courts. For a long time, judges were recruited only from males. The tide began to turn in 1958, in the city of Tegal in the northern part of Central Java, when fifteen women were appointed honorary judges and one was appointed as a fully sworn-in judge. In the same year the wife of a Pamong Pradja official announced her candidature to be a judge and was approved. This ignited a debate and protests among the *'ulamā'* who questioned whether or not a woman could be a judge. Arguing that it was a necessity to appoint women to become judges, as male judges there were not fully qualified, the Director of Religious Justice at the Ministry of Religious Affairs at that time made a considerable effort to ensure the *'ulamā'* would accept the appointment of women judges and to convince them that what he was doing was right.[100] Now, with the qualifications laid down in the Act and applied to both male and female university graduates, the appointment of women judges in the Islamic courts has a solid legal foundation.

Applicants with the proper qualifications as laid down in the Act should pass different types of exams, including a test on their knowledge of Islamic law through the reading of *fiqh* texts. Realizing that many applicants, especially from IAINs did not have sufficient judicial knowledge, the Ministry of Religious Affairs, in cooperation with the Department of Justice, organized projects to develop and train its would-be judges. In 1992 to 1994, for example, the Ministry of Religious Affairs ran one project whose implementation was entrusted to the faculty of Islamic Law of the Institute for Islamic Studies (IAIN), now UIN, of Jakarta. The project, which ran four months of every year for three years, educated and trained aspiring judges who had not yet become civil servants. The main goal of the project was to socialize the Act of 1989 and the *kompilasi*.[101] Therefore the subjects taught in the project were oriented more toward practical matters pertaining to members of the judiciary. The participants were tutored in judicial sciences and trained in trial procedures, resolving cases, and making judgments. To ensure the best tuition, most tutors were judges from both religious courts and the Supreme Court, including Bustanul Arifin, Yahya Harahap, Bismar Siregar, and Thahir Azhari. No lecturers from the Institute of Islamic Studies (IAIN) were involved in the teaching activities.[102]

The establishment of the project was particularly related to the need to recruit new judges. With the expansion of their jurisdiction, the religious courts needed more judges to deal with the increase in cases put forward to them. For this, the Ministry of Religious Affairs recruited newly graduated students from the faculty of Islamic law. When they finished the program, they were sent to various religious courts, particularly newly established ones in remote areas. When the positions of judges were considered to have been adequately filled, the project was terminated. The training of the would-be judges recruited from among civil servants already employed in the provincial and branches of the Ministry of Religious Affairs, and with adequate knowledge of either Islamic law or national law, continues up to the present time.

V.5 *The Need for the Unification of Legal References*

The application of the Islamic Judicature Act of 1989 required the religious courts to have a more solid foundation, especially in terms of their substantive law. It has been widely acknowledged that, although they were established centuries ago, the Islamic courts so far have never had a uniform legal reference to which their judges could refer in resolving cases brought before them. Finding themselves in this unenviable situation, in deciding cases Muslim judges would for guidance refer to various classical *fiqh* texts of their choice, a practice which had resulted in uncertainties about legal transactions among Muslim society who sought justice in religious courts, since two cases of the same nature might receive two different rulings. As mentioned above, in 1958 the unification of substantive laws of the religious courts had been attempted. The circular letter from the Ministry of Religious Affairs limited the number of *fiqh* texts to be referred to by judges in religious courts and stated that Muslim judges should refer to only thirteen *fiqh* texts. Although a step in the right direction, this limitation did not halt the discrepancy of decisions on some cases which were virtually and exactly the same. In fact, although referring to only thirteen *fiqh* books after 1958, religious court judges still decided the same sorts of cases on different grounds, so that there were inevitably often divergent decisions handed down. The logical conclusion was accordingly to assume that their decisions had failed to remove persistent uncertainties in Muslim society.

Yahya Harahap, a Supreme Court judge, described how tragic the effect of the decisions based on *fiqh* books could be. He took an example of a case decided by a first instance-Islamic court with the reference of a certain *fiqh* book. Should the loser (be they defendant or plaintiff) take the case to the appellate court, where reference could be made to another *fiqh* book with a view on the case opposite to that of the *fiqh* book used by the first-instance court, the appellate court would reverse the decision. These two different decisions would inevitably result in conflict among the disputants. Each of the disputants would comply only with the reference which accorded with their own interest. Such a confusion of judgments could not be tolerated, as it produced discrepancies and robbed the Islamic courts of their credibility.[103]

In order to solve the problems and guarantee certainty in Muslim society, Yahya Harahap felt that a unification of legal references within the religious courts was essential. Therefore, he demanded that Indonesian Muslims attempt to codify and legalize Islamic familial rules. This entailed, he further argued: *first*, to complete the pillars of the religious court; *second*, to make legal application uniform; *third*, to strengthen the idea of *ukhuwah* (Islamic brotherhood); and, *fourth*, to deter the settling of disputes in the non-formal sector.[104] The necessity to compile a legal code of Islamic familial rules was therefore not merely relevant to guaranteeing certainty among Muslims seeking justice in the religious courts, but also to resolving other problems arising from the absence of a uniform law.

Turning to the first goal, it should be noted that there are three pillars of the religious court. The first is the existence of a well-organized judicial institution, and this has been met in the 1970 Act on the basic regulation of judicial authority. The second is that there be functionaries, namely, judges and advocates, and this was fulfilled as soon as the religious court was established. The third is uniform reference.[105] This last pillar, which is also relevant to the second goal, has remained an unattainable goal for the Islamic courts and thus should be resolved without further delay. While the first and the second goals are to address the discrepancy in the religious courts, the two last goals are more concerned about solving problems resulting from the failure of classical *fiqh* texts, as well as of the statutory law, to meet the general conditions in which contemporary problems in Indonesia occur. Although the 1974 Law of Marriage and a few clauses of the 1989 Islamic Judicature Act had made reforms and dealt with material laws, many outstanding matters had elicited no response. Inevitably, there had been problematic cases which had resulted in conflict and debate among Muslims. Moreover, many Muslim citizens, *'ulamā'*, and even members of the elites believe that familial matters are personal matters and should be free of intervention by the government. Above all, although there had been an attempt to adduce a proposal for the application of a national inheritance system in the 1960s, because of certain political aspects combined with the strength of the opposition by traditionalist *'ulamā'*, no Islamic legal codes on inheritance in particular or uniform substantive laws on issues have been issued in Indonesia, let alone in the religious courts.

A new day had dawned when the Indonesian president at that time, Soeharto, issued a Presidential Instruction identified as the *Inpres (Instruksi Presiden/* presidential instruction*)* No. 1/1991 about the socialization of the *Kompilasi Hukum Islam* (Compilation of Islamic Law). This *kompilasi* was to act as the substantive law which ought to be referred to by all the religious courts judges in making judgments on issues brought before them. With the *kompilasi*, it was hoped that the disparity between references used by judges and its consequence of producing divergent judgments on similar cases would come to an end.

V.6 From the Ministry of Religious Affairs to the Supreme Court

Just at the time when the religious courts had been gaining their firm institutional foundation and begun to anchor their juridical power, a challenge emerged. The government issued Law No. 35/1999, which reevaluated and replaced some articles in Law No. 14/1970 on the basic regulation of judicial authority. The articles which were replaced are Articles 11, 22 and 44. The most intriguing case of these replacements is Article 11, which governs the transfer of the administrative, structural, and financial authority of all the domains of the courts, from the executive, where each court fell under its own departments, to the Supreme Court, forming what is called a "single roof" judicial system.[106] As a consequence, the administration, structure, and finance of the religious courts, which had since independence been under the auspices of the Ministry of Religious Affairs, had to be transferred to the Supreme Court. This then would mean that the Supreme Court, which previously had been assigned responsibility for only such "technical juridical" matters, as noted in the Act No. 7/1989,[107] as giving guidance to judges in relation to the application of law both substantially and procedurally,[108] would be responsible for all the matters pertaining to the religious court.

This law inevitably caused debates in the Ministry of Religious Affairs. In response to these debates, the Minister of Religious Affairs organized a meeting with religious scholars (*'ulamā'*) and judges, at which three opinions were adduced. *First,* the transfer of the administrative authority of the Ministry of Religious Affairs over the religious courts would take place within five years. This was raised as a reference to Article 11A (1) of the regulation, which governs the time of transfer in general.[109] The

Article stated that the transfer could be done within a certain period, five years at most after the law had been issued. *Second*, the transfer could be done at any time. This opinion was the outcome of the understanding of a committee meeting on Article 11A (2), which specifically administers the time of transfer for the administrative authority of the Ministry of Religious Affairs over the religious courts to the Supreme Court. This Article states that the time of such a transfer is not defined.[110] *Third*, the transfer would be effectuated only if there was a basic amendment which, they maintained, should touch upon the scope of the judicial system as defined in the Constitution of Indonesia, *Undang-Undang Dasar 1945*, as shown in Article 24.[111] Taking account of these opinions, it has to be assumed that the religious scholars, as well as officials in the Ministry of Religious Affairs, would raise some objection to the law.

However, the law could be claimed to be lenient, as it allows an interval time for the implementation of transfer; but it withheld Muslim scholars from amplifying the debate. In fact, the lenience of the law even gives them time to evaluate what the law requires.[112] Although debate about the "single roof" system in the Ministry of Religious Affairs continues, since 30 June 2004 the religious courts have been totally under the control of the Supreme Court. On that day, the Minister of Religious Affairs under Megawati's Soekarnoputri's government, Said Agil Husin al-Munawar, symbolically handed over the Directorate of the Islamic Justice to the Head of the Supreme Court, Bagir Manan. This event marked the end of the "dual roof" system, in which religious Courts were organizationally, administratively and financially under the aegis of the Ministry of Religious Affairs, but judicially under the Supreme Courts. Through the creation of the "single roof" legal system, many feel that the status of the religious courts has been elevated, and is now more integrated into the national judicial system.

II The Making of the *Kompilasi Hukum Islam*

The issue of the Presidential Instruction on the socialization of the *Kompilasi Hukum Islam* in 1991 was a crucial event in the dynamics of Islam and the religious courts in Indonesia. Despite the fact that Indonesia is the largest Muslim country in the world, it is not an Islamic state in the sense that it has not adopted the *sharī'a* or the Islamic judiciary system. Its constitution and legal system are secular in nature, though some elements of Islam are integrated into their bodies.[1] One of the consequences of this is that the demands for the application of the *sharī'a* have been made repeatedly, and such demands have lain at the core of a series of tensions and conflicts in the country.

The enactment of the *kompilasi*, codifying the classical Islamic legal doctrines scattered in various *fiqh* books into a modern legal text, seems to have thawed the long congealed relationship between Islam and State in Indonesia. This event was a hallmark heralding the turning point in the New Order policy toward Islam, which had been previously marked by hostility, manipulation, and marginalization. By authorizing the *kompilasi*, the State demonstrated not only its rapprochement with Islam but also its support for the process of Islamization taking place in its political arena. In the eyes of some Muslims, this meant that Islamic law was increasingly gaining proper legal status in the national legal system.

This chapter is concerned with the process of making of the *kompilasi*, attempting to show how some different elements have contributed to its body. The first aspect to be examined is the political processes which led to the *kompilasi*'s enactment. Having extrapolated these, there will be an investigation of those ideas which contributed to its making. Having established the foundations, then the actual process of how the *kompilasi* was made and who was involved will be scrutinized. Finally, there will be an examination of what the enactment of the *kompilasi* has entailed within the scope of Indonesianization of Islamic law and in the political interest of the State.

I Islam in the New Order

I.1 *The New Order and Marginalization of Islam*

It must be stated at the outset that the history of the *kompilasi* is inextricably linked to the dynamics of State-Islam relations during the New Order. The "New Order" is the term commonly used to refer to the governmental system in Indonesia launched in 1966 and ending in 1998. This term is used to differentiate the Indonesian Government under Soeharto from its predecessor under Soekarno, which is now referred to as the "Old Order". The New Order came to power in 1966 when Soekarno, the first President of Indonesia, reluctantly signed a letter designated *Supersemar* (letter of command of 11 March), giving Soeharto authority to take all measures necessary to ensure the security of the State. The Temporary People's Consultative Assembly (MPRS) ratified the *Supersemar* and eventually appointed Soeharto the second President of Indonesia in 1968.[2]

It is generally believed that the establishment of the New Order and the simultaneous fall of the Old Order was the result of a combined effort undertaken by various parties, in which Muslim forces were the backbone. They stood on the frontline in calling for reforms and for the resignation of Soekarno, following the abortive [alleged] Indonesian Communist Party (PKI) coup in 1965. Having believed that they had made a significant contribution to the emergence of the New Order, Muslims immediately expressed new hopes for the granting of a greater role to Islam in the political arena of the State. They expected that the New Order would support their attempts to rehabilitate Muslim politics, which had been suppressed by Soekarno's regime, and allow them to play a decisive role in it.

One of the Muslim hopes was centered on the revival of the largest Islamic political party, the Masyumi (*Madjlis Syura' Muslimin Indonesia*, Consultative Council of Indonesian Muslims), banned by Soekarno in 1960. A variety of Islamic forces took to the streets to advocate its rehabilitation. The demonstrators felt that this was a historical necessity to which the New Order should acquiesce. In this context, it is important to note that the Masyumi was initially established in 1942, with the support of the Japanese occupation Government, as a successor to the Majelis Islam A'la Indonesia (MIAI), a Muslim umbrella organization set up in 1937 under the joint sponsorship of the Nahdlatul Ulama (NU) and the Muhammadiyah. In 1945, a new Masyumi was established as the party which would represent all Indonesian Muslims. In the first general election in 1955, this party won the second largest number of votes after the nationalist party, the *Partai Nasional Indonesia* (PNI). Later, Soekarno banned it after accusing some of its leaders of being involved in the Revolutionary Government of the Republic of Indonesia (PRRI) rebellion of 1958.[3]

The demand for the rehabilitation of the Masyumi proved fruitless.[4] On 21 December 1966, the Army officers who stood behind Soeharto issued a statement, which implied their opposition to whatever they considered to be an attempt to deviate from the Pancasila, the ideology of the State, and the Indonesian Constitution. From their point of view, the Masyumi was among those groups which had abandoned the true principles of the Pancasila.[5] In 1967, Soeharto issued a letter confirming the statement. This letter stated that the refusal of the Army to contemplate the idea of rehabilitating the Masyumi was soundly based on legal, constitutional, and psychological considerations.[6]

Considering that there seemed no possibility of reviving the Masyumi, Muslim leaders looked to another alternative which they thought could realize their original goal. They began to think of organizing a new political party under a different name. A committee consisting of seven Muslim leaders was formed to do the groundwork. The task of this committee was to arrange the formation of the Parmusi (Indonesian Muslim Party), a new party designed as an alternative to the Masyumi, so as to accommodate Muslim modernist forces in its fold. Although the Government agreed to the formation of this party, it objected to the inclusion or participation of important former Masyumi leaders in it. In a meeting between with the committee members, Soeharto confirmed that no single former Masyumi leader was to be permitted to hold a leading position in the new party. Soeharto recommended that Muhammad Roem, the appointed leader in the Congress of the Parmusi held in Malang, withdraw from the leadership.[7]

While demanding the rehabilitation of the Masyumi, Muslims also campaigned for the implementation of the Jakarta Charter (Piagam Jakarta), a document originally produced by the Committee of Nine (Panitia Sembilan) during the constitutional debates in 1945, as a form of compromise between the secular nationalist and Islamic nationalist groups. In this document there is a stipulation that the State was to be established on the principle of *Ketuhanan yang Maha Esa dengan Kewajiban Menjalankan Syari'at Islam bagi Pemeluk-pemeluknya* (Belief in One God with the obligation for adherents of Islam to cleave to Islamic law), giving a constitutional status to the *Shari'a*.[8] These "seven words" were briefly incorporated into the constitution, but then quickly removed from the draft, following the objections raised by the Christian-nationalist group.[9] After being hotly but fruitlessly debated for many years under Soekarno, the Jakarta Charter question was outlawed under Soeharto as destabilizing.

In spite of the obvious discontent and frustration, the New Order continued to dismiss Muslim demands in its search to anchor the hegemony of its power. Having carefully observed the factors contributing to the collapse of the Soekarno regime, the New Order persisted in its attachment to the Pancasila, and constructed a new system which got rid of the ideological debates which had made much of national interest and had ignored such development goals as achieving economic progress. After it had paved the way by heavily emphasizing the need to de-politicize expressions of religious belief, the New Order then began to implement the party fusion policy which reduced the number of political parties. With the exception of Golkar, the Government party, in 1973 the New Order pressured the nine existing parties which participated in the general election in 1971[10] to group themselves into no more than two different clusters. The Muslim parties, namely, Parmusi, NU, Perti (Partai Tarbiyyah Indonesia, and PSII (Partai Serikat Islam Indonesia), were merged by the Government into a single body identified by a name which had nothing to do with religious affiliation, the United Development Party (Partai Persatuan Pembangunan/PPP). Other minority parties which basically consisted of Christian and nationalist parties, including the Roman Catholic party, the Protestant party, and the remainder of the former Indonesian Nationalist party, were united as the Indonesian Democratic Party (Partai Demokrasi Indonesia/PDI).[11]

While forging ahead with these projects, the New Order introduced an intensive program of ideological training, called the *Pedoman Penghayatan dan Pengamalan Pancasila* (Guidelines to Experiencing and Implementing Pancasila). Through this program, the position of the Pancasila was strengthened. The New Order simultaneously glorified the Pancasila in a plethora of slogans, transmitted through educational institutions, the media, State ceremonies and other societal activities. Any expressions which sounded as if they might jar with the Pancasila were repressed and were swiftly labeled either "left extreme", identical to "communist", or "right extreme", identical with those aspiring for the establishment of an Islamic state. In such a heavily hegemonic atmosphere, the space for participation by society appeared to be limited. Nearly all aspects of societal life fell under the control of the State.

Interestingly perhaps, keeping pace with its attempts to marginalize Muslim politics, the New Order sponsored the proposal for a marriage law at the beginning of the 1970s. This bill represented an attempt to unify laws relating to the act of marriage itself and other related fields conforming to the various customary *(adat)* and religious laws. It was also a response to Indonesian women's questions about their legal position in the event of polygyny and divorce.[12] Despite this apparently progressive gesture, Muslims perceived this proposal as being informed by political interest, as through adducing this proposal it seemed the New Order was apparently seeking to reduce the role of Islamic institutions which were beyond State control, and at the same time, strengthen the role of civil administration.[13] The bill required the civil registration of marriages and court approval for divorce and polygyny among Muslims, as well as entrusting the issues to the general courts. Such provisions sent Muslims the message that the State intended to elevate the general courts above the religious courts, and as such was deemed unacceptable to them.

What perturbed them even more deeply was they believed that this proposal offended their religious beliefs, as it included some points which contradicted Islamic rules. The bill introduced tight regulation of polygyny, which was directly opposed by a number of *'ulamā'*, who sought to maintain the practice. It also recognized the legal consequences of adoption and permitted marriage between a Muslim woman and a non-Muslim man. These were subject to criticism, particularly from those elements of the society which perceived them as contradicting Islamic rules.[14] Some feared that if, for example, the two later provisions mentioned above were passed then the law would make it easier for Muslims to adopt children, with the associated legal consequences, and for Muslim women to marry non-Muslims.

Perceived, rightly or wrongly, as a New Order project to control Islamic institutions and as being incongruous with Islamic laws, the proposal set off a wave of protests from Muslims and was inevitably considered further evidence of Government hostility towards Islam.[15] Unsurprisingly, it provoked a massive Muslim reaction. When Parliament discussed it, no less than 700 women from various women's groups,[16] as well as hundreds of Muslim youths, temporarily occupied the floor of the Parliament building,[17] while a massive demonstration was staged outside the building. In this situation, a lobbying session was held between the Muslim groups represented by the United Development Party (PPP) and the Government represented by the military group. In this lobby, a compromise was reached by agreeing to the removal of some articles pertaining to issues considered contradictory to Islamic principles. After it was revised, the draft was then passed as the National Marriage Law in the Parliament on 22 December 1973 and ratified as Law on Marriage No. 1/1974.

The ulterior motive of the New Order behind the enactment of the Marriage Law seems to have been to ensure its firm grip on power and leadership and to be certain to maintain its control of society constitutionally. The New Order was convinced that the economic development it had made its main platform could only be reached if political stability was a guaranteed constant. In this case, the New Order utilized the institution of law as an instrument of social engineering, and this can be seen in the character of the law.[18] Not only does the law mark the change from revolutionary law to development law, but legislation had also crossed the threshold at which law becomes one of the instruments of social control by the Government.

The Government decision to amend and then pass the law might also have been influenced by the threatening political climate in which, for the first time since the inception of his presidency, Soeharto experienced a crisis in political support. Beginning quite modestly in 1970, students began to criticize a variety of the policies he promulgated. Later they took to the streets to express their discontent. The peak of the demonstrations occurred on 15 January 1974, known as "Malari Affair", when thousands of students besieged the Parliament building.[19] Around about the same time, Muslims began to be critical of Government policies which they considered to be weighted in favor of Christians or of secularization, at the expense of the weakening power of Muslims in the political arena of the State. At that time, some hard-line Muslim groups began to dare to oppose Soeharto openly. Nevertheless, although motivated by such a political crisis, the amendment was still a first and major victory for the Islamic faction against the New Order regime and the secularists.

Despite the setback, the New Order remained undeterred and continued its attempts to marginalize Muslim politics. These attempts culminated in 1983, when the New Order enforced the idea of the Pancasila as the sole basis of all existing political organizations, referred to as the *Asas Tunggal*. The enforcement was issued on 16 August 1982. In this case, both PPP and PDI, the only two legally permitted political parties, with the exception of Golkar, had no choice but to endorse the Pancasila as their ideological basis. In its party congress held in August 1984, PPP proclaimed that it had replaced Islam with the Pancasila as its ideological basis. On this occasion, PPP also changed its symbol from the *Ka'ba* (denoting the holy shrine in Mecca to which Muslims orient their faces during their five daily prayers) to the *bintang* (the Star, one of the five Pancasila symbols).[20]

I.2 Politics of Islamization

Fully aware of the restraints imposed by the New Order regime on the overt expression of Muslim politics, from the beginning of 1970s, Indonesian Muslims began to turn their interest towards the spheres of economics and education. This change of direction was bolstered by the Government policy of speeding up the process of development and modernization, which was initiated in 1969 with the *Pelita* (Pembangunan Lima Tahun), or Five-year Development Plan. Within the scope of this program, Muslims began to participate in higher education, given a significant fillip at that time by the rapid migration of rural masses who sought new lives in the big cities of Indonesia. The enrolment of more Muslims with a *santri* (Islamic student) background in modern schools and universities resulted in the intellectual growth of Muslims, which stimulated the emergence of a new Muslim middle class and, simultaneously, resulted in the acceleration of the process of what came to be called *priyayization.* This phenomenon allowed *santris* the mobility to spread into various sectors of activities and the Government services, as well as to penetrate the modern business structure.[21]

These new intellectual Muslims no longer represented a backward and marginal group; they now formed a potent new socio-political group, which held certain ideas and harbored a pool of considerable skills. They were extremely anxious to modernize Islamic thought and rejuvenate religious understanding. To achieve their purpose, most of them chose to become activists in Islamic student organizations such as the Himpunan Mahasiswa Islam (HMI, Islamic Students Association), known as one of the most renowned in the country. They believed that Muslim comprehension of their religious messages would not stagnate. Nurcholish Madjid, a graduate of IAIN Jakarta, who for two consecutive periods served as the national chairman of HMI (1966-1969 and 1969-1971), formally instigated the necessity of the renewal of Islamic thought in his paper entitled *Keharusan Pembaharuan Pemikiran Islam dan Masalah Integrasi Ummat.* He pointed out that Indonesian Muslims were suffering from stagnation in religious thinking and had lost the "psychological striking force" in their seemingly fruitless struggle. In fact, Nurcholish observed, the majority of Muslims were unable to differentiate values which are transcendental from those which are temporal. Furthermore, Nurcholish suggested that Muslims should be able to liberate themselves from the tendency to transcend values and to "secularize" their perceptions of the worldly issues, which included social matters, culture and politics.[23]

This newly emerging generation of Muslim intellectuals therefore did not share the idea of establishing an Islamic State, nor did they aspire to the goal of an Islamic State. Instead, they considered the realization of a just, participatory construct of the State as their goal. This should best be achieved not only through the participation of Islamic parties, but also through the participation of the bureaucracy.[24] In this regard, they argued that Islam does not oblige its adherents to establish an Islamic State.[25] However, they did believe that Islam provides a set of ethical values on which to base political principles, such as justice (*'adl*), consultation, (*shūra'*), and egalitarianism (*musāwā*). They argued that the current form of the Indonesian nation-state had adequate foundations to encourage the realization of these Islamic socio-political precepts. Therefore they proclaimed that the Indonesian nation-state deserved to be accorded religio-political legitimacy and acceptance by Muslims.[26] Their acceptance of the current form of the State was coupled with their new perception of the Pancasila. They considered this ideological foundation as reflecting the substance of Islamic teachings.[27] A number of them even argued that Pancasila could be compared to the Constitution of Medina in that both substantially recognized the relationship between religious values and the affairs of the State.[28]

Their positive feelings towards the current form of the State of Indonesia and its ideological basis did not seem to weigh heavily upon them. Initially they were probably assured by the proclaimed promise of the Government about the stability of the current form of the Indonesian nation. In fact, the President once stated and adamantly assured the Muslims that with the sole foundation of Pancasila, the Indonesian nation-state would not be turned into a secular state.[29] No matter how their new thoughts about the current form of the Indonesian nation-state and its ideological foundation evolved, it provided a basis in which the new generation of Muslim intellectuals struggled to achieve the articulation and the realization of Islamic socio-political ideals. This new Islamic political activism can be said to have elicited many positive results. The most evident of these has been the political reconciliation between the State and Islam,[30] which was demonstrated by the agreement of the former to issue a number of policies highlighting the religious interests of the latter.[31]

In 1990, Soeharto personally supported the establishment of the *Ikatan Cendekiawan Muslim se-Indonesia* (Association of Indonesian Muslim Intellectuals, ICMI), an organization composed of many Government bureaucrats and academics. The foundation of ICMI under the leadership of B.J. Habibie, Soeharto's close confidant and Minister of Research and Technology, as well as chairman of *Badan Pengkajian dan Penerapan Teknologi* (Board for the Study and Implementation of Technology, BPPT), was suggested by some scholars as a way to reach out to the large and growing group of Islamic intellectuals and educated *santri* Muslims previously located outside the general political sphere, and who had often felt alienated from the Government. This organization has also often been perceived as a vehicle for bringing Muslim thinkers and activists a step close to power.[32]

The President's authorization for the formation of the organization pleased most Indonesian Muslims. It had also convinced them that the organization would be able to promote the Islamization of the Indonesian State. Nevertheless, Hefner claims that it came as a surprise to some Western scholars, who were convinced that the Soeharto Government was deeply opposed to anything that might expand Muslim influence in Indonesian politics and society. To non-Muslims and secular-nationalists, the foundation of this organization was not only a surprise, but also a threat. Hefner has said that non-Muslims and secular-nationalists considered Soeharto's action a dangerous departure from non-sectarian principles.[33]

Within this context, the New Order also introduced several policies demonstrating its accommodating attitude towards Muslim interests in the legislature. In 1989 the Government issued a new regulation on school curricula which explicitly recognized the role of religious instruction at all levels of education. The former educational curricula had covered only the fields of science, technology, and the arts. The new regulation also guaranteed that Muslim students attending Christian schools would receive Islamic religious instruction.

In the same year, the Government again demonstrated its accommodation, this time in relation to the development of the religious courts through the enactment of the Islamic Judicature Act (*Undang-Undang Peradilan Agama No.1. Th 1989*) dealing with the legal procedures to be applied in the religious courts, whose process of legislation very clearly reveals the extensive role of the State. In the climate of increasing tolerance between Muslims and non-Muslims developing since the 1980s,[34] Muslims assumed that the DPR debate on the draft submitted by the Government to the Parliament (DPR) on 28 January 1989 would run smoothly. In this they were sorely disappointed. At the time DPR was discussing the draft, the matter was also widely debated outside DPR. A vehement debate arose between those in favor of the draft and those who were not. Whereas almost all the Islamic groups supported it and were pleased with it, the other groups opposed it, [35]claiming that it sounded all sorts of warning bells. Especially those in favor of the unification of laws questioned whether or not the proposed Act, which naturally regulated Muslim legal family issues, was actually in keeping with the principle of the unification of the law in the Indonesian legal system. The most fundamental concern underlying their objection to the Act was their suspicion that it would be a cover for the realization of the acceptance of the Jakarta Charter, which would oblige Muslims to implement Islamic law.[36]

In this case, the Government stepped forward, convincing all parties of the need for such an Act. When the debate in the DPR dragged on for several days (about seventy-six hours), the Coordinating Minister of Social Welfare, Alamsyah Ratuprawiranegara, urged the Golkar (Golongan Karya) party to agree with the Act. The reason he gave was that the approval should not be reached by a show of votes, as this would embarrass the President. Having been forced to agree with the Act, the Golkar finally submitted. PDI (Indonesian Democratic Party), which was still debating the bill, was persuaded by the Army to approve it. Again, the Army played mediator between the pro- and anti-law groups, as it had done in the proposal for the Law on Marriage, but this time as a counterforce. Whereas in the case of Marriage Law the Army had persuaded PPP (United Development Party) to acquiesce, in this case it turned its attentions to the PDI.[37]

To assuage the objections of non-Muslim and secular-nationalists, Soeharto himself responded to their qualms and assured all the groups of the necessity of the Act. He said that the Muslim community was in need of a special law on Islamic judicature to govern its family life. He also argued that the Act did not contradict the Pancasila, the sole fundamental basis of the nation, as some groups had stated. Instead, the Act should be seen as an implementation of the Constitution of the 1945 and the Pancasila.[38] Adopting the same tone, Munawir Sjadzali, the then Minister of Religious Affairs, commented that the draft of the Act would be concerned only with the procedures and structures of the religious courts and that their jurisdiction would be limited to marriage, inheritance, religious endowment (*waqf*) and alms-giving (*zakāt* and *ṣadaqa*). Many such scholars of Islamic law, such as Ismail Sunny and M. Daud Ali, also did their best to convince doubters that the Act would not jeopardize the State's principle of the unification of law. They hastened to stress that the Act was not a cloak under which to usher in the Jakarta Charter.[39] Finally, having weighed the reasons given by the Muslim scholars and accepted the guarantee of Soeharto, various factions in the DPR approved the draft. After the revision of some clauses,[40] the draft was then agreed upon and ratified on 29 December 1989 as Act No. 7/1989.

In 1991, the Government also passed a new regulation on school uniforms, which reversed its policy on *jilbab* (head coverings). Under this new regulation, the Government decided to allow Muslim girls to wear long skirts and *jilbab* (head coverings) to State schools, instead of short skirts and being bare-headed, and ratified the regulation into *Surat Keputusan* or SK No. 100/C/Kep/D/1991. Hence, Muslim girls who wished to wear a *jilbab*, because of their religious beliefs, might now do so without fear of being punished. Before the passing of this new regulation, Muslim girls attending the State schools were forbidden to wear the *jilbab*, even though they simply wanted to honor their religious doctrines, and those who wore the *jilbab* during school hours were considered to be violating the school uniform code (SK No. 052/ Kep/D/1982). The Minister of Religious Affairs and the Minister of Home Affairs also issued a joint decision on the Guidance of Badan Amil Zakat, Infaq and Sadaqah (BAZIS)/ the Board of Amil Zakat, Infaq, dan Sadaqah (No. 29 and 47/1991). In spite of these new decisions, the State did no more than supervise and guide the implementation of *zakāt*. They did not deal with 'zakat payment', which is the obligation of *muzakki* (zakat payer) but with 'zakat management'.

Two years later, the Government reluctantly agreed to stop running the national lottery, which had existed under a whole series of different names: Porkas (Pekan Olahraga dan Kesehatan, Weekly Donation for Sport and Health); KSOB (Kupon Sumbangan Olahraga Berhadiah,

Donation Coupon for Sport with Prizes); TSSB (Titipan Sumbangan Sosial Berhadiah, Allocation of Philanthropic Donations with Prizes), but was later popularly referred to as SDSB (*Sumbangan Dermawan Sosial Berhadiah*, Philanthropic Donation with Prizes), and was reported to have raised a large sum of money to enable the State to fund sporting events, welfare programs and other such undertakings. Being considered a form of gambling, a pastime forbidden in Islam, Muslims were strongly opposed to it and made repeated demands the Government abolish it, and in 1993 the Government finally closed it down.[41]

II Historical Ideas behind the Making of the *Kompilasi*

As has been stated above, the shift in the State policy towards Islam coincided with the fact that many Muslim leaders now abandoned their attempts to establish an official Islamic State, but were content to strive to infuse society with Islamic precepts and move towards a gradual Islamization of the country. In terms of realization of Islamic law, they no longer spoke of a general but only a partial realization, that is, the application of certain elements, which included merely familial matters. They strove to integrate the principles of Islamic law into national law through the regulations issued by the Government. Considering that the national legal system was still in its formative stages, it was therefore perfectly feasible that Islamic principles might be introduced into national law. This feasibility was remarked upon by a previous Minister of Justice, Ismail Saleh, who said that the national legal system was an open system, which meant that it always considered any laws existing in the world as its raw material as long as they were not contradictory to the Pancasila values, the Constitutional norms, and national interests, and were in line with the legal requirements of the Indonesian State and nation.[42]

To mark the realization and legislation of Islamic family law, Muslims now have what has come to be called the *Kompilasi Hukum Islam*. From the perspective of legal development among Indonesian Muslim scholars, this piece of State legalization reflects a long struggle by a number of Muslims for the application of Islamic law in Indonesia. The preliminary struggle took place in 1950s when the idea of the formulation of an Indonesian school of Islamic law emerged.[43] In the 1980s, the same agenda re-emerged in the form of the re-actualization of Islamic law, which developed in the direction of the unification of legal references in the religious courts. In this section I will present these ideas, mainly because they have survived and influenced the present debate on the nature of Islamic law, and led to the enactment of the *kompilasi*.

II.1 *The Formulation of an Indonesian Madhhab: Hazairin and Hasbi ash-Shiddieqy*

The *kompilasi* owes its origins to the idea of formulating a distinct Indonesian school of Islamic law, proposed by Hazairin (1905-1975) in the 1950s. A scholar of both Islamic and *adat* law at the University of Indonesia, he sought to bridge the gap between Islam and *adat*, by advocating the development of a distinctive body of Islamic law. He was convinced that the reform of Islamic law was not an individual matter, but rather a collective task to be completed by representatives of the community, working in close partnership with the State. He wanted to see problems in the Muslim community solved by formal institutions with the authority to act on religious issues.[44] For this purpose, he once suggested that by the formation of *Dewan Fatwa* (Fatwa Council), the institution of the mosque could be utilized to issue decisions on questions of religious law, and serve the People's Representative Assembly (MPR) as an associated body.[45]

Hazairin focused his attention on family law issues, observing that a number of the ideas of the classical *'ulamā'* were no longer appropriate to the contemporary Indonesian situation. He took inheritance law as an example, claiming that the rules of inheritance proposed in the classical *fiqh* texts were not relevant to the actual socio-cultural conditions in Indonesia. He argued that the traditional Arab social customs were incorporated into the body of Islamic law of inheritance. He illustrated this by pointing out that the traditionally accepted preference for male agnatic relatives in Islamic law had no clear textual precedent in the Qur'ān. It tended to be based on *ḥadīth* or *ijmā'* accommodating the particular situation prevailing in early Arabia.[46] Therefore, in order for Islamic rules on inheritance to become the living law of Indonesian society, they must be interpreted according to actual conditions in Indonesia. In this case, he found that a majority of Indonesian Muslims tended towards the bilateral system of marriage, and consequently this system would best serve as a model for a new and unified system of Islamic inheritance to be applied in Indonesia. Accordingly, he proposed a national inheritance system based on the principle of bilateral descent.[47]

Understanding that certain passages in the Qur'ān relating to inheritance issues do appear to be fixed, Hazairin preferred to interpret the extra-Qur'ānic system of determining heirs which grew out of the traditional social customs of Arab society. The Qur'ānic stipulation of the allotment of half-shares to daughters was, in his opinion, based upon a clear and authoritative scriptural foundation which could not be ignored.[48] Therefore, instead of interpreting such passages, he focused on rules which could be interpreted under the bilateral rubric. In this regard, Hazairin stated that in classical *fiqh*, after certain fixed shares of an estate have been awarded, the reminder of the estate is divided in such a way that agnatic relatives (related through males) take priority over uterine relatives (related through females). This way of dividing the residuals of an estate is understandable to a person who follows or relates it to Arab society norms, in which the family system is patriarchal.[49] This analysis, he continues, can be more fully confirmed by the fact that the Shi'īte jurisprudence does not subordinate uterine relatives to the agnatic.[50]

Hazairin found that the systems of inheritance offered in the classical *fiqh* texts and applied in Indonesia do not provide a good solution to the problem of dividing up an estate. With this conviction, he introduced the concept of *mawālī* (replacement heirs), besides *dhawū al-farā'iḍ* and *dhawū al-qarābat*.[51] By doing so, he tried to cope with not only such gender issues as *mawālī* , which includes all generations regardless of their sex, but also with the issues of justice in general in the Indonesian sense.[52] Hazairin believed if something had not been established in the texts of the Qur'ān and *ḥadīth*, but was felt to be among the concerns of Muslim society today, a new line of law should be developed. In this regard, Hazairin found that the share due to those grandchildren whose parents have died before an estate is divided is not explicitly regulated.[53] If this is the case, he says, it is unjust. He was convinced that the Qur'ān must have dealt with this matter and would not have left such a situation which could wreak disaster on human beings. His idea was that Verse 33 of Chapter 4, which talks about replacement or representation (*mawālī*), provides guidance for handling and solving the problem.[54]

For the majority of Indonesian Muslim leaders, Hazairin's ideas were too radical and extreme, and inevitably elicited opposition. In fact, these ideas won no positive response until 1961, when Hasbi ash-Shiddieqy, a professor at the State Institute for Islamic Studies (IAIN) in Yogyakarta, argued the need to reformulate a new school of Islamic law taking greater account of the social and historical context of Indonesia. Hasbi thought that what had traditionally been established as Islamic law among the founders of *madhhab* should actually be thought of as "Arab *fiqh*".[55] Realizing that, in their contemporary societies, both Arab and Indonesian, members are faced with many new questions, Hasbi saw a need to find different ways of problem-solving. In Hasbi's eyes, the Arab *fiqh* is already outdated and unsuitable, not only for grappling with actual contemporary situations in Indonesia, but also for addressing problems faced by the Arabs themselves.[56] In this context, Hasbi argued that Islam could only remain a vital source of guidance in the lives of Indonesian Muslims, if the methods of understanding scripture and law could be re-conceptualized in accordance with the specific conditions and the current needs of Indonesian society.[57] For this purpose, he called for a new and more directly relevant method in order to achieve the appropriate interpretation and application of principles from the original source to particular cases and conditions.

To realize the creation of *fiqh* with a peculiarly Indonesian setting, Hasbi demanded that the State play a role. He stressed the necessity for Indonesian Muslims to conduct a "collective *ijtihād*", facilitated by an institution officially recognized by the Indonesian Government.[58] Here, Hasbi sought to demonstrate that the establishment of a more appropriate place for Islamic law in the modern Indonesian State would not be successful if it were to take the form of a movement by one of any of the Islamic groups against the State. Rather, it would be the task of an organized body of *ahl al-ḥall wa al-'aqd,* formed from the corps of Muslim scholars with a wider knowledge of Islamic law.[59] Proposing this concept of *ijtihād,* Hasbi seemed to emphasize his belief that *ijtihād* should not be attempted arbitrarily.[60]

Hasbi and Hazairin's ideas have some parallels with the supposition that the theory of *ijtihād* has to be developed in keeping with contemporary situations. In the case of Indonesia, it is argued that, if in the past the practice of *ijtihād* could be exercised by a qualified *mujtahid* using his original ideas and independent personal opinion, in modern times its exercise would better if it were integrated into the working of such collective bodies or organizations the Majelis Ulama Indonesia (Indonesian Council of *'Ulamā'*/MUI), NU, and the Muhammadiyah. Thus it is no longer the right of individual *mujtahid,* but must be accomplished collectively by a recognized and responsible body.[61]

Hasbi and Hazairin's visions on the formulation and the application of the Indonesian *fiqh* emphasized a sense of Indonesian-ness, in terms of both of the specific local conditions prevailing in Indonesia and the specific character of the Indonesian State, particularly in relation to its legal policy based on Pancasila, the ideology of the State. There is no doubt that these ideas are a reflection of thinking which lay at the core of the Islamic legal discourse at that time. Although they gained no widespread acceptance during their lifetime, or currency in and support from the Soekarno regime, as in the context of political competition rife at that time, this regime tended to see Islam as a threat and even introduced some repressive policies to control Islamic groups. Nonetheless, their ideas helped lay the groundwork for the development of Islamic law in the 1980s.

II.2 The Re-actualization of Islamic Law: Munawir Sjadzali

The idea of formulating a distinct Indonesian school of Islamic law proposed by both Hasbi and Hazairin seems to have taken on a new life in the 1980s. It fell within the scope of re-actualization of Islamic teachings proposed by a prominent and high-ranking Muslim and statesman,

Munawir Sjadzali (1925-2005), who served as a long-time senior official in the Department of Foreign Affairs before his appointment as the Minister of Religious Affairs in the last two consecutive cabinets of the New Order (1983-1993). His ideas gained significance in the new wave of intellectualism among Muslims during the New Order, born of the need to deal with the failure of reactionary Muslim leaders to realize their political agendas in the early years of the Soeharto regime. With a background in Islamic studies and having written an MA thesis entitled "Indonesia's Muslim Parties and their Political Concepts", he had a particular interest in Islamic issues. While serving as Ambassador to the United Arab Emirates in 1976-1980, he collected many works on Islam. His long years of service in the Department of Foreign Affairs, as he himself recognized, had prevented him from becoming involved as early as some of his fellow scholars in the discourse on the new Islamic intellectualism.[62] His appointment as the Minister of Religious Affairs brought him back to Islamic discourse and encouraged him to become engaged in the new line of Islamic intellectualism, and to socialize his ideas on the re-actualization of Islamic teachings.

Sjadzali's ideas on Islamic re-actualization have generally been considered to have contributed to the development of a new theological underpinning of political Islam. The hallmark of his religio-political ideas was manifested in the publication of his *Islam dan Tata Negara* (Islam and the State Order) in 1990. However, the central point of his ideas was general in the sense that he encouraged Muslims to exercise religious *ijtihād* objectively, in order to make Islam more responsive to the contemporary and local needs of the Indonesian nation. Looking specifically at the development of Islamic law, his encouragement can be understood from an examination of his discussion on the principles of Islamic inheritance, particularly on the share of children of the deceased. The stipulation of the Qur'ān that a son inherits twice as much as daughter was, according to him, under some conditions contradictory to the very notion of justice. Sjadzali argued that the decision noted in the Qur'ān – that a female receives only a half-share of that of the male from an estate – is not a final decision. In view of the character of gradualism in the establishment of Islamic law (*tashrī'*), it is still awaiting completion. The fact that in the era of paganism Arab females were considered property and chattel, and did not have any rights to property, meant that the process of giving equal status to females could not be accomplished in one go. He argued that the text needed a gradual reworking to accomplish the abrogation of the old pagan rule, as direct and complete process would have caused instability in societal and familial life.

Using the analogy of the assumption that the abolition of slavery had not been realized by the time the Prophet died, Sjadzali assumed that the process of giving the female equal status to the male in claims to an estate had also not been finished, hence this process should be accomplished when conditions allowed. He argued that if we think that the slavery can still be legally practiced, as rules governing it are still in the Qur'ān, we have then contradicted the modern principles of justice and equity. Therefore, as those rules militate against a basic human right, we must set them aside and make ourselves guilty of the institution of slavery. It is on these same grounds, and based on his personal experiences, that Sjadzali affirmed equal shares in an estate should be given to a female, although the Qur'ān still says that female was allotted only half that accorded to male.[63]

The importance of Sjadzali's ideas to supporting the suggestion of the equal shares of female and male in an inheritance lies beyond the rhetoric of the inheritance issue.[64] He was clearly inclined to point out that there are some Qur'ānic stipulations which are no longer appropriate to the requirements of the contemporary era. In fact, he observed that there was an inconsistent and ambivalent attitude among many Muslim leaders toward Islamic law. Even though the Qur'ān has prohibited usury (*ribā'*) and granted a son twice the portion of a daughter, he thought that most Indonesian Muslims, including *'ulamā'*, had used the banking service themselves and had taken anticipatory action in the event of their demise through the concept of *hibah*, namely giving or distributing their property to their children while they are still alive, to assure equal distribution among their offspring.[65]

Believing that Islam is a dynamic religion, Sjadzali therefore suggested that Muslims undertake a re-actualization agenda to make Islam more compatible with the local and present circumstances in Indonesia. Although he nowhere specified a legislation of Islamic law in the form of code, his ideas on the re-actualization of Islamic law were interpreted as a call for the creation of a school of Islamic law more appropriate to modern Indonesian needs, and one which would more narrowly define the parameters of all future debates on national law reform, particularly on inheritance issues, as those of Hazairin had done.

III The Process of Creating the *Kompilasi*

III.1 Bustanul Arifin's Proposal

What we have discussed above reflects the evolution of the idea of the application of Islamic law in Indonesia in relation to the changes in the State attitude towards Islam. Munawir Sjadzali's idea of the re-actualization of Islamic law was clearly a continuation of Hazairin's and Hasbi's thoughts about the creation of a distinct Indonesian school of Islamic law. Sjadzali seemed to attempt to give new resonance to their ideas after the State had succeeded in reinforcing its domination over Muslims, as proven by the acceptance of the sole national ideology, Pancasila, by Muslim organizations. All these ideas have provided a basis for the various attempts to ensure the inclusion of Islamic law in the legal system of the State. Within this context, the idea of the making of the *kompilasi* came to the fore.

Bustanul Arifin played an enormously important role in the dynamics behind the creation of the *kompilasi*. His role was officially approved by his appointment as chairman of the Special Chamber in the Supreme Court treating judicial appeals from religious courts, which was established through the negotiation of the Ministry of Religious Affairs. Once this special chamber had been accomplished, the cooperation between the Ministry of Religious Affairs and the Supreme Court strengthened, even more so after Bustanul Arifin assumed the position of its chairman in 1982. This cooperation led to the process which culminated in the passing of the Islamic Judicature Act. It was reported that the draft of the Islamic Judicature Act itself had been prepared when K.H Ahmad Dahlan led the Ministry of Religious Affairs in the 1970s. Nevertheless, the Government only got round to doing something about it in 1982. Its response was signaled by the proposal of the Ministry of Justice to set up a committee, led by Bustanul Arifin.[66]

Having succeeded in making the Act, as the Chief of the Special Chamber in charge of monitoring the development of the religious courts, Bustanul Arifin seems not to have been fully satisfied with his attempts to apply Islamic law in general, and to develop the institution of a religious court in particular. In fact, like the other Muslim judges, he was still bothered by the fact that the religious courts did not have any systematic and uniform legal reference, and that Indonesian Muslims still embraced various perspectives on Islamic law.

To solve such problems, Bustanul Arifin shared with the other Indonesian Muslim scholars and judges the idea of creating a unifying Islamic legal code, which would assume a strong legal enforcement. To realize the idea, in 1985 Bustanul Arifin, backed up by Muslim judges and officials of the religious courts, proposed the project of codifying Islamic family rules to the President. In this case, Bustanul Arifin was well aware that the year 1985 was the most apposite time for his project proposal. At that juncture, as will be described below, the President needed more political support in order to impose his *asas tunggal* policy. Arifin also made sure he adduced a good reason to the President to explain why it was necessary the project be undertaken. To cultivate the President's support, in this case he cleverly utilized the argument pertinent to the State ideology, Pancasila, on which the President always highly insisted. When he met the President, Bustanul Arifin told him that Indonesian Muslims held various perspectives on Islamic law and that this could be a potential threat to the position of the Pancasila. To ensure the safety and survival of the Pancasila, he argued, the State would be well-advised to unify these various perspectives into one codified text, the *kompilasi*.[67]

III.2 Approval of the Project

Being very sure that both the timing and the reason for his proposal were attuned to the political interests of the State, Bustanul Arifin felt highly confident that the project of codifying Islamic familial rules would become a reality. What he predicted did indeed come true. The President agreed to the proposal and actualized it by approving a joint decision of the Minister of Religious Affairs and the Supreme Court announcing the project. This joint letter was ratified into *Surat Keputusan Bersama* (SKB) Number 07/KMA/1985, and was followed by the SKB Number 25/1985, dealing with the pragmatic business of the establishment of a special commission. It was not long before this commission, consisting of officials of both the Supreme Court and the Ministry of Religious Affairs, named Bustanul Arifin as its head.[68] Not only did the President agree to the proposal, he was ready to fund it. It was reported that the President was irritated by the vacillating stance of the Ford Foundation, which had initially agreed to fund the project but delayed its support. In Presidential Decree No. 19/1985, the President underlined his personal readiness to fund the project and provided Rp 230,000,000.00, a large amount of money, which was withdrawn not from the State budget but from his personal capital.[69]

Although the proposal had been approved by the President, the project's name was not yet settled. Initially, Bustanul Arifin, who was supported by the then Minister of Religious Affairs, Munawir Sjadzali, intended to use the word '*kodifikasi*/codification' instead of '*kompilasi*/compilation' for their project. However, the proposal of these Muslim scholars, who although in this case supposedly spoke on behalf of Muslims first and foremost represented the tendencies of the Government party, in suggesting such a specifically technical legal term, raised strong objections among a number of *'ulamā'*. They were unhappy about its overt sense of legal technicality and suspected it to be an attempt by the Government to show a preference for one elastic school of *madhhabs*. To eliminate the criticism and obtain the approval of the *'ulamā'*, it was decided to define the project as a *kompilasi* of Islamic rules, rather than *kodifikasi*.[70] More importantly, such a definition was intended to avoid any implication that the Government was engaged in the creation of Islamic doctrine.

At this juncture it is important to note the literal meaning of the English word of *kompilasi*, namely, compilation, which implies something basically very different from *kodifikasi* (codification). The word "compilation" is the noun from the verb "to compile", which has two meanings: act or process of collecting materials for making a book, statistical table, etc; and that which is compiled, as a book made up of material gathered from other books.[71] In contrast, the word "codification" is the noun from the verb "to codify" meaning "to systematize," which means the process of collecting and arranging systematically, usually by subject, the laws of state or country, or the rules and regulations covering a particular area or subject of law or practice.[72] Looking at the definition of both terms, many agreed that the product of the project – whose aim was to compile laws governing familial issues on the basis of the various opinions covered in various *fiqh* texts – was better defined as the "compilation."

Once the term *kompilasi* had been chosen, the project was approved by both sides and formally launched. However, although the term agreed was *kompilasi*, the intention to introduce the legal opinions deemed most appropriate to the local culture in Indonesia remained intact, because the fundamental idea of producing a unified legal code of Islamic familial rules was to meet the demands of modernizing Indonesian society. Therefore, the project was not only to compile Islamic rulings applicable in Muslim society, but also to introduce other various legal opinions, even those from unconventional and liberal *madhhab*. In keeping with this purpose, besides the fact that they were interviewed and invited to seminars to air their opinions, in the years of preparing and accomplishing the project, the *'ulamā'*, were also intentionally challenged by extreme and liberal ideas on Islamic law. Strategically the idea of what had become known as the "re-actualization of Islamic law" of Munawir Sjadzali was put on the frontline, in order to embed the law in society. This was, said Bustanul Arifin, intended to make the *'ulamā'* pay attention and not be shocked that some reforms to Islamic law would be presented in the *kompilasi*.

> So that that the *'ulamā'* would not be concerned only with the doctrines of the *fiqh* books to which they personally adhered, some issues were thrown open. This was to prompt the *'ulamā'* to be receptive to opinions other than those to which they were strongly committed. The opinion of Munawir Sjadzali on making the inheritance portion between male and female equal was raised for example. Stung into action by Munawir Sjadzali's extreme opinion, the *'ulamā'* busied themselves looking in *fiqh* books other than those they regularly studied and reading them. They even opened and read books in Indonesian written by some reformist scholars.[73]

Even though the ideas proposed by Sjadzali were not incorporated into the *kompilasi*, some other reformist ideas such as that of Hazairin, as will be made clear in the next discussion, were integrated into the *kompilasi*. It was, Bustanul Arifin remarked, partially because of the strategy mentioned above.

III.3 Bridging the State and the Society

The approval of the *kompilasi* project by Soeharto and by a number of Muslim leaders led to the process which was to effectuate its accomplishment. As mentioned earlier, the decision to realize the project was attributed to the cooperation between the Supreme Court and the Department/Ministry of Religious Affairs. To tackle the project, within the scope of their co-operation, under the direction of Bustanul Arifin, the committee formulated five stages in which it could gather data and collect opinions on issues for which rules would be compiled. These steps to some extent demonstrated the willingness of Bustanul Arifin to bridge the interests of the State and the society.

The first step was to examine the texts of Islamic jurisprudence (*fiqh* books) of various *madhhab*, covering 160 issues of Islamic family law. To this end, several State Institutes of Islamic Studies (Institute Agama Islam Negeri/IAIN) were given the task and the basic regulation was set out in a Letter of Cooperation, signed by the Minister of Religious Affairs and the Rectors of the chosen IAINs. The letter announced the decision to have the *fiqh* books examined by seven IAINs. Each IAIN was responsible for analyzing certain *fiqh* books.[74]

In total, there were thirty-eight *fiqh* books to be examined. Besides the thirteen texts listed in the Circular Letter of the Ministry of Religious Affairs of 1958, to be used as references of the religious courts (see I.V.1.), another twenty-five *fiqh* texts which are read and studied in some traditional Islamic boarding schools (*pesantrens*) were also to be considered, including:

1. *Nihāyat al-Muḥtāj* by al-Ramlī (1004-1595),
2. *I'ānat al-Ṭālibīn* by Sayyid Bakri al-Dimyāṭi (d. 1893 AD);
3. *Bulghāt al-Sālik* by Aḥmad ibn Muḥammad al-Sāwī (d. 1825 AD),
4. *Al-Mudawwana al-Kubrā* by Shahnūn ibn Sa'īd al-Tanūkhī (d. 854 M),
5. *Al-'Umm* by Muhammad 'ibn Idrīs al-Shāfi'ī (767-820 M),
6. Bidāyat al-Mujtahid wa Nihāyat al-Muqtaṣid by Ibn Rushd (1126-1198 M);
7. *Al-Islām Aqīda wa Sharīa* by Maḥmūd Shalṭūṭ (1893-1963 M),
8. *Al-Muḥalla* by 'Alī 'ibn Muḥammad 'Ibn Ḥazm (994-1064 M),
9. *Al-Wajīz* by Abū Ḥamīd al-Ghazālī (1058-1111 M),
10. *Fatḥ al-Qadīr 'alā al-Hidāya* by Muḥammad 'Ibn 'Abd al-Wāḥid al-Siwāsi (d. 1457 M)
11. *Fiqh al-Sunnah* by Sayyid al-Sābiq,

12. Kashf al-Qinā' i 'an al-Tadmīn al-Sinā'i by 'Ibn Rahhūl al-Madānī (1727/8 M)
13. *Majmū` Fatāwā Ibn al-Taymiyya* by Aḥmad 'Ibn Taymiyya (1263-1328 M),
14. *Al-Mughnī* by 'Abd Allāh 'ibn Aḥmad al-Qudāmā (1147-1223 M),
15. *Hidāya Sharḥ Bidāya al-Mubtadī* by 'Alī 'Ibn Abi Bakr al-Marginānī (1196 M),
16. *Mawāhib al-Jalīl* by Muḥammad `ibn Muḥammad Khaṭṭāb (1497-1547 M),
17. *Ḥāshiyat al-Radd al-Mukhtār* by Muḥammad Amīn `ibn `Umar `ibn 'Ābidīn (d. 1552/1836),
18. *Al-Muwaṭṭa* by Mālik ibn `Ānas (d. 795 M),
19. *Ḥāshiya Irfat Dasūkī 'alā Sharḥ al-Kabīr* by `Ibn `Arafa al-Dasūkī (d. 1815 M),
20. *Badā'i al-Sanā'i fi Tartīb al-Sharā`ī* by Abū Bakr 'ibn Mas'ūd al-Kasānī (d.1191 M),
21. *Tabyīn al-Ḥaqā'iq* by Mu'inuddīn 'Ibn Ibrāhīm al-Farābī (d. 811/1408),
22. *Al-Fatāwā al-Hindiyya* by al-Shaikh Niżām,
23. *Fatḥ al-Qadīr* by M. ibn Ahmad al-Safati al-Zainabi 1244/1828,
24. *Kanz al-Rāghibīn* by Jalaluddin M. al-Mahallī (864 H), and
25. *Nihāyat al-Zayn* by ibn 'Umar al-Nawāwī al-Zāwī (d. 1298 H).[75]

These books represented the preferences considered important in gathering diverse opinions on the issues concerned in the *kompilasi*; not only from those of the Shāfi'īte school.[76] The inclusion of *Majmū' Fatāwā Ibn Taymiyya* which pertains to the Ḥanbalīte school, and the Māliki *al-Muwaṭṭa*, and *Fatḥ al-Qādir* which are based on Mālikīte doctrines, and the *Tabyīn al-Ḥaqā'iq* and *Fatāwā al-Hindiyya* which adopts Ḥanafīte doctrines, at least marked an attempt to consider comparative thought and was considered to be absolutely essential to the development of Islamic law in Indonesia, in keeping with the emergence of a new paradigm of Islamic law in which pluralism played an important role.

The second step was to conduct interviews with 181 influential *'ulamā'* from ten chosen areas, including Aceh, Medan, Palembang, Padang, Central Java, West Java, East Java, Ujung Pandang, Mataram, and Banjarmasin. While some were independent *'ulamā'*, others were affiliated with certain Islamic organizations. They were interviewed collectively in one place and at one time. Importantly they were given a chance to express their opinions on the issues of Islamic family law and to elucidate the arguments on which they based their opinions.[77] This was considered an appropriate way of tackling this matter, as the *'ulamā'* could respect each other's opinions as well as present or introduce different opinions derived from different schools of Islamic law. To collect the *'ulamā'*s comments and opinions on matters of Islamic injunctions as meticulously as possible, a questionnaire was also distributed among them.

The interviews with the *'ulamā'* were extremely important because of the basic assumption that the *kompilasi* was aimed at systematizing and compiling Islamic rules to govern family issues, which so far had been applied by the Muslim community and religious court judges in Indonesia based on the *fiqh* texts. *'Ulamā'* who enjoy credibility for their knowledge of Islamic law and have been presumed to be its guardians are considered well-acquainted with which rules have been applied in Muslim society. By interviewing *'ulamā'*, it was hoped that creating the *kompilasi* could be accomplished in a climate replete with aspiration and accommodation, and the *kompilasi* could eventually present fixed laws for the Muslim community.

The involvement of the *'ulamā'* was also intended to make the *kompilasi* more acceptable to Muslim society. Bustanul Arifin said that by involving *'ulamā'* from various regions, Indonesian Muslims would feel that the opinions of their *'ulamā'* would also have been heard and considered. Their involvement, Bustanul Arifin added, was also related to the fact that different *'ulamā'* have their own individual tendency to refer to various *fiqh* books. Realizing this fact, Arifin and the other members of the committee even decided to invite them to the national seminar to discuss the draft (see below). He remarked that the success in issuing the *kompilasi* could be attributed to the *'ulamā'* support of the project.

> When the *kompilasi* was composed, the *'ulamā'* were asked their opinions on some issues and were invited to the seminar. This was to make the *'ulamā'* feel that their opinions were considered. The *'ulamā'* were very optimistic, as they had their own interests in proposing or socializing the *fiqh* books studied in their *pesantren*. They could be proud to stand in front of their *santri* and tell them that their *fiqh* books had been brought to the formal State forum.[78]

In this regard, he noted, "I have now become much more convinced of the correctness of my thesis that, if we want to talk about and develop Islamic law, *'ulamā'* must be involved, indeed they must be made the basic foundation".[79]

The third step was to examine the jurisprudence of the religious courts. Judicial decisions of the religious courts throughout the country, which were collected in sixteen books, were analyzed to find the strongest argument to support certain issues. The Directorate of Religious Justice at the Ministry of Religious Affairs was assigned the role of studying these books.[80]

The next step was to make a comparative analysis of the Islamic family law applied in various other Muslim countries. Considering that various Muslim countries had succeeded in codifying Islamic family law, the members of the project felt that a comparative study should necessarily be undertaken there to see how Islamic law had been applied and how judicial procedure was prepared. Morocco and Egypt[81] were then chosen to be the areas where the comparative studies were made. Besides these two countries, Turkey, with a majority Muslim population, was also visited.[82] Important information was acquired from this comparative study; the system of courts; how the *sharīʻa* was integrated into national law; and the sources on which the applied laws of the family issues were based in the three countries.

After the phase of collecting data was completed, the team began to make a draft, which after completion was presented to a national seminar. The holding of a national seminar to discuss the draft seemed to associate the draft with a more accommodating climate. It also implies that the *kompilasi* team considered the interviews with the *ʻulamāʼ* inadequate to count as their approval of the draft. Indeed, in the seminar the draft, which although based on the data sought and obtained from various phases – interviews, exploring *fiqh* books, comparative studies, and evaluation of jurisprudence – had been hammered out only within the team, was now launched to a wider audience representing various elements in the Muslim community, and was thrown open to discussion.

The seminar was held on 2-6 February 1988 and attended by 124 participants.[83] They represented *ʻulamāʼ* from such Muslim organizations as NU and the Muhammadiyah, legal scholars from Islamic universities or institutions, Muslim intellectuals and officials.[84] The majority of the participants were male, in fact only four were female: Aisyah Amini, a representative of the legislative assembly; Huzaemah Tahido, a professor in Islamic law and a lecturer of the Islamic Institute for Islamic Studies (IAIN), now State Islamic University (UIN), Jakarta; Tuty Alawiyah, a senior and popular preacher and a director of the modern boarding school As-Shafiʼiyyah; and Nawangsih, a Supreme Court judge.[85] The general task of the national seminar was to discuss the issues of Islamic family law including marriage, inheritance, and endowment, to form the material for the *kompilasi*. The participants in the seminar were divided into three committees, each of which discussed and then compiled laws on the three fields of Islamic family law to be included in the *kompilasi*.[86]

However, although the seminar was to discuss the draft, it was reported that the participants were not given enough opportunity to give meaningful input. According to some participants, the draft was not circulated well enough in advance of the meeting, which meant that they could not study it adequately, and the organizers did not allow them to argue against points and speak their minds.[87] It then seems to be clear that, as Cammack has noted, the objective of the seminar was to secure agreement rather than to invite discussion on issues on which disagreement was highly likely. In short, it was to achieve a consensus among all the parties involved in the *kompilasi* project.[88]

The consensus of the Indonesian *'ulamā'* indeed played a crucial role in creating the *kompilasi*, as its final shape would not depend on the decision of the committee, but on the collective approval of the *'ulamā'*. By collecting 124 professionals ranging from professors of religious law, jurists, judges, and rectors of IAIN, and leaders of all the major Muslim organizations in the country to the seminar, and also consulting the opinion of the Council of the Indonesian 'Ulamā' (MUI), the Muhammadiyah, the Nahdlatul 'Ulama and other, minor, Muslim organizations, the committee expected to have gathered enough representatives of all the Muslim scholars in Indonesia to represent all shades of opinion. More importantly, this attempt at the convocation of all leading segments of Muslim Indonesian society was evidently to invoke the concept of *ijmā'* or consensus among the Indonesian Muslim scholars. Although, as will become clear in the next chapter, a number of its articles were debated as soon as the *kompilasi* was finished, the formulators announced that the *kompilasi* constituted a product of the consensus among the Indonesian *'ulamā'*.

The draft of the *kompilasi* was basically completed and approved in the national seminar in 1988, but because of the legal theory that the *kompilasi* was to be a substantive law for the religious courts which, at the time, did not have access to the procedural law governing the legal procedures of the religious courts, its ratification was suspended until the religious courts were given a legal procedure to govern their practice. Then, after the religious courts had acquired the formal law on legal procedures in 1989 by the passing of the Act, in 1991 the *kompilasi* was signed by Soeharto, signaling it was to be applied as a substantive law of the religious courts and ratified by Presidential Instruction or *Inpres* No. 1/ 1991. This legal force behind the *kompilasi* was then followed by the Decree of the Minister of Religious Affairs or *Keputusan Menteri Agama* (KMA) No. 154/ 1991, instruction of the application of the *kompilasi*.

The *Inpres*, after it mentioned the points of its considerations and its legal grounding, instructed the Minister of Religious Affairs to disseminate the *kompilasi* in the governmental institutions and society and to realize the instruction as well as possible. Although it is not a statute, the *kompilasi* has a quite strong legal base in the *Inpres*. Moreover, as a follow up of this presidential instruction, the Minister of Religious Affairs issued his decree as KMA (Keputusan Menteri Agama) NO. 154/ 1991 on the realization of the *Inpres*. After it refers to the *Inpres* as its consideration, and to a number of the legal regulations, the decree stated its decisions as to strongly suggest the Ministry of Religious Affairs and the other implicated governmental institutions disseminate the *kompilasi*, and use it as a reference to the greatest possible extent in resolving the issues it covers. The instruction of the President to use it is indeed not a fixed obligation, but the decree of the Minister strengthens it as a strong suggestion (for the full content of *Inpres* (the Presidential Instruction) and KMA (Ministerial Decree), see appendix).

IV State Accommodation of Islamic Law or Political Project?

The enactment of the *kompilasi* by no means represented the intention of the State towards an actual Islamization. It is only part of the negotiations undertaken by the State to deal with increasingly vocal demands in society. The choice of the familial aspects of the Islamic law to be accommodated demonstrated the effort made by the State not to cede legitimacy among its Muslim citizens, who were well aware of the fact that many Muslim countries had codified this integral part of Islamic law. It has become the most widely applied element of Islamic law in the Muslim world today, and an arena which can be negotiated by existing governments. In Indonesia, for instance, it has survived and developed by degrees according to the political will of the State, and also because of the struggles by Muslims to achieve this.

If we trace back the historical records of the development of Islamic law in Indonesia, it is not difficult to understand why family law assumes such an important place in the process of Islamizing the legal system. Since the spread of Islam, Islamic family law, more than any other element, has been observed by the Muslim community in Indonesia. Admittedly to some extent assimilated with *adat* law, Islamic family law has been observed by Indonesian Muslims as a matter of religious obligation and an important concern. By determining the validity of marriage, for example, they decide whether a child is born under a legal or a void contract of marriage. Children of an illegal marriage are illegitimate, and as such disqualified from inheriting from their parents or other relatives.

It is apparent that while in many Muslim countries, Western-inspired legal codes eventually replaced the *sharīʿa*, the areas of Islamic family law were retained. Ziba Mir-Hosseini has argued that the survival of Islamic family law is attributable to several reasons:

> *First*, the Islamic family law has traditionally been the most developed areas of Islamic law in which the *ʿulamāʾ* have the highest control. *Secondly*, in their modernizing scheme the colonial gov-

> ernments were, either consciously or unconsciously, arranging the Western liberal distinction between public and private realms. Family law could then be left in the hands of the *'ulamā'* as it was deemed to be private and hence politically less significant. *Thirdly*, in this way the modernizing governments (or colonial powers) paid lip service to the *sharī'a* and avoided an open confrontation with its guardian.[89]

Furthermore, it has been also widely assumed that family law is an element of Islamic law most liable to be subjected to the administrative intervention of the State. Discussing secularism and law in Egypt, in which he focuses heavily on the Islamic family law, Talal Asad referred to 'Abduh's report on the *Sharī'a* courts written in 1899. Asad writes that 'Abduh approached the fundamental social function of the *Sharī'a* courts through something which has come to be called 'the family'. According to 'Abduh, Asad continues, the *Sharī'a* judges look into matters which are very private and listen to what others are not allowed to hear. In their practice, 'Abduh recommended that the *Sharī'a* courts should be independent of State control, but he urged that their system be integral to Government. 'Abduh further stated the *Sharī'a* courts – which are in effect "the family courts" – are very important, as without them society would be in danger of moral collapse.[90]

The emergence of nation-states in many countries in the Muslim world has apparently changed the outlook that the *sharī'a* had managed to avoid being identified with the temporal power. In fact, the governments of these countries were in a position to effect a radical change. They were influenced not only by Western theories of government and sources of legitimacy, but were also pressurized to modernize.[91] Although family law is the only area of the *sharī'a* which can be maintained, its administration was not free of the intervention by the states moving in the direction of the modern States.

Moreover, the project of national development aimed at realizing domestic stability seems to have favored the Islamization of family law in Indonesia. The Indonesian Government seemed to be aware that, as Islamic family law was often perceived as the badge of Muslim religious identity, uncertainty about its legal status was believed to introduce instability into the lives of Muslims. The Government also realized that instability in their lives could destabilize the whole nation. On this assumption and on the grounds that law should be developed, as it would create stability for the nation, the Indonesian Government felt Muslim demands on legislation relating to the legal status of Islamic family law should be urgently accomplished. It was the stability of Islamic family law, whose areas, namely marriage, divorce, inheritance, endowment, testamentary disposals, and gifts have been firmly observed and practiced in their daily life since Islam was first disseminated in the archipelago, which stimulated the Indonesian Government to act to administer it legally or to rationalize it.

If we follow the theory of legal development, this legal agreement or rationalization of the State is principally not surprising. According to Weber, a radical legal change occurred during the Enlightenment and "... the formal quality of the law has proceeded from a primitive legal procedure which irrationally conditioned by revelation to increasingly specialized juridical and logical rationality and systematization."[92] It is a fact that, through the *kompilasi*, the Islamic rules, particularly on familial issues, have been now displayed and presented in a systematized and formally logical manner. Unlike those in the basic *fiqh* books, all of which are written in Arabic, the Islamic doctrines of familial issues are now presented in the Indonesian language. Following the modern style of legal systematization, these Islamic doctrines previously scattered throughout various *fiqh* books are now presented in systematic numbered articles, and formed into a small handbook resembling the formal form of 'law'. This new, modernized form of substantive law for the religious courts is consequently believed to be able to smooth the path for judges in finding legal consideration on which to base their judgments.

Nonetheless, I doubt that the enactment of the *kompilasi* was merely determined by the desire of the State to run the project of Islamization of family law, and was importantly motivated by the emergence of intellectual Muslims who shared new thoughts on political Islam, as a number of analysts believed.[93] Other significant leading forces were assumed to have participated in this event. To observe them, the issue would be better placed in the framework of the changing personal behavior of Soeharto, rather than the broader context of the State. In other words, although it is one of the accommodative attitudes of the State, the enactment of the *kompilasi* was resolved by Soeharto's ambition to shore up his legitimacy and by his personal political interests, an ambition which led him to cultivate Muslim political support for his presidential position. In this regard, it is worth noting that, as Annelies Moors has remarked, twentieth-century Islamic family law has indeed become a powerful political symbol. Moors pointed out the case of the reforms in Islamic family law in Iran instigated by the Pahlevi regime but which were immediately abrogated in order to demonstrate the commitment of the state to the Islamization of society.[94] Viewed from this perspective, it is no exaggeration to say that the enactment of the *kompilasi* was one of the tactical moves taken by Soeharto to enable him to remain in power.

One of the arguments often adopted by the advocates of this theory is that the *kompilasi* was promulgated in a period when Soeharto was undergoing what has become known as his legitimacy crisis, which expanded markedly after the end of the 1980s. In this period, his grip on the military was weakened. The military was reported to be looking ahead to a time when they, as individuals and as an institution, would still be players without Soeharto.[95] Meanwhile, Soeharto was in crucial need of such support, as this period was characterized by growing concern about his succession. In this situation, there is strong evidence that Soeharto turned to the Muslim community as the majority group from which he might expect the political support. To cultivate their support, Soeharto's first step was to woo and satisfy the Muslim community by transforming Islamic law into legislation. In fact, a number of prominent Muslim figures and Islamic socio-religious organizations were very vocal in their clearly audible support for Soeharto's next presidential term in 1993.[96]

Another argument is that the issuing of the *kompilasi* happened just before Soeharto left for Mecca in 1991 to make the *Hajj*,[97] an Islamic ritual practice which is usually not undertaken by members of the *abangan* Muslim group, in which Soeharto was often included. It is true that Soeharto's trip to Mecca reciprocated that of the leader of Saudi Arabia to Indonesia after the tragedy at *Mina* in 1990, which claimed a hundred Indonesian lives. On this visit, he talked with the Saudi Arabian Government about the plan to build hospitals as memorials to the victims.[98] This visit was certainly significant in strengthening and refining his ambition to demonstrate his closeness to Muslims.

These two arguments are very closely related to the ways or strategies adopted by Soeharto as a means to cultivate Muslim political support. I have other arguments which clearly authenticate the assumption. One of them is that, as has been mentioned above, Bustanul Arifin expressed to the President his conviction that the importance of the enactment of the *kompilasi* was to save the Pancasila from the threat of the determination of some Muslims to apply the *sharīʿa*. What Bustanul Arifin presented as reasons for enacting the *kompilasi* was compatible with Soeharto's aspiration to remain in the running for his presidential leadership. Soeharto had proclaimed that he intended to run for the leadership according to the Constitution, of which the Pancasila was the main and sole foundation, and he would support the development of any aspects of national life. He also proclaimed his support of any legalization of law to regulate the nation but only insofar as it did not contradict the Pancasila.

From another perspective, Suharto's political interest, which worked behind the scenes of the enactment of the *kompilasi*, met more readily with approval because of its legal status, namely a Presidential Instruction, which has lower status than a Statute or even Governmental Regulation, but which enjoyed the all-important backing of the President. Muslim scholars who approved the formalization of the *kompilasi* realized that the Presidential Instruction ranked more lowly in the structure of the national legal order, and essentially they would have wished to have had it enacted as a legal Statute passed by Parliament. However, they realized that to have it enacted by Parliament would take some time, while the religious courts had urgent need of substantive law, following the promulgation of the Islamic Judicature Act regulating their legal procedures. Moreover, in some cases, Statutes, even though passed, remain unenforceable while still waiting for the implementing regulations which have to be issued by the executive branch of the Government.[99] By choosing such a legal status, Muslims also anticipated the growing protests and opposition from some nationalists and non-Muslim leaders in the legislature, as had indeed happened with the legislation of the 1974 Law of Marriage and the 1989 Act. Given the urgency and the sensitivity of the issue, they therefore bore in mind that it would be effective and wise to choose a 'bypass road',[100] or to have a *kompilasi* undertaken by Presidential Instruction. Their decision may also have been inspired by the fact that in a country with a strong executive system, an executive instruction may be politically as effective as an enacted statute. The fact that the document was characterized only as a *kompilasi* may also have suggested they did not think that legislative approval was necessary.

Therefore, for Muslims the decision to have the *kompilasi* enacted through the Presidential Instruction was based on mature consideration, and was clearly only an alternative, which is still having to be paid for by a continuous debate on its legal enforcement (this issue will be discussed in the next chapter, when analyzing the application of the *kompilasi* in the religious courts). Meanwhile, for Soeharto it was highly likely first and foremost a coincidence with his own interest. In fact by his own instruction, Soeharto had the opportunity to demonstrate his personal willingness to realize the Muslim interests more clearly.

It is intriguing that the political interest of Soeharto in the enactment of *kompilasi* was in no way hidden from the knowledge of Muslims. As can be understood from the way he proposed the project, Bustanul Arifin himself, its chief architect, was aware of it. He even remarked:

> It is true that the *kompilasi* was proposed and then enacted within the growing accommodating atmosphere between Muslims and the State. But many thought that the State had a political interest in it. If the State did have such an interest in the enactment of the *kompilasi*, it would have been normal. We have an interest in applying Islamic law in a more focused (*terarah*) way, and the State has also an interest, in the form of political support from Muslims. In principle, the application of Islamic law should have been the agenda of the State, without being ridden by its own political interests (*tanpa adanya embel-embel politik*), but most of ruling groups are outsiders (*minhum*) (he then explained what he meant by *minhum*, namely Muslims but without having an inter-

> est in Muslim needs or non-Muslims). So, in this case it was applied by what is called 'the choice between utilizing (*menindas*) and being utilized (*ditindas*).' If we (Muslims) did not utilize the State, the State would have utilized us; *Al-amr bi al-shauka* (ruling or order required in an emergency)[101] and *wa makarū makara Allāh* (if they (in this case Government) exploit, God will do the same).[102]

What Bustanul Arifin meant by the State explicitly referred to Soeharto in person. The key words in this interpretation are his phrase "ruling groups" and his expression "*al-amr bi al-shauka*," which originally indicated the main ruler, that is, the President.

The political motives of Soeharto behind the enactment of the *kompilasi* were moreover expressed more straightforwardly in Arifin's report on the accomplishment of the project. Bustanul Arifin said:

> Given this opportunity, the committee felt obliged to deliver a message from the all *'ulamā'* who took part in the project of the *kompilasi*, a message which constitutes an expression of gratitude to God. This message runs as follows: (We) (the *'ulamā'*) ask the honorable Chief Justice of the Supreme Court and the Minister of Religious Affairs to deliver our thanks and respect to the upright President who has revealed his political will and given concrete support in the form of funds for the accomplishment of the project of the *kompilasi* through his Presidential Decision (*keputusan Presiden*) or *Kepres* No. 191/Sosroch/1985.[103]

It is therefore not surprising that looking at its contents and form, the way it was enacted and the elements contributing to its creation, some specialists in Islamic law in Indonesia, as well as its formulators, had attributed several pejorative phrases to the *kompilasi*, such as "*Fiqh dalam Bahasa Undang-Undang*" (*fiqh* in the language of State laws),[104] and "*Fiqh Islam Berwawasan Pancasila*" (Pancasilaized *fiqh*), "*Fiqh Madzhab Negara*" (State School of Islamic law) and others.[105]

III Debates on the *Kompilasi Hukum Islam*

The *Kompilasi Hukum Islam* consists of three chapters: marriage, inheritance, and endowment, which are presented in 229 Articles. The chapter on marriage rules on nineteen issues, including the foundation of marriage, engagement, requirements and conditions for a marriage, a dowry, prohibitions in marriage, agreements in marriage, marriage during pregnancy, polygyny, the cancellation of a marriage, the annulment of a marriage, rights and privileges of spouses, property in marriage, child care, guardianship, dissolution of a marriage, consequences of dissolution of a marriage, reconciliation, and the waiting period (*iddah*). The chapter on inheritance deals with five issues, including heirs, portions of heirs, problems raised by *awl* and *rad* (means of calculation), a will or bequest, and gifts. The chapter on endowment includes functions, elements, conditions, procedures and registration of *waqf*, and settlement and supervision of property.

Although on most issues the *kompilasi* generally adopts the classical Islamic legal doctrines, especially that of the Shāfi'īte *fiqh* texts, it introduces a number of reform aspects. These aspects reflect the inclusion of local customs, State interests and new tendencies which have assumed a place in the Indonesian Islamic discourse. By doing so, in the *kompilasi* an attempt has been made to achieve an amalgamation between the classical legal doctrines of Islam, State interests, and local tradition or *adat*. There can be no doubt that the drafters of the *kompilasi* realized that the plurality of legal norms could be ignored. By accommodating local customs, giving the State a place, and paying due attention to such new issues as gender, they have apparently sought to demonstrate that these domains can be integrated into the practice of Islamic law and do not stand in isolation from one another.

What they have done is indeed relevant to what sociologists and anthropologists have observed in regard to the plurality of norms in the application of Islamic law. Referring to the particular case of Morocco, for example, Léon Buskens outlines the relationship of the *sharī'a*, State law, and local customs, from which basis he has proposed the theory of the "triangular model." By constructing such a model, he wants to show that apart from the *sharī'a*, norms related to State law and local customs are very important to any study in order to understand the diversity of norms governing Muslim behavior.[1] In the same vein, John R. Bowen stresses the blend of different norms in the application of Islamic law in the Muslim world. Referring to the Islamic familial cases in France and Indonesia, for example, he has demonstrated that *adat* has very much shaped the rules governing Muslim life.[2]

Although the *kompilasi* has been proclaimed as the product of the consensus of the Indonesian *'ulamā'*, this does not mean that the controversy surrounding it has abated. Debates still rage, especially in relation to the aspects of reform it has introduced. Some legal experts and Muslim scholars and *'ulamā'* were satisfied with points raised and addressed, but others have contested them, arguing that they lack Islamic rationales and clearly deviate from traditional Islamic doctrines. Yet other groups, such as Muslim feminists, have criticized the provisions of the *kompilasi* as being as yet inadequate and unsatisfactory to address contemporary Indonesian problems, citing such concepts as justice and gender equality. They have accompanied these criticisms with demands that the *kompilasi* be revised.

In this chapter I will explore reaction to and criticism of the reform aspects introduced in the *kompilasi* which have arisen among Indonesians. I will address the issue by looking at specific questions relating to the reforms. After displaying the reform aspects, I will study the arguments and the tendency in their criticism, as well as the key concepts and interpretations of Islam they have used. Bearing in mind the differentiation between modernist and traditionalist groups of Indonesian Muslims, the discussion will be focused on the two largest Muslim organizations, NU and the Muhammadiyah, each of which represents such a trend. Arising from their disappointment in the lack of improvement of their legal status and the audibility of their voices, the critical responses launched by woman activists should certainly not be overlooked. Finally, this chapter will discuss the proposals for future reforms, and reveals a heated debate on the drafts of the reformed *kompilasi* proposed by a number of institutions.

Before we delve into the debates, it is relevant to study the way in which *adat* and the State have contributed elements to defining the form of the *kompilasi*. According to a number of scholars, both are the most essential aspects to be considered in assessing the dynamics of Islamic law in Indonesia.[3]

I The Reform Aspects in the *Kompilasi*

I.1 *The Influence of Adat*

The influence of *adat* or local norms is most apparent in a number of rules in the *kompilasi* concerning the issue of inheritance. Although the *kompilasi* generally adopts the traditional *fiqh* doctrines and incorporates all of the relevant Qur'ānic texts, giving a son, for instance, as great a share in inheritances as that of two daughters, and maintaining the rule of *'aṣaba,* – that nearest male agnate takes what remains – it applies the system of representation of heirs and obligatory bequests found nowhere in the classical *fiqh* texts. The system of representation of heirs has been adopted to solve the problem of orphaned grandchildren, whose parents predeceased their own parents. According to the classical Islamic system of inheritance, orphaned grandchildren are excluded from shares in their grandparents' estates. All schools of Islamic law agree that an orphaned grandchild has no right to a share from his or her grandparent if there are other living children (sons). Following this rule, some Muslim countries have denied the predeceased heirs and their heirs or descendants any share of an inheritance as long as there are other living sons. This rule is believed to have created problems for Muslims. Lucy Carroll explains:

> In a tribal society where the surviving son took over responsibility for the children of his deceased brother in the extended family group, the traditional rules of succession may not have occasioned much hardship. But in a society where nuclear families are more common, the total exclusion of one line of the deceased's descendants appears both unjust and unjustified.[4]

As there is a prevailing sense that it is unjust to deprive orphaned grandchildren of their right to the estates of their grandparents only because their parents predeceased their parents, some countries have attempted to solve the inequity. Two solutions have been proposed; namely, obligatory bequests and a system of inheritance by right or representation of heirs. The former was first adopted by the Middle Eastern countries; the latter by Pakistan.[5]

The *kompilasi* apparently prefers to adopt both rules, with some adjustments to conform to the local system of society. Article 185 of the *kompilasi* states that the inheritance position of a predeceased heir may be assumed by his heirs.[6] This preference is in accord with the practice of giving a right of inheritance to orphaned grandchildren, which had been established among certain Indonesian Muslims through the system of *plaatsvervulling*. This practice had even become a law in Medan, where the Appellate General Court once decided in a judgment that when a child of deceased heir had died, before the deceased, and the former had left behind a child or children, the children of the child or grandchildren of the deceased had right to the deceased's estate on behalf of their father.[7] This means that the system of representation of heirs is not totally novel in Indonesia. Although it constitutes a widespread problem in many Muslim countries, it has local foundation in the legal practice among Indonesians.

Nonetheless, as the *kompilasi* preserves the established ratio of 2:1 in the shares between males and females, it has been assumed that the application of the representation of heirs may generate some problems. One such problem is that the aunt will get a smaller share than her nephew. When someone dies, leaving behind a daughter (A) and a predeceased son's child (B), A will be given a one-third share, while B, as the representative of his father, will be granted two-thirds. Realizing this problem, as the aunt (A) receives less than her nephew (B), the *kompilasi* establishes that the portion of the substitutive heirs must not exceed the portion of the other heirs whose positions are equal to the substitute heirs.[8] Following this additional rule, the portion of B is thus not two-thirds but one-third, the same portion as A. The remainder of the estate is equally distributed to both A and B. Consequently, each of them receives a half.

The same holds true for the system of an obligatory bequest applied by the *kompilasi*, to grant an adopted child a share of his or her adoptive parent's estate. Based on this concept, an adoptive parent has the right to inherit from his or her adopted child. However, the application of the concept is only possible if the child or parent leaves no will. Article 209 states that if they die intestate, both adopted child and adoptive parent will be granted an obligatory bequest amounting to as much as one-third of each other's estates.[9] By using this concept, the purpose of the *kompilasi* is to avoid a 'pure' practice of inheritance among adoptive and adopted parties as practiced among Indonesians, especially Javanese. At the same time, it does not fully ban such a practice. It must be said that the practice of adoption is popular among Indonesian families in general. In spite of the variations in application from one society to another, several principles are uniformly embraced. These principles rule that the adopted child is automatically included in the circle of the adoptive family, that the relationship of the adopted child and his or her biological parents is severed, and that the status of the adopted child is equal to that of a biological child.[10]

The drafters of the *kompilasi* sensed that, although the full attribution of adopted children to their adoptive parent or vice versa may be disallowed, as it contradicts the Qur'ānic text, the tradition of inheriting from each other should be retained as, they argued, it would not be fair if each of the parties were to be left with nothing when the other party dies. However, they thought that the system by which the adoptive parties could give and receive each other's estate should not be attributed the position of both parties as real children or parents. It is in the context of eliminating the practice of inheritance between adoptive parties, but granting them a share from each other, that they preferred the institution of obligatory bequest to be applied.

The accommodation of *adat* is also reflected in the provisions of the *kompilasi* on some marital matters, such as the regulation of joint property between married couples. The institution of the joint property (in Indonesian *harta bersama; harta gono gini*) had been firmly held and had been internalized in the social life of Indonesian society. A husband and a wife who have been bound in the contract of marriage have the same rights to the property acquired during their marriage. When the marriage is ended, each of them has the right to the same share of that property. This is based on the fact that in Indonesia, although adhering to the principle that the head of the family is the husband, both husband and wife often work outside the home. In Solo, for example, women generally earn money from their multifarious activities. In a family which runs a home industry such as *membatik* (traditionally designing and printing on cloth), for instance, women play more important roles. They buy the cloth, design the patterns, and even manage the firms.[11] In other regions, likewise women do not just stay at home but go to farms, markets and other places to earn their own living. In due consideration of these facts, it would then be unreasonable for wives to be left behind with nothing when their marriage ends, while the husbands have full rights to that property.

Taking the Indonesian culture or social reality of accumulating wealth into account, the Indonesian Government formally legalized this established tradition in the Marriage Law of 1974. Article 35 states that property which is acquired during a marriage becomes joint property. However, there is no detailed rule governing the division of that property when the marriage ends. It is merely said that should the marriage be dissolved by divorce, the joint estate should be dealt with according to the respective laws (Art. 37).

The *kompilasi* deals more thoroughly with this institution. There are thirteen Articles (from Article 85 to 97) discussing the situations. Article 85 decrees that the admission of the existence of the joint property by no means rejects the possibility of the ownership of the individual property, by either a husband or a wife. To protect the joint property from any attempt by either party to jeopardize it, the *kompilasi* rules that a wife and or a husband may request a religious court to denounce the joint property ownership. Article 95 states that a wife or a husband may request a religious court to claim the joint property if either of the parties is addicted to drugs, gambling, alcohol or the like. Furthermore, the *kompilasi* rules that the dissolution of a marriage requires equal division of the joint estate. Should the marriage end in divorce, women have the same rights as men to the estate which they acquired through their joint efforts during their marriage with a half-share for each. Likewise, when the marriage ends in the death of one of the parties, the surviving party has the right to half the estate, and the other half constitutes the inheritance of the deceased.[12]

The issue of joint property has never been dealt with in the classical *fiqh* doctrines. However, a number of Muslim scholars have concluded that the Islamic legal bases for the dispersal of joint property can be found in the discussion of *shirka* (cooperation).[13] Admittedly there is no mention that *shirka* can exist between a husband and a wife in a marriage. In fact, the discussion of *shirka* is not included in the chapter on marriage (*bāb al-nikāḥ*), but in the chapter on trade (*bāb al-buyū'*). *Shirka* literally means cooperation or a contract between two or more persons or institutions. As an institution which involves two parties, *shirka* is considered a legal form of business in so far as either of the parties does not violate or deviate from the terms of the agreement.

The majority of Muslim jurists agree that there are two forms of *shirka*: cooperation in ownership (*shirkat al-amlāk*) and cooperation in contract (*shirkat al-'uqūd*). Joint property can be categorized as cooperation in ownership. Basically, the cooperation in ownership is different from the institution of the joint property, as cooperation of ownership is business-oriented, while the institution of joint property tends to be a social contract and can be disassociated from the marriage contract. However, as some principles, such as the rights and the duties of both parties engaged in the co-operation of ownership tend in the same direction as those pertaining to the institution of joint property, both husband and wife have the same duty to protect and the same right to spend the joint property. The institution of the joint property can be claimed to be cooperation of ownership in the marriage.[14]

Indeed, a marriage is a contract between a husband and a wife. When the contract or transaction of marriage is concluded, the cooperation or reciprocity between the two parties automatically commences, including cooperation in acquiring property. In this sense, a wife does not have to directly involve herself in earning money to have the right to the joint property. On the assumption that the wife has been considered to be cooperative by taking care of the household and child or children, when the husband goes out to work, this absolves her of the duty to go out to work.[15] Some Muslim scholars have argued that without having to make an agreement as soon as the marriage is concluded, the property acquired during a marriage automatically becomes joint property of the husband and the wife. This is strengthened by the fact that in Indonesia, as has been discussed before, women (wives) have been accustomed to work to earn their own living, which makes their involvement in creating property during their marriages unequivocally evident. Following this line of reasoning, and the fact that for a very long time Indonesian people have been attached to *adat*, in the *kompilasi* it was felt necessary to include the institution of joint property in the Islamic legal system.

Besides the rules regarding the representation of heirs, obligatory bequests, and joint property, the *kompilasi* introduces another novel rule which treats the inheritance rights of a father. Though it is not explicitly related to the local norms, the rule establishes the local familial system, namely a bilateral system. Article 177 rules that the father takes a one-third share if the deceased left no children, and if the deceased left children, he receives one-sixth. The provision that the father takes a one-sixth share when the deceased has children is taken directly from the Qur'ān IV: 11. However, the granting of one-third to the father when the deceased did not leave children is grounded neither in the Qur'ān nor traditional *fiqh* doctrine. According to the traditional Islamic system of inheritance, the father is granted the remainder of the estate as *'aṣaba*.[16] It is recognized that by granting the father one-third, the drafters of the *kompilasi* initially intended to make the rules of inheritance fully bilateral, equalizing the position of all male and female relatives. They argued that under the same conditions, the mother takes one-third of the estate of the deceased. Although the drafters had an explanation for their decision, the rules generated some criticism. When the document of the *kompilasi* was ratified in 1991, the Nahdlatul Ulama (NU) protested and requested the provision be changed. The largest Muslim organization in Indonesia even went as far as to announce that it would reject the *kompilasi* entirely unless the rule was amended.[17]

In response to the protest, in 1994 the Supreme Court, after consulting the Ministry of Religious Affairs, issued a circular letter stating that the intent of the provision was for the father to take a one-third share of the estate when the deceased left no children, but did leave a husband and a mother. In other words, the rule means that the father takes one-third if he inherits together with only the husband and mother of the deceased.[18] After the wave of protest this elicited and the response of the Supreme Court to the issue, confusion and obfuscation about the application of the inheritance rule to the father emerged among Muslims, ironically. Issuing such a clarification – while taking cognizance of only one circumstance, namely associating the father only with a husband and a mother, which denotes that the deceased is a female (wife) – the Supreme Court failed to clarify the provision and hence did not quell the debate, given the fixed consideration that the father may share the estate with other heirs, such as the mother and the wife – should the deceased be a male (husband).

Accordingly, although at the time the clarification was issued, the NU understanding that in such a case the residue of the estate would be one-third, – after the husband has taken one-half of the estate and the mother has claimed her one-third of another half or of the remainder, or one-sixth – accepted the explanation of the Supreme Court, the criticism and protest still raged among Muslims. Ichtiyanto, a former director of the Islamic Justice at the Ministry of Religious Affairs, repeatedly expressed his repudiation of the provision, urging that under such conditions the father should be granted a residual part of the estate. Although he realized that the residue of the estate to be granted to the father would be equal to one-third if the other heirs were a husband and a mother, he asserted that it is not equal to one-third but more; namely, one-half,[19] if the other heirs are a mother and a wife, instead of a husband. By this demonstration he indubitably showed that the provision is confusing and must be modified.[20] It can be inferred that, although its formula was not changed and still remains written as it stands in the *kompilasi*, the initially intended one-third rule is not applied as it was formally qualified in more detail in the circular clarification. This means that the *kompilasi* failed to introduce a new rule and has remained consistent to the traditional doctrine.

I.2 State Policy

I.2.1 *Marriage*

According to the classical doctrine of Islamic law, marriage is concluded by offering and accepting in the presence of witnesses. Two Muslim males or one male and two females are required to witness the contract of marriage.[21] There is no need for a contract of marriage to be registered. Nowadays, some Muslim countries have realized that a contract of marriage needs to be registered in order that records may be kept. Therefore laws have been passed to regulate the registration of marriage. However, the principles taken to make the rule effective are different. In Pakistan, for example, the State has passed a regulation stating that a failure to obey the law makes both the parties involved in the contract legally liable to imprisonment or a fine.[22] In Singapore, a penal sanction is also applied to those who do not register their marriages.[23] In contrast, in Morocco, which also demands the registration of marriage as an administrative requirement, as do both Pakistan and Singapore, and even makes the signature of two professional witnesses (*'udūl*) one of the conditions of the validity of marriage,[24] does not impose a sanction on those who disobey the rule.[25]

In this case, Indonesia is also no exception. The *kompilasi* states that a marriage should be concluded in the presence of an official marriage registrar or must be registered. Failure to register a marriage affects the validity of marriage, and judicial relief is denied in the case of an unregistered marriage. This means that the *kompilasi* allows no room for an unregistered marriage. However, it does differentiate between the religious validity and the State legality of marriage and therefore does not deem a marriage religiously invalid if the parties concerned fail to register their marriage.[26] It seems clear that the *kompilasi* is anxious not to deviate from the classical doctrine of marriage. This is different from the case of Iran, which adopts the Shi'īte legal school, where registration is obligatory and failure to do so invalidates a marriage in terms of religion.[27]

The *kompilasi* has applied the concept of "dual validity" so as to preserve the point of view of classical Muslim scholars, that only religious requirements can decide whether or not a contract of marriage is valid; therefore the registration of marriage cannot be considered the main factors in deciding the religious validity of marriage, only as an administrative requirement.[28] Indeed this concept emerges as the result of the compromise between the traditionalists and modernists, and inevitably still fuels debates among Muslim scholars in Indonesia.

Positioning the registration as a purely administrative affair, the *kompilasi* does not rule on the sanction for those failing to comply with it. The 1975 regulation elucidating the application of the Marriage Law does mention the sanction, but it is applied only to the registrars. It states that should a registrar fail to register a marriage, he will be fined 7,500 rupiahs. It tends to be rather hazy on specifying under what conditions the failure of the registrar will be condemned to pay the fine. As I shall discuss later, though this law is still in force, many marriages in Indonesia are still not registered.

Alongside insisting on the obligation to register, the State also intervenes in the matter at what age a boy or a girl can enter into married life. Marriage may not be concluded before the age of consent which for women has been fixed at sixteen and for men at nineteen. Girls and boys who seek to marry before the age of puberty must obtain the court's permission. In addition, the State laws also decree that women and men who seek to marry after the age of puberty, but before the age of legal majority which has been fixed at twenty-one, must obtain their father's permission.[29]

I.2.2 Polygyny and Divorce

Keeping pace with the growing demand for gender equality, the *kompilasi* has also striven to heed women interests, paying special attention to the issues of polygyny and divorce, which are still hotly debated by Muslims.[30] This specific attention ties in with the State agenda to empower women in accordance with the program of economic development. Muslim modernists tend to view it as a conditional act. They argue polygyny is tolerated only on the grounds of necessity, for example, for the protection of widows and orphans after a war, which is exactly what had happened in the time of the Prophet. The stipulation which is laid down in the Qur'ān insisting that all wives should be treated equally seems to stress that polygyny is basically discouraged, as it is believed to be difficult for a man to fulfill such a demand. In this context it is stressed that Muhammad was married to a number of women, as an example of his self-sacrifice and self-denial, instead of his seeking of enjoyment and pleasure.[31] Bearing this proviso in mind, in order to avoid the abuse of polygyny, polygynous marriages are permitted only if the permission of the court has been obtained. This permission is made dependent on such requirements as the consent of the previous wife. By including this restrictive condition, the modernists consider the Qur'ānic standard of "equal justice" no longer a matter for the moral conscience of the individual, but rather a legal matter to be decided by the court.

This is contested by conservative Muslims, who assert that polygyny is a husband's absolute right and that he is legally free to exercise it, provided he follows the limit of the maximum number of wives at any one time. Consequently they regard polygyny not a matter to be resorted to only in times of dire necessity. Their view is that the practice of polygyny is better than the practice of having unlawful mistresses and girlfriends.[32]

In various Muslim countries, ideas with intent to reform have been introduced to restrict the practice of polygyny or even abolish it altogether.[33] Syria, Iraq and Morocco, for instance, have introduced some restrictions. In Syria, a man is permitted to practice polygyny if the court is satisfied that he is financially able to maintain multiple wives properly. In Iran, besides requiring that a man be financially capable of supporting polygyny, he must guarantee that he can treat the co-wives with equal justice. Even when these requirements are fulfilled, the polygynous marriage cannot be entered into unless the present wife consents to the marriage or has been sentenced to imprisonment, is addicted to drink, drugs or gambling, has disappeared, is certified insane, or is afflicted with incurable disease. Iraq stipulates that a man who wants to embark on polygyny must treat the co-wives equally.[34] In Tunisia, the practice of polygyny is completely prohibited.[35] In the Indian sub-continent, Muslim modernists have argued that the ideal marriage in Islam is monogamy. It is true that before the partition of India and Pakistan, polygyny was a common practice among Muslims. However, in Pakistan, polygyny has recently decreased in the wake of some restrictions placed upon its practice by the Muslim Family Law Ordinance (MFLO).[36]

In Indonesia, the issue of polygyny has attracted considerable attention from women activists for a very long time. Some efforts had been made to fight to have it prohibited or, failing that, at least to restrict its arbitrary practice. Various seminars on this issue had been held by Muslim Women's Organizations.[37] These protracted struggles only gained a positive response from the Government in the 1970s. With the ratification of the 1974 Marriage Law, the Indonesian Government did place boundaries on the practice of polygyny by putting a number of conditions on the legal conclusion of a polygynous marriage. Permission for such a marriage has to be obtained from the religious courts, and this is the one crucial condition for a husband to have more than one wife, if both the parties concerned wish to do so (Art. 3 (2)). A husband can enter into a polygynous marriage only on the grounds that his wife is unable to perform her duties as a wife, or because she is suffering from some physical defect or incurable disease, or she is unable to bear descendants (Art. 4). Furthermore, it stipulates that the marriage can be conducted if the wife of a husband wishing to resort to polygyny consents, and the husband is financially capable of maintaining co-wives and their descendants. In addition, he has to be prepared to treat the co-wives equally (Art. 5). All these regulations were adopted into the *kompilasi* of Articles 56, 57, and 58.[38] These Articles insist that the polygynous marriage can be solemnized only if these all conditions are fulfilled, and if one of the stated reasons exists. Failure to fulfill the requirements collectively incurs the prohibition of its practice. Above all, the approval of the court is absolutely essential and this means that the polygynous marriage can only be legally recognized if it is approved in the court.

Like polygyny, divorce is now also restricted in Indonesia. In classical Islamic legal doctrines, divorce is a man's absolute right. No intervention could be made in his exclusive right. Therefore it follows that the approval of a court is not needed. The man can exercise this right without having to provide any reason. Before 1974, divorce could be unilaterally effective when a husband uttered the formula of divorce. He was only required to come to KUA to finalize and register it. Meanwhile, a Muslim woman had to appear before a judge and assure that judge that her husband had committed an act included in the categories which are stated in the marriage agreement, usually called *ta'līq ṭalāq*, if the husband had refused to divorce her. After 1974, both man who wants to repudiate his wife, and a woman who wants to file for divorce, what is known as *khul'*, must appear before a judge and convince the judge that one or more of the sanctioned reasons are present.[39] The first task of the judge is to verify whether there is a valid reason or justification as specified in the limitation list for divorce or *khul'* grounds. If the judge has satisfied him or herself that a valid reason is present, the judge can order a husband to repeat the formula of divorce, or can grant a wife's request to have the marriage annulled.[40] These provisions have been adopted and elaborated by the *kompilasi*.

II Criticism of the *Kompilasi*

The *kompilasi* which has been put into effect has a number of reformist ideas incorporated in it. Some Indonesian Muslim scholars are satisfied with it, but others are disappointed. Debates on and repudiations of some of its provisions have inevitably arisen among them. Even some of the *'ulamā'* involved in its making have clearly expressed their uneasiness with some matters as the ultimate decision lay in the hands of the project committee, the majority of whom were Government agents. The fact that those attending the seminar were not given sufficient time to study it properly and give their informed comments in the forum, as mentioned in the previous chapter, were taken as a sign that the voices of the *'ulamā'* were not fully taken into consideration. A number of *'ulamā'* even said that they did not get any idea that a number of rules introduced in the *kompilasi* are in contradiction to the *sharī'a*. Moreover, the *kompilasi* is considered to have been weakened by employing the authority of the President. Above all, in relation to the interests of women, no representatives of feminist groups attended the seminar. The female participants, whose names have been recorded in the previous chapter, were not drawn from their ranks and, more importantly, do not share the same views and interests as the feminists.

II.1 Fiqh Texts versus the Qur'ān

It is impossible to abstract the debate on the *kompilasi* from the classical contestation between traditionalists and modernists, represented in organizational form by NU and the Muhammadiyah, and their attempts to engage in the discourse of the application of Islamic law in Indonesia. It is important to recall that the establishment of the Nahdlatul Ulama should be seen against its historical background. NU was formed when the Muhammadiyah, which was set up in 1912, began to exert its influence among traditionalists by calling upon Muslims to return to the original scriptural sources, the Qur'ān and *ḥadīth*. By adopting this slogan, the founders of this organization had the development of an Islamic practice appropriate to the challenges of the modern age in mind. They leveled the accusation that the stagnation of the Muslim world was the result of the blind adherence to the teachings of earlier generations of Muslim thinkers, which they thought was the practice among traditionalist Muslims.[41] As a reaction to what they considered an unjust criticism, some prominent *'ulamā'* in Java began to voice their interests as representatives of the traditionalist practice of Islam, on the basis of the *kitab kuning* (yellow books in Arabic script), and to provide a more sustained response to modernist encroachment. On 31 January 1926, a new body called the Nahdlatul Ulama (the Revival of the *'ulamā'*) was set up.[42]

It is understandable that these two organizations have always been engaged in competition, if not confrontation, with each other. This is particularly apparent in the ways they view Islamic legal problems and consequently the way they seek references to support their legal stances. NU has tended to seek to understand Islam and find answers to current problems by referring to *fiqh* texts. Its *'ulamā'*, including those who claim *Baḥth Masā'il* membership, feel that it is presumptuous to refer to the Qur'ān and the Prophetic tradition. They have even claimed any person who directly cites Qur'ānic verses to support their way of thinking is *sesat dan menyesatkan* (misled and misleading).[43] This is in sharp contrast to the Muhammadiyah which, in its attempts to understand Islam correctly, is inclined to refer directly to the Qur'ānic verses; and suggests that every Muslim has the right to interpret the Qur'ān. In the eyes of this organization, true "Islam" is what the Qur'ān and the Prophetic tradition say.[44]

In an intriguing juxtaposition, NU has now become much more moderate and flexible than the Muhammadiyah Rifyal Ka'bah. A Supreme Court judge, one of the elite members of the Muhammadiyah, has confirmed this fact. In an interview with *Suara Hidayatullah*, he criticized the attitude of the Muhammadiyah's *Majlis Tarjīḥ* (Council for Opinions), in its perspective on modern issues and the methods adopted by its members in demonstrating their arguments. The point of his argument is that the *Majlis Tarjīḥ* is too Qur'ānic- and *ḥadīth*-oriented, while there are only a few people among Muhammadiyah activists and even its *Majlis Tarjīḥ* members who truly understand the Qur'ān and the Prophetic traditions. As a Muhammadiyah activist, in essence he agrees with calls for Muslims to refer to the Qur'ān and *ḥadīth* in seeking answers to contemporary problems, but he is very unhappy about how superficial the *Majlis Tarjīḥ* members are in understanding of the Qur'ān when they are called upon to solve complicated Islamic questions. Through this practice of referring directly to the Qur'ān and *ḥadīth*, Ka'bah is anxious that in its reformulations of Islamic law, the Muhammadiyah is often too adamant and more conservative than the NU.[45] While nowadays a rapprochement is assumed, as they have to some extent attempted to draw closer to each other, a lingering contestation is still apparent when it comes to viewing social problems and finding the

Islamic rationale for their views, and this is well reflected in their debates on the *kompilasi*.

From what I have been able to observe, NU feels that the provisions of the *kompilasi* have been formulated without consulting the *fiqh* texts properly. Irfan Zidny, the chairman of the *Sharī'a* council of this organization, has insisted that, even though the Qur'ān, followed by the *ḥadīth*, are the main sources of Islam, the *fiqh* texts remain the primary references to be consulted in seeking precedents for points of Islamic law.[46] His opinion reflects the position of the NU's *Baḥth al-Masā'il* when it attempts to deal with legal questions posed by its members.[47] Explaining the procedure this council follows in issuing *fatwā* (religious decrees), Zidny stated that: *firstly*, they identify the problem or case, and *secondly*, they look at *tafsīr* books, but should no *tafsīr* book deal with it, they go to *fiqh* books, but such *mu'tabara* ones as *al-'Umm* of al-Shāfi'ī and then after that to commentaries. [48]

Zidny argues that the *kompilasi* is still an unacceptable work, above all because a number of its provisions have deviated from the classical doctrines of the *fiqh* texts. He is adamant that if any rule can be located in *fiqh* books, it should be followed unreservedly.

> We are not *mujtahid*, we are *muttabi'* (followers). Our leading '*ulamā'* who are endowed with the capacity to understand the fundamental sources of Islam have interpreted the Qur'ān, *ḥadīths* and the like and what we need to do now is to follow what they have interpreted. If they are silent about cases with which we are now confronted, then we have to struggle to solve these and find the rules which govern their solution. If there are already rules on them, it is not our task to find other laws, but simply follow them.[49]

Zidny pointed out some examples to bolster his arguments, such as the matter of divorce, to demonstrate the deviation from the *fiqh* texts of the *kompilasi*. He argues that divorce is automatically put into effect as soon as a husband utters the required formula. In this respect, the religious court needs only to record it and not to legalize it.

His position of adhering closely to the *fiqh* texts can also be gleaned from his views on the prohibition of inter-religious marriage between a Muslim man and a non-Muslim woman, as this is ruled upon in the *kompilasi*. Referring to some *fiqh* books, he argues that the majority of the founders of the Sunnite schools of Islamic law permitted this. Without making reference to the Qur'ānic text, which also explicitly permits it, he views the position adopted by the *kompilasi* on this issue as quite a radical departure from the prevalent opinions in the classical *fiqh* texts. Zidny's opinion is not the same as that propounded by liberalist and feminist groups. Setting out the opinions of all the Sunnite legal schools, he proposes that the *kompilasi* should consider the possibility, however remote, of the existence of purely *ahl al-kitāb* (the People of the Book) women, and differentiate women of this kind from those of other religions, thereby allowing a Muslim man the latitude to marry such a woman believer. If the *kompilasi* is truly trying to be as careful as possible in this matter, as it relates to faith issue, it should at least consider al-Shāfi'ī's view, which places a strict condition on such a marriage. The woman's profession of *al-kitāb* must not be disrupted by the conversion of one of her descendants to another faith (*kitābiyah khāliṣa*) when permitting such a marriage, is how he analyses the matter.[50] In even more unequivocal tones, he has proposed that the *kompilasi* should not prohibit such a marriage but allow it under very strict conditions, as is the view of the al-Shāfi'ī school.

Interestingly, he supports the concept of *waṣiat wājiba* used by the *kompilasi* to solve the problem of adoption, deeming it an appropriate rule. Indeed, this sort of issue was not dealt with in the *fiqh* books, so it cannot be considered to deviate from *fiqh* doctrine. This quite clearly demonstrates that it is those rules which deviate from the *fiqh* doctrines which are the target of his criticism. Doubtless, such a standpoint has been influenced by the central position of *fiqh* books among the NU *'ulamā'*.

In contrast, the Muhammadiyah is of the opinion that some provisions of the *kompilasi* have ignored Qur'ānic texts. This organization announced that referring directly to the Qur'ān is a must in the deductive precedents in Islamic law.[51] It is also from this context that, in contrast to the adherents of NU who resort repeatedly to the *fiqh* books in criticizing rules in the *kompilasi*, Muhammadiyah legal experts tended to refer directly to the Qur'ānic text to provide arguments for their criticism of the *kompilasi*. When asked about the rule on inter-religious marriage, Ichtiyanto, from a modernist background and a former Director of the Islamic Justice at the Ministry of Religious Affairs (1977-1982), also criticized the position taken by the *kompilasi*. However, unlike Zidny, who tended to base his views more on references to the opinions of the four leading Sunni schools, Ichtiyanto has tended to explore the Qur'ānic verse which states that it is lawful to marry women from the People of the Book. He has interpreted the words *wa al muḥṣanāt allāi 'ūtū al-kitāb* as an explicit sign allowing a Muslim man to marry a woman of the Book. This includes Christians.

Besides the belief that it is quite hard to find women of the Book as intended by the Qur'ān, Ichtiyanto has understood that the position adopted by the *kompilasi* reflects the prevailing concern among Muslim leaders about the campaign to propagate Christianity among Indonesian Muslims, and of their perception that inter-religious marriage is a covert tactic of Christianization. In this context he has emphasized that the departure of the *kompilasi* from the Qur'ānic text is therefore in the sake of public interest (*maṣlaḥa*). However, he has maintained that whatever the reason was, such a prohibition is in contradiction to the text of the Qur'ān which reads "... do not forbid what is allowed by God." As some provisions of the *kompilasi* contradict what God has decided, he claims that the drafters of the *kompilasi* have strayed beyond the Qur'ān and become *mu'tadīn*. He also understood that such a prohibition would have a negative effect on Muslim interests. In fact, such marriages had still been performed even after the *fatwā* of the MUI, which was restricted exclusively to Qur'ānic quotations, as he himself tended to do, and adduced no *fiqh* texts as arguments prohibiting such a marriage. Even worse, he added, such marriages were conducted and registered by the civil marriage registrar.[52]

What has just been said shows incontrovertibly that as far as the Muhammadiyah is concerned, the Qur'ān and the *ḥadīth* are unquestionably the main references which must be consulted directly in deciding Islamic legal issues. Another Muhammadiyah legal expert, Ma'rifat Iman, has criticized the tendency of judges in the religious courts to quote too many *fiqh* books, at the expense of the Qur'ān, in constructing the argument for their judgments.[53] Furthermore, Ichtiyanto censured the *kompilasi*, whose creation, he believed, involved for the main part *'ulamā'* from and representing NU, and was more conservative than Shāfi'īte jurisprudence itself. In this regard, he accused the NU adherents of not referring directly to the *fiqh* texts written by al-Shāfi'ī, such as *al-'Umm*, but *fiqh* books written by the Shāfi'ite followers.[54]

II.2 Islamic or Adat Law?

The debate on the *kompilasi* also involved Muslim scholars and legal experts from both NU and the Muhammadiyah, who questioned whether or not it was appropriate to call this Islamic law. The first point at stake concerns the adoption of the *kompilasi* of *adat* law, first and foremost in inheritance issues with a bearing on the system of representation and obligatory bequest. The accommodation of the local practice of joint property does not seem to have elicited any heated debate. Yahya Harahap comments on this, saying that this conformity can be attributed to the assumption that the maintenance of this institution offers more advantages than disadvantages. Therefore, because of regard for public interest (*maṣlaḥa mursala*) *'urf* can be observed, unless it contradicts the Qur'ān and the *ḥadīth*. Harahap argues that the institution of the joint property can be admitted legally and applied. On the system of social stratification, the conformity as shown in the *kompilasi* is also perceived as granting equal or egalitarian status to a husband and a wife in a relationship.[55]

In my opinion, it is certain that, although it relates to material goods or estates, the question of joint property differs from such matters as the representation of heirs and obligatory bequests, which also relate to estates. The big difference is that the question of joint property is associated with the estate of living persons for which a ruling has not been found, as it was not dealt with in either the *fiqh* or the Qur'ān. Meanwhile, such matters as the representation of heirs and adoption relate to the estate of a deceased or dead person, and rules of distribution pertaining to this are abundantly defined in both the Qur'ān and the *ḥadīth,* and legally defined in the *fiqh*. Such rules involve parties (heirs) whose shares have been defined, and would have been inconvenienced if other parties were suddenly designated to share with them. It seems that these are the specific considerations which have led to acceptance among Muslims of the ruling on joint property, and to debate in the cases of representation of heirs and adoption.

It may be true that local tradition and Islamic doctrine can be harmonized, as shown in the matter of joint property. Since the reformed ideas introduced are not always felt to represent justice among people, the two rules are, though not publicly contested, inevitably still questioned. Considering that inheritance rules are dealt with abundantly in the Qur'ān, *'ulamā'* have continued to remain very sensitive about the reforms introduced on this issue by the *kompilasi*. It is not difficult to recall how Munawir Sjadzali's proposal to offer 1:1 ratio for the shares of males and females instead of 2:1 was strongly opposed by Indonesian Muslim scholars, as it was considered to have deviated from explicit text of the Qur'ān. Besides taking issue with the methodological approach which Sjadzali used in quite a liberal manner, the criticisms also focus on the empirical levels on which Sjadzali based his ideas. Many Muslims consider the way Sjadzali applied terms like *naskh* and *maqāṣid al-sharī'a,* although the general context was familiar to them, as too liberal. They even thought it went so far as to endanger scriptural bases and Muslim religious beliefs.[56]

Incontrovertibly, Sjadzali also received support from different scholars. Yahya Harahap, a former Supreme Court judge, is one of Sjadzali's supporters, and offers a somewhat promising argument. He speculates that the half-share of a female in an estate, compared to the male, is the minimum limit. Accordingly, should a situation which requires more than half exist, the limit can be raised to an equal share as male, or even more than that. He expands on this by assuring that a female's right to an estate is absolute, but the ratio of two to one is elastic and therefore can be changed. He goes on to draw an analogy of this with the case of, for example, murder. He argues that killing is harmful and therefore whoever commits a murder must be punished, but the forms of criminal penalties applied are not rigid. They can be adapted to the situation or condition which prompted the murder.[57] Here, he wants to emphasize that there is a difference between some fixed injunctions which cannot be changed and those that can be interpreted conditionally.

Criticism of Sjadzali's ideas reminds us of Hazairin's initial proposal for the system of the representation of heirs (*mawālī*) in inheritance, which inspired the application of the representation of heirs in the *kompilasi*. In the seminar on national inheritance held in 1964, Toha Yahya Omar, a graduate of al-Azhar University, and Mahmud Yunus, a well-known Indonesian professor of Islamic Studies, strongly reacted to Hazairin's idea and accused it of deviating from the established Islamic rule of inheritance of both the Sunnīte and Shī'īte schools. The debate in the seminar focused on the discussion of Verse 33 of Chapter 4 (al-Nisā'). There was no agreement between them in interpreting the verse, as they diverged enormously in the matter of the *i'rāb* (grammatical explanation) of the verse. While Omar and Yunus positioned the words *al-wālidāni* and *al-'aqrabūna* as 'hāl' from the word *mawālī* and mentioned that the subject of the word *taraka* is the word *kullin*, Hazairin considered them to be the subject of the word *taraka*. [58] Reviewing this issue, another Muslim scholar, Ismuha, said that both interpretations could possibly be applied. He tended to support Omar and Yunus in considering the *ḥadīth* transmitted by Bukhārī.[59]

In contrast to that of Sjadzali, Hazairin's idea was incorporated into the *kompilasi* and there may be some good explanations for this. The most cogent argument is that the idea of representation had been adopted earlier in another Muslim country, Pakistan, to deal with the same matter. Wisely, Hazairin did not challenge the explicit text of the Qur'ān, as in the application of his concept he retained the ratio of 2:1 for male and female.[60] Another pertinent reason might be that the local traditions of various regions in Indonesia concur almost exactly with the idea of the representation of heirs. No less important is the idea that freeing the orphaned grandchildren from poverty errs on the side of justice. It is an idea with which other Islamic countries have been concerned, although they have differed in finding its solution; Egypt and other Middle Eastern countries chose the adoption of the obligatory bequest, and Pakistan opted for the acceptance of the doctrine of representation.[61] Nonetheless, like Pakistan,[62] the inclusion of the system of representation of heirs into the *kompilasi* by Indonesia has, as mentioned earlier, provoked debate from diverse camps among Indonesian Muslims.

Some scholars of Islamic law, including Amir Syarifuddin, a professor of Islamic Law at the State Islamic University in Jakarta, concerned with the re-actualization of Islamic law, and Roihan Rasyid, a former lecturer of the State Institute for Islamic Studies in Yogyakarta, have maintained that the application of the representation of heirs is positively grounded in Islamic law and hence they have supported the rule. They mention that the system has been customarily practiced among certain groups of Indonesian Muslims through the system of *plaatsvervulling*. As local tradition (*adat* or *'urf*) constitutes one of the sources of Islamic law, they have argued that the local practice of the representation of heirs could be legalized through the legal maxim of *'al-'āda muḥākama*. However, they gave due notice that the adoption of this established local practice could not be absolute, and some modification was required. A number of modifications were therefore duly applied. The portion of the representative heirs is not to exceed the portion of the other heirs whose positions are equal to the substituted heirs, and this principle was, as mentioned in passing earlier, indeed set down in the *kompilasi*. Therefore, if the deceased leaves two heirs, including one daughter and one grandchild of a predeceased son, the estate is divided equally between them. Each gets one-half. This limitation is a necessity as long as the ratio of 2:1 is preserved. This is to prevent injustice to an aunt. Furthermore, the principle of the representation of heirs is not to be applied if a deceased leaves behind heirs including a father, a mother, a husband or wife, and a sister(s) or a brother(s) whose shares will be lessened by the presence of a representative heir, unless they consent.[63] This last principle was not adopted by the *kompilasi*, but its advocates have insisted that it must be applied by judges dealing with such a case.

Unlike Syarifuddin and Rasyid, Minhajul Falah and Thoha Abdurrahman, both specialists in inheritance (*farā'id*) from the Faculty of Islamic Law at the State Islamic University in Jakarta and the State Islamic University in Yogyakarta respectively, have strongly contested the idea. Their contention is that the *kompilasi* has ignored a more appropriate way of solving the problem of grandchildren, namely an obligatory bequest, by adopting such a precarious solution. They argue that the application of this system not only deviates from the established classical Sunnite system of inheritance, but it also creates some problems if applied in broader and more complex issues of inheritance.[64] They have also asserted that the adoption of the concept was too imprudent and not well thought-out, giving the impression that it is the local tradition which grants grandchildren the right to inherit from their grandparents, following the concept of *plaatsvervulling* rather than the Islamic classical legal system.[65]

As a better foundation, they have proposed some *ḥadīth* texts, such as that of Ibn Mas'ūd, which reads:

> "In the case of heirs including a daughter, a daughter of a son, and a sister, the Prophet Muhammad decided that for the daugh-

> ter is a half of the share, for the daughter of a son is one-sixth so as to make up the two-thirds, and the remaining share is awarded to the sister" (Transmitted by Bukhārī).[66]

The purport of their argument is that this *ḥadīth* indicates that the Hazairin's interpretation of the *mawālī* is not correct, and simply proposed to legitimize a direct adoption of *plaatsvervulling* or "representation of heirs" which had been practiced by some Indonesians for a long time.

Besides denouncing the concept as having no Islamic basis, these scholars have also criticized the term "representation" itself. They contend that a person does not have any inherent right to the property of his or her ancestor until the latter dies. When a person dies before the death of one of his or her progenitors, the pre-deceased person cannot be considered to have a claim in inheritance from his or her progenitor who will have died after him or her. Instead, he or she should be regarded as a *pewaris* (praepositus) and not *ahli waris* (heir). Consequently, there must be no claim through a deceased person that any of his generation or his heirs can act as his representative. In more direct words, they questioned how a deceased person can be substituted or represented in heir-ship while he himself cannot be regarded as an heir or, to put it another way, how children can inherit a right which is not credited to their parents. Following this logic, they then concluded that representation cannot occur between predeceased persons and their predecessors; and the only case to which the representation can be applied is therefore a case in which an heir dies before the distribution of the estate, considering that he or she was alive when his or her progenitor died.[67]

Just as with the principle of representation of heirs, the application of the institution of obligatory bequest to legitimize adoptive parties to a share in an estate has also aroused debate among specialists on Islamic law. One view holds that the abolition of the established practice of full adoption, which permits the adoptive parties to inherit from each other in the Muslim community, is impossible to realize fully. Adherents of this view find support for their interpretation in the principle that *'urf* or customary law can be maintained for the sake of public interest. Consequently, they argue that the system of *wāṣiya wājiba* is the appropriate solution to the problem. They have also pointed out the fact that adoptive parties constitute close relatives or friends who deserve to inherit from each other. Ichtiyanto, one of the proponents of this idea, has referred to the concept developed by Hazairin that *pertaulanan* or "friendship" constitutes one of the principles which bring the parties concerned to give, make a bequest, and even inherit to and from each other. He recalls the Prophetic Tradition, which demonstrates that the Prophet once showed his very close relationship with his friends by giving them his things and making a bequest to them. Citing this legal action of the Prophet, he concludes that giving shares between adoptive parties as ruled in the *kompilasi* has an adequate Islamic rationale.[68]

In accordance with their inclination to use the system of obligatory bequest to solve the problem of the rightful inheritance of grandchildren, some scholars have contested the application of obligatory bequest as a means to deal with the adoptive problem in regard to inheritance. Holding true to his inclination to apply the obligatory bequest to the problem of orphaned grandchildren, Minhajul Falah, for instance, has stated that the application of the concept of obligatory bequest to the problem of adoption is not relevant. Adoption, he maintains, could not affect inheritance among the adoptive parties, though by means of the institution of obligatory bequest. Adopted children may have spent a large amount of money from his or her adoptive parents, yet they are not to be granted shares from the deceased's (adoptive parent) estate by a religious court. If it can be acknowledged that an adopted child played a significant role in developing his or her adoptive parent's estate during their lifetime and is thereby considered to deserve a share from his or her adoptive parent's estate, the division of the estate must be carried out by applying the concept of *mushāraka*, as regulated in *fiqh*.[69]

Similarly, Roihan A. Rasyid has accused the *kompilasi* in this regard of having departed from the Qur'ānic text, which clearly decrees that the status of both the adoptive parent and the adopted child is not to be transformed into that of real parent and child, and therefore they cannot inherit from each other, except by obligatory bequest. The Prophet Muhammad's marriage to the divorced wife of Zaid Ibn Thābit, his adopted child, is a clear signal that adoption did not result in any prohibition of marriage between the Prophet (the adoptive parent) and the ex-wife of his adopted child, as she was not considered to be his daughter-in-law during her marriage with Zaid Ibn Thābit. This should be taken as a basic assumption that it does not produce any other legal consequences including those affecting inheritance. Above all, there is no classical *fiqh* text which discusses the matter, and neither has the *jurisprudence* in Indonesia nor that of other Muslim countries tackled the question. Therefore, if neither the Qur'ānic injunctions, the Traditions of the Prophet, the decisions of the Companions, nor the practices of a particular society (*umma*) readily lead to the conclusion that the application of the institution of *wāṣiya wājiba* as a means to deal with the adoption problem in regard with inheritance in the *kompilasi* is in accordance with the collective viewpoint of the community, there is no critical reason to uphold Article of 209 of the *kompilasi*.[70]

Essentially, the upsurge in debates on both issues is not surprising. It is reported that almost none of the *'ulamā'* involved in the making of the *kompilasi* agreed with the proposal for the regulation that adoptive parent and their adopted child inherit from each other, which is what had happened for a long time in some regions of Indonesia. Yahya Harahap, who was in charge of testing the opinions of *'ulamā'*, admitted that the *'ulamā'* refused to countenance the *adat* law of adoption. But the necessity of bridging the contradictory rules of adoption between *adat* law and Islamic law left the drafters of the *kompilasi* no option but to ignore the objections of the *'ulamā'* and introduce the institution of *wāṣiya wājiba* to accommodate the two conflicting rules.[71] As has been discussed before (see p. 99), Hazairin's initial proposal for the system of representation of heirs to deal with the problem of orphaned grandchildren was likewise contested.

To add to the confusion, the introduction of these two systems in the *kompilasi* is somewhat peculiar in the sense that in the case of representation, it introduces an additional rule, namely a limitation on the portion of the representative heir, which Pakistan, while adopting the same doctrine, did not legislate. This limitation rule has indubitably given an extra edge to the debate. Moreover, the fact that the two issues to be resolved by these two systems have both been ineluctably practiced by Indonesian society has turned the debate towards a more principal point, questioning whether it is Islamic or *adat* law which provides the basis for the maintenance of their practices. Or, in other words, has *adat* adapted to Islam or vice versa in answering the problems?

Bearing in mind that the majority of Muslim scholars agree in principle with granting a share of the deceased estate to orphaned grandchildren, and have preferred the institution of *wāṣiya wājiba* to deal with it, I arrive at the question of why the *kompilasi* preferred the concept of representation of heirs to the institution of *wāṣiya wājiba* to solve the problem of grandchildren. I assume that the drafters of the *kompilasi* realized that there is yet another problem which needs to be resolved, namely, that of adoptive parties. Having decided that the problem of adoption could not be solved by the concept of the representation of heirs, they chose to employ the concept of representation of heirs to the problem of orphaned grandchildren. At the same time, they had a tendency to employ one solution to one problem rather than employ one and the same solution to two problems by, for instance, the employment of the legal concept of obligatory bequest to the separate problems of orphaned grandchildren and adoption. With their minds firmly set on their own path, they insisted on the application of the principle of the representation of heirs, despite its lack of rationale in the Qur'ānic texts, to the problem of orphaned grandchildren, and the obligatory bequest to that of adoption.

Exploring the employment of the concept of obligatory bequest, if we refer to the Qur'ān, we discover that the Qur'ān (II: 180) commands a Muslim to bequeath part of his or her estate to his or her relatives.

Although some Muslim jurists have agreed that the verse was abrogated by the verse on inheritance (IV: 7), others have maintained that the abrogation is only to be applied to those relatives who had been entitled to the definite shares elucidated in the Qur'ān.[72] Accordingly, they have believed that making a bequest is still recommended for those not entitled to definite shares of deceased estates. Ibn Ḥazm even considered that should a person have failed to make a bequest during his lifetime, a religious court is obliged to make a testament on behalf of the deceased.[73]

Adopting this point of view, some Muslim countries, especially Egypt as mentioned before, have employed the regulation of bequeathing to solve the problem of orphaned grandchildren whose shares in their grandparents' estates, according to classical system of inheritance, would otherwise have been blocked by their uncles.[74] Regardless of the inclusion of the different specifications of each rule on this issue, these countries have agreed that orphaned grandchildren should be given shares in their grandparents' estates. As the consequence of employing the principle of bequeathing, the shares of orphaned grandchildren should be limited to one-third.

The opinion of Muslim jurists that *wāṣiya* could still be applied to relatives not entitled to definite shares of a deceased estate was utilized by the *kompilasi* to deal with a different problem. Facing a particular local problem of adoption whose practice is popular in Indonesia, particularly in Java – albeit in contradiction to Islamic doctrine as it allows adoptive parties to inherit from each other as real parents and children – the *kompilasi* preferred to retain the established practice of adoption rather than to abolish it. The drafters of the *kompilasi* refused to challenge the Qur'ānic doctrine, which clearly undermines the full attribution of an adopted child to his or her adoptive parent and vice versa. The practice of giving and receiving of parts of each other's estates, as in the case of the practice of ordinary inheritance between natural parents and children, is then thought to have been ended. It is in the institution of obligatory bequest that they have found an Islamic legitimization for maintaining the practice of inheritance between adoptive parties. Applying the regulation of obligatory bequest to adoptive parties, they have observed that the relationship between an adopted child and his or her adoptive parent is so intimate that it is interpreted by adoptive parties as concerning close relatives (*al-aqrabūn*). Having decided this, they ignored the established principle that a blood relationship is the valid perquisite for the distribution of the deceased's estate to his or her heirs.[75] Instead of recommending both adoptive parents and adopted children make bequests to each other before they die, the *kompilasi* has decided that a certain share, namely one-third, of their estates should be allotted to each of them after one or the other has passed away.

II.3 Marriage According to What Law?

The debate that reflects the question on the Islamic legal basis of the *kompilasi* touches also upon the issue of marriage. Some Muslim scholars agreed that the registration of marriage cannot be regarded as one of the requirements of its religious validity, and can be only considered an administrative matter. They perceive the registration of marriage as aimed at preventing the practice of illegal marriage (*nikah di bawah tangan)* and functioning only administratively.[76] Ali Yafie, one of the leading *'ulamā'*, asserted that Islamic law is different from European civil codes considering marriage as merely a private affair, and thus regarding registration as a principal thing. Islamic law focuses more on the religious conditions and sees registration as administrative. It then affirms that registration of marriage cannot be regarded as one condition of the validity of marriage in Islam.[77]

In contrast, Amir Syarifuddin, a professor of Islamic law at the State Institute for Islamic Studies (IAIN) Padang (1983-1992), demanded the registration be one of the conditions for the religious validity of marriage.[78] In proposing such an idea, he wanted to abolish dual validation of a marriage and to demonstrate that what has been established in one of *fiqh* books is not ultimate and final doctrine; Muslims can still change. He found support in the comparative knowledge of Islamic legal schools (*al-'ilm fi muqāranat al-madhāhib*). These clarify that *sharī'a* is indeed one, but *fiqh* has varied interpretations. The *fiqh* of the Ḥanafī, for example, had reduced the conditions for validating a marriage to those put forward by Shāfi'ī in case of *wālī*. For him, it is clear that the *fiqh* could be amended, as it was a product of human reasoning. Thus the Indonesian *'ulamā'*, through their collective *ijtihād*, could add one or even more conditions of the validity of marriage, such as the registration of marriage, in accordance with the public interests of the Indonesian Muslims.[79]

Regardless of the different perceptions on the issue, it can be argued that on the one hand, the rule of the compulsory registration of marriage has been to some extent a form of successful adoption of reform ideas in Indonesia. Reasons for that are: firstly, failure to register marriage affects the validity of the marriage, although only in the eyes of the State; secondly, judicial recourse is denied in unregistered marriages; and lastly, marriages should be witnessed directly by the Marriage Register Official in order to ensure the marriages are registered. However, looking at the overall provisions of marriage, the *kompilasi* contains some ambiguities. First, dualism appears, as it admits the validity of the marriage if it fulfils religious requirements or if it is concluded according to the rules of religion, but claims it illegal in the view of the State if it is not registered. Accordingly, marriage validity becomes twofold, according to religious doctrine and State. Second, it does not regulate sanctions for those who do not register their marriages. Third, it provides a way for the unregistered marriage to be confirmed through the institution of *ithbāt nikāḥ*. Although it is regulated that the *ithbāt nikāḥ* can only be applied in certain cases, such as divorce, loss of the original certificate of marriage, doubts as to whether or not the marriage concluded is lawful, marriages conducted before the application of Marriage Law of 1974, and marriages concluded by the parties who are legally allowed to marry, it at least gives space for couples to ignore the rule of registration of marriages. With these conditions, couples see the opportunity for them to confirm their marriages in the future, as shall be discussed in the next chapter in greater detail.

II.4 Subordination of Women?

Other issues which have unleashed a gale of criticism are concerned with the rules of polygyny and divorce. The majority of Muslim scholars and judges have viewed the restrictions on polygyny introduced in the *kompilasi* as an appropriate position to be taken by the Indonesian Muslims and a dynamically advanced step in the discourse on Islamic law. Yahya Harahap, for example, thinks that this position has been adopted in the public interest or *maṣlaḥa*. Referring to the Qur'ān: 3 which sets out the rule of polygyny, he argues that the level of its legal basis is only reached with permission or *ibāha*. Even this level of permission should be historically traced, as it was at the time permitted relevant to the situation or conditions of the society in the period of early Islam.[80]

Some *'ulamā'* and judges interviewed have agreed with the *kompilasi* and maintained that polygyny can be exercised if the reasons and requirements are met. One or more reasons must be first met, and then the conditions of the consent of the wife, being capable of treating his co-wives justly, and being financially capable of maintaining more than one wife, are subsequent upon the valid reason. Therefore, although a husband can present requirements, if no reason can be adduced, he has no right to enter into a polygynous marriage. Contrarily, they further said that if one of reasons covered in the *kompilasi* does exist, the consent of wife is no longer necessary.[81] Nonetheless, it must be noted here that, as will be discussed in the next chapter, it often happens that judges fulfill the request of a husband who can prove that he is capable of maintaining his co-wives and whose wife states her consent, although he has provided none of the reasons enumerated in the *kompilasi*.

The rule of divorce put forward in the *kompilasi* is also seen as a reform by the majority of Indonesian Muslim scholars, as its purpose is to serve the public interest. Amir Syarifuddin and Bustanul Arifin, two leading scholars of Islamic law, support the rule by upholding the interpretation of the Shī'īte School of the word *washhidū* following the words *dhawai 'adlin* in a Qur'ānic verse. They claim that this interpretation is more appropriate than those of other schools of Islamic law, which are interpreted only as a recommendation (*ibāha*). This is because, besides its relevance to the Prophetic saying, 'The most detested allowed action by God is divorce', it is in the spirit of the Qur'ānic text which stipulates that divorce must follow several procedures, such as the process of attempted reconciliation (*al-ṣulḥ*). Following the interpretation of Shī'īte, the *kompilasi* therefore rules that the divorce can be effective only if it is carried out/ pronounced before two qualified persons who must be defined as judges, they confirmed.[82]

Nevertheless, Muslim feminists have taken issue with this and argued that the reforms in this aspect are not adequate to ensure justice for women. To express their interests more effectively and systematically, they have established women's study centers, which frequently organize seminars to discuss protection for abused women, orphaned children and other vulnerable groups such as single mothers. Among such groups are the Team Pengarusutamaan Gender (the Team of Gender Interests) of the Ministry of Religious Affairs, APIK (Asosiasi Perempuan untuk Keadilan, Association of Indonesian Women for Justice) under the supervision of the LBH (Lembaga Bantuan Hukum, the Association for Legal Aid), Rahima, most of whose members are young NU adherents, Rifka al-Nisa, Yasanti, LSPPA (Lembaga Studi Pengembangan Perempuan dan Anak) and others. Similar centers can also be found in a number of State Institutes of Islamic Studies (IAINs) in Indonesia. This indicates that the main public actors in debates about family law are no longer merely men, but women who are imbued with notions of gender equality. They actively explore the gender discourses which have developed throughout the Muslim world.[83] In doing so, they benefit from national and international support concerned with the issues, acting in accordance with the United Nations "Convention on the Elimination of All Forms of Discrimination against Women".[84]

Some activists in the groups have openly expressed their disappointment in a number of provisions regarding women's issues in the *kompilasi* and other legislation presented by the State. They have accused the State of marginalizing women's interests in favor of the opinions of '*ulamā'* and other established groups, which happened earlier in the case of the 1974 Marriage Law.[85] Their argument is that since the Law upholds the voices of the '*ulamā'*, unsurprisingly, those provisions which were then adopted into the *kompilasi* are far removed from a sense of justice for women.

One clear example, they claim, can be seen in the provisions in the *kompilasi* on polygyny, which have not yet been conducive to the restriction of the practice. The members of several women's study centers have regarded the stipulations regulating the practice of polygyny as being gender-biased. They have insisted that it is not fair if husbands may enter into a polygynous marriage when their wives are unable to perform their duties as wives, or if they suffer from physical defects or an incurable disease, or they are unable to provide descendants.[86] They have strongly criticized the reasons for which men are permitted to take another wife, and have observed that it is unfair that such physical problems afflicting wives are taken as reasons for husbands to enter into a polygynous marriage or to have other wives.[87] In their eyes, the goal of marriage, namely to establish a happy family, is the responsibility of both husband and wife. So, if one of them has a problem, the other party should understand and share in the problem. If the wife has a physical infirmity, such as being unable to bear descendants, it is unfair if the husband takes another wife for the sake of own his interest, because that infirmity not only becomes the husband's problem, it also a source of the wife's dissatisfaction. They also question the Article which indicates that the consent of wives is not needed at all times or is not an absolute requirement. Indeed, the *kompilasi* states that for one or more reasons, a husband wishing to enter into a polygynous marriage can just do it if the consent of wives is impossible to gain (Art. 59). This rule asserts that in such an event, the physical infirmity of a wife weighs more strongly than such conditions or requirements as the consent of the wife.[88]

They also pose pertinent questions about the conditions or the assumptions often taken as a reason for entering into a polygynous marriage among Indonesian Muslim men, which states that statistically the number of women is far higher than that of men. They argue that this assumption might be only true in a comparison of older rather than younger people. Referring to other data, they concede that the number of elderly women is indeed higher than that of elderly men. The finding can be considered accurate on the basis of the medical assumption that the immunity of women is better than that of men, so that the life expectancy of women is higher than that of men. Accordingly, they conclude, polygynous marriage should be applied only to older women, if the statistical finding of this comparison of number of women and men is to be deemed valid grounds to conclude polygynous marriages.[89]

To Muslim feminists, the abandoning of the supreme right of the husband in the case of divorce in the *kompilasi* is also not a total reform. They feel the *kompilasi* is still inclined to support male superiority. The difference in words used to denote acts of divorce by both parties, the wife and husband – being *cerai gugat* for wife and *cerai talak* for husband- is claimed to prove this assertion.[90] The term *cerai gugat*, used in the *kompilasi* to denote divorce requested by a wife, is asserted to maintain a superior right of husband in an act of divorce as, they argue, the words *gugat cerai* imply that a wife cannot divorce her husband but instead can only ask her husband to divorce her. The word *gugat*, accordingly, is deleterious to women facing a lawsuit. Women who want to petition for divorce must face a long and difficult trial process in the court, as they are considered to be plaintiffs. Therefore, claiming the use of two different wordings as a cover for gender bias, they have demanded that the wording be removed and replaced by the same wording as is used for a husband's petition for divorce.[91]

The preservation of the classical *fiqh* concept of *'iwāḍ* or compensation in the *kompilasi* – in Indonesian, *ganti rugi* or *tebusan*, and which has to be paid by a woman to a husband when a woman petitions for a divorce in the form of *khul'* or *ta'līq ṭalāq* as a monetary compensation for her petition for divorce – also came under fire. Some feminists have argued that this rule is a clear indication that the *kompilasi* still maintains that divorce is the absolute right of a man.[92] This preservation of patriarchal ideology is also taken as proof that the law is often easier for a man to negotiate than a woman, a tendency which has led women to move to solve an internal domestic conflict and to fight for their rights against men in a lawsuit with the assistance of a lawyer.[93]

In requiring further reform on the issues, the feminists seem to have ignored the objections of a number of *'ulamā'* to the point of departure of the *kompilasi* in the case of divorce, particularly, from the classical doctrine. In fact, if modernists give solid support to the provision that a divorce can be considered valid only if it is pronounced before the court, traditionalists, such as Zidny, as mentioned before, maintain that the court cannot disallow the proclamation of divorce by a husband outside the confines of a court.[94] Although not as frank as Zidny, Ali Yafie also seems to disagree with the rule. He looks at this issue in a way he viewed the rule of the registration of marriage. He argues that, contrary to the European civil code of marriage which stresses the administrative matter in what is considered a private issue as the principal matter, Islamic law stresses the religious conditions. Therefore, he regards the intervention of the State as limited to administering and recording such cases. He has also affirmed that he believes that the court cannot repudiate the validity and force of a husband's pronouncement of the divorce formula. Although the modernists have different and more innovative views than the traditionalists, what the feminists demand in relation to the issues of polygyny and divorce does not seem to be in concert with either of these factions.

To sum up all the discussions, it seems there can be no shadow of a doubt that there have been various perspectives about Islam in general, and Islamic (family) law in particular, among Muslims as individuals and as members of Muslim organizations. Basically, realizing the fact that the text of the *kompilasi* leaves many unanswered questions and that it did not incorporate a number of recommendations, the drafters of the *kompilasi* deemed it necessary to leave open the possibility of future developments through interpretation. Through the final provision of the *kompilasi*, they had indeed allowed space for such possibilities by requiring that, in their judgments, "... judges should consider the values of living law in order that their judgments shall conform to the sense of justice."[95] Nevertheless, this provision does not seem to have been enough to prevent the emergence of plenty of debate, and does not seem to have satisfied groups of Muslims whose identities and interests have not been covered in the *kompilasi*.

III Proposal for Future Reforms

III.1 Points Proposed to Reform

As demonstrated above, the *kompilasi* has engendered an avalanche of criticism since it was issued in 1991. Aware of this situation and of the question of its legal status, many different groups of Indonesian Muslims feel that a review and reform should be attempted. On 19 September 2002, the Ministry of Religious Affairs set up an institution called the "Badan Pengkajian dan Pengembangan Hukum Islam/Institution for Studying and Developing Islamic Law (BPPHI)." The task of BPPHI is to study and develop the *kompilasi*. To achieve this purpose, the institution has proposed holding seminars, workshops and other activities to assist it in its work. Its members consist of Islamic legal professionals representing various Islamic organizations like NU, the Muhammadiyah, and the Council of Indonesian *'Ulama* (MUI).[96]

The founding of BPPHI is reported to tie in with the plan for upgrading the legal status of the *kompilasi* from a Presidential Instruction (*Inpres*) to a Statute (Undang-Undang). Said Agil Munawar, who was Minister of Religious Affairs at the time, said that the legal status of the *kompilasi* should be upgraded to statute. If this were to be accomplished, he added, an institution which would conduct an intensive examination and promote the development of Islamic law should be established.[97] In keeping with this plan, the personnel of the institution would also be responsible for carrying out the study of contemporary Islamic law to be proposed as a draft statute.

On 27 August 2003, the Ministry of Religious Affairs organized a seminar on the *kompilasi*, which I attended.[98] Although the announcement said it would be held by the Ministry of Religious Affairs, in practice the seminar was organized by the Team of Pengarusutamaan Gender or Pokja (Kelompok Kerja) untuk Masalah-Masalah Perempuan (Working Team for Women's Issues)' and very much revealed gender interests. Half of the participants in fact represented feminist groups, while the other half represented various elements of Muslim life, such as NU, the

Muhammadiyah, the religious courts, the Supreme Court, the Council of Indonesian *'Ulamā'*, Islamic institutions and researchers interested in the subject. In this seminar, Wahyu Widiana, the then Director of the Religious Justice at the Ministry of Religious Affairs (Ditbinbapera Depag), reported that since its establishment, BPPHI has been continuously engaged in discussing and analysing the rules in the *kompilasi*. Surveying the various discussions and debates held by BPPHI, Wahyu announced that BPPHI had recorded a number of proposals on rules to be revised. They were as follows: (1) Registration of marriage: registration must be made one of the conditions for the validity of a religious marriage and not be seen simply as an administrative affair; (2) Minimum age of marriage for both girls and boys: that of girls is proposed to be raised from 16 to 18 and that of boys from 19 to 21; (3) Mutual responsibilities between spouses; (4) Marriage during pregnancy: it is proposed that this rule be removed as it is considered to legalize free sex; (5) *Ithbāt nikāh*; its application can only be limited to certain situation as divorce; (6) Provision of sanctions in the case of the failure to meet some stipulations made in the *kompilasi*: it is proposed that the failure to some stipulations may incur imprisonment and payment of a fine; and (7) the clause "resulting in disharmony" attached to apostasy as grounds for divorce in Article 116 (h) to be removed.

Apart from these points, in keeping with their criticisms, some other detailed revisions proposed by feminist groups present in the seminar were also noted. A number of feminist activists representing various women's centers also vociferously contested provisions in the *kompilasi* they considered to exhibit a gender bias. Besides polygyny and divorce, they questioned provisions which they thought had been adopted in their entirety from classical doctrines and put women in a subordinate position. They pointed out the rules of guardianship in marriage, which stipulate that only males are appropriate to fulfill that role. They concluded that the Articles of the *kompilasi* dealing with the issue overall do not allow any room for female relatives, including mothers, to be guardians for their daughters' marriages.[99] They also corrected the fixed perception enshrined in the *kompilasi* of the superiority of a husband over his wife in their rights and obligations. They rejected the provisions of the *kompilasi* stating that the husband is the head of the family, that the husband is obliged to govern and supervise his wife, and that the husband should educate his wife in terms of religion without considering any possibility that husband's religiosity might be weaker than that of his wife.[100] They also rejected the rule stating that a baby has to follow his or her father's religion, which, they argue, indicates that the drafters of the *kompilasi* have automatically assumed that a father's religion is better than that of a mother.[101] They even find the *kompilasi* unfair when it insists that a wife should obey and respect her husband and considers her a disobedient wife (*nāshīz*), a predicate which leads to her losing rights to maintenance, if she neglects her duties, whereas it does not apply the same rule to a husband or, in other words, it does not consider the possible disobedience of a husband.[102]

They are also critical of the lower minimum age of marriage for girls than for boys.[103] Establishing 16 years old as the minimum age for girls, which is lower than that for boys (19), is seen by them as a legitimization of women as only second-rate citizens, there to obey men who are regarded as the first rank and are naturally assumed to be leaders. They have argued that by deciding to lower the age for girls, the *kompilasi* gives proof of an unequivocal expression of the wish to make it proper and appropriate for women to obey the men who are, in terms of age, older. Considering that these all provisions only exacerbate the subordinate position of women, the groups demand that they be amended.

Observing that the points criticized by the feminists are numerous, it is more than evident that the feminists are convinced that the *kompilasi* is still unreceptive to their interests. A leading feminist associated with the Islamic Liberal Network (Jaringan Islam Liberal/ JIL), Musdah Mulia, has stated that the *kompilasi*, by laying down some rules which she thought still put women and children in subordinate positions thereby preserving men's power, is still very conservative and does not exude a spirit of wanting to protect women and children.[104] On another occasion, she has even alleged that the *kompilasi* preserves "barbaric" rules and accordingly has insisted that the agenda of future reforms will eliminate such "barbaric" rules, such as one which states that a polygynous husband could gather all his co-wives in one place.[105]

III.2 Controversy on the Counter Legal Draft of the Kompilasi

Aware of the plan to upgrade the legal status of the *kompilasi* to a Statute and the amendment of its contents, a number of feminist organizations or institutions have been attempting to contribute to this. Although a formal institution, namely BPPHI, has been specifically set up for this purpose within the Ministry of Religious Affairs, and has made a draft which introduces a number of changes, other institutions have also felt they have right to contribute to its amendment. The Team of Pengarusutamaan Gender headed by Musdah Mulia has even drawn up and proposed a counter-draft, challenging the draft proposed by the Ministry of Religious Affairs to Parliament. Entitled Counter Legal Draft of the KHI or CLD-KHI, this draft includes such suggestions as a ban on polygyny, insistence on a contract of marriage, the obligation of both spouses to give *mahr*, the *iddah* for men, permission for inter-religious marriage: issues which had been highlighted in the critical debate of the *kompilasi* as mentioned above. This draft would allow spouses to make an agreement on the period of the marriage they are about to enter into. If ended, the period of marriage can be extended if both parties wish it to be so. Both the spouses must give each other *mahr* (dowry) and both of them can be parties who declare *'ījāb* (offer of contract) and *qabūl* (acceptance). If the marriage ends either in divorce or the death of one party, a husband, just as is expected of a wife, must undergo a transition period within which he is not allowed to marry another woman. The length of the period for a husband is defined as the same as that defined for a wife. A Muslim man or woman can marry a non-Muslim woman or man according to the tolerance and freedom of the implementation of their faith. With such rules in it, the draft has also been arranged for submission to Parliament.

In several interviews, Musdah Mulia has asserted that she has been fearless in fighting for gender equality and therefore had no plan to stop her struggle fighting for the rights of women. She is not alone, as she has obtained considerable support from female activists and liberalists, both involved and not involved in the team.[106] Ulil Abshar Abdalla, the Director of the Islamic Liberal Network, for example, thinks that CLD is progressive and a great step forward, and should be supported. Maria Ulfah, the chairperson in *Fatayat*, a women's organization of NU, endorses this opinion, saying that what the team has produced has to be respected as it is a more progressive and humane, and is more relevant to the conditions in contemporary Indonesia.[107] Abdul Muqsith Ghazali, a member and the spokesperson of the working group, and Wahid Marzuki, a member of the working group, said that in light of the existing law, the *kompilasi* is too Arab-centric, and they have based proposed reforms on authentic legal bases.[108] No text indicates that changing the established rules is prohibited, and therefore this implies that change is ultimately allowed, he argues. With such support, Mulia is pursuing her intention to bring the draft before Parliament where, she is sure, her supporters will defend it, and that some of its rules or even the whole, may be considered.

The team has paid great attention to socializing this draft. On 4 October 2004, a seminar was held, formally opened by the Minister of Religious Affairs. Understandably, as it put forward such controversial proposals, it provoked considerable debate and was harshly criticized by various Muslim groups, including those in MUI and established Muslim organizations. They condemned the draft as being in contradistinction to Islam, and sent a letter to the Minister of Religious Affairs demanding he take action.[109] In response to the MUI protest, the minister swiftly complied with the demand by sending a formal letter warning the head of the team to stop attempting to socialize the draft and to submit the original draft to the ministry.[110] The minister also sent another letter to MUI, informing it that he had warned the director of the team and, to assure MUI that he did not specifically support the team, and that he had never issued a letter authorizing the formation of the team.[111] By writing such a letter, the minister also formally declared the detachment of the draft.[112]

Specialists in Islamic law and judges also commented on the draft. Rifyal Ka'bah, a Supreme Court judge attached to Muhammadiyah, in the seminar held by Yarsi University (Universitas Yayasan Rumah Sakit Islam) on 29 October 2004, asserted that the team had overstepped the mark, and by proposing such a draft, it had assailed the legal opinions of prominent and qualified scholars of the Islamic law schools as the Shāfi'ī and others. He also claimed the members of the team were not adequately qualified to be *mujtahid*.[113] Tahir Azhari, the professor of Islamic law at the University of Indonesia and Hasanuddin AF, the professor of Uṣūl al-Fiqh and the Dean of the Faculty of Islamic Law of the State Islamic University in Jakarta, openly said that the draft had introduced rules contradictory to the texts of the Qur'ān and *ḥadīth*, and warned the people behind the draft not simply to rely on their feelings when trying to reform Islamic rules. Neng Zubaeda, a member of MUI, strongly contested the draft. He said that Islam in Indonesia is in danger, as feminists who are themselves Muslims have proposed reforms to family law which were too far-reaching. She went on to say that, as human beings, they place far too much value on worldly affairs and are neglecting the afterlife.[114] While advocating that inter-religious marriage has to be allowed, thereby agreeing with the team, Ichtiyanto has contested other reforms and claimed that the feminists often neglect the Qur'ān, and in doing so become *mu'tadīn* (going beyond the Qur'āni texts). He has stated emphatically that, in proposing to amend or abolish a number of rules they found gender-biased, the feminist activists are too emotional and are referring only to their own interests. Therefore he stigmatizes this as a selfish agenda, which does not consider the interests of other groups. Therefore, although they appeal to universal principles of human rights, they tend to be self-oriented, he concluded.

Furthermore, at the request of several Muslim groups who are aware of the existence of that controversial draft, a professor of Islamic Law who graduated from the Azhar University and is now a lecturer in the Faculty of Islamic Law of the State Islamic University in Jakarta, Huzaemah Tahido, wrote a small book to counter the provisions suggested by the team.[115] This book was widely disseminated in religious courts and reprinted twice. In her book, she attempts to analyze the points of the *kompilasi* criticized by the team by referring to the texts of the Qur'ān and the *ḥadīth*. She declares that a number of the contents in the draft drawn up by the Team are *bid'a* (unlawful innovation or heresy). She also accuses the team of ignoring the deductive method in Islamic law, which is based on the maintenance of the *maqāṣid shari'iyya*, of which the aim is to protect life, reason, family or reproduction, religion, and property.[116]

In my interview with her after she published the book, she said that she agreed with some reforms like the equalization of the minimum age of marriage for boys and girls, but the laws on divorce and polygyny should be maintained as they are set both in the Marriage Law and the *kompilasi*. On the issue of polygyny, she said:

> Islam has given an appropriate rule on the issue and that the conditions put in both the Marriage Law and the *kompilasi* upon which the polygyny could be conducted are logical. Imagine if a husband wants to have children and his wife cannot fulfill his wish. What is he to do if his wife does not offer him a solution, when he really wants it? So, there must be a rule to regulate this. And, under the rule provided in the *kompilasi*, he may be given a chance to have offspring by another wife. The consent of the wife is necessary, but if she is reluctant to give permission when there is a real reason, it can be ignored.[117]

It is particularly interesting to note that the Counter Legal Draft also unleashed a wave of criticism and protest among radical Muslim groups. Hizbut al-Tahrir, for instance, stood in the van to stage demonstrations to disparage the draft as the "Komunis" (*Kompilasi Hukum non-Islam*, or the Compilation of Non-Muslim Law' and as the '*Kompilasi Hukum Inkar Syari'at* (the Compilation of Law Deviating Sharī'ā').[118] The Majelis Mujahidin Indonesia sent a personal delegation to the Ministry of Religious Affairs to deliver a letter of protest to the Minister. In an open-minded fashion, this organization also invited the team to hold a discussion.[119] An association of Muslim university students, called KAMMI (Kesatuan Aksi Mahasiswa Muslim Indonesia/Association of Action of Muslim University Students), also protested the draft and expressed its gratitude when the draft was declared rejected. They accused the team of conspiring with Western secularists who, they claim, emphasize such wayward principles as liberalism and feminism.[120]

> This controversial draft has also attracted criticism from Muslims at the grassroots level. It has become a topic discussed among, for instance, the people on the Internet and the members of *pengajian* (village-based Islamic learning gatherings). Preachers or tutors at the *pengajian* had inevitably been addressed with questions about the issues covered in the draft, which they have often found difficult to answer. Many people are dubious about the legal basis of the reforms and have asked why the legal doctrines to which they are completely attached are being challenged. This has

> aroused the curiosity of the tutors who naturally have wanted to know more about the reforms and the argumentation supporting them. As a result, they have consulted persons whom they consider to be authoritative. Some have talked to people against the reforms and some others with those for the reforms, attitudes which have led to a more open debate. A tutor at one *pengajian* who consulted a person about the reforms admitted to understanding where the team is coming from, but finds it hard to make her community accept it.

The resistance to the draft has basically been linked to several factors. Under the impression that it is BPPHI which is formally given the authority to review points in the *kompilasi*, many have questioned if the feminists' separate proposal will be given a hearing. Moreover, besides the conservative *'ulamā,* – who also include those claiming to be modernist – still the most dominant group in interpreting Islamic law, the viewpoint on the principles they cite when proposing reform change in keeping with the times, conditions, and with different places. This in turn leads to the emergence of divergent views about what, for example, "justice" is. There are those who argue that if the share of a male is twice as much as that of a female, it could be considered as 'just' in one time and one place, it may equally be thought 'unjust' in another time and place, and that 21 years old is the appropriate minimum age for marriage among girls in urban areas, but might not be for those in rural areas.

Not surprisingly, class looms large as a contributor to the conflict, and particularly in explaining why not all women for whom the feminists struggle support the reforms. Feminists mostly come from urban areas and are generally upper or upper-middle class and are economically stable. They are also well-educated and the majority are independent women. The problems which lower-class women experience may be different from those experienced by their more socially elevated sisters. Therefore, the attempt to abolish polygyny, as an example, may not be agreed with or accepted among rural women. They may prefer to share a husband with another woman, instead of being a widow without a man supporting her. Rather than arguing against the notion of male breadwinners, lower-class women, as will be clear in the next chapter, may prefer to question the failure of men to fulfill their economic duty.[121]

IV Between the *Kompilasi* and the *Fiqh* Texts

One of the main objectives in creating the *kompilasi* was to unify the legal reasoning used by judges in Indonesian religious courts in order to achieve legal certainty for Indonesian Muslims seeking resolution of familial problems. Since the issuing of this Presidential Instruction, judges in the religious courts have indeed been required to base their judgments on the *kompilasi*, which presents a systematization or *rationalization* of the material law of *fiqh*. This was intended to prevent reliance on two different rulings in deciding two cases of the same nature, a situation which had frequently occurred in the judicial practices of the religious courts.

This chapter sets out to analyze the judicial process in the religious courts, in order to establish whether or not the goals mentioned above have been achieved. This is to be done by examining the decisions handed down by some of the judges. In doing so, this chapter will examine in detail the continuity and change evident in the judicial practice of the judges since the issuing of the *kompilasi*. A detailed examination of the judges' judicial practice, especially the way they seek and adduce legal bases for their judgments, is particularly important in establishing to what extent the judges have accepted the existence of the *kompilasi*, and in discerning the character of Islamic justice dispensed.

I Legal Judgments: Form and Structure

There is a more or less standard formula prescribed for the judgments issued by judges in the religious courts before and after the issuing of the *kompilasi*. It usually begins with *Bismillahirrahmanirrahim* (In the name of God, the merciful and the compassionate), followed by the sentence *Demi Keadilan Berdasarkan Ketuhanan Yang Maha Esa* (In the name of Justice founded on the divinity of Almighty God). The *Basmalah* used at the beginning of the judgment is to attest to the Islamic character of the religious courts. The sentence *Demi Keadilan Berdasarkan Ketuhanan yang Maha Esa* is to stress the goal of the judicial practice of the court, namely justice inspired by religious values. This phrase constitutes the first principle of the ideological foundation of the country, namely the *Pancasila*, and is not peculiar to the religious court. Other courts also include this phrase in their judgments.[1] This formula is prescribed in Law No. 1/1970 on the judicial system in Indonesia.[2]

The prescribed form continues by stating the name(s) of the plaintiff(s) followed by that of the defendant(s). The nature of the case (problem) brought before the court is described next, consisting of the statements, pleas and counter-pleas of the plaintiff and defendant, complete with the statements or testimonies of witnesses. This is followed by an exposition of the legal considerations or deliberations. This is based on information supplied by both sides, by the hearing itself, and by the argumentations based on the laws, the texts (*naṣṣ*) of the Qur'an and the Sunna, or from *fiqh* books, followed by the decisions of the judges on how they have adjudged the claim. It ends by stating the time, day, and date on which the judgment is passed. It also includes the names of the judges and the clerk who dealt with the case, followed by their signatures.[3]

There are two kinds of judgments issued by the religious courts: *penetapan* (decree) and *putusan* (decision). A *penetapan* is handed down when the judges decide a case on the basis of a *permohonan* (petition) from one party, called the petitioner or plaintiff. In this case, no other party is involved as defendant (*termohon*). A frequently encountered example is the request for a decision about whether or not the plaintiff is an heir to a deceased *praepositus* (*pewaris*), or whether or not a group of people are the heirs of a certain person. As the *penetapan* is based simply upon a request from one party, it is legally valid for the plaintiff only. It has no executorial force. By contrast, a *putusan* is issued when the judges decide a case on the basis of a *gugatan* (claim) involving two parties, plaintiff and defendant. In this case, the judgments automatically have both condemnatory and executorial character. One such example is the dispute over the legal status of a person or of a group of people in an inheritance or a divorce.[4]

I must mention, however, that the differentiation between these two forms of judgments is somewhat confusing and hazy. It is stipulated that cases of polygyny and divorce initiated by a husband are categorized as cases of *permohonan*, which implies that they do not embrace the element of disputation and therefore do not involve a defendant. However, it is then stipulated that they are to be heard under the procedure for cases of *gugatan*, by which the wife is given the right to defend herself from the accusations of her husband and oppose his intention to divorce or enter into a polygynous marriage. This ambiguity in the rules, for both a divorce initiated by the husband and for polygyny, is seen as a revelation of the bifurcated position adopted by the formulators of both the Act and the *kompilasi*, in achieving reform and their lingering inclination towards the *fiqh* doctrines.[5] Given the vagueness of the distinction, in this discussion I shall not differentiate between the two types of judgments in the religious courts, and hence use the term 'judgment' to refer to both kinds of cases.

In deciding the cases brought before them, judges in the religious courts adduce legal reasoning in support of their judgments. They sum up the information received from the plaintiff or from both the plaintiff and the defendant, as well as the testimonies given by witnesses. Before the *kompilasi* was issued, they usually composed their legal considerations with citations from the Qur'ānic texts (*naṣṣ*) and the Prophetic Traditions, as well as statements or opinions of *'ulamā'* taken from the *fiqh* book(s). In some judgments, all these references are cited, and in other cases only one or two of them are mentioned. If the citation includes all the references, the ranking order of the references follows the hierarchy of the sources. The Qur'ānic texts are put in the first rank, followed by the Prophetic saying(s), and then by the opinions of *'ulamā'* derived from the *fiqh* books. However, some judges ignore such an arrangement and list the references as they prefer.

It is understandable that such sources were selected, for at that time there was no unified, substantive legal code which could otherwise be consulted. It is true that since 1974 there has been a Law of Marriage, and that since 1977 there has been a Governmental Regulation on Endowment (*waqf*). As their names suggest, these relate to two specific areas of Islamic law; the 1974 Law of Marriage deals only with rules concerning marital affairs, and the 1977 Government Regulation merely concerns endowment. The regulations for inheritance and other matters such as gifts and *wāṣiyat* had not yet been legally codified at this time. Accordingly, although judgments on marital issues began to be based on the Law of Marriage and those on endowments on the 1977 Government Regulation, those on inheritance, gifts and *wāṣiyat* were based entirely on such references as the Qur'ān, the Prophetic Traditions, and the *fiqh* books. In addition, the Law of Marriage does not cover all familial issues disputed in the Muslim community. Marriage during a pregnancy resulting from pre-marital sexual intercourse was, for example, not mentioned in the Law, even though such cases were often brought to the religious courts.[6] Consequently, the application of the Law of Marriage and the Government Regulation on *waqf* did not entirely end the citation of such references as the Qur'ān, the Prophetic Traditions, and *fiqh* books. Even a number of judgments on cases which had been dealt with decisively in the Marriage Law listed only these references as legal reasoning, thereby ignoring the Law of Marriage.[7]

Muslim judges cited these references as follows: *menimbang dalil dari al-Qur'ān yang berbunyi...* or *dalil dari ḥadīth yang berbunyi...* or *dalil dari kitab 'A' yang berbunyi...* (considering the argument in the Qur'ānic text which reads..., and or the text in the Prophetic Traditions which states..., and or the opinions in the *fiqh* book 'A' which says...). The citations were written before the decision stating whether or not a judge acquiesced in the petition or the claim and were put under separate headings. The judges usually wrote the original texts of every reference – from the Qur'ān, the Prophetic sayings, and the statements of certain *'ulamā'* from certain *fiqh* books – followed by their own translations into the Indonesian language. They also included attributes of the references such as the relevant chapter and verse for the Qur'ānic texts, the names of the transmitters for the Prophetic sayings, and the page reference for the *fiqh* books, and sometimes the volume of the *fiqh* books if necessary.

After the passing of the Marriage Law, a number of judges introduced quotations of these references from the Qur'an, *Hadīth* and *fiqh* books in the judgments on marital issues, adhering to the articles in the Marriage Law of 1974, if the Law was cited. Used in this manner, in some judgments such references were no longer considered main references but simply supporting legal reasons, indicated by the words used to initiate these citations, which sometimes read, *Kami perlu juga mengemukakan dalil yang berbunyi.../* "In addition to this, we need also to refer to the argument (legal text in the Qur'ān, *Hadīth* and *fiqh* books) which says..." However, in several judgments these references were mentioned and placed first in the list, which meant they were cited earlier than the Marriage Law. No matter how they were positioned, quotations remained frequent and dominant.

There is no significant difference between the types of cases in which the doctrines from the *fiqh* books, the Qur'ānic verses, and the *ḥadīth* texts are displayed. In cases of all types, the references are quoted interchangeably. In spite of this, I found that although citation of the *fiqh* books was sometimes also noticeable, in inheritance cases the judgments were presented more frequently with a citation from the Qur'ānic and *ḥadīth* texts. This may be because the rules of inheritance are clearly presented in the Qur'ān. Therefore, in resolving issues of inheritance the judges felt obliged to go directly to the Qur'ānic verses.

In most marital cases, judges in the religious courts tended to quote *fiqh* books for their judgments. Yet, they sometimes also explored the Qur'ānic texts. It is apparent that the citation of the Qur'ānic verses was intended to give their decisions on certain cases a more solid Islamic legal basis. I discovered that, besides stating a number of legal doctrines found in the *fiqh* books, judges always quoted the Qur'ānic texts stating "but if their intention is firm for divorce, Allah heareth and knoweth all things" (II: 227) for the judgment on divorce requested by a husband; "if ye fear that ye shall not be able to deal justly with the orphans, marry women of your choice, two or three or four" (III: 3) for the judgment on polygyny; and "divorced wives shall wait concerning themselves for three monthly periods" (II: 228) for the judgment related to the *'iddah* of a divorced wife. Meanwhile, in tackling cases of divorce requested by a wife, *ḥaḍāna* (custody), *walī 'aḍal* (the reluctant guardian) and others, the judges often simply quoted the legal doctrines from the *fiqh* books and rarely had recourse to the Qur'ānic texts.

These facts, plus the inescapable conclusion that most cases handled by the religious courts are marital issues, indicate the crucial position of the *fiqh* books in the judgments issued by judges in these courts. From the legal perspective, this is a coherent and logical phenomenon. As has been mentioned before, the use of the *fiqh* books had been formally recommended in 1958 when the Ministry of Religious Affairs limited the use of the *fiqh* books to thirteen. Still, it is interesting to note that, although there was such a restriction, the names of which have been listed in the previous chapter and most of which, except *al-Fiqh 'ālā al-Madhāhib al-'Arba'a,* contain Islamic law on the basis of the Shāfi'īte texts, the judges have always felt free to use *fiqh* books other than these thirteen as their references. However, as I have just remarked, the Shāfi'ite texts are predominantly preferred. Scrutinizing the judgments issued before the *kompilasi* was applied, I found that certain *fiqh* books besides the thirteen recommended were often quoted, including *I'ānat al-Ṭālibīn* by Sayyid Bakri al-Dimyātī, *al-Muhadhdhab fi Fiqh Madhhab Imām al-Shāfi'ī* by al-Shirājī, and *Minhāj al-Ṭullāb* by al-Anṣārī, all of which are also Shāfi'īte *fiqh* texts.

II Change and Continuity

The format of the judgments issued by the judges in the religious courts after the application of the *kompilasi* is generally similar to what it was before. It starts with *Bismillahirrahmanirrahin,* and is followed by the phrase *Demi Keadilan Berdasarkan Atas Ketuhanan yang Maha Esa.* It then mentions the names of the plaintiff and the defendant, gives a description of the case followed by the information from the plaintiff, defendant, and witnesses, presents the legal considerations, gives the decision and then closes by mentioning the names of the judges and clerk dealing with the case, along with the date when the judgment is handed down. The only obvious difference occurs in the part concerning legal considerations. In this part, besides the mention of the information provided by the plaintiff and the defendant, the citation of articles from the *kompilasi* relevant to the cases is also included. This still begs the question: does the *kompilasi* automatically replace the position of the *fiqh* books?

In 2000, the Directorate of Religious Justice at the Ministry of Religious Affairs (*Direktorat Pembinaan dan Pengembangan Peradilan Agama/Ditbinbapera*) conducted research in which it monitored the application of the *kompilasi.* The research results reported that the *kompilasi* had been widely used by judges in the religious courts as the reference for their judgments. But this research discovered that not all judgments issued since 1991 used the *kompilasi* as a reference.[8] Analyzing 484 judgments issued in 1996, 1997, and 1998 from various religious courts spread across Indonesia, especially Surabaya, Yogyakarta, Bandung, and Jakarta, it came up with 300 judgments of the first-instance religious courts which used the *kompilasi* as a reference, and 116 which did not. It then concluded that in the first-instance religious courts, the percentage of judgments using the *kompilasi* as reference is far higher than that of those which do not.[9] Interestingly, it seems that in the appellate religious courts the *kompilasi* is rarely used. It found that of sixty-eight judgments only thirty-one used the *kompilasi*. It then concluded that the use of the *kompilasi* by judges in the first-instance religious courts has been more frequent than by those in the appellate religious courts.

Table 4.1 *Decisions of the First-Instance Religious Courts and Appellate Religious Courts with and without the citation of the Kompilasi*

No	Cases	1996, 1997, 1998 First Instance Religious Court		1996, 1997, 1998 Appellate Religious Courts	
		With *kompilasi*	without *kompilasi*	with *kompilasi*	Without *kompilasi*
1	Divorce (wife petition)	94	36	6	12
2	Divorce (husband petition)	95	25	7	9
3	Custody (*ḥaḍāna*)	17	8	3	5
4	M. annulment	31	6	8	3
5	Guardianship	11	11	-	-
6	Polygamy	35	20	1	3
7	Joint property	17	10	6	5
	Total	300	116	31	37

Source: "The Report of the Monitoring of the Application of the *Kompilasi*", Ministry of Religious Affairs, 2001

The research was an important contribution to the management of the development of the religious courts. The Ministry of Religious Affairs had at least confirmed that the existence of the *kompilasi* was widespread and accepted among the judges. Although mindful of its usefulness and necessity, I have identified some weaknesses in the research. The first point which might be viewed critically is that the aim of the survey of the Ministry of Religious Affairs on this issue was to establish whether the *kompilasi* had been successfully applied. It seems to me that the objects of the survey were selected to support the aim. Tellingly, the courts chosen were those located in large urban areas like Jakarta, Surabaya, and Yogyakarta where those elements which support the application of the *kompilasi* are met.

Furthermore, the research did not show accurately why the *kompilasi* had not yet been fully accepted as a reference by some judges. Nor did it demonstrate specifically why the *kompilasi* was used as a reference less in the appellate religious courts than in the first-instance religious courts. It merely concluded that judges in the appellate religious courts were less legally aware than those in the first-instance religious courts. In the part displaying the dependent variables, explaining why the *kompilasi* was not yet fully used as reference, the research enumerated a number of related factors. I think there is some ambiguity in this presentation of the factors explaining why the *kompilasi* has not been well used. It tended to explore reasons such as the dichotomy in various understandings of Islamic law among the traditional Muslim scholars, which I feel relates more to the issue of why the substance of the *kompilasi* has not been well applied. On the other hand, the research is on solid ground when it states that the *kompilasi* has been generally applied, and that the absence of the citation of the articles of the *kompilasi* in a number of judgments did not mean the judges had deviated from the provisions of the *kompilasi*, but implied their application in an implicit manner. What I mean is that the research, using the categories of citing or not citing the *kompilasi*, clearly focused on whether or not the *kompilasi* was taken to be a reference or legal consideration, and did not attempt to report on to what extent the substance of the *kompilasi* has been applied, as it did not display any example of judgments which indicated this. Meanwhile, the reasons why a number of judgments were not backed up by the *kompilasi* are related more to the issue of the application of its provisions. There is therefore vagueness in precisely what it is about the *kompilasi* which is being observed; the application of its contents or the citation of its articles in the judgments.

In addition, the research reported that a few judgments did not use the *kompilasi* as reference, but gave little information about the sources to which these judgments referred. It recorded that the sources quoted included the Law of Marriage and others. *Fiqh* books are not noted. Why the research did not take note of this is uncertain and questionable.

Similar research was also done by Nuryamin Aini. Focusing on the judgments produced by the religious court of South Jakarta, Aini found that the *fiqh* texts are still considered crucial within the religious court of South Jakarta. Although he observed the application of the *kompilasi*, as did the Ministry of Religious Courts, Aini did not look into the use of the *kompilasi* more comprehensively, as he did not observe it through the perspective of the application of its contents. Therefore, although he did discuss and mention few reasons why the *fiqh* texts are still dominant, Aini did not answer why and in what cases the *kompilasi* has not been well applied.[10]

To fill this gap, I have resolved to look more deeply into the use of the *kompilasi* by the judges in the religious courts in their search for the legal considerations for their judgments. For this purpose, I shall take account of not only their quotation of the *fiqh* books, but also ask whether or not the legal doctrines of the *fiqh* books have been maintained in dealing with the cases for which the *kompilasi* sets different rules, in order to discover whether or not the *kompilasi* has been fully applied.

III The Central Position of the *Fiqh* Texts

After examining 118 judgments collected and chosen at random from various religious courts including South and East Jakarta, Cianjur, Tasikmalaya, Rengkasbitung (Lebak), and Bogor and from other courts in West Java and from the Supreme Court, mostly issued between 2000 and 2001 with a few ranging from 1992, I discovered that seventy-seven judgments used the *kompilasi* as reference. However, its citation did not appear alone, but was placed alongside other references like the Qur'ān, the Prophetic Traditions and *fiqh* books. Seventeen decisions used only the *kompilasi,* thereby ignoring the other references. Twenty-four of them include only such references as the Qur'ān and *fiqh* books. Therefore, although almost all the judgments have cited the *kompilasi* as a reference, references resorted to previously are still cited by the judges.

The table unequivocally shows that the judges in these areas have formally recognized the existence of the *kompilasi*, revealed in their use of the *kompilasi* as their main reference. This still did not preclude them referring to other references in use before the *kompilasi* was issued, the *fiqh* books in particular. Moreover, although the *kompilasi* is quoted, in most judgments, its quotation is coupled with excerpts from *fiqh* books. In short, this figure confirms that quotation of *fiqh* books is still dominant. It shows that the quotation of the *fiqh* books is quantitatively more frequent, being 101 times; that is, seventy-seven plus twenty-four times, than that of the *kompilasi,* being ninety-four times, or seventy-seven plus seventeen times. The conclusion which has to be drawn is that the judges are very reluctant to dispense with citation of *fiqh* books. Logically, by citing only the *kompilasi,* the judges have indeed basically referred to them anyway, as the articles in the *kompilasi* are grounded on the *fiqh* books.

Table 4.2 *Decisions with only kompilasi, with kompilasi and other references, and without kompilasi*

No	Cases	2000		2001	Total
		only *kompilasi*	*kompilasi* with others	without *kompilasi*	
1	Divorce (husband petitions)	5	27	3	35
2	Divorce (wife petitions)	7	39	6	52
3	*Ithbāt nikāh*	2	-	3	5
4	Polygyny	-	2	3	5
5	Maintenance	-	2	-	2
6	Guardianship	1	2	-	3
7	Joint property	-	3	1	4
8	Inheritance	-	1	4	5
9	Child custody	2	1	4	7
	Total	17	77	24	118

*The category of "with other references" means that *fiqh* books are quoted besides the *kompilasi*.
*The category of "without the *kompilasi*" means that *fiqh* books are quoted without making reference to any provisions in the *kompilasi*.

In their attitudes toward quoting legal doctrines from *fiqh* books, judges have displayed behavior deserving of some comment here. Looking over the judgments in my collection, I found that certain *fiqh* books are more frequently cited by the judges of all the religious courts than are others, including 1. al-Dimyāṭī's *I'ānat al-Ṭālibīn*, 2. al-Bājūrī's *Ḥāshiya Kifāyat al-Akhyār*, 3. Sharqāwī's *Ḥāshiya 'alā al-Taḥrīr*, 4. *Al-Anwār*, 5. *Al-Muhadhdhab*, 6. al-Rāfī's *Mu'īn al-Ḥukkām*[11], and 7. Suyūṭī's *Al-Ashbāh wa al-Naẓā'ir.*[12] It should be noted that these seven books are those which were also often cited before the *kompilasi* was issued. Not all of them are among the thirteen recommended *fiqh* books. Of the seven books mentioned above, only two are included in that group, namely, al-Bājūrī's *Ḥāshiya Kifāyat al-Akhyār*, and Sharqāwī's *Ḥāshiya 'alā al-Taḥrīr*. However, all the books pertain to the category of Shāfi'īte texts.

In contrast, there are some recommended *fiqh* books which were seldom or even never cited by the judges. These books include: Shamsūrī's *al-Farā'iḍ*, al-Jazirī's *al-Fiqh 'alā al-Madhāhib al-Arba'a*, Sayyid Uthmān's *al-Qawānīn al-Shar'iyya*, and Ṣadaqāh Dakhlān's *al- Qawānīn al-Shar'iyya*. Although seldom or never cited, this does not mean that these books are not well used among the Indonesian *'ulamā'*. The last book in the list, Sayyid Uthmān's *al-Qawānīn al-Shar'iyyah*, a discussion of the methods of judicial practice and the legal rules on familial issues, for example, has been certainly well known among a number of the senior *'ulamā'* and earlier judges (*penghulu*).[13] Pijper noted that this book was once used as a reference for a case of divorce related to apostasy committed by a couple, which was heard in the religious court of Bogor in 1920.[14] Among the *penghulu* of the religious court of Palembang, this book was also frequently used.[15]

Despite its earlier appreciation, I did not find any later judgments referring to this book in my collection. Although written in Arabic script, the book is composed in the Malay (Indonesian) language, and for this reason has not been included among the subjects in the syllabi of the Islamic boarding school (*pesantren*) in the past.[16] Consequently, it is not widely known among the young *santri*, hence the ignorance of it among later Muslim judges.[17] Interestingly, the fact that the book is written in the Indonesian (Malay) language has prevented it from winning preference among those later judges who do happen to be acquainted with it. Indeed, the Arabic script carries great authority in the eyes of the traditionalist *'ulamā'*, while legal doctrines expressed in the Indonesian language are considered to have less legitimacy among judges for purposes of written legal consideration in their judgments. They are of course taken as legal reflections, but it is rare that these are written down as legal considerations.[18] In the judgment on the case of the divorce related to apostasy mentioned by Pijper, the use of the book was not in fact primary. It was mentioned that the judgment was based on the opinion of Sayyid Uthmān, but it was then stressed that Sayyid Uthmān followed the legal text of the Nawāwī's *Minhāj al-Ṭālibīn*[19]. In the judgments mentioned by Rahim, the reference to this book was also often accompanied by other *fiqh* books such as al-Bājūrī*'s Ḥāshiya Kifāyat al-Akhyār.*[20]

This leaves the question of why Sayyid Uthmān's work was included among the group of thirteen recommended *fiqh* books. It seems that it was because the book, composed by this well-known Batavian scholar of Arab descent, is considered one of the *mu'tabara* (reliable) *fiqh* books.[21] Another reason was probably related to the fact that the selection of the thirteen *fiqh* books was not made simply for the purpose of providing legal references for judgments, but also to provide the bases for the legal procedures in the religious courts, discussed comprehensively in Sayyid Uthmān's *al-Qawānīn*. It was also, as has been mentioned above, because it was one of the references used by the *Raad Agama* which the *penghulu* were reported to have often consulted.[22]

Another fact which should be mentioned is related to the existence of a book entitled *Alasan Syar'i Penerapan Kompilasi Hukum Islam* (The Islamic Rationale of the Application of the *Kompilasi Hukum Islam*), published by the Directorate of Religious Justice at the Ministry of Religious Affairs. This book consists of articles from the *kompilasi*, especially the chapter on marriage, giving the corresponding Islamic grounds for each article from the Qur'ān, the Prophetic Traditions, and *fiqh* books.[23] An official in the office pointed out the publication of this book was intended to illustrate that the articles of the *kompilasi* derived their Islamic legal rationales from the Qur'ān, the Prophetic Tradition, and the *fiqh* books.[24]

Despite the existence of this book, I found that judges in the religious courts felt free to quote doctrines from *fiqh* books other than those used in the book. From my observations, almost all the judgments in cases of divorce related to the utterance of *ta'līq ṭalāq* or conditional divorce, for example, are backed up by the legal doctrine from Sharqāwī's *Ḥāshiya 'alā al-Taḥrīr*, which reads, "Whoever makes his *talak* dependent upon an action, the *talak* occurs with the existence of that action according to the original pronouncement."[25] Meanwhile, I discovered that Article 116 (g) of the book, which deals with this issue, is based on the legal text from al-Bājūrī's *Ḥāshiya Kifāyat al-Akhyār*, page 153, which reads, "And if the *talak* is made dependent on a conditional action, that conditional divorce occurs when that action is present."[26]

Although the meanings of the two legal doctrines do not differ, the fact that the judges did not cite the text recorded in the book, but mentioned instead another text from the other *fiqh* books, leads me to at least two assumptions. First, the Directorate of Islamic Justice had failed to socialize the book. In fact, almost all the judges interviewed were not familiar with the book. Instead, they often consult a small book which contains a compilation of legal texts from the Qur'ān, *ḥadīth*, and *fiqh* books, which was published a long time before the *kompilasi* was made,[27] and/or copies of earlier judgments dealing with the same case. Second, the judges wanted to maintain their strict adherence to or preference for certain *fiqh* books. In other words, the judges still wanted to enjoy the freedom to choose the *fiqh* books of their preference, and not to be tied to those recommended by the Directorate of Islamic Justice.

It is of interest to note, however, that as do the judges, the officials of the Directorate of Islamic Justice have also displayed a degree of freedom in using the *fiqh* texts. In composing the aforementioned book, they frequently used *Fiqh al-Sunna* by Sayyid Sābiq (1915-2000). Written in the 1940s, this book brought the four Sunnite schools of Islamic law together in a comprehensive analysis of the basis of the Qur'ān and Sunna. The book has since been translated into a dozen languages and is used by Muslims throughout the world, including in Indonesia. It was not included in the thirteen *fiqh* books, but was included among the thirty-eight *fiqh* books to be analyzed in the making of the *kompilasi*. This book was the most frequently used reference, according to Ali Yafie, because it cites the Qur'ānic texts abundantly and hence is considered to be a more accurate and reliable source for the judicial practices of the religious courts. However, he noted that the privileged position of that book is being slowly undermined today by Wahbah al-Zuhaylī's *al-Fiqh al-Islāmiyy wa Adillatuhu.*[28] Another reason might be the fact that the book has been chosen as material for the Arabic language test for would-be judges, as shall be discussed below.

The other references recommended by the Directorate of the Islamic Justice, according to the book, include *al-Ashbāh wa al-Naẓā'ir* by Jalāl al-Dīn al-Suyūṭī, *al-Aḥwāl al-Shaḥṣiyya* by Yūsuf Mūsā', *Tarshīḥ al-Mustafidīn* by Alwī bin Aḥmad Saqqāf, *al-Fiqh al-Islāmiyy wa Adillatuhu* by Wahbah al-Zuhaylī, *Kifāyat al-Akhyār* by Taqī al-Dīn Abū Bakr Dimshāqī, *Mabādī Awwāliya* by Abdul Ḥāmid Ḥakīm, *'Uqūd al-Lujayn* by al-Nawāwī al-Bantanī, and *Minhāj al-Ṭullāb* by Zakariya al-Anṣāri. Interestingly, none of these books is included in the group of thirteen recommended *fiqh* books or in the thirty-eight books chosen to be analysed in the making of the *kompilasi.*

From these findings, it is clear that both the judges and officials of the Ministry of Religious Affairs freely chose *fiqh* books according to their own preference, and that the freedom to select *fiqh* books has no connection with their knowledge of what *fiqh* books were actually recommended to them as references. In fact, even the officials of the Ministry of Religious Affairs who were responsible for the project of the *kompilasi*, and who most likely were acquainted with or who must have been familiar with the *fiqh* books recommended for use, did not follow what was specified.

Ironically, the reluctance of judges to leave the *fiqh* books behind is not complemented by accuracy in displaying the page references in the books. I found that the page of Sharqāwī's *Ḥāshiya 'alā al-Taḥrīr* on which the statement "... whoever makes his *talak* dependent upon an action, the *talak* occurs with the existence of that action according to the original pronouncement," occurs, for example, was often noted differently. Some judgments noted that the statement was found on page 302, and others on page 238.[29] A number of factors may have contributed to this inaccuracy. Since judgments are often rewritten or retyped by clerks, the latter might have mistyped the page number quoted from the originals, so that it sometimes appears differently. However, this factor seems to be insignificant, as the difference is too great for 302 to become 238 or vice versa. There is also a possibility that the books have been printed several times and the judges therefore refer to different editions when they state the page reference. Their admission that they rarely refer to the original *fiqh* books, however, makes it dubious that the inaccuracy crept in this way. Another reason may have been because judges often relied only on memory when quoting the legal doctrines, and mentioned the relevant places or pages without checking in the original books.[30] The most apparent reason may have been that the judges often only copied the citation of the legal opinions of certain *'ulamā'* from previously issued judgments. By referring to the earlier judgments, a number of which I found, particularly in the cases mentioned, too often display different page references from the same books for the same quotation, later judges could therefore not avoid making mistakes in their citations. Regardless of these facts, one should ask to what extent the application of the *kompilasi* has influenced the actual judicial process in the religious courts.

IV In the Public Utility

In what appears to be the majority of cases, judges in the religious courts have followed the provisions of the *kompilasi* in deciding the legal cases brought before them. This is apparent in the judgments of the religious court in South Jakarta (No. 19/pdt.p/1997/PAJS), which refused a request for confirmation of marriage (*ithbāt nikāḥ*) on the basis of the fact that it was requested by only one party, while the other party (the alleged husband) denied that the marriage had ever taken place. The *kompilasi* insists that the confirmation of marriage must be requested and agreed upon by a couple for their own welfare. Similarly, the judges of the religious court of Tasikmalaya, by decision No. 11/pdt.p/ 2001/ PA.Tsm, permitted a person to conclude a polygynous marriage only after the petitioner (the husband) could prove the existence of one of the grounds enumerated in the *kompilasi*, namely that his wife had an incurable disease, and after he produced evidence of his capacity to finance his co-wives plus evidence of his first wife's consent. In earlier cases, the judges of the religious court of Nganjuk refused to give a husband willing to take a second wife permission, because it was known that the first wife, though having no child at the time the petition was submitted, one of the reasons for his petition for polygynous marriage, was proven to be still medically capable of bearing a child. The admission of the husband that he had had sexual relations with the prospective second wife, which was then also put forward as a reason for the petition, convinced the judges to dismiss the request, arguing that a man could not take another wife to satisfy his extraordinary sexual appetite because this was not mentioned in the *kompilasi*.[31]

However, this does not mean that all provisions in the *kompilasi* are followed with approval by judges. Some judgments have in fact demonstrated that in a number of cases they have deviated from the *kompilasi* and referred to the *fiqh* books instead. They are apparently not worried that their decisions will be overturned by higher courts.[32] There are fundamental reasons behind their decisions to abandon the *kompilasi*. Among these reasons is their intention to uphold public interest. As a matter of fact, many judges argue that deviation from the rules prescribed in the *kompilasi* is sometimes needed to create public good or to guarantee the satisfaction of justice for the parties or one of the parties engaged in a case. Therefore, in certain cases a number of rules in the *kompilasi* are not to be obeyed absolutely.

IV.1 Ḥaḍāna

The rule concerning custody (*ḥaḍāna*) of a child under age twelve is the best example in this context. Article 105 of the *kompilasi* grants *ḥaḍāna* of a child younger than twelve to his or her mother if his or her parents are divorced. Although they agree with this rule and mostly follow it, in practice, judges sometimes conclude that it is not always good to give all mothers this responsibility without due consideration; a small number of mothers of bad character, such as those addicted to drugs or those planning to marry another man, could be considered inappropriate to this task, and hence could be deprived of the responsibility. As the choice of giving the right of *ḥaḍāna* to one of the divorced parties aims to ensure the welfare of the children, judges maintain that such a rule is not always to be followed and can be ignored for some reasons, such as those mentioned above.

Accordingly, in some cases judges have decided to grant the rights to the father.[33] The religious court of Bogor once ordered a mother to be deprived of the right of *ḥaḍāna* because it considered her incapable of taking care of her children, for the reason that she planned to marry again soon after she divorced her first husband. The court based its decision on the *fiqh* doctrine, stipulating that one of the qualifications for a mother to be given the right of *ḥaḍāna* is that she has no plans to marry again soon and that she has *iffah* (full of love and care). The *fiqh* books cited in this case are Dimasqī's *Kifāyat al-Akhyār,* Vol II, 152,[34] and Bājūrī's *Ḥāshiya Kifāyat al-Akhyār,* Vol. II, 198. The statement from the former reads as follows: "And to retain charge of a child the guardian must possess certain qualities such as reason, freedom, good religiosity, love, trustworthiness, has achieved a settlement with the child, and has no plans for remarriage. If he or she fails in one of these capacities, he or she loses his or her right to custody."[35] The doctrine from the latter reads as follows: "[The guardian must be] caring and honest and someone failing to pray has no right of custody."[36] In another case, the religious court of Rangkasbitung gave the right of *ḥaḍāna* of the children younger than twelve to their father on the basis of the consideration that the mother was not pious in her religion and that all the members of her family were non-Muslims. As a basis for its decision, it mentioned the legal doctrine from al-Bājūrī's *Hāshiya Kifāyat al-Akhyār,* Vol. 3, 203 stating that "... there is no right of *ḥaḍāna* for the mother who is religiously deviant."[37]

In principle, the *kompilasi* stipulates that *ḥaḍāna* of children should be first passed to women on the mother's side if the mother is deemed incapable.[38] But the fact that familial relationships are so close in Indonesia provides a foundation for some judges to give the right of *ḥaḍāna* directly to the father, as giving it to, for example, an aunt or grandparent on the mother's side can mean in effect still giving it to the mother. It seems that such a decision was taken to ensure that the *ḥaḍāna* of the children, particularly in the case where the mother and her family have become religiously deviant (*fāsiq*) or apostate, lies in the right hands and that the demands of public utility have been satisfied.[39] In this respect, it should be mentioned that the *kompilasi* indeed rules that to guarantee the safety of the children physically and spiritually, a religious court can transfer the right of *ḥaḍāna* from one nominee to others. Although it is not clear whether the spiritual aspects to be guaranteed also include (Islamic) religion, judges in the religious courts interpret that this is so, and the public utility emphasized by them also has a bearing on religious interests.

The same holds true in the case of *mumayyiz* children (those who have reached maturity or those, according to the *kompilasi*, aged twelve or older). The *kompilasi* states they are free to choose one of their parents to be their guardian.[40] But some judges have preferred to abandon this rule when they felt that Islam was threatened. In Judgment No. 746/1991/PA.MDN, for instance, the religious court of Medan decided to give the *ḥaḍāna* of the disputants' two underage children to their mother and agreed with the decision of the other two children, aged twenty and seventeen years, to live with their father who happened to have reverted to his previous religion, Christianity. In this decision, they followed the *kompilasi*.

This judgment elicited criticism from some Islamic legal experts and judges. Satria Effendi, a professor at the State Institute for Islamic Studies (IAIN) in Jakarta, who regularly analysed decisions issued by the religious courts, criticized the judges who handed down the judgment for having not been circumspect enough of the possibility that the father may have harbored bad intentions to influence his two older children. He argued that under such conditions, the children should not to be given their right to choose freely with whom they will live. Judges must choose for them who is the best guardian in terms of their (Islamic) religiosity. He went on to say that the majority of *'ulamā'* including the Shāfi'īte agreed that such a condition robs people of the right of *ḥaḍāna* of their children. Therefore, if in a Muslim family a spouse commits apostasy and this results in a divorce, the *ḥaḍāna* of their children must automatically be given to the party who is still Muslim.[41] As the basis for this he referred to the opinions of the majority of classical *'ulamā'*, including the Shāfi'ītes, who hold that being Muslim is one of the absolute qualifications for a person to be a guardian; non-Muslims or apostates will automatically lose their rights of custody.[42]

IV.2 Ithbāt al-Nikāh

The rule of *ithbāt nikāḥ* in the *kompilasi* is another example which has sometimes been ignored by judges from this perspective. The *kompilasi* rules that the *ithbāt nikāḥ* can only be obtained by couples in unregistered marriages if a number of conditions are met, one of which is that their marriage had to have been concluded before the passing of the Marriage Law in 1974. However, it often happens that couples coming to the courts reported they had been married after 1974, but wanted to have their marriages legally registered through the procedure of *ithbāt nikāḥ*. If the judges follow the provision of the *kompilasi* strictly, these marriages cannot be registered. Several times, though, the religious court in East Jakarta complied with their demands, and by so doing ignored and deviated from the *kompilasi*. The judges announced that their decisions were based on an attempt to guarantee the virtue of the couples. Specifically, the judges mentioned the fact that the applicants had one or more children and therefore supported the applicants in their decision to register their marriages. "Law is made to endow the people with virtue. If the law made fails to bestow decency on the people, then we should ignore it and create a new one," argued the director of the court.[43]

In such cases, judges attempt to provide a legal basis for their decisions by exploring the legal doctrines prescribed in the *fiqh* books. The source most often cited is Ba'alawī's *Bughyat al-Mustarshidīn*. It contains a legal doctrine which states "if there is an admission of one party, a wife, to be married to a man (her husband), or of a husband to be married to a woman (his wife), and they have successfully presented evidence of the fulfillment of the religious conditions of their marriage, these could be taken as the proof of the marriage between the couple."[44] As the citation is seen as insufficient to support their need to deviate from the *kompilasi*, they insist on an Islamic legal principle which states that "the rule or the law is applied and ignored in accordance with its reason," in order to confirm that what they did is in accordance with true Islamic legal procedure.

IV.3 Age of Marriage

Another example is the rule concerning the age of marriage for girls and boys. The *kompilasi* (Art. 15) and the Marriage Law (Art. 7) both stipulate that girls and boys can enter into marital life if they have attained the age of sixteen years (girls) or nineteen years (boys). Broadly speaking, judges agree with the rule, but for a number of reasons they occasionally ignore it and give permission to those under the minimum statutory age to marry. It is true that the Law allows the dispensation for marriage to be given to those under the required ages.[45] Yet the fact that, although the *kompilasi* does not confirm it, judges still grant it purely on the consideration that the boys and or the girls have met the qualifications legitimized in the *fiqh* books, is unequivocal proof that judges are too free in applying the rule of dispensation and have preferred the provisions of the *fiqh* books to those ruled in the *kompilasi*.

The reasons for such a case are when the parents of a girl or a boy under the ages of sixteen and nineteen respectively consider that the couple have been intimate with each other to the point where it is feared that pre-marital intercourse has occurred between them. Alternatively, a parent may argue that they are already old enough, the couple is already sufficiently mature and they wish to see their child married, and will not brook the refusal of the registry officials to marry their daughter or son. As a result, they bring the case to the court, requesting formal permission to marry their child. After hearing and considering the reasons and the situation of both the girl and the boy, which may be, for example, that the girl has reached maturity, and this is indicated by the fact that she is menstruating, a number of judges may find that they should approve the request and issue a decision stating that the girl or the boy can be officially married with her boyfriend or his girlfriend and therefore direct the official registrar of the place of origin of the girl or the boy to marry them.[46]

To support their decisions, judges pointed out the legal doctrine which states that "the claim of a girl that she has reached her maturity may be accepted because she has experienced menstruation,"[47] presented in al-Dimyātī's *I'ānat al-Ṭālibīn*, vol. II, 314; and/or the legal doctrine that states "the guardian of a boy may marry him if he sees in it something beneficial and good,"[48] presented in al-*Muhadhdhab*, vol. II, 40. To strengthen their decisions, they refer to an Islamic legal maxim which states that "avoiding deficiency must be prioritized over the bringing of advantages."[49] In doing so, they have tried to show that marriage at ages younger than those specified in the *kompilasi* is more appropriate as it will prevent negative consequences.

From these examples, we can see how cultural assumptions, legal approaches, and substantive law are all deeply interlinked. Therefore, it appears that judges often do not decide cases in accordance with the dictum of the law, but because the social utility demands this to be so. In Islamic law, judges frequently encounter the concepts of *istiḥsān* and *istiṣlaḥ*, forms of legal reasoning by means of analogy. These concepts incorporate the idea that analogies may be described with a clear eye to the social well-being at large rather than to a strict set of logically required results.[50] Nonetheless, although we have already seen a number of cases in which legal presumptions are really little more than the judicial recognition of local assumptions, we observe that, through their judgments, judges always need to demonstrate that they have not deviated from the Qur'ān and other sources of Islamic law. They are convinced that the legal doctrines from the classical texts constitute the best sources for their judgments when they thought the strict application of the new code of law or the *kompilasi* would cause harm and prevent serving the public good. These three examples indicate that the deliberate ignoring of the *kompilasi* by judges and their continuing reliance on the *fiqh* books is because the *kompilasi* is casuistically perceived as an inappropriate text to be followed.

V Against the Deviation of the *Kompilasi* from the *Fiqh* Texts

In other cases, judges reject the rules in the *kompilasi* because they claim that in some cases they have deviated too far from the classical *fiqh* doctrines. In cases of inheritance, for instance, they often abandon its provisions, which happen to be currently hotly debated by Muslim scholars and judges themselves, including the rule of representation of heirs. One judge I interviewed argued: "If I faced a case of inheritance related to the rule of representation of heirs, I would not follow the rule in the *kompilasi*, as I do not agree with it."[51]

Another judge said,

> I shall solve the problem involving representative heirs as regulated in the *kompilasi*, but in part. I shall not acquiesce in the rule of limitation which states that the representative's portion should not succeed the portion of the heirs whose legal entitlement to the estate is equal to the represented heirs, because I do not agree with the additional clause on such a limitation.[52]

Indeed, a number of judges have disagreed with the application of the principle of representation of heirs to deal with the problem of the inheritance of grandchildren. They have maintained that the problem of grandchildren must be solved by the application of the concept of *wāṣiya wājiba* in force in Egypt. They argue representation means that one takes the whole other's position. They realize that once such a ruling is applied, injustice will be an inevitable consequence, and they are aware that the limitation of the portion of the representative heirs was to anticipate and prevent the injustice. Because of this, the *kompilasi* is simultaneously accused of not yet being in state to apply the full concept of the representation of heirs. Hence, they have proposed that the *kompilasi* apply the institution of *wāṣiya wājiba*. One of the judges even criticized

Hazairin, who is considered to be the first proponents of this concept. He said that Hazairin did not fully comprehend the Islamic system of inheritance: "Hazairin was not a professor of Islamic law but of *adat* law. His knowledge about Islam was so restricted he was inadequately equipped to undertake *ijtihād* in this issue."[53]

Other judges who have agreed with the application of the principle maintain that the problem of grandchildren is better solved by resorting to the concept of representation of heirs. They offer a number of reasons for this; the principle of representation of heirs has its Islamic rationale in the Qur'ān, that is, in the concept of *mawālī*, as developed by Hazairin, while the concept of *wāṣiya* is abrogated by the Qur'ānic verse. Another reason is that, they claim, a grandchild constitutes a close relative of the grandparent (*praepositus*) and has a genetic relationship with him. Hence, the term 'representation of heirs' is far more appropriate to such a relationship than is the term '*wāṣiya wājiba*'. Arguing that the *wāṣiya wājiba* could be applied only to relatives with no genetic relationship, the inheritance of grandchildren who do have a genetic relationship is not to be solved by the institution of *wāṣiya wājiba*, but by the principle of representation of heirs: "If we utilize *wāṣiya wājiba* in this case, we seem to be excluding the grandchildren from the family circle and positioning them as outsiders."[54]

However, they have a different view of the limitation of the portion of the substitutive heirs. Some said that this has been very just. They argue that unless it is limited, the portion of the daughters of the deceased would be less than those of the grandchildren, and this would be unfair. They believe that justice must be administered equally to all heirs and not to some at the expense of others. So, the limitation is to meet another principle, that of general justice, rather than general equity among the heirs. Some judges have said that it has been more than enough for the grandchildren to be allotted such a limited portion, at least the same share as the other heirs whose positions are equal to the substituted heirs:

> Under such a rule, it has been more than enough for the grandchildren who are, according to the classical Islamic rule of inheritance, basically excluded from the share, to receive the same as or a lesser portion than that of their aunts. Compared to the portion to which they would be entitled in their own position as grandchildren (should there be only aunt (s) or daughters of the deceased), the portion is still bigger.[55]

Some judges have maintained that representation of heirs can be applied, but without any limitation on the portion of the substitutive heirs and hence intimating they consider the limitation a deviation from the whole principle. They have demanded that the representative or substitutive heirs must be given whatever the one for whom they are substituting would receive, should they still be alive. One judge pointed out:

> I am in agreement of the application of representation of heirs, as it meets the principle of justice and equality. The system of 'representation of heirs' is more appropriate than the concept of *wāṣiya wājiba* for dealing with the problem of grandchildren, as *wāṣiya wājiba* can, I think, only properly be applied to those who do not have a genetic relationship or *nasab*, whereas grandchildren are still the descendants of the *pewaris*, namely the grandparents. I believe that the limitation introduced in Article 185 of the *kompilasi* is a deviation from or inconsistency in the application of the whole concept. If we want to apply the concept of representation, we should be consistent and award the whole portion of the represented heirs to their representatives.[56]

Another judge offered a stronger argument in adopting a position against the rule of limitation, saying:

> If the representative party consists of only one, the limitation rule so as to anticipate the committing of an injustice to an aunt may be proper. But does it fit a case where the represented heir leaves several children, two or more perhaps? They (the representative parties) should share the portion and therefore each of them will receive less than their aunt.[57]

Parallel to this is the fact that a number of judges also see a misapplication of the institution of an obligatory bequest. They claim the institution of an obligatory bequest should be applied to solve the problem of grandchildren. They also consider that an over-exaggeration should the practice of adoption result in the applying of *wāṣiya wājiba* to both an adopted child and the adoptive parent. One of the judges questioned the sincerity of the adoptive parents in this case. He said:

> If the adopting parent did not orally or in written form make a bequest to their adopted child, why must the court oblige itself to give the portion from the grandparent's estate to him or her (the adopted child)? What would people say about a case in which the adopting parents did not intend to do so, but the court went ahead and did it?[58]

Despite having said this, he did not want to leave the adopted child with nothing. In fact, he remarked that the *kompilasi* plainly recommends the adopting parent give or leave to his adopted child during his or her lifetime and vice-versa. He said that the direct instruction in the *kompilasi* to the religious court to give one-third to the adoptive parties when one of them dies is too facile.

Adopting the same tone, a female judge said, "I do not think that the religious courts need to involve the institution of obligatory bequest (*wāṣiya wājiba)* to deal with the problem of adoption."[59] However, she saw the possibility of applying the concept to grant adopting parents a share from their adopted child, considering that it would have been they who had spent plenty of money to raise the adopted child. She argued that, if the adopting parent made no *wāṣiya* (testament) naming their adopted child as heir, then no act of *wāṣiya* should be accomplished or assumed. Likewise, the religious courts do not need to oblige themselves to distribute a part of the deceased adopting parents' estates to their adopted child. The adopting parent who receives no *wāṣiya* from his adopted child may be granted a share from the deceased adopted child's estate by the court. It seems that she saw the practice of adoption as merely an act of kindness on the part of the adopting party, for which he or she deserves a reward from the adopted child.

The reflections in this debate reveal that a number of judges are quite adamant in their repudiation of the *kompilasi*.

V.1 Daughter versus Collaterals

The first example is related to the inheritance rule of the deceased who leaves behind a daughter and collaterals (brother(s) and sister(s)), as best illustrated by two following cases. The first is identified as No. 830/G/1991/PA.Pkl, and then No. 69/G/1992/PTA.Smrg, and No.184/K/AG/1995/MA, and the second is identified as No. 85/pdt.6/1992/V/PA.Mtr, and then No.19/Pdt.G/1993/PTA. Mtr, and hence No. 86/K/AG/1994/MA.[60] The first case involves a daughter and several sisters, all of whom were designated as co-heirs with the former by the first-instance religious court of Pekalongan and the appellate court of Semarang. The second case, which attracted great attention from legal analysts and scholars, involves a brother and a daughter.[61] It is not known whether or not the litigants understood what the *kompilasi* says about their case, but the heirs of the brother of the deceased in the second case came to the first-instance religious court claiming a share in the property on the basis that, as the brother of the deceased, their progenitor deserved to share with the deceased's daughter – although the daughter was still alive, the brother had died when the case was filed at the court, but was, of course, alive when his brother (*praepositus*) deceased. The court concluded that the case bristled with too many problems, as the property disputed was not clearly defined and, as the petition was considered not to have met the procedural requirements, therefore they rejected the case.[62] Being dissatisfied with the decision, both the plaintiffs and the defendant took the case to the appellate religious court. It agreed the brother be given a share.

In ruling that the brother, in the second case, as the sisters in the first case, should share with the daughter, it is clear that the appellate court of Mataram and the lower courts of Semarang adopted a juristic interpretation of a relevant Qur'ānic verse, which states that the collaterals, sisters and brothers, are granted rights in inheritance if the deceased leaves no child or *walad* (IV: 176). It is common knowledge that the majority of Sunni scholars have understood from this verse that, when the deceased leaves a child or *walad,* the collaterals are excluded from the share and that, so as to reconcile the practice of the Prophet who once gave sisters equal shares with daughters, they have interpreted the word *walad* in this verse to refer to male children only,[63] which means that in the existence of a daughter the collaterals can be granted a share. It is on the grounds of this traditional Sunnite interpretation that the word *walad* refers to males only, that these religious courts granted the brother a share.

In both cases, the daughters appealed to the Supreme Court, and the judges in the Supreme Court reversed the decision of both appellate courts. They agreed that the daughters excluded the brother (in the second case) and sisters (in the first case) from a share, stating that as long as the deceased left children, either male or female, the rights of inheritance of the deceased's blood relations, with the exception of parents and spouse (not a blood relation), are blocked. Interestingly, in this respect they referred to the view of Ibn 'Abbās, one of the companions of the Prophet, who interpreted the word *walad* in the verse mentioned above as both male and female children – a position which unleashed criticism from a number of scholars and judges as they considered these Supreme Court judges, as will be discussed below, had misunderstood Ibn 'Abbās – and did not, as of course the two appellate courts had, mention the *kompilasi* as their basis at all.

Then what does the *kompilasi* say about this? Why did they not refer to it? The *kompilasi*, Articles 181 and 182, states that the rights of inheritance of collaterals can only be granted in the absence of *anak. Anak* is the exact translation of *walad.*[64] So, the *kompilasi* rules as the Qur'ān says. In principle, the word *anak* refers to both a male and female child. However, it seems that the use of the word is still confusing to some judges who question whether it, as the word *walad* in the Qur'ān, refers only to males as in the Sunnite interpretation, or to both males and females as in Ibn 'Abbās interpretation. In fact, when I asked some judges about this debate between the appellate courts and the Supreme Court, a number of them commented that the debate had been generated because the *kompilasi* is ambiguous. "If the Qur'ānic word *walad* is interpreted differently in this context, why does the *kompilasi* still use its general translation?" They questioned why it (Article 182) did not use the clear and definite compound nouns of *anak perempuan* (daughter) and *anak laki-laki* (son) together when intending that both of them take precedence over the collaterals, and use the word *anak laki-laki* alone when the purpose is to state that only *anak laki-laki* exclude collaterals from inheritance.

This issue has provoked a heated debate among both judges and specialists in Islamic law. This debate can be followed in the monthly publication of the Directorate of Religious Justice of the Ministry of Religious Affairs, *Mimbar Hukum*, from which it can be discerned that the position of the classical Sunnite doctrine among Indonesian Muslims, particularly specialists in Islamic law and judges, remains so strongly entrenched to the extent that many of them have dared to take a position against the *kompilasi* and even against the decision of the Supreme Court. Even though the Supreme Court's decision had gained support from a number of judges,[65] the opposition to it is too significant to ignore.

In one of its issues, the journal published articles by Baidlawi and Rahmat Syafe'i, who presented the interpretations of the word *walad* given by earlier jurists, including that of Ibn 'Abbās, and connected these to the debate aroused by judicial practices, particularly in relation to the second case. Intending to counter the view of the Supreme Court, in their articles both Baidlawi and Syafe'i wrote that it is true that Ibn 'Abbās interpreted the word *walad* as referring to both a male and a female child, but it is a mistake to understand that his inclusion of female child under the word *walad* is his intention to exclude a brother. Therefore the Supreme Court would be in error if it took his view as its legal basis for its decision. Ibn 'Abbās, they continued, meant that it is only sister(s) and not brother(s) over whom daughter(s) takes precedence. In other words, they wanted to emphasize unambiguously that Ibn 'Abbās thought that when the deceased left behind male and female children, or only a male child, the right of collaterals, both brother(s) and sister(s), are superseded. But if the deceased left behind only a daughter, it is only the right of sister(s) and not of the brothers which is superseded, therefore it is only when she is contested by sister(s) that the daughter is considered *walad*. Explaining this, the writers wanted to say that should the deceased have left only a daughter as in the (second) case discussed, the claim(s) of the brother(s) to the share has clear foundations in the views of both the Sunnite jurists and Ibn 'Abbās'. Therefore, they argue, the Supreme Court was mistaken when it cited and referred to Ibn 'Abbās' view to support its decision of granting a full share to the daughter and at the same time of excluding the brother from a share, as

Ibn 'Abbās himself did not intend it to be so.[66] By understanding the opinion of Ibn 'Abbās in this way, they also seemed to convey that the decision of the Supreme Court that a daughter can take precedence over collateral(s) was correct and had legal basis, namely, the view of Ibn 'Abbās, only in the Pekalongan case in which a daughter disputed with sisters.[67]

Several remarks can be made on the basis of these two cases. First, it may be true, as Cammack has stated, that the Supreme Court probably wanted to give direction to the future development of Islamic inheritance doctrine and tried to be consistent with the premise developed that male and female relatives enjoy an equal position under the law.[68] The fact that the Supreme Court judges did not refer to the *kompilasi* or to theories proposed by a number of Indonesian legal experts, for instance Hazairin's bilateral theory, but to Ibn 'Abbās's view, demonstrated its lack of confidence in the *kompilasi* and its inclination towards the legal doctrines from the *fiqh* books, such as those used in the first-instance and appellate religious courts. Second, although the Ministry of Religious Affairs has no authority to evaluate the legal products of the religious courts, it feels a need to analyze and study the judgments issued at all levels of the religious courts, including the Supreme Court. It must be noted here that if what the Supreme Court practices implies the development of judicial model when appeals are made, what the Ministry of Religious Affairs does, as reflected in *Mimbar Hukum*, constitutes a kind of a legal reflection confirming that there are other opinions on one case which might also be proper or indeed even more proper to apply.[69] Moreover, Indonesian Muslim scholars also still argue that, as they often invariably find that no two cases are precisely the same, since people are not exactly the same, therefore the judges could justifiably reach different judgments as long as the reasoning process remains consistent.

V.2 Children of Pre-deceased Heirs

Another example is related to the rule of representation of heirs. In 1993, the first-instance religious court of Central Jakarta awarded shares to the representatives of heirs who were in this case 'the plaintiffs' in its Judgment No. 0259/Pdt.G/1992/PA.JP. The judges in the court based their decision on Article 185 in the *kompilasi*, which states that the right of inheritance of a predeceased heir can be assumed by his heirs. The appellate court in Judgment No. 025/1993/PTA.JK corrected the earlier judgment and decided that, because the deceased had died in 1985, long before the *kompilasi* was issued, the representative heirs could not be awarded shares. The reasoning is that before the application of the *kompilasi*, such a case was solved by resorting to the classical *fiqh* doctrines, which did not recognize the system of representation of heirs. The orphaned nephews, who claimed the shares, just as did the orphaned grandchildren of their grandparents, did not inherit from their deceased uncle. In its Judgment No. 221/K/AG/1993 the Supreme Court found in favor of the decision issued by the appellate court.[70] Interestingly, in another case in which the deceased (*pewaris*) had also died before the *kompilasi* was issued, the Supreme Court agreed that the orphaned grandchild inherited as the representative heir of his predeceased parent.[71]

According to a number of judges I interviewed, these two cases should have been solved using the rules laid down in the *kompilasi* as, although the deceased died before the *kompilasi* was issued, the case was brought after the *kompilasi* was put into effect. They argued that they had never been given any further explanation about the specification of the time of the legal enforcement of the *kompilasi* when facing such particular inheritance cases.

> All we know is that as soon as the *kompilasi* was issued, it had legal effect. Therefore, we apply it in all the cases brought before us after it was put into effect. We never consider the time at which the deceased died, for instance. If we had to, I am quite sure that the *kompilasi* in that case would never be applied as most inheritance cases often report that the deceased (*pewaris*) died long time ago, before the *kompilasi* was issued.[72]

A number of judges said that they would decide matters on the grounds of the old rule, namely the Sunnite view, if faced with such a case. However, they would not take into consideration the fact that, in any case they were handling where the deceased died before the *kompilasi* was issued was an argument, they would rely on their legal conviction that it is the old rule of the majority of the Sunnite *'ulamā'* and not the new rule in the *kompilasi* that is the correct rule.

The admission of a number of judges that they have never been given any explanation about any statutory limitation on the enforcing the rules of inheritance, and hence their understanding that they had to apply the rules of the *kompilasi* as soon as it was issued; and that they did not have to take the time of death of the deceased (*pewaris*) into consideration, confirms there is some ambiguity in the *kompilasi,* as well as inconsistency in the judges' understanding of the *kompilasi*. One clear example is the (first) case mentioned above, namely the inheritance case related to the rule of inheritance of collaterals. It was reported that in this case, the *pewaris* had also died a long time ago, before the *kompilasi* was issued (sometime before 1930). If the time of the death of the *pewaris* is to be considered, the grounds for the decision of the Mataram appellate court, which awarded the brother a share with the sister, is then appropriate.

However, the appellate court seemed merely to want to adopt the classical doctrines and was not concerned with the time of death of the *pewaris*. Likewise, when deciding to give the daughters the whole share and to exclude the brothers in the Mataram case, that is when issuing Judgment No. 86/K/AG/1994/MA, the Supreme Court was not aware of nor concerned about that detail. The position it adopted was not in keeping with that adopted when solving the case of representation of heirs, that is when issuing Judgment No. 221/K/AG/1993/MA.

The obvious inference is that while some judges were eager to follow the *kompilasi*, others did not hesitate to abandon the *kompilasi* because of their preference for the classical *fiqh* doctrine, which in this case does not recognize the concept of representation. In this respect the *kompilasi* seems to have failed in guaranteeing legal certainty for Muslims, because litigants in such cases may be awarded judgments under the old ruling; that is, classical Sunnite jurisprudence, while others are awarded theirs under the new ruling, the *kompilasi*. Realizing the deleterious effect of such practices, Zain Badjeber, one of the Muslim scholars of Islamic law who often gives analytical views on the decisions made by the courts from a procedural point of view (*hukum acara*), has strongly suggested that the time of the legal enforcement of the *kompilasi* for such cases of inheritance be clearly defined, so that the uncertainty often created could be eliminated in the future.[73] Like most of the judges interviewed, he also stressed that the case brought to the religious court should be treated according to the legal considerations of the time when or where the claim was made or litigation was brought, and not of the time when the legal action (*peristiwa hukum*) occurred.[74] Since the *kompilasi* has now been accorded the status of the formal reference of the religious court, the latter must solve cases by recourse to the new rules covered in the *kompilasi*.

V.3 Apostasy within Marriage

Another example which demonstrates judges' preference for the legal doctrine from the *fiqh* books and decision to ignore the provisions in the *kompilasi* concerns the rule of apostasy in its relation to the marital relationship. Intending to give a more detailed reason for why the *fiqh* books are still needed, a female judge at the religious court of Bogor mentioned the example of cases for which she thought rules are not completely covered in the *kompilasi*. She said:

> The *kompilasi* (Article 116: h) implies that if one of a married couple (whether this be wife or husband) commits *riddah*/apostasy, a petition for divorce can be granted. But this raises some questions. Is the wife entitled to *nafkah* during her *iddah*? When is

> then the period of *iddah* considered to begin, at the time the apostasy is committed, or at the time the case is brought to the court? Facing such a problematic case, we need to consult other sources. And it is to the *fiqh* books that we first refer."[75]

This example is quite interesting. The *kompilasi* mentions that apostasy can be taken as grounds for divorce. The consequences of this divorce actually can be solved by a number of articles in the *kompilasi*, regulating the period of *iddah* and the *nafkah* for the divorced wives. Article 153 (2b) states that if the marriage is dissolved by divorce (without stressing any differentiation of how or for what reason the divorce occurs), the period of the *iddah* starts after the pronouncement of the divorce in the court. That is, for those who are menstruating, it lasts for three cycles or at least ninety days; and for those who are not menstruating it lasts ninety days, and for those who are pregnant it is until the birth of the child. Many judges are confused about this issue. The source of their confusion is their understanding that the marriage is automatically dissolved as soon as the apostasy is committed, whereas they are required to treat this case just as other divorce cases arising for other reasons. Were they to consider it as only one of the reasons for dissolving a marriage, they would not be confused, and would account for the consequence of the dissolution of marriage, since the divorce is pronounced in the court. Quite apart from this, they still doubt that should the wife have committed apostasy, she still has right of *nafkah* as well as *mut'a* from her husband, as they tended to consider her as *nāshij* (disobedient). In this respect the judge I interviewed argued that "because the *kompilasi* is silent on this, we need to resort to *ijtihād* by referring to the *fiqh* books."

The drafters of the *kompilasi* apparently want to place apostasy in the same position as the other grounds for divorce mentioned and therefore to give the couples the freedom to decide whether their marriage should continue. They do not intend to dissolve a marriage at the precise moment one of the parties commits apostasy. Nevertheless, for a number who tend to refer to the legal doctrine of the *fiqh* books, stating that one of the consequences of the apostasy is the dissolution of the marriage and that it must be acted upon as soon as the apostasy is committed,[76] a loophole is left open to decide whether apostasy can automatically break up a couple at the time the apostasy is committed, or when the couple should come to the court to petition for divorce. Tending to favor the *fiqh* doctrine, they consider that a divorce between a couple was contemporaneous with the committal of the apostasy and not with the time the divorce decision is issued.

A related matter is that while the *kompilasi* tends to stress the element of disharmony resulting from the act of apostasy, the majority of judges are inclined to stress the act of apostasy itself.[77] Mukti Arto, one of the former chief judges of the religious courts, said that a petition of divorce on the grounds of apostasy does not acquire any attempts at reconciliation. He argues that the difference in religious faith between the couple will automatically result in disharmony. Therefore, what should be done is to advise the apostate to return to Islam.[78] Another judge strongly suggested that the clause 'resulting in disharmony in the marital life' attached to the word '*murtad*/apostasy' found in Article 116 (h) be eliminated, as it makes the rule itself vague. He asserts that the essence of the clause has been covered in the same Article (116: f), which mentions continuous quarrelling as one of the grounds for divorce. If the clause is maintained, the aim of Point (h) is obscured, that it is apostasy or disharmony to be considered. Apostasy can stand by itself as adequate grounds for the judges to end the marital relationship of a couple. They are not burdened by the necessity of proving the existence of disharmony resulting from the act of apostasy.[79]

As a matter of fact, judges in the religious courts are inclined to decide a case of apostasy on the basis of the apostasy itself. The decision of the judges of the religious court of Tasikmalaya illustrates the case. They decided to grant the petition for a divorce from a woman who claimed that her husband had reverted to his previous religion, shown by the fact that he attended a church congregation every Sunday. In their legal summation, they mentioned that there was no need to summon the husband to appear before the court, because the court is not competent to try a non-Muslim. They added that the act of apostasy will unquestionably produce disharmony in future should the marriage be permitted to continue.[80] This case clearly reveals that it is the act of apostasy itself which leads the court to end the marriage. Reconciliation, and even hearing from the party who is apostate, is therefore unnecessary.

Another judgment issued by the religious court in Rangkasbitung implies more concretely that reconciliation is not to be striven for in a divorce sought when one of a couple has become apostate and that the difference of religious faith was the strongest motivation which led the judges to comply with the petition. It is recorded in the judgment that a man petitioned for divorce because he claimed that he had frequent disagreements with his wife, and they had been separated since April 2003. It is also recorded that the husband admitted since January 2004 to have reverted to his former religion, Christianity, which he had embraced before marrying his wife. The wife, who contested the husband's petition, stated that not everything her husband had stated was true, and that she still wanted to save her marriage although the husband had reverted to his former religion. In dealing with this case, the judges decided to terminate the marriage. What is of interest is that in their legal considerations they clearly stressed the apostasy of the husband, attested to by the fact that since January 2004 the husband had been active in one of the churches in Rangkasbitung. They then referred to Article 116 (h) of the *kompilasi,* which mentions that apostasy constitutes one of the grounds for divorce. It also cited the legal text from *al-muhadhdhab,* Vol. 2, p. 54, which states, "If a couple or one of each becomes an apostate, the marriage is to be annulled... if the apostasy occurs after a sexual relationship has been commenced, the divorce occurs after the expiry of the *iddah* period."[81] In giving such a judgment, the judges ignored the objection of the wife contesting the husband's petition and had adduced the act of apostasy as the main grounds for divorce, whereas it was clear that the apostasy had basically been committed after the couple had been involved in arguments for a long time and had separated. They did not even seem to consider the possibility that, by stating that he had reconverted to Christianity, the husband had merely intended to back up his petition and ensure that it was granted.

I must mention here that before the issuing of the *kompilasi* and the Marriage Law, there were many cases which demonstrated that the judges in the religious courts accepted apostasy as a condition which could break up a marriage automatically, a position relevant to the *fiqh* doctrine applied at the time. Understanding that under such a condition the religious court would make no difficulties in granting their petition for divorce, many women reported to have committed apostasy to rid themselves of their husbands. Their attempts indeed succeeded.[82] The same position was also adopted by judges of the religious courts after 1974, which however tends to run counter to the Marriage Law, as it does not categorize apostasy into the group of the grounds on which the divorce can be granted.[83] This tendency continued to strengthen after the issuing of the *kompilasi* in which apostasy is considered as valid grounds for, but not automatically confirming, the dissolution of a marriage. It limits the act of apostasy as grounds for divorce to the existence of disharmony arising from the act. In this regard, it is worth mentioning here that a new draft of the Marriage Law to be submitted to Parliament by the Ministry of Religious Affairs seems to have adopted the dominant position of judges towards this issue, and mentions that apostasy alone, without being limited to the existence of disharmony, can break marriages – see again the points proposed for revision on page 129 in the previous chapter.

From the discussion above, it can be clearly inferred that judges in the religious courts only accept the reform aspects introduced by the *kompilasi* which do not deviate greatly from the *fiqh* books. It seems that the *kompilasi* has not had the force to shift the central position of the established *fiqh* doctrine among Indonesian Muslims. Even though it seeks to impose the registration of marriage and limit the age of marriage for couples and insists that divorce should follow due legal process, it still does not have the power to interfere in the religious validity of a marriage for which religious conditions and qualifications have been fulfilled. Similarly, the *kompilasi* has failed to eliminate the cases of injustice arising from the application of the Islamic law of inheritance by promoting the bilateral system of inheritance, which places the male and female links in the same position. It has no power to force judges in the religious courts to abandon the *fiqh* doctrines in dealing with the cases of inheritance. Paradoxically, they have continued to demand the institutionalization of Islamic law by the State, an insistence which is not complemented by their readiness to depart from the legal doctrines prescribed in the *fiqh* books.

V The *Kompilasi* and the Need for Religious Legitimacy

In the previous chapters, the discussion has concentrated on the role of the *fiqh* texts in the judicial practices of judges in the Indonesian religious courts, even after they had the *kompilasi* available to them. Presenting a number of cases, I have also discussed to what extent the judges have used the *kompilasi* as the basis of their legal decisions, and at the same time discovered the motives behind the judges' preference for maintaining the *fiqh* texts. Nevertheless, a fundamental question remains unanswered. Why do they feel it necessary to continue referring to the *fiqh* books in rendering judgments on the cases brought before them? Why do they need to confirm and support their judgments with the references from the *fiqh* books, although they have found adequate grounds in the *kompilasi*? In short, why has the *kompilasi* not been able to change this traditional feature of the religious courts? This chapter will reveal that, besides the motives mentioned in the previous chapter, there are more fundamental roots for the maintenance of the *fiqh* texts in the judicial practices of the Indonesian religious courts.

I The Question of the Legal Status of the *Kompilasi*

To deal with these questions, first and foremost we have to understand that the *kompilasi* was put into effect only in the form of a Presidential Instruction, which has less legal force than a Statute, and therefore is considered to be loosely binding. Indeed no sooner was it issued than the legal status of the *kompilasi* was subject to a vehement debate. Bismar Siregar, a former Supreme Court judge, commented that the *kompilasi* was not a law book, and judges had a right to interpret its provisions.[1] Other legal scholars even considered the *kompilasi* in its present form to have no formal and juridical authority which can be fully applied by the judges, because judges are supposed to abide by the Statutes (*undang-undang*).[2] In response to these opinions, some other scholars and judges who supported the making of the *kompilasi* asserted that, even though it was put into effect in the form of a Presidential Instruction, the *kompilasi* has a strong legal position, so that all judges should abide by it. Bustanul Arifin, for instance, asserted that the *kompilasi* has the same legal power as a Law or a Statute, although he cautioned that the *kompilasi* is "only the commencement of a process".[3] Yahya Harahap, another Supreme Court judge, stated that all the parties engaged in the judicial process in the religious courts should acquiesce in the rules covered in the *kompilasi*. He even proclaimed that, if the judges still referred to the *fiqh* books, they were not pronouncing law but *fiqh* doctrines.[4]

As explained in the previous chapters, the aim of the making of the *kompilasi* was to unify a variety of material rules derived from various *fiqh* books, covering issues related to marriage, inheritance, and endowment which had been previously applied in the Indonesian religious courts.[5] By decree, the Minister of Religious Affairs ordered all Government employees to rely on it "to the greatest possible extent" and proclaimed it publicly as the law of the country.[6] Despite this instruction, judges have differed on whether the *kompilasi* can be a basis for their decisions. In the seminar on 'Critical Debate on the *Kompilasi*' held by the Department of Religious Affairs, the former Director of Islamic Justice, Wahyu Widiana, said that the judges have often argued that they are reluctant to follow the *kompilasi* because it is only a Presidential Instruction enjoining the Minister of Religious Affairs to promote it.[7]

A number of judges betrayed the same reluctance, revealing the fact that they often heard cynical comments about the legal status of the *kompilasi* from *'ulamā'*. They claimed that this sort of comment indubitably affected their attitude towards the *kompilasi*. Some judges have even publicly and unequivocally expressed their doubt about its legal status, although it is included in the texts of the judgments they have handed down. Furthermore, in their rulings some judges have clearly stated, "(...) As the *kompilasi* is not a Statute (still *Inpres*), its legal position is the same as that of the *fiqh* books. So here, we feel a need to still refer to the *fiqh* books for our judgments and do not have to mention the rule in the *kompilasi* and give it precedence over the *fiqh* books." Those judgments have then revealed an abundance of legal doctrines from the *fiqh* books, as well as from the *ḥadīth*, and have not cited any article from the *kompilasi*.[8] By adopting this position, they have accorded the *kompilasi* the status of an unwritten source, like that of the *fiqh* books, and they even feel that the *fiqh* books embrace a more certain legal position. In fact, several judges, as illustrated earlier, have cited the *fiqh* books alone and ignored the *kompilasi*, and on some cases have even preferred the *fiqh* books to the *kompilasi*.

II The Maintenance of Tradition

II.1 The Distinguished Position of the Fiqh Texts

The most cogent matter is their attitude, merely elicited by their doubts about the legal status of the *kompilasi*. Recalling the replies given by almost all the judges I interviewed when asked whether or not their citation of and their preference for legal doctrines from the *fiqh* books would be minimized or even pushed to one side when the *kompilasi* became a Statute, the answer was 'No'. In other words, concealed behind the façade of their doubts about the legal status of the *kompilasi,* there is apparently a more intrinsic reason, or another more profound explanation, for their attitude. Although their ambiguous attitude towards the *kompilasi* can superficially be attributed to its equivocal legal standing, almost all the judges could not guarantee that upgrading the legal status of the *kompilasi* from Presidential Instruction to Statute would be enough to undermine the central position of the *fiqh* books in the religious courts. In fact, a few judges have repudiated the plan to upgrade the legal status of the *kompilasi* from Presidential Instruction to Statute, and one of their reasons is their uneasiness that judges would be more bound by and committed to that would-be law, and ignore the *fiqh* books and no longer cite them.

This reason exposes the possible disappointment and worry if the peculiarity of the religious courts underlined by the distinguished position of *fiqh* books were to be eliminated by the more solid and stronger legal status of the *kompilasi*. Even those judges who stated their approval of the plan generally also wanted to preserve the *fiqh* books. One of the judges said that if the aim of upgrading the legal status of the *kompilasi* were to oust the position of the *fiqh* books, this would not be supported by the judges, as almost all of them wanted to maintain the use of the *fiqh* books.[9]

The reluctance of the judges to abandon the use of the *fiqh* books in their judicial practice after the upgrading of the legal status of the *kompilasi* to that of a Statute indicates their wish to use the *fiqh* books not only in cases for which the *kompilasi* (and subsequently the Statute) does not provide context, or takes different position from the *fiqh* texts. This reluctance apparently has to do with the distinguished position enjoyed by the Islamic tradition among Indonesian Muslims. Although ideas of reform are very much part of their religious discourse, the position of tradition remains strong among them. In fact, the majority of them are traditionalists attached to the largest Muslim organization in the country, the Nahdlatul Ulama. Among this group, the position of the *kitab kuning,* to which the religious courts were historically and culturally oriented, is quite central.[10]

Comprehension of the influence exerted by traditional and cultural elements on judges is strengthened by an examination of their educational background and the system of their recruitment, in both of which the *fiqh* book remains one of the exam subjects. Most candidates graduated from *pesantren* before continuing their studies at the State Institute for Islamic studies (*Institute Agama Islam Negeri*/IAIN). In the *pesantren,* the tradition of studying and analyzing *fiqh* books has always enjoyed a considerable position.[11] Although they have adopted a modern curriculum, the *pesantren* still also include *fiqh* texts as an area of study. *Fiqh* books therefore have become an everyday subject among the students in *pesantren.* The familiarity which *pesantren* graduates have with the *fiqh* books is formally revived and refreshed as soon as they apply for a position as a judge in the religious courts. In fact, in order to aspire to this position, applicants should first pass an examination in subjects including the reading of certain *fiqh* books.[12] A failure to read the *fiqh* books may disqualify an applicant from being appointed a judge. Zuffran Sabrie, a senior staff member at the Directorate of Religious Justice in the Department of Religious Affairs, said that being able to read *fiqh* books is and has always been an absolutely unconditional qualification for being a judge in the religious court. Therefore, the test in reading *fiqh* books is assumed to be the best way to determine whether or not a candidate judge is capable of undertaking this task.

In this regard, while considering the test as the best way to measure a person's ability to master the *fiqh* books, Sabrie realized that the test does not always meet the goal. Not everyone who has passed the test of reading the *fiqh* books, he said, could be adjudged fully capable of reading them. Moreover, while the program of the test for reading *fiqh* books is still maintained, from time to time the standard has been lowered. This is because of the imbalance between the pressing need to recruit new judges and the decline in the applicants' capability to master the *fiqh* books.[13]

In the past, the qualification of being able to read the *fiqh* books fluently presented no difficulty to judges, especially as a number of them were selected from the *'ulamā',* who had graduated from *pesantren* where various *fiqh* books, ranging from those with extremely complicated grammatical structures to those with simple sentences, were read.[14] After the issuing of the 1989 Islamic Judicature Act, as mentioned earlier, judges were selected from graduates of the faculty of Islamic law at the IAIN and the faculty of national law at public universities, and their ability to read *fiqh* books leaves some question marks.[15] In order to comply with the qualifications, the *fiqh* book selected as material for examinations is now one of the easiest and the simplest, namely *Fiqh al-Sunna.*[16] This book is composed using a simple language structure and covers basic *fiqh* matters showing no preference for any jurisprudential methodology. It was hoped that by taking the simplest *fiqh* book, more judges could be selected.[17]

The upshot of this is that judges display an unsatisfactory mastery of Arabic. Moreover, although the book used is the simplest one, not all the judges selected actually passed the test with a good mark. A few were considered to have a poor mastery of Arabic but were selected so as to fill the judicial vacancies.[18] The results of the test between 1991 and 1992 supply plenty of evidence to back up this assertion. The investigation reported that among the 250 applicants selected in 1991, only four passed with a high mark, and among the 248 applicants selected the following year, only two achieved a high score.[19] Accordingly, there has been a gap between the idealism and the reality in terms of employing judges who have mastered Arabic adequately. Sabrie expressed his opinion in these words:

> We have to maintain the central position of the *fiqh* books in our environment, that is the religious court, and this is why we should employ judges capable of reading Arabic. I realized that the reading test for Arabic could not be regarded as the optimal way to do this as we still found judges employed in religious courts with no ability to read Arabic, even though they had passed the test. But what is a better way than this? I am sure that the quality of judges of the religious court in terms of Arabic will be worse if the test is not utilized.[20]

A glance at what Sabrie stated and the stipulations the Department of Religious Affairs has applied for recruitment seems to be irrelevant to one article in the 1989 Islamic Judicature Act governing the qualifications for candidate judges. This article states that a graduate of a faculty of national law can become a judge in a religious court if he or she understands Islamic law.[21] No qualification of being able to read *fiqh* books is mentioned in any article. Today there are Islamic legal books written in languages other than Arabic. So, without having the ability to read and understand *fiqh* books written in Arabic, a person can understand Islamic law from his or her reading of Islamic legal books written in other languages and can be judges in the religious courts.

Interpretations of the article advanced by Muslim legal scholars and judges in the religious courts suggest the relevance of the test of the mastery of Arabic to the article. Huzaemah Tahido, a professor of Islamic law at State Islamic University Jakarta, for example, has insisted that applicants who are graduates either of the faculty of Islamic law or national law can be recruited as judges of religious courts only if they understand Islamic law from their own reading of *fiqh* books, or in other words, only if they are able to read *fiqh* books. She claims that a person cannot be judged to be capable of understanding Islamic law if he or she cannot read the *fiqh* books (Islamic legal books written in Arabic).[22] Similarly, the vice-chairman of the religious court in East Jakarta has said that the qualification of understanding Islamic law must be interpreted as being able to read the *fiqh* books. He argues that a person can be regarded to have understood Islamic law, only if he or she can read the *fiqh* books. As understanding of Islamic law is one of main qualifications to be a judge in the religious court, being able to read *fiqh* books is accordingly an absolute qualification, he emphasized.[23]

Following their interpretation, it is then evident that what is required is not whether or not a candidate has graduated from a faculty of Islamic law or national law, but whether he or she has the ability to comprehend *fiqh* books. Why has the qualification of being able to read *fiqh* books not been stated clearly and expressed unequivocally, but is instead encapsulated in the clause 'understanding Islamic law'? The answer seems to be connected to the fact that in its pursuit of modernization, the State has continued to attempt to free all its civil institutions from religious symbols. In addition, to state clearly that the would-be judges should be capable of reading the *fiqh* books would contradict the whole aim of its national project – making the *kompilasi* – in which the legal rules are systematized in a modern manner, replacing those written in Arabic and scattered throughout various *fiqh* books. Therefore, although the articles allow graduates from the faculty of national law with some knowledge of Islamic law to become judges, the qualification of being able to read the *fiqh* books often prevents them from applying altogether or induces only a small number of them to aspire to being judges in the religious courts. Consequently most applicants selected are Islamic law faculty graduates who have been taught Arabic texts in *pesantren*.

II.2 The Internalization of the Fiqh Texts

If the educational background of the majority of the applicants was the *pesantren*, where the *fiqh* books were accorded a central position, and then the faculty of Islamic law, and if at the very start of their career they have also been required to demonstrate their understanding of *fiqh* books – even after the issuing of the *kompilasi* – it is not surprising that the tradition of using and studying *fiqh* books is so institutionalized, it might even be said internalized, among religious court judges, that their judicial behavior will be strongly influenced by this tradition. To cite the legal doctrines from the *fiqh* books is a tried and tested practice and need which they are unable to ignore. As demonstrated earlier, for a number of them the legal doctrines in the *fiqh* books have even become unchallenged truth.

Here, it is feasible to argue that while such an intensity of feeling for preserving an established tradition in a society, particularly among judges in the religious courts in this case, persists, any formalization of law (even at the higher levels of the legal system) will not have a great effect on law enforcement. Therefore, the thesis which states that the rule or law which had been judicially established will be loyally obeyed, as it has fulfilled the formal element of its legality, it will not always be valid. It is an incontrovertible fact that the formal juridical dimension embraced by the *kompilasi* does not effectively motivate the judges to apply it to its fullest possible extent. They still prefer the *fiqh* books should the *kompilasi* adopt a different stance. Even should they agree with the *kompilasi*, they still exclusively explore the legal doctrines in the *fiqh* books. To understand this attitude, we may turn to Hart's statement that the enactment of a law by Parliament or through other instruments of legislation is not enough to effectuate the validity of a law. The law must be internalized by such insiders in the legal system as judges and lawyers, and in a wider sense by all citizens.[24] In the case of the Islamic law, merely enacting a law and claiming it to be Islamic will not be sufficient to ensure its validity if it is not linked to its real sources, namely, the Qur'ān, the *ḥadīth*, and the *fiqh* texts, as it is only through such linkages that the process of the internalization of the law claimed to be Islamic can be accomplished. And the way to ensure that the insiders believe that the law is Islamic law and is based on the sources mentioned is to link each provision of the law to a specific rule or general principles contained in those sources.[25]

What Lawrence M. Friedmann has proposed also seems to be relevant to this case. According to Friedmann, the application of law is to be communicated in three dimensions, namely: the structural; the substantial; and the cultural. He suggests that application will only be effective if all three dimensions have been considered. Therefore, although the law has been substantially and structurally systematized, it will not have been applied well if, for example, a society has failed to alter its cultural attitude and traditional practices.[26] Even though the three dimensions share an equal position in this issue, it is not impossible that one of them may play a more significant role than the others in a certain society. The cultural factor can be, for example, considered more dominant than the other two factors in the case of those groups in the community which have strongly maintained their traditional model in solving cases.[27]

In this regard, one particular phenomenon is worth mentioning here. The greatest attempt to maintain and express the preservation of the use of the *fiqh* texts is among the senior judges. The judges in the first-instance religious courts reported that the senior judges in the appellate religious courts often strongly recommend they preserve the use of the *fiqh* books, and even vehemently claimed judgments in which no Arabic texts or the legal doctrines from the *fiqh* books have been cited to have been issued outside the religious courts.[28] Indeed, as has been mentioned above, research into the comparison between judgments issued by judges in the first-instance religious courts and by those in the appellate religious courts found that the judgments issued by the latter are more frequently grounded on *fiqh* books, and many of their judgments were overturned by the Supreme Court judges.

It seems that the psychological and sociological aspects invariably contribute to the practice of the judges in the appellate religious courts in ruling on the cases brought before them. They have been working as judges for a very long time, beginning in religious courts in rural areas, and their rank is usually lower than their counterparts in the urban religious courts. Then they are appointed judges or even directors of religious courts in both rural and urban areas, and later still as judges in the appellate religious courts and the Supreme Court. This wide experience and seniority have played a large part in their legal maturation process, and have often led them to an overstated attitude in deciding the relevant legal considerations. Such a position is readily understandable if these psychological and sociological aspects, which have led to their independent decision to rely on the *fiqh* books, are coupled with the fact that they have been very accustomed to using the *fiqh* books. In the seminar organized by the Working Team for Concern with Women's Issues of the Department of Religious Affairs, Wahyu Widiana, the former director of Religious Justice, noted the senior judges' custom of taking legal references for their judgments. He revealed that these judges often feel more dependent on tradition than do junior judges, and consequently ignore the formally codified law in favor of other references of their own preference.[29]

Without casting aside all these phenomena, it must be noted here, however, that as some judges confessed, the citation of the legal doctrines of the *fiqh* books relevant to the provisions in the *kompilasi* seems to have decreased slightly over time. Surprisingly, this gradual elimination can be attributed to computers, as in a number of courts computers are used for writing the judgments, and these either do not have Arabic script at all, or, if it does exist, there are not enough skilled people to operate the program. The decrease was gradually completed by purposely leaving empty spaces for later entry of the Arabic script from the *fiqh* books by hand. Over the course of time, a number of judges who found this time-consuming often ignored the quotation of the legal doctrines from the *fiqh* books in their judgments, making a conscious decision no longer to leave space for inserting Arabic script. Nonetheless, for those who have still found it necessary and who are very strict about it – and there are many – such a technical problem does not prevent them from displaying Arabic statements taken from the *fiqh* books. These judges continued to allow space for the citation of Arabic legal doctrines and then filled it in manually in their own handwriting. Eleven of the judgments in my collection have handwritten Arabic texts.

III The Significance of the Arabic Language

III.1 Religious Identity

The tendency of the judges in the Indonesian religious courts to continue quoting the *fiqh* books becomes more readily explicable when we observe the debates among Indonesian Muslims around the issue of defining what is "Islamic" and what is not. By debating such an issue, they are actually trying to inscribe a religious identity. In this context the Arabic language plays a crucial role, especially in giving people their religious identity. It simultaneously also emerges as a source of authority. A person's authority in Islamic knowledge is often determined by their mastery of Arabic, or more precisely the *fiqh* books. For judges in the religious courts, there is always a need to demonstrate this mastery by preserving the use of the *fiqh* books in their judicial practices so that their authority as the guardians of Islamic law can be acknowledged and accepted by society.

A number of judges were adamant that they feel more certain and on firmer ground with citations in Arabic in their judgments. The judgments are considered to be more accurate and binding (*afḍal*) on account of the insertion of the Arabic texts. The transfer of the Islamic legal doctrines expressed in Arabic, as covered in the *fiqh* books, to a more understandable and articulate language presented in the *kompilasi* is considered to be useful only in a few cases, as a tool to help to understand the rules required to be applied. In fact, although the judges refer to the *kompilasi* and in doing so follow its provisions in deciding some cases, they often mention only the codes of its articles and rarely or indeed never display its full texts or provisions. Instead, they afterwards cite the opinions of the earlier *'ulamā'* in a full statement in Arabic. "We simply have to be different from the other courts," said almost all the chairmen and judges of the religious courts in which I conducted my research. "We are 'religious (Islamic) courts (judges)', and need to show our identity," they argued. A few judges who do not read the *fiqh* books fluently are accordingly also persuaded to cite the Arabic legal statements from the *fiqh* books. In this regard, it is interesting to mention here that since 2004, judges of the religious court in Cianjur have written the sentence *basmallah* at the top of the judgment in Arabic script, whereas before this was always written in Latin script.[30] One of its judges mentioned that this is to demonstrate their religious identity, namely: that they are judges of the religious court. Highlighting the doctrine that to write and read even a letter in Arabic script constitutes religious merit or *'ibādah,* another judge stated that it is for religious merit.[31]

III.2 Religious Justification

The Arabic language and script do indeed enjoy a privileged position among the Indonesian Muslims, particularly traditionalist *'ulamā'*. They think both represent noble values in themselves; hence they not only adhere to the Arabic language, but also to Arabic script. Therefore, when they write in and translate the *fiqh* works into vernacular languages, they have done this almost without exception in Arabic script.[32] Aware of this, judges feel that they need comply with this orientation. The judges assume that if they do not follow or respond to the legal awareness of the community, the community will abandon the religious court. In fact, they have sometimes heard that a certain community often claims the religious courts are no longer Islamic when it finds no Arabic texts cited in its decisions. Conversely, the community will be highly satisfied at finding the judgment supported by Arabic statements. Quoting the *kompilasi* is not enough to demonstrate that they really know and comprehend the *fiqh* books, or have mastered the classical sources of the rules of the *kompilasi.*[33]

This is palpable in the attitude displayed by judges when making judgments on cases in which they agree with the provisions of the *kompilasi.* In these cases, judges usually mention the article of the *kompilasi* and then proceed to quote one or more opinions of the *'ulamā'* drawn from certain *fiqh* books. The case of a divorce related to the utterance of *ta'līq ṭalāq* is probably the best example. The *kompilasi,* Article 116, rules that a divorce can be concluded on the basis of the existence of various reasons, one of which is a husband's violation of one or more points falling under *ta'līq ṭalāq*. This reason is listed as Point (g) of Article 116. In deciding such a case, the judges usually mention Article 116 Point (g) of the *kompilasi* as one of the legal bases for their judgments, but then also quote the *fiqh* doctrine from Sharqāwī's *Ḥāshiya 'alā al-Taḥrīr,* which reads, "Whoever makes his *talak* dependent upon an action, the *talak* is co-terminus with the performance of that action according to the original pronouncement." This is the case in almost all the judgments in divorce cases in my collection.

In the judges' view, demonstrating their mastery of the *fiqh* books is also of particular importance in reinforcing their position as religious authorities outside the circle of traditional authority, the *'ulamā'*. Broadly speaking, the litigants rarely bother about the legal basis taken by the judges in deciding disputes or cases brought before them. Most of the litigants who come to the religious courts are not overly concerned about the legal reference for the judgments handed down to them. They focus on the core of the judgments themselves.

> I do not care on what judges base their judgments. The important thing for me is the substance of the judgment. If the judgment has fulfilled my petition satisfying my sense of justice, I can accept it. Frankly speaking, I am ignorant of the (Islamic) law. I trust the judges, and that is why I came here (to the religious court) to solve my problem.[34]

My analytical investigation of how losing parties who appealed against the decision in their cases replied, and countered their opponents, as described in the copy of the judgments also demonstrated that many litigants were rarely bothered by the legal references derived from the texts of either *fiqh* books or other sources. Their greatest source of wrangling is the judges' legal considerations or reasoning, extracted from the statements or information from both the plaintiffs and defendants, and their witnesses. Some have sometimes proposed and questioned the use of the specific points of Islamic law, but often (Muslim) lawyers who are qualified in Islamic law play a role here.

Many judges admitted the ignorance of the legal references for the judgment among the majority of the litigants. Yet they realized that the *'ulamā'* around the litigants are sometimes, in fact quite often, curious to know the legal basis of their judgments, as often before coming to the courts litigants had consulted the local *'ulamā'* about their problems:

> Most of the people who turned to the religious court to solve their problems did not care about the arguments adduced or the considerations we espoused. To whatever authority the judgments referred is not very important for them. They can accept the judgment in as far as they can sense it is just. As judges we should always base our judgments on the rules or grounds available to us. The *kompilasi* is now our reference in making judgments. We need to socialize it and the best way to do this is by applying it in our judgments. However, as judges we need to understand the legal awareness of the community, particularly that of the groups of *'ulamā'*. Although we have been well trained in using the *kompilasi* and have told them that it was composed from the *fiqh*

> books, we could not in fact budge their deep admiration for the *fiqh* books.[35]

Nonetheless, a number of judges admitted that in a few cases, references to the *fiqh* books are necessary in order to convince the litigants, particularly a defendant. In the case of divorce petitioned by a wife but strongly opposed by her husband, for example, a judge feels a need to put forward opinions of earlier *'ulamā'* which explain the rules pertaining to the case specifically and clearly. A number of judges said that in such a case, the husband often argued that he still loved his wife and they had never quarreled. Meanwhile the wife, while also admitting that they had never had a serious clash, felt that she could no longer live together with her husband. Hearing the case and not being able to persuade the wife to retract her petition, the judges grant the petition. In doing so, the judges usually mention Article 116 of the *kompilasi*, but go on to give a more relevant legal basis for the case. For this purpose, they quote the legal doctrine which reads, "(...) If the hatred of a wife towards her husband has grown more aggravated, her petition for divorce can ultimately be approved in the court" (al-Anṣārī's *Minhāj al-Ṭullāb*, vol. IV, 346).[36] They believe that referring to the opinions of earlier *'ulamā'* in the *fiqh* books can convince the defendant that their approval of the petition is based on a sound Islamic legal basis.

It can be inferred from this fact that the judges, while citing the *fiqh* books, have not deviated fundamentally from the provisions of the *kompilasi*. In the first case of *ta'līq ṭalaq*, it is very clear that the judges adopted the provisions of the *kompilasi*, but also needed a justification or seal of legitimacy from the *fiqh* books. The second example indicates that the judges needed to reveal the Islamic legal basis more explicitly; and by so doing they believed that the litigants, particularly the one ruled against, would be satisfied and accept the judgment. All of the examples indicate that judges often felt the need for more legitimacy and justification to endorse their judgments, and are convinced that the *fiqh* texts can fulfill this need.

III.3 Shafi'ite's Doctrine

Why are Indonesian Muslims, the *'ulamā'* and therefore also the judges, so concerned about revealing their religious identities, and why do they consider the Arabic language to be one the signifiers of their religious identity? The answer seems to be partly related to their rigid adherence to the Shāfi'īte school. Indeed, in contrast to the other Sunnite schools, particularly the Ḥanafītes, Shāfi'ītes believe that learning Arabic is obligatory upon every believer in order that he or she be able to perform his or her religious obligations properly. Al-Shāfiʿī (d.829/204), in his *Risāla*, stated:

> It is obligatory upon every Muslim to learn the Arab tongue to the utmost of his power in order (to be able) to profess through it that there is no God at all but God and Muhammad is His servant and Apostle', and to recite in it (i.e. the Arabic tongue) the Book of God, and to utter in mentioning what is incumbent upon him, the *takbīr*, the *tasbīḥ* and the *tashahhud* and others. Whatever learning he gains of the language which God made to be the language of him (Muhammad), by whom He sealed His prophethood and by whom He revealed the last of His Books, is for his (man's) welfare, just as it is his (duty) to learn (how) to pray and recite the *dhikr* in it... Calling the attention of the public to the fact that the Qur'ān was revealed in the Arab tongue in particular is (a sincere piece) of advice to (all) Muslims.[37]

This long statement clearly demonstrates that for al-Shāfiʿī it is the duty of every believer to learn as much Arabic as is needed in order to be able to be a good Muslim. The emphasis on the obligation to learn Arabic by al-Shāfiʿī can be interpreted to mean that he was aware of the existence of non-Arabic speaking Muslims. Informed about the existence of languages other than Arabic, it seems that al-Shāfiʿī, and his followers, anticipated that the Muslims would be ignorant of Arabic and even replace it with other languages. Meanwhile, as the language of the Qur'ān, the first source of Muslim theology, law, and ethics as well as the vehicle of the fulfillment of ritual obligations, the Arabic language is considered by them to play a role in assessing the quality of the Muslim religious beliefs. In this connection, Wiegers has pointed out that the famous Tilimsan-born *muftī* al-Wansharīshī (d. 1508) issued a *fatwā* at the request of someone about a man who wished to remain in Marbella after the conquest of his native town by the Christians. Overwhelmingly reflecting the view of al-Shāfiʿī, in his *fatwā* al-Wansharīshī stated that this was not allowed. This negative answer was interestingly prompted by his supposition that it would be impossible to practice Islam among polytheists, arguing that the religion of minorities is endangered in a number of ways, including their language.[38]

As Shāfiʿīte adherents, the majority of Indonesian Muslims have by and large adhered to what Shāfiʿī thought about ritual practices, including the significance of Arabic texts which should be used for the performance of worship. Consequently, Arabic has occupied a fundamental place in their religious lives.[39] I am aware translations of written Arabic books into Indonesian and some local languages have been made by Indonesian Muslim scholars and the publication of Islamic books in these languages has been also attempted, which a number of scholars argue implies that religious authority has been split and has not rested solely on *'ulamā'*, but also on writers of books, journals, and newspapers.[40] While numerous scholars have realized that modernization is inescapable as a method to spread Islamic reform, others are determined that there must be a group which solicitously guards the Islamic heritage, including the Arabic texts, in which their Islamic authority lies. They are convinced that modernization cannot be unhesitatingly espoused, but should be balanced by the preservation of the Islamic heritage.[41] Accordingly, they also think that the modernization of Islamic law must be worked out within the boundaries of Islamic legal principles.

Pragmatically, the modernization of Islamic law does not seem to have exerted any considerable influence on Indonesian Muslims, and has failed to generate a coherent intellectual determination to displace traditionalism. Lev has suggested that in the 1970s this was because, besides the modernist scholars who worked on legal modernism, there were those whose writings were not sufficiently provocative to unleash anything approaching a national debate,[42] leaving the way free for the traditionalist party to dominate Islamic politics and gain the upper hand in a difficult coalition with dominant ruling groups.[43] Unfortunately, Muslim modernists have not cooperated with non-Islamically oriented groups in support of family law reforms.[44] Now, even such modernist groups represented by the Muhammadiyah seem so reluctant to deal with contemporary legal discourse that they have become more conservative than their traditionalist counterparts.[45] As indicated in the previous chapter, while the traditionalists wish to maintain *fiqh* texts as the instrument for their method of the deduction of Islamic law, the modernists appear even more reactionary and insist on strict reference to the Qur'ān and *ḥadīth*. A number of religious court judges affiliated with the Muhammadiyah confirmed the necessity of mentioning Qur'ānic verses relevant to the cases brought before them in their judgments.[46]

III.4 For the Sake of Religious Responsibility

The unique position of the Arabic language in the religious courts may not seem so very surprising, and can be logically understood when we recall the religious doctrine which emphasizes that judges in the religious court have a religious responsibility, namely: they are not only responsible for the present life (*dunya*), but also responsible for the Hereafter (*al-akhīra*). They are very much tied by the religious doctrine which states that in deciding legal cases, the judge is standing with one of his legs in the realm of enjoyment (paradise) and the other in the realm of frustration and irritation (hell). Saddled with such a burden, it is understandable that they need to say a special prayer or even meditate and reflect (*bertafakkur*) before they decide the cases before them. Consequently it seems that they feel that, to articulate religious nuances and fulfill their heavy religious responsibility, they need to still quote the Arabic texts from the *fiqh* books.[47]

Interestingly, some judges tend to exaggerate in this regard. Scrutinizing their judgments, I found that they sometimes quoted legal doctrines from the *fiqh* books or texts from the Qur'ān which had no particular relevance to the cases they were handling. Let us take the examples of judgments on the cases of divorce petitioned by wives because the husbands, according to the wives, have committed one of the mistakes which could provide grounds for divorce as enumerated in the agreement of *ta'līq ṭalāq*. Almost all the judges, when they decided to grant the petitions, besides quoting the *kompilasi* and the legal doctrine which states, "Whoever makes his *talak* dependent upon an action, the *talak* is set in motion as soon as the action is accomplished," often also cited the Qur'ānic verse which reads, "Fulfil every engagement, for (every) engagement will be inquired into (on) the Day of Reckoning" (al-Isrā':34).[48] This verse indeed talks about the responsibility of and the obligation upon a party in a contract to discharge his or her agreement. To put it down as a legal consideration in such cases is not particularly relevant. Clearly hampered by the significance of the citation of the legal doctrines from the *fiqh* books, a number of them also often tend to cite an excess of Arabic statements. A number of judgments on the cases of *nafkah* and *mut'a* litigations are among those revealing this. In the judgments in which the judges agreed to the petitions of wives, for example, they quote more than three legal statements from three different *fiqh* books, namely: from al-Bājūrī's *Ḥāshiya Kifāyat al-Akhyār,* Vol. 3, 203 which says that "a woman divorced with *rujuk* has a right to a settlement, financial support during the *iddah*, and clothes;"[49] from Nawāwī's *Minhāj al-Ṭālibīn,* 116: "And the (amount of) the financial support for the divorced woman is decided according to that given during marriage;"[50] and from Dimsaqī's *Kifāyat al-Akhyār,* Vol. 2, 132 which reads, "A divorced woman has a right to financial support according to the *ijmā'*."[51] Simply to provide a religious character, judges often quote the same Arabic texts for totally contradictory judgments. When they permit and or refuse to give permission to husbands (as the petitioners) to enter into a polygynous marriage, they quote the same Qur'ānic text: "And marry good women, two, three, or four, but if you are fearful of being unjust marry only one," without placing an emphasis on which part of the text is taken as legal consideration or giving any further interpretation. Interestingly, sometimes a legal principle is added which states *dar'u al-mafāsid muqaddamun 'alā jalb al-maṣāliḥ* (avoiding deficiency must be prioritized over bringing advantages), so as to show that giving the petitioner permission to enter into a polygynous marriage is more beneficial and appropriate than allowing them (the petitioner and the prospective wife) to indulge in forbidden sexual intercourse (*zinā*).

IV In the Name of *Ijtihād*

IV.1 Insufficiency of the Kompilasi

There is a deep-seated idea prevailing among judges in the religious courts that performing *ijtihād* is an obligation upon them. This belief has also contributed to the central position of the *fiqh* texts. In this respect, they see the *kompilasi* to be deficient, as it has not ruled on all Muslim familial issues. In solving cases for which the *kompilasi* has not set the rules, judges accordingly should look at other references to find some grounds on which they can base their judgments. In their opinion, the *fiqh* books are still the best reference because of their sheer comprehensiveness in dealing with Muslim familial issues.[52] The chairman of the court of Bogor, Jaenuddin, said:

> *Kitab kuning* (*fiqh* books) are more advanced than the *kompilasi* itself. There are some views held by '*ulamā*' which can solve contemporary problems. It is true that the *kompilasi* has just been recently composed (a few years ago), while the traditional *fiqh* books were composed hundreds of years ago; but, the traditional *fiqh* books are more oriented towards the future than the *kompilasi* itself. In fact, we often find the rules for a contemporary problem in the *fiqh* books and not in the *kompilasi*.

In several cases judges admitted they needed to clarify the provisions of the *kompilasi*. Some judges find the *kompilasi* is not very clear about the correct ruling on certain cases, such as that on *verstek*, which regulates that should the defendant not attend court even though he or she had been formally summoned to do so (subpoenaed), he or she forfeits their rights in the case, and the claim or petition of the plaintiff can be granted. The judges agree with such a provision. The crux of the problem is that the provision does not clearly explain how the petition can be accomplished. In this case, judges believe they should resort to *fiqh* books to find an explanation. A number of *fiqh* books deal with the issue and state that the case can be solved by evidence (*bayyina*) produced or shown by the plaintiff; "... and the pronouncement of justice on a person absent in the court on account of his or her laxness is acceptable if the claimant has enough evidence to support his or her claim" (Ibn Hajar's *Tuḥfah al-Muhtāj*, Vol. 10, 164), or "... whoever is summoned to come to court but does not respond is considered prejudiced and has no right to it (to be heard)" (*'Ulūm al-Qur'ān*, 405).[53] They cite these legal doctrines in order to enlighten the litigants, particularly the plaintiff. One judge argued that the necessity for publicly citing the opinions of *'ulamā'* is also because an incident of *verstek* in the religious courts is not to be considered full or pure *verstek*. What he meant is that the case of *verstek* remains to be supported by evidence. The *kompilasi* does not deal clearly with this matter.[54]

IV.2 Supplementary Ijtihād

Their association of the significance of the *fiqh* texts and the resorting to *ijtihād* on the assumption that the *kompilasi* has not dealt with all modern familial issues is indeed logical. What they end up doing in practice leads me to state that the significance of the *fiqh* texts and *ijtihād* does not rest merely on such an assumption. As I have discussed at length, a number of judges still feel that they need to perform *ijtihād* in cases in which, they sense, the *kompilasi* has set unclear rules or in which the rules of the *kompilasi* for certain conditions would not be beneficial if followed. For example, they think that the rule for divorce on the grounds of *riddah* committed by one member of the couple is not complete. Meanwhile, I would say that if on that certain issue the *kompilasi* is understood comprehensively, he or she will see that it does give a clear ruling. Therefore, I think that their supposition that the *kompilasi* is deficient in this respect can be attributed to their preference to adherence to the *fiqh* doctrine and, as in some issues the *kompilasi* goes beyond *fiqh*, they feel a need to correct it by resorting to *ijtihād*. One judge stated that, having been equipped with a uniform legal reference, judges should not be reluctant to perform and/or be prevented from performing *ijtihād*. "The *kompilasi* is a standard source for all the judges, but when judges want to refer to other sources as they find that the *kompilasi* is silent about the issue facing them, this is permissible." He cites the issue of polygyny as one of areas in which the *kompilasi* still falls short. While he knew that being hypersexual is not mentioned as a reason for entering into polygyny, he maintained that judges could give a man permission for such a marriage only because he is hypersexual. As the *kompilasi* did not say anything about the issue of a hypersexual man, this is an indication that judges can develop new rules on the issue on the basis of the public good, he argued.[55]

Nevertheless, we need to see if he gave a correct example to support his claim that the *kompilasi* is insufficient. Polygyny has been exhaustively treated in the *kompilasi*. It mentions reasons and requirements for which the request to enter into a polygynous marriage can be met. It indeed did not categorize the hypersexuality of a husband as a reason, therefore it can be assumed that it would withhold consent from someone wanting to enter into a polygynous marriage on the grounds of such a condition and should not be seen to be silent on the issue. Thinking the way the judges does seems to indicate that the exercise of *ijtihād* is always essential in order to meet contemporary human needs. Assuming the truth of the argument, that *ijtihād* is legally allowed, the judge recalled a*ḥadīth* which implies that judges earn their fee even if they are mistaken in their reasoning on *ijtihād*. He also said that the products of their *ijtihād* automatically become positive law and are not open to debate. He bases this claim on a legal principle: "The ruling of the judge ends disputes among Muslims." What he said may be true but by giving such an example, it seems that he is proposing arbitrary or free *ijtihād* as he merely prioritizes the needs of a certain group, males, and ignores those of another, females. He also seems to want to introduce a new model of *ijtihād*, which can be called supplementary *ijtihād*.

Decisions by judges of the religious court of Cianjur on a case of a polygynous marriage clearly demonstrates that judges sometimes dare to take a controversial decision based of this a kind of *ijtihād*. As has just been mentioned, the *kompilasi* enumerates the reasons and conditions under which a man can enter into a polygynous marriage. The judges of Cianjur, however, once gave a man permission to enter such a marriage on grounds not mentioned in the *kompilasi*, namely that he was asked by a woman or his would-be second wife to protect her and her wealth. The woman was a rich widow and had no relatives whom she could ask for help when needed. She then grew close to the man who lately had happened to assist her in dealing with variety of her affairs. Fearing that slander (*fitna*) is a pernicious element in society, they decided to legalize the partnership by marriage. Stating as the reason that he would often go and spend much time with the woman when she needed his help, the man came to the court with the woman to ask permission to marry. The first wife, who is still quite young, even younger than her husband's prospective second wife, has given her husband children, and has no physical problems also appeared in court and stated her agreement with her husband's intention to marry another woman. Seeing in the man's intention to marry the woman he had the good of the woman at heart, judges decided to acquiesce in the request. Although this reason is not mentioned in either the 1974 Marriage Law or the *kompilasi*, or indeed in the *fiqh* texts, they believed that the practice of *ijtihād* which they claim recommended this course of action has legalized their decision.

While I am not intending to say that what they did reflects a wrong interpretation of the scope of the *ijtihād*, I want to point out that, although the exercise of *ijtihād* is legally permissible, it is essential to be aware that this, particularly in regard with solving cases in a court, has some limitations.[56] In his book *Kedudukan dan Kewenangan Kekuasaan*

Pengadilan Agama, Yahya Harahap describes that judges have some degree of freedom in solving the cases with which they have to deal, but the freedom accorded the judges is bounded by the existing rules:

> A judge is not allowed to create a rule and make it a legal basis for solving a case he or she is hearing... In regard to the right of a judge to interpret law, he or she is not allowed to do so in their own way, exceeding existing rules or Statutes. The interpretation of the law is acceptable only if it employs valid approaches or methodologies... It can therefore employ the legal principle of *maṣlaḥa mursala* on the basis of the argument of the *'ulamā'* that public utility changes and is a continuous process. It is essential that when utilizing this legal principle of *maṣlaḥa mursala* a judge feels that public utility is being served.[57]

In this regard it is relevant to mention that Indonesian Muslim scholars have often argued that *ijtihād* which can be performed at this time is the *ijtihād fī al-madhhab* or *ijtihād muntasib* (the independent legal reasoning based on the legal doctrines of the established schools of Islamic law). *Ijtihād muṭlaq* (absolute independent legal reasoning or based on personal interpretation of the main sources of Islamic law) is no longer considered to be appropriate and is attributed only to the practices of the founders of the schools of Islamic law.[58] Consequently, if the first category of *ijtihād* refers to that in which its practitioner has absolute freedom in deducing laws from the original sources, the second means that its practitioner is bound to follow the principles laid down by the founders of the existing *madhhab,* so that most of the laws deduced will concur with those expressed in the *madhhab* professed.[59]

Indeed, in exercising *ijtihād,* the judges of the religious courts have claimed to have applied the concept of *ijtihād* in *madhhab,* and therefore always refer to the *fiqh* texts in which the opinions of the founders of the Islamic law schools are presented. In doing so, they have admitted they have not adhered strictly to the *fiqh* texts of one certain school, but looked at various *fiqh* texts of all the schools of Islamic law, but particularly Sunnīte ones, in order to find the opinion most appropriate to the case they have to resolve. Therefore, when they find that the *kompilasi* is not clear about the legal status of some cases brought before them or do not agree with the rules of the *kompilasi,* they have turned their attention to the *fiqh* books or Arabic texts. Nonetheless, it is also observed that when there is no law referring to certain cases, as already mentioned, or that the *kompilasi* has indicated its law implicitly, they often adduce an extra or supplementary interpretation according to their personal insights by employing principles borrowed from the *uṣūl fiqh* books. By exercising this way of finding the proper legal ruling, they consider themselves to be exercising *ijtihād*. They interpret the word *ijtihād* in such a case as exploring the energies to discover the relevant legal status of the cases in sources of Islamic law other than in the formally given source provided, namely, the *kompilasi,* and to find a new and more appropriate law than that implied in the laws provided to meet the contemporary needs of the seekers of justice. It is because of the exercising of this sort of *ijtihād* that the *fiqh* books or Arabic texts are still central in the judicial practice in the religious courts.

VI Judges, 'Ulamā', and the State: Legal Practices of Society

The fact that, despite the very existence of the *kompilasi*, the *fiqh* texts remain central to the judicial practice of judges in Indonesian religious courts seems to constitute a reflection of the ambivalence of Indonesian Muslims about accepting the results of the institutionalization of Islamic law initiated by the State. On the one hand, they believe that Islamic law is a sacred law whose domain is beyond State control, and consider the authority of the *'ulamā'* on the interpretation of Islamic law to be exclusive. The *'ulamā'* are regarded as the guardians of Islamic law, the people by whom actual Islamic legal cases facing the society should be solved. On the other hand, they are aware that the role of the State in the arrangement of legal relations among its citizens cannot be ignored, and thereby its intervention in relevant matters is needed. In this context, the institutionalization of the Islamic law within the framework of the national legal system is frequently perceived to be a necessity.

This chapter is an investigation into the complicated relations between judges, *'ulamā'*, and the State. It begins with a description of the position of the judges in the eyes of Indonesian Muslims, especially in their relationship to the presence of the traditional religious authority, the *'ulamā'*. It then proceeds to show how the Muslim community to some extent still relies on *'ulamā'* to solve its legal familial problems arising from marriage, divorce, and inheritance. It will also address how their perceptions and acceptance of the *kompilasi* affect the judicial practices among judges in the religious courts.

I Judges and their Position in Society

Unlike the traditional religious authority, judges for the religious courts are appointed by the State as officials charged with a specific duty, namely to hear and judge Islamic legal cases which occur among Indonesian Muslims, particularly in the fields of marriage, inheritance, and *waqf*. They are better conceptualized as agents of the State, which has bestowed its authority on them, giving them the responsibility to undertake religious tasks. In contrast to the *'ulamā'*, who enjoy widespread acceptance in society and are considered the absolute guardians of the *sharī'a*, judges in the religious courts occupy an ambiguous position; they are forced to play a double role, as State officials in their relationship to the State and *'ulamā'* in the eyes of the people. Herein lies a dilemma; as State officials they have to follow the rules implemented by the State, but as *'ulamā'* they have to follow the *sharī'a* and consequently be fluent in quoting the *kitab kuning* and interpreting the Qur'ān and the *Sunna* if they are to be accepted as respected religious authorities. This task is more difficult if the local *'ulamā'* are personalities who are regarded as competent in the Islamic *sharī'a* after proving this to society. In comparison, the judges are State-appointed employees with qualifications approved by the State and are often persons who are strangers in certain local societies.

During the early years of Independence, the dilemma which dichotomized *'ulamā'* and judges in the religious courts still lay concealed, as judges in the religious courts at that time were, as in the colonial period, recruited from among the local *'ulamā'* who were considered to have the knowledge and capacity to define Islamic law and settle disputes. Generally speaking, they were informally trained in the traditional Islamic schools (*pesantren* and *madrasah*), equivalent to senior high school, in which they studied with some leading *'ulamā'*.[1] In the 1980s, particularly after the promulgation of the Islamic Judicature Act in 1989, the dilemma clearly emerged, as all judges in the religious courts are now without exception to be recruited from among university graduates. They are no longer required to have the background of a specific Islamic education or an association with leading local *'ulamā'*.

When we examine the educational background of judges in the religious courts, we nevertheless will find that their association with *pesantren* remains strong. Most students in the Sharī'a faculty of IAINs have a background as *pesantren* or at least *madrasah* graduates. It is no exaggeration to say that the Sharī'a faculties or IAINs in general are often considered to be a continuation of *pesantren* or *madrasah* at a higher level. Therefore, though not directly recruited from the *pesantren* but from the IAIN and other educational institutions, judges in the religious courts generally have a certain linkage with *pesantren* and come from traditional religious backgrounds. Moreover, as has been mentioned before, the Ministry of Religious Affairs itself demands the ability to read and comprehend *fiqh* or Arabic texts, with passing a reading test being one of the requirements to become a judge.

In fact, most of the judges in the religious courts I interviewed graduated from the faculty of Islamic law at IAINs. Before studying at IAIN, most had been enrolled in *pesantren*. Even though studying at university, a number of them had continued their studies in *pesantren*. One of the judges in the religious court of Bogor admitted that while studying in the faculty of Islamic law in one of the private Islamic universities in Bogor, he broadened his knowledge of Islamic law in a famous *pesantren* in the same city.[2] It should be noted, however, that some of the judges graduated from the faculty of civil law in public universities. They also have the insights into Islamic law and other religious subjects as if they had also studied in *pesantren*. But in terms of their comprehension of Arabic texts, this cannot conceal the fact that a few judges do not have thorough comprehension of Arabic texts. One such example is a judge in the court of Cianjur; he graduated from the faculty of civil law in a university in Bandung and admitted he was not able to read and comprehend Arabic texts. Nevertheless, although it is emphasized that they administer State law, the judges' very backgrounds often prompt them to present themselves as guardians and supervisors of social life and the *sharī'a*. Accordingly, this shapes the actual content of the judgments reached.

In line with the circular letter of the Supreme Court, stressing that judges in the religious courts should continue to pursue their legal education, some judges, particularly those holding degrees from the faculty of Islamic law, are continuing their legal education in the faculty of national law in a number of mostly private universities. Both the chairman of the religious court of Rangkasbitung and his vice are registered as students in the faculty of law of a private university in Jakarta. Their aim in enrolling for further education in the field of law is to broaden their knowledge of legal procedure, which will give them more confidence in their professional relationship with judges of other courts, lawyers, and Government officials. It has the added advantage that, when they have higher degrees in law, promotion to higher positions is easier for them.[3]

Most judges have no local ties with the society in which they work. Only some of them have a close relationship with the local people. Importantly, many of them are involved in such social activities as being *imām* or *khaṭīb* of Friday prayer. Since they undertake these activities in their home communities and not where they work as judges, this does not create an intimate bond with the local society.[4]

The lack of social interaction between judges and the local society is basically linked to several factors. Firstly, the applicants selected to be judges are not evenly spread over all the regions of Indonesia. It often happens that applicants from one region tend to preponderate. This can stem from the fact that those from one region are more qualified to be selected as judges than those from others. Accordingly, the judges selected are sent to regions from which no or fewer applicants have been drawn.[5]

Secondly, so that judges may develop their careers and to avoid too close an interaction between judges and the society in which they work, which might lead to personal relationships which are assumed might have a possible affect on and prejudice judicial freedom and the administration of justice in society, a schedule handling the transfer of officials and judges is arranged. It is not regulated in any law, but the practice of mutation has become recognized by convention. It is recommended and regulated that a judge be employed in one particular religious court for five years only, after which he or she should be transferred to another court.[6] The circulation of judges from one court to another is therefore a usual occurrence in the Indonesian Islamic judicial institution. The purpose of these two circumstances, that is, the placement of judges not drawn from the local region in which the court is situated and their mutation, seems to be designed to promote unity in legal practice from a national point of view, and simultaneously to exclude infiltration by local custom as much as possible.

Thirdly, some judges appointed to one religious court do not settle down and make their homes in the region where they work. The examples of the chairmen of the religious courts of Cianjur and Rangkasbitung, and some of their judges prove this. Not provided with appropriate housing, these two chairmen were unable to establish their social position in the local community, as they had to leave every week to visit their families in other cities. When I came back to the court of Rangkasbitung for the third time, I discovered that the director and his deputy had been moved to other courts and their successors had been working there for four months. While the new director had brought his family to live in Rangkasbitung, the deputy who said that he might be moved again to another region at the middle of the year 2005 had decided to have his family stay in Subang which he visited every weekend. This is a big problem for many judges, as for their livelihood they rely greatly on their salary as State officials. Whereas privately they are not well enough off to improve their lives, the Government pays them a relatively small amount in salary and has not provided them with appropriate housing.

II Legal Awareness in Society and the Judges' Judicial Attitudes

The promulgation of the 1989 Islamic Judicature Act and the issuing of the *kompilasi* indicated that a number of aspects of Islamic law, including marriage, divorce, and inheritance, have been accepted and regulated as part of the national legal system. Under the 1989 Islamic Judicature Act, Indonesian Muslims faced with such familial problems should address themselves to religious courts, where the problems will be adjudicated and solved according to Islamic laws interpreted by the State or by State laws. However, while the laws have attempted to come up with substantive rules with a built-in compromise and with the requisite organs of State to be involved in implementing them, several aspects have created ambivalence among Indonesian Muslims, which has shaped judicial practice among judges in the religious courts.

II.1 Getting Divorced Outside the Court

The ambivalence of Indonesian Muslims towards the outcome of the institutionalization of Islamic law by the State can be seen first and foremost in the issue of divorce. The *kompilasi* establishes that a couple who wants to get divorced should go to the court to ask permission to pronounce the divorce formula, or to ask the court to dissolve (*faskh*) their marriages, or to initiate a *khul'* divorce for which the financial compensation is to be paid by the wife to the husband. In reality, many people who want to get divorced summon only a religious leader or one of their relatives to witness their pronouncements of the divorce formula. Some even simply write letters to or shout at their wives, stating that from that time on they are repudiated.[7] Having spoken the formula, many go to the Offices of Religious Affairs at the sub-district level (*Kantor Urusan Agama* or KUA), which since 1974 has been no longer competent to legalize their divorces.

Indeed, before the issuing of the Marriage Law in 1974, divorces could be petitioned at KUA. Beginning in late 1954, couples wishing to divorce had to go to the *Badan Penasihat Perkawinan, Perselisihan, dan Perceraian* (the Advisory Board for Marriage, Disputes, and Divorce, BP4) for counseling before they went to KUA. With the approval of the members of the board, which appeared in the form of *Naskah Penasihat* (Advisor's Note), they then went to KUA to finalize their divorces.[8] After the head of a KUA gave approval, the petition for divorce was accepted. The husband then pronounced the divorce, and the marriage was thereafter dissolved religiously, legally, and administratively. However, as the pronouncement of divorce is an essential legal procedure in the obtaining of a divorce, when a wife wanted to have her marriage dissolved but her husband did not, or was unable to pronounce the formula, she was expected to present the case to a religious court. This gave rise to a great deal of misunderstanding, leading people to think that a wife always had to go to the court to obtain divorce. This was incorrect, as a wife could also go to her local KUA to petition for divorce and her petition could be approved if her husband agreed to divorce her with or without *iwaḍ* (monetary compensation). In short, before the Marriage Law was introduced, petitions for divorce were dealt with by KUA and only in some cases had to be brought before the religious courts.

Since 1974, all petitions for divorce are required by law to be brought to the religious court, and the local KUA receive reports of or documents pertaining to divorce from the religious court. The 1989 Islamic Judicature Act and the *kompilasi* elaborated on the rule by providing some more details about the procedure for divorce. A plaintiff has to write his or her claim and submit it to the court. The case is heard in the court within thirty days at most after it has been registered. The court hearing consists of three sittings, each with a different aim. The first sitting attempts to arrange a reconciliation between the couple and requires them to be counseled by the *Badan Penasihat Perkawinan, Perselisihan dan Perceraian* (Advisory Board for Marriage, Disputes, and Divorce Settlements, BP4). Presently, no questions are asked about whether or not couples have attended BP4. Therefore, while counseling is still recommended, the advisory note issued by the BP4, which formerly had to be brought to court, is no longer required. This is because, besides also having a role in attempting to reconcile the litigants, religious court judges must work independently from intervention by other parties or institutions.[9] The second session discusses the result of the efforts at reconciliation. If the petition for divorce is not retracted, the third hearing is arranged to complete the arrangements for divorce.

Ironically, in spite of the rule, Indonesian Muslims who live in rural areas, as mentioned above, still tend to follow their own road in seeking a divorce. In general, for many people in the villages in the countryside, going to the court to obtain a divorce is more a burden than a necessity. Indeed, some villages in Cianjur province, for instance, have limited access to the town of Cianjur. Therefore to go to the religious court located in the regency capital, an unfamiliar environment for some rural people, they would have to spend large amounts of time and money, as they sometimes have to walk to reach the main road where normal public transportation like a bus is provided, and then take particular public transport, such as an '*ojeg*' (hired motorcycle).[10] To make matters worse, the hearing is conducted not in one session but in three, for each of which they would be required to spend more time and money. Moreover, because the hearing requires witnesses, they have to bring witnesses whose transportation costs must also be covered by the litigants.[11]

Initially it is to be expected that such procedures might prevent people from divorcing. Instead, the difficulties of procuring a divorce in the courts have encouraged some of them to avoid courts and conclude a divorce in a way they regard as religiously lawful (*sāḥiḥ*).[12] Presenting their cases to the *'ulamā'* who maintain that, according to Islamic law, the pronouncement of divorce by the husband is the essential legal element to effectuate a divorce and therefore are prepared to approve the divorce, is one of the best options. Above all, local norms are thought to have a bearing on ignoring the rules laid down by the State by some people, and also on the preservation of the legal doctrine produced by earlier legal scholars. In most regions of West Java, such as Cianjur and Rangkasbitung, the practice of returning seriously ill wives to their families is common. The basic reason for this is to help wives in achieving a speedy recovery, but often husbands do not take the wives back when their health improves. Instead, they come in person or send letters to pronounce a divorce. The tendency of the local norms to be on the side of the classical doctrine of divorce can also be seen in the practice of what is known as *pegat sentak* (suddenly broken marriage), a form of divorce resulting from serious problems. This way of procuring a divorce is considered lawful by the society and does not have to be heard before a court, especially not if the village in which those seeking the divorce live is far away from that court.[13]

It is no surprise that in Cianjur, for instance, divorce cases brought to the religious court number only around thirty to forty a month. This has to do with the intervention of KUA in the judicial tasks of the religious court. The deputy-director of the court in this town said that KUA officials often told the disputants that the costs of the hearing in the religious court were exorbitant. These officials then suggest that to resolve their legal problems, the disputants should resort to KUA. Ironically, for their efforts in solving the case, they sometimes demand costs higher than those determined by the court. They are particularly prone to this if one of the disputants is a woman worker (*Tenaga Kerja Wanita*, TKW) who has just returned from an Arab country. Assuming that they have managed to save a large amount of money and thereby can afford to pay the high costs demanded, KUA officials have not been slow in requesting high prices from their clients. Lacking in legal knowledge and sometimes anxious to avoid the complicated procedures in the religious courts, the disputants are often happy just to follow what KUA officials have suggested.[14]

The intervention of KUA officials in the judicial tasks of the religious courts is also relatively common in Rangkasbitung. The chairman of the religious Court of Rangkasbitung said that if KUA officials had not assumed the duty of the judges, more cases would have been registered at the religious court. He was convinced that the frequency of divorce is far higher than is indicated by those registered in the court. Accordingly, the religious court of Rangkasbitung often had no hearing in a day, since the divorce cases brought before the court, as the chairman told me, amount to only thirteen or even just eleven a month. If we look at the statistical data issued by the Ministry of Religious Affairs, there is proof that what the Director said is true. The statistics record that in the year 2000, for example, the court received only 160 divorce petitions initiated by both the wife (126) and the husband (34). From this number of divorce cases, we can conclude that the average number of the divorce cases it received per month in that year was twelve cases.

Table 6.1 *Divorce Cases Registered in the Court of Rangkasbitung in 2000*

Category	*Amount*	*Estimated rate per month*
Women's petitions	126	10 to 11
Men's petitions	34	3
Total	160	13 to 14

Source: Statistical data recorded by the Ministry of Religious Affairs, 2002

The statistical data for 2004 recorded that this court received more or less the same number of divorce cases, namely 142 cases, initiated both by wife (99) and husband (43).

A slightly different picture is found in the religious courts in Jakarta. The religious court of South Jakarta, for instance, hears more than fifteen divorce cases a day. This number is dealt with only in one court session. Meanwhile, there are sometimes two sessions in one day. I attended two sessions of divorce hearings in the religious court of South Jakarta. The session I first attended heard eighteen cases of divorce. The hearings began at 9:30 in the morning. Two of the cases had reached the final stage of the process and were decided, while some were just at the first stage and others were in the process of discussing whether or not reconciliation could be possible. If we compare what I witnessed in 2002 with the statistical data from 2000, it is obvious that the court of South Jakarta is one of the busiest courts in Indonesia. It is recorded that in that year the court heard 1375 divorce cases initiated either by wives, 935, or husbands, 440. From this number we can reckon that the court received 114 divorce cases per month and that, with sixteen hearing days per month, from Monday to Thursday per week, the court must have heard approximately seven divorce cases per day. Because one case cannot be heard in just one session but is spread over three sessions, the court must hear and judge twice as many cases than the rate per day, or seven cases each day.

Table 6.2 *Divorce Cases Registered in the Religious Court of South Jakarta in 2000*

Category	*Amount*	*Estimated Rate Per Month*
Women's petitions	935	78
Men's petitions	440	36
Total	1375	114

Table 6.3 *The Estimated Rate of Divorce Cases Tried Per Day*

Monthly rate of registered divorces	114
Working days per month	16
Daily rate of trial on initial cases + Cases of ongoing proceedings	7 plus*

*As has been stated above the rate can be twice as high.
Source: Source: Ministry of Religious Affairs, *Himpunan Data Statistik Perkara Di Lingkungan Peradilan Agama Seluruh Indonesia Tahun 2000,* Ditbinbapera, 2002.

Looking at the intervention of KUA, it should be noted here that KUA is a government institution, placed at the intermediary level between *'ulamā'* and the religious courts. The personnel of every KUA consists of a head, deputy-head, one or two assistants, all of whom serve as marriage registrars (*Pegawai Pencatat Nikah*, PPN), and administrative staff. Under the division of PPN, a number of assistant marriage registrars (*Pembantu Pegawai Pencatat Nikah,* P3N) have been appointed to help the former (PPN) deal with marriage issues. In carrying out this duty, KUA officials often co-operate with *'ulamā'* and tend to consider themselves more as guardians of the *sharī'a* or *'ulamā'* than as State officials, and hence differentiate sharply between the *sharī'a* and the Islamic law interpreted by the State. But while the effect of this tendency does not show up so strongly in the areas of Jakarta, outside Jakarta it is clearly marked. What two officials of the KUA at Warung Gunung, Rangkasbitung, described clearly supports this assumption. Although they will not handle and legalize divorce proceedings directly, the officials of this KUA often legally permit the sanctioning of divorces concluded outside the court. They do this by registering marriages of couples who claim that they have been divorced but are unable to show divorce certificates. This fact demonstrates that they tend to see the judicial process of divorce as merely a State and an administrative affair. Note the opinions in the following statement by one of them:

> Because we know that according to Islamic law divorce is considered to be effective when a husband utters the formula of divorce, we cannot refuse to remarry a couple one or both of whom have admitted to having been divorced, although they could not show us certificates of their divorces. Often we have asked them first to go to a religious court to arrange the divorce, but they hardly comprehend what we ask. Instead, they came again another time, still without certificates of divorce and insisted that we marry them and admitted that they had lived together for months. We, as

> Muslims who do not like to see adultery (*perzinahan*) committed, had no choice but to marry them.[15]

Another KUA official said, "We were often considered arrogant if we refused to register their marriage. We know the people here well and find it difficult to be very strict in applying the law."[16]

What these two officials stated is relevant to the admission of a woman originally from Bandung, who divorced her husband informally but remarried formally. She recounted that several years ago, she married a man in one of the KUA in Bandung, but divorced after only three years of marriage. She then moved to Rangkasbitung and found a new (unmarried) man to marry. With the man she went to the KUA in Warung Gunung to request its officials to marry them. Having admitted that she was a divorcée, she was required to present the certificate of divorce. Because she divorced informally, she could not comply with the request but told the officials that she would live together with the man even though they would not marry them (or, in her words, commit *kumpul kebo*, living together out of wedlock). When they heard this threat, the officials, she told me, married them and registered their marriage. Instead of the certificate of divorce, she was asked to present a letter of declaration from the village head stating that she was a widow (*janda*).[17]

Several other factors must also have contributed to the attitude of KUA officials in dealing with such matters. The majority of KUA officials, particularly outside Jakarta, are graduates of senior or even just junior high schools. Only a few have graduated from universities.[18] With such a limited educational background, they are supposed to be less independent and tend to follow the *'ulamā'* in their interpretation of Islamic law. Moreover, KUA officials themselves are inclined to attempt to hold onto their previous position in which they were given an extensive authority to handle divorce cases. Some retired KUA officials, who once enjoyed extensive power in handling divorce cases, often still feel they are competent to involve themselves in them. This conviction is intensified by the fact that many rural people do not know that this authority has been removed from them. Importantly, a local KUA has increasing contact with society in its area as most of its officials, particularly those serving as *Pembantu Pegawai Pencatat Nikah* (P3N), are recruited from among the local religious leaders or *'ulamā'* (*tokoh desa* or *tokoh agama*). Above all, this institution is established in every district (*kecamatan*), and consequently its officials are firmly rooted in local society. This fact, which enables KUA officials to gain a deeper insight into the marital problems faced by society, also prompts certain officials to be more realistic and urge that the authority for solving divorce cases be returned to the KUA. One director at one of the KUA surveyed stated frankly that if the authority to solve divorce cases is returned to KUAs, unregistered or informal practices of divorce will drop, if not be eliminated completely.

The fewer number of cases registered at religious courts in rural areas, particularly Rangkasbitung and Cianjur, is also associated with the fact that it is not only KUA officials who intervene in solving cases of divorce. Local *'ulamā'*also feel they have the right to do so. They support the handling of divorce cases by KUAs, and often handle the cases themselves. The judges of the court of Rangkasbitung claim that, broadly speaking, the *'ulamā'* in Banten are still conservative. The fact that the obligation to register both marriage and divorce resonate of the Shi'īte legal school is perceived to be the main reason the *'ulamā'* are reluctant to adopt the rules on such issues laid down in both the Marriage Law and the *kompilasi.* It must be noted that, as has been mentioned above, the phrases 'register it *(faktubūh)'* and 'and call two just persons (to witness) *washhidū dhawai 'adlin)'* in the Qur'ānic verses expounding on the issue of the registration of marriage and divorce are not regarded as imperative and therefore do not lead to any form of compulsion in the Sunnite schools of Islamic law; it is only the Shi'īte who interpret them as compulsory. "If adopting the legal opinions put forward by Sunni schools of Islamic law other than the Shāfi'īte is already hard, following the legal opinions of the Shi'īte school would be almost impossible for them," commented one of judges at the court of Rangkasbitung.[19] For many *'ulamā'* in this region, divorce is an absolute right of husbands which is beyond the reach of judicial affairs. It does not have to be dealt with in KUA or in the religious court.

It seems particularly intriguing to note that, in Rangkasbitung in particular, the attempts of the religious court to solve familial problems among Muslim people are also frequently confronted with obstacles placed in its way by a group of persons called *jawara* or warriors, [20] who have sought to intervene in cases dealt with by the court. They often collaborate with such local leaders as *kepala-kepala desa* (village leaders). Alternatively the village leaders themselves are *jawara* or ex-*jawara*. There are many cases in which a *jawara* is bribed or asked by a party to help him to divorce or not divorce. As a result, the other party is forced to comply with the orders of the *jawara* and his allies. Any disobedience on their part might encourage the *jawara* to harm him or her. In some cases, the *jawara* have dared to come to court and create a disturbance, or even go so far as to put the officials or judges of the court in danger. The vice-chairman of the court of Rangkasbitung said that a *jawara*, who is also a village leader, once appeared in the court and approached the clerk shouting at him not to proceed with a divorce case brought by one of his people, and threatened to harm him should he do so.[22] He also said that he would handle the case instead as he felt that he, as village leader, had the right to do so. Other judges also recalled that a *jawara* bribed by a man whose wife petitioned the court for a divorce had once come to one of them demanding he not grant the wife's petition for a divorce.[23] A plaintiff in one of cases whose hearing I attended used a *jawara* as a witness. In contrast to an ordinary witness, the *jawara* witness looked more aggressive and tried to involve himself in deciding the case. Because of the likelihood of such a problem, many who want to put their familial problems in order in court must bear such consequences in mind.

These are the particular instances which prompt judges of the court of Rangkasbitung to say that Rangkasbitung constitutes a unique region. Both the chairman and the vice-chairman, who have worked in the court of Rangkasbitung before, have also served as judges in other parts of West Java, Subang and Indramayu, and they could see a clear difference in the legal awareness levels between the former and the latter regions. They feel that this has something to do with the fact that in Indramayu and Subang, Islam is not as so strong as it is in Rangkasbitung.[24]

II.2 Seeking State Legalization

Accepting the intervention of KUA and *'ulamā'* and the established belief that a husband has unlimited power in the matter of divorce, divorce cases brought to the religious courts have different natures. Besides petitions purely and simply for divorce, the court of Rangkasbitung heard cases that had already been heard by KUA and local *'ulamā'*, and were considered to have been settled between the couple themselves. The litigants in these cases came to the court merely for the sake of obtaining letters or certificates of divorce. They usually told judges that they had been divorced before KUA officials or before local *'ulamā'*, and that they had come to the court in order to obtain *kartu kuning*, meaning a yellow certificate, that is, certificate of divorce (*akte cerai*).[25] One of the judges of the religious court in Rangkasbitung even recalled that a woman once came to him saying that she had been divorced by her husband. She showed him a small cigarette paper, on which there was a statement written by her husband that since a certain (mentioned) date she was no longer his wife. She said that, as she considered herself a divorced wife, she had come to the court merely to obtain a certificate of divorce.

> You see how people in this region still believe that divorce is effected when a husband utters the formula of divorce, wherever and whenever he wishes and the wife accepts it. They come here just to confirm the divorce. They do not see divorce as a matter which needs to be heard here (in court). We are apparently con-

> sidered administrative staff that deal only with papers and are sought after they have realized that they need us.[26]

Similar situations occur in Cianjur. Frequently wives come to the religious court to claim divorce from their husbands, but interestingly they often admit that their husbands had actually divorced them either before KUA officials or local *'ulamā'*.

Some couples knew that what they followed in the local KUA was not acceptable as a formal divorce procedure, but for the sake of simplicity they decided to acquiesce in that decision. Some others did not realize anything was amiss. In both cases the role of KUA officials is highly significant. In a number of cases, they issued the litigants with certificates of divorce, which were technically speaking forgeries.[27] For those who were aware that it was essentially against the law of the State, the certificates issued by the KUA officials, which they knew to be invalid, could be a help to them in arranging their affairs, even though they knew what the consequences would be should the nature of the certificate be identified by the relevant officials. For those ignorant of this, the certificates were sufficient to convince them that the procedure they had followed was the right one. I was told that the court of Cianjur had heard two cases of divorce handled by the regional KUA in which the litigants had been issued with certificates. The cases came to light when the holders of the fraudulent certificates wanted to remarry and went to another KUA in Cianjur for this purpose. They claimed they were widows, showing their certificate of divorce to one of its officials. This official who was not happy about the authenticity of the certificates came to the court of Cianjur to confirm this. After they had been carefully checked, it was confirmed that the registration numbers on the certificates were not recorded in the court.[28]

Among these people, the reasons for registering their divorces or possessing the certificates of divorce varied. One was to fulfill the requirement for entering into a new marriage with another man or woman. A divorced man could (still) actually marry a woman before the *'ulamā'* without having to have valid evidence of divorce from his former (first) wife, as described in more detail below. Sometimes the new (prospective) wife whom he wants to marry demands that a formal and or legal marriage be concluded in front of the registrars, for which a certificate of divorce is needed. The marriage and remarriage stories of one of my respondents illustrate this. He said that he married his first wife informally and, after seven years of marriage, a serious dispute erupted between him and his wife. He then left his wife, stating that he had divorced her, and since that time he had had a love relationship with a widow. Feeling that they were compatible, they managed to get married, but the widow, who had been married before, demanded that they marry officially. Although his marriage to his former wife was not officially registered and hence he could state before the registrar that he was an unmarried man, he could not do so, as his identity card revealed that he was married. Above all, his prospective wife and her family did not agree.[29] The only road open to him was first to register his divorce in the court, which would issue him with a certificate of divorce, and then he could be married officially. For a divorced wife, the certificate is also needed for the same purpose if, in the future, she finds another man to marry after her *iddah* (waiting period) has lapsed.

Some couples come to the courts because they are afraid that should they pass away, their spouses, whom they said had been divorced, might claim a share in their estate; and they wondered if their claims might be granted in the courts in the absence of the valid evidence of divorce.

II.3 Dilemma Faced by Judges

Facing such divorce cases, judges in the religious courts are usually in a dilemma; should they annul the divorce and then re-issue it, or admit it and then grant what is demanded? Several judges who are determined to apply the State law strictly tend to decide such cases by adhering to the regulated divorce procedures and considering the informal divorces had not occurred, particularly in cases brought to the courts during recent years, although husbands convincingly stated that they had divorced their wives. When they see an instance in which a wife still questions the reason she was divorced, or in which she does not realize that her husband had actually divorced her, the judges always rehear the case. Judges do the same in a case in which a husband who was understood by his wife to have divorced her denies that he did so. After assuring the facts of the case, they ask the husband to pronounce the divorce formula again or declare that the wife's petition is granted, and affirm that the divorce will be absolute after the husband's pronouncement of the divorce in court, or after the decision has been given executorial force. One case, whose hearing in the religious court of Rangkasbitung I attended, clarifies this. A husband (DM) petitioned for divorce and admitted to having divorced his wife and even to have married another woman. The wife (SH) rejected this and said that she did not want to be divorced, and preferred to share him with the (second) woman. The judges explained to them that the husband had now entered into a polygynous marriage, to which the wife has agreed, but the husband has not. While the husband kept saying that he came to the court merely to formalize the divorce, the judges required them to reconsider what they had done and reconcile and come to the court again the coming week. Although adopting such a position, these judges often do not care whether or not the litigants adhere to their decisions in terms of their consequences in relation to other legal matters.[30]

In other cases, judges decide differently. Considering that, if they annul the divorce, there will be inevitable consequences such as in the matter of *iddah*, they tend to accept the case and grant the litigants the certificate of divorce, stating that the divorce had occurred on the date on which the husband uttered the formula. In these cases, judges do not consider the declaration of divorce in the courts to affect the divorce, but simply register it. Such cases happen particularly when husbands, asked by judges whether or not they, when pronouncing the formula, really intend to divorce their wives, admit that they mean it, and when their wives accept their husbands' clarification.

From the investigation of the character of divorces registered in the courts of both Cianjur and Rangkasbitung, several points have emerged. First is that the decision of some judges to admit the occurrence of a divorce out of court and legalize it by granting the divorce certificate tells us that, although the *kompilasi* is applied for the confirmation (*ithbāt*) of marriage, a divorce which is concluded out of the court can be proposed in the court for its legal confirmation. Second, it seems interesting that, while one of the religious courts in Malaysia assigns registration of divorce as one category of cases registered in the court, Indonesian religious courts have no statistical records of such cases under the heading of *ithbāt* of divorce.[31] Arguing that no *ithbāt* of divorce is ruled in the law, all the cases are recorded under the general heading of divorce. Finally, debate on the validity of divorce and its consequences often occurs between litigants and judges, a situation which clearly demonstrates the repudiation of the State control over their application of Islamic law by Indonesian Muslims.[32]

The ambiguous position of the judges in the case of divorce might also be linked to the vagueness of the State law itself, reflected in the language or semantics of its articles ruling on the issues concerned. The Marriage Law treats the issue of divorce briefly and obscurely. From the perspective of some Muslims it merely regulates the occurrence of legally significant events rather than introducing new legal meanings. Consequently, a divorce concluded outside court might be illegal but is nonetheless effective. The 1989 Islamic Judicature Act clarified the vague position of the Marriage Law in the case of divorce, and explicitly declared that the procedure for divorce initiated by men requires court authorization. Nevertheless, it also remains vague on the question of whether obedience to its procedures is necessary for the divorce to be valid. The approach taken by the *kompilasi* is clearer, although it does not explicitly suggest that an extra-judicial divorce is invalid, merely stating that a divorce without judicial approval does not have legal force.[33] Despite this, it seems that, as the main agents having authority in its application, judges have not been able to resolve the difference in the interpretation of the divorce rules.

A similar ambiguity in how to deal with cases of divorce can also be found among NU *'ulamā'*, reflected in the *fatwā* issued by this organization in 1989. This *fatwā*, which commences with a list of six standard *fiqh* texts on divorce rules, makes several pronouncements.[34] A declaration which takes place in court is considered the first divorce. If a declaration has occurred outside the court and this is followed by a declaration before the court, the latter counts as the second. However, if the second declaration in the court occurs before the expiry period within which remarriage is not permitted, only one divorce is considered to have taken place. If a litigant comes to the court just to register a divorce which had already taken place, the declaration in court is not taken into consideration. It seems obvious that NU members simply cannot eschew their belief that the *fiqh* texts are the primary foundations on which to solve the cases and that the State rules for divorce merely complement the *fiqh* texts, not replace them. Indeed, from the perspective of argumentation, this *fatwā* reinforces the primary position of the *fiqh* texts in governing the religious legal practices of Indonesian Muslims.[35]

II.4 Unregistered Marriage

The reluctance of some Indonesian Muslims to arrange their religious legal affairs according to the rules laid down in the *kompilasi* is also found in cases of unregistered marriages. The judges in the religious courts of Rangkasbitung and Cianjur suggested that people living in villages in the countryside are ignorant of the existence of the *kompilasi*.[36] For the villagers, finding the money to pay the costs of a marriage before the official registrar is a big problem. Although it is not a large amount of money,[37] a number of villagers simply cannot afford to pay the cost required by KUA, even though they really want to marry.[38] Besides, as they are struggling to make a living, they often do not even consider the necessity of seeking to record marriage legally. They only realize that the legal records are necessary when they have to deal with other legal matters which might crop up in the future.[39] Partly because of these considerations, terms like *kawin kampung, kawin di bawah tangan or kawin siri,* literally meaning 'marriage according to village rules', 'informal marriage' or 'clandestine marriage', in contrast to *kawin negara* or *kawin resmi* (marriage according to the State law or formal marriage), are still often bandied about, indicating that unregistered or informal marriages are still common.

Evidence of the existence of informal marriages is clearly revealed in cases of *ithbāt nikāh* (marriage confirmation) brought to the courts. I was told that the court at Cianjur, where unregistered marriages are believed to be plentiful, had recently confirmed (*mengithbatkan*) a massive 6,000 unregistered marriages. However, it should be noted that this number consisted mostly of marriages concluded before the issuing of the 1974 Marriage Law. It is also recorded that in 2000, the court of Cianjur legally confirmed a significant number of unregistered marriages, namely 104 cases, and three years later registered thirty-one cases. Although this was fewer than the number registered three years before, it is still a significant number compared to those registered in other courts. The pattern was repeated in Cibinong, where in 2000 ninety-seven unregistered marriages were confirmed.

The courts of Jakarta dealt with far fewer instances of unregistered marriages. In 2000, the court of South Jakarta registered seventeen cases and the court of East Jakarta only fifteen cases.[40] It has been generally perceived that people in urban areas are more motivated to seek, and are more aware of having, formal and legitimate evidence of such events than their compatriots in rural areas. Among them, the practice of informal marriages is believed to be quite rare. It must be noted that informal polygynous marriages are not absent in urban areas. In some slum neighborhoods in the urban areas, couples did not marry at the local KUA. For various reasons, such as the difficulty of obtaining the consent of the existing wife or wives, some people preferred to enter into polygynous marriages without consulting KUA. In Cinere, South Jakarta, for instance, a number of influential figures had entered into polygynous marriages which they did not register.[41] Likewise, although since 1993 there have been no polygynous marriages registered in the KUA office at Koja, North Jakarta, a number of polygynous marriages had taken place there. Husbands admitted that they concluded their first marriage before the registration officials, but the second marriages only before the *'ulamā'* of the region.[42] In the penal provisions in the Government Regulation of 1975, concerning the application of the 1974 Marriage Law, it is stated that whoever is found guilty of violating the provisions of marriage and polygyny shall be punished by a fine not exceeding 7,500 *rupiah*s (less than one Euro). Still, with such a small penalty, it was reported that, as they found it difficult to gain the consent of their existing wife or wives and hence to seek judicial permission, many husbands preferred paying 7,500 *rupiah*s to obtaining the consent of the wife, if they are reported to have entered into an illegal polygynous marriage.

In some areas, people are simply not bothered by the unregistered status of their marriages and for this reason, the number of cases cannot be concluded on the basis of the frequency of *ithbāt nikāh* registered in the courts. In Rangkasbitung, for instance, only a few couples come to court to seek legal confirmation of their marriages. In 2000, it confirmed ten unregistered marriages and in 2003 only two. These were believed to constitute only a small percentage of the existing unregistered marriages in this region. The judges in the court of Rangkasbitung were convinced that there have still been many unregistered marriages concluded both before and since the issuing of the 1974 Marriage Law. What the survey team of the physical and social conditions of KUA in rural areas, including Rangkasbitung, found confirms this. It drew the conclusion that, because the money from the activities connected to marriages and reconciliations (NR/*Nikah Rujuk*) coming into the KUA treasury is small, KUA in Rangkasbitung rarely registered marriages and reconciliation activities. Despite this, they believed that marriage activities are high in this region.[43] Pertinently, while they had heard that polygyny is frequently practiced among people, KUA officials of Warung Gunung, Rangkasbitung, almost never registered such marriages. One of its officials said that while he believed that polygynous marriages were widespread in the region where he works, almost no polygynous marriage had been registered in KUA during the two years he had been employed there. Two couples wishing to enter into a polygynous marriage, he said, did come to him, but because they could not show him decisions of religious courts permitting them to conclude the marriage, he did not officially register their marriages, although he decided to marry them. He said to me that at their marriage he functioned not as an official registrar of marriage but as an *'ulamā'*.[44] A judge confirmed this when saying that it seems ironic that while polygynous marriages are commonly practiced among Muslims in his region, almost no case of polygyny or request for permission to enter into such a marriage (*perkara permohonan ijin poligami*) was registered with the court.

The fact that people in some areas, particularly in Rangkasbitung, are not worried by their unregistered marriages and make no attempt to seek official confirmation of their marriages either, and that cases of *ithbāt nikāh* are relatively few, can be traced to a number of factors. Among them are a prevailing tolerance and the entrenchment of bribery or illegal public services provided by certain institutions. Among these, those which arrange such private documents as birth certificates are the most relevant. There is a regulation which states that the certificate of the parents' marriage is required to obtain birth certificates for children, for which purpose, as will be described below, some couples intentionally came to the courts to confirm their informal marriages. Although legally required, certificates of marriage are in some cases often ignored, if those requesting the certificate of birth are familiar with the officials in the civil offices at which the birth certificate is to be issued, or if the former are prepared to pass the latter some "money of understanding" (*uang pengertian*/ bribe).

One of my respondents, a female teacher, admitted to having always helped the parents of her pupils arrange to obtain the birth certificates of their children. She explained that when children are nearly through with primary school education, they are required to submit birth certificates in order to obtain a diploma signifying completion (*Surat Tanda Tamat Belajar*/STTB). The birth certificate had actually been required when they registered at and commenced school for the first time, but this requirement is met only in rare instances and the schools often turn a blind eye to their non-appearance, but do require pupils to submit them at the end of their education. Although given six years to arrange the birth certificate, the pupils in the highest class still did not have them when they were urgently needed. The problem is that their parents could not apply for them, as they did not possess a marriage certificate. Understanding that it might be quite impossible or would take long time for parents to confirm their marriage by obtaining this from the court, she (the teacher) took steps to arrange the making of birth certificates for her students. Of course, her first step was not to go to court to obtain the certificate of marriage of the parents of her students, but to go directly to the office of civil registrations to request it, before which she collected an amount of money from the parents. In the office, she explained the case to an official whom she knows well and when an agreement about the money of understanding or bribery was reached, in the guise of helping, the official promised to comply with the request, although the marriage certificate which is officially required could not be presented.[45] With such alleys open, parents whose marriages were not formally registered but were required at a certain time to present the birth certificates of their children did not feel any great compulsion to register theirs as yet unregistered marriages.

While the motivation of couples whose marriages are unregistered to come to the court to seek legal confirmation (*ithbāt*) of their marriages is obvious, namely to obtain a marriage certificate, the reasons they need such a certificate vary. Some did it because they needed the certificates to fulfill one of the requirements for obtaining the birth certificates of their children – although it was mentioned above that many obtained the certificates illegally (informally), others wished to follow the normal procedure. Some came to the court to obtain a marriage certificate to collect the pension or the salary of their deceased spouse (husband) who had been a civil servant.[46] In my analysis of the judgments, I also observed that some couples requested the certificates to legalize their disputed marriage status. One such case will be discussed below.

Paradoxically, the most often noted reason for the confirmation of a marriage is divorce. Often, although they married informally, couples (particularly women) who petition for divorce wished to do so officially; especially if there is a problem with the custody of their children or joint property. To obtain a divorce before the religious court, couples should first assure the judges that they are a married couple. To prove this, they need to possess and submit the legal certificate of marriage. Accordingly, couples in unregistered marriages have to arrange for the confirmation of their marriages in court before they petition for divorce. The *kompilasi* rules that one of the reasons upon which the confirmation of marriage can be demanded is the initiation of divorce proceedings. The Judgment of the Court of South Jakarta No. 423/Pdt.G/1997/PAJS illustrates this. It recorded that a woman (FN) married a man but did not register their marriage. After the birth of her first child, as her husband failed to provide financial support, she petitioned for divorce. Because their marriage was not registered, she was unable to submit the certificate of marriage and consequently arranged first for the confirmation of their marriage so that the court could be assured that it would part a married couple. As the purpose of her confirming her marriage was to obtain a divorce, referring to the *kompilasi* as well as to the specific Islamic texts stating that the admission of a woman of her marriage to a man is enough evidence of the existence of marriage between them, the judges usually grant such a petition.

The majority of judges in the religious courts display some ambivalence in dealing with such cases, particularly when the conditions of the marriages to be legalized do not comply with the rules in the *kompilasi*. Relying on the concept of *maṣlaḥa* and the willingness to show his flexibility, one judge said:

> Let us say there is a couple who has children but did not register their marriage. If someone informs me of this, should I come and say that their marriage is not valid? No, I would not challenge the *'ulamā'* who had married them. Or, say that the couple comes to us requesting us to validate their marriage and the wife states that she had indeed married her husband, can I contest this? No, I would not do that. As far as I am concerned, the marriage of the couple is indeed religiously lawful. Besides, they might find themselves in serious trouble, should I not validate it.[47]

Another judge who connects this case with the perception that marriage constitutes a contract between two persons says:

> Registration of marriage is indeed necessary, but regarding it as one of the requirements required for the validity of a marriage runs counter to the Islamic legal principle stating that a contract made between two persons constitutes a rule or law for both of them and each of them is tied by the rule. Accordingly, the contract they made has been effective since the contract was made.

> The effect of the unregistered marriage is therefore not the invalidity of the marriage religiously but is the denial of their judicial relief. [48]

Judges recognize that rigidity and idealism may often be cast to the wind when considerations about public interest are appealed to. Not being tied by the directives of *ithbāt nikāh* regulated in the *kompilasi*, one of which is if the marriage was concluded before the issuing of the 1974 Marriage Law, and concerned with what is best (*maṣlaḥa*) for the couples, they tend to handle such requests as confirmation of a marriage concluded after 1974 flexibly, so that difficulties arising in connection with pensions, legitimacy of children and so on can be then resolved.

It should be noted that the utilization of the concept of *maṣlaḥa* in this issue is strictly limited to the marriages of which the conclusion, according to them, fulfilled the conditions stipulated under Islamic law, as appears in the case of *ithbāt nikāh*. One of the judgments in South Jakarta proves this.[49] It explains that in 1994 HR (husband), a married man, married EK (wife) in the front of an *'ulamā'* (*nikah di bawah tangan*) and promised to renew their marriage in front of the marriage registrar or according to State law. Because the husband broke his promise and even showed signs of leaving her, this second wife went to the religious court requesting it to confirm the marriage legally. Unfortunately for the wife, the court did not grant the petition. The court's decision is basically relevant to the rule that a case of *ithbāt nikāh* constitutes a request and therefore has to be requested with the agreement of the two parties, the husband and the wife. That the court did not utilize the concept of *maṣlaḥa* to deviate from the established rule and hence did not legalize the marriage, whereas the (second) wife would benefit had the court legalized it, seems relevant to the fact that their marriage was assumed to have fallen short of the religious requirements. In this respect, although the husband admitted that the marriage had been concluded, he disagreed with its existence, as at the time he was under pressure and claimed that he did not pay *mahar,* thereby denying that they had lawfully married, even according to standards of religious law.

Another important consideration in the decision may have been the fact that the husband was not a single person but had a family, whose stability might have been disturbed had the judges legalized the husband's second marriage. It seems that by refusing to validate the marriage, the judges were not intending to create an advantage for one party if this might have been supposed to produce a potential problem for another party. In other words, the judges will employ the concept of *maṣlaḥa* only when it produces a real advantage and does not trigger an obviously negative effect. Another case clearly proves that such a consideration is taken into account significantly in such cases. Two judges in

Rangkasbitung explained to me that they had refused to confirm a woman's marriage with a civil servant who was about to retire. Before the judges, the woman admitted she had married the man unofficially and wanted to confirm their marriage to make proper arrangements of their private affairs. The woman submitted the letter of statement issued by a village head, affirming that they were married, and presented witnesses who stated that they knew of the existence of their marriage for the consideration of the judges. From their interrogation in the hearing, the judges understood that the husband had another (formal) wife and children and was suffering from a serious illness, a condition which had prevented him being present in the court, and consequently did not grant the request. While in their judgment they based their decision on the lack of evidence that the couple was in fact married, they actually had other significant considerations in mind. First, whereas he had no child in his marriage to the second wife, the husband had a number of children with the first formal wife. Second, it was strongly suggested that the main aim of the woman's request to obtain confirmation of the marriage was to gain a share of any property and pension, of which the assessment would be upset should they legalize her marriage to such a man.[50]

The flexible attitude of the judges toward the cases of *ithbāt nikāh* also seems to be prompted by the ambiguous provision in both the Marriage Law and the *kompilasi*. Article 7 (3) of the *kompilasi* regulates that *ithbāt nikāh* can be proposed to courts only if: (a) the marriage is to be dissolved by divorce; (b) the marriage certificate is lost; (c) the legality of the marriage is in doubt; (d) the marriage was conducted before the issuing of the 1974 Law of Marriage; and (e) the marriage was concluded by a couple who were permitted to marry, according to the Law. At a glance, the *kompilasi* seems to limit the chances of the legalization of unregistered marriages only to those complying with the conditions mentioned in the *kompilasi*.

However, looking carefully at the conditions prescribed in the laws, it is immediately striking that the conditions are so confusing that judges could easily misinterpret and misuse them. Point (b) is, for example, seen to be a loophole allowing the misuse of the institution of *ithbāt nikāh,* if we relate it to the time when the lost marriage certificate was issued. If the lost certificate was issued after the passing of the 1974 Marriage Law, *ithbāt nikāh* in the court is superfluous, because the holder of the lost certificate can simply ask the KUA which issued it for its duplicate. Meanwhile, if it was a certificate issued before 1974, *ithbāt nikāh* can be indeed proposed but on the grounds of the reason mentioned in point (d). Such an ambiguity can be taken as a reason for couples who married outside KUA after 1974 to request *ithbāt nikāh,* stating that their marriage certificate was lost, and for judges to grant the request. The reason mentioned in point (e) is much more ambiguous and allows a chance for the misuse of the institution of *ithbāt nikāh*. From the clause 'according to the 1974 Marriage Law', it can be inferred that the marriage meant in this point is a marriage concluded after 1974, which contradicts point (d), and that, even if it is not the subject of the process of divorce, on this ground the unregistered marriage can be presented to the court for legal confirmation.

II.5 Inheritance

All the religious courts outside Jakarta face the same problem in cases of inheritance. When I visited the religious court of Bogor in 2003, I was told that one case of inheritance had been registered and was being prepared for hearing, but it was very rare for this court to hear a case of inheritance. In 2004, the court of Rangksbitung registered only one inheritance case and the court of Cianjur heard two inheritance cases. This is in contrast to the religious courts in Jakarta, which hear inheritance cases relatively often. The religious court of South Jakarta, for instance, accepts one or even sometimes two cases of inheritance per month or twelve to fourteen cases per a year. Likewise, though less frequent than those in South Jakarta, the religious court of East Jakarta sometimes registers and hears such cases. In general, however, inheritance cases registered in the religious courts in Indonesia are very few in number, as indicated by the statistical data of the cases registered at the religious courts throughout the country in 2000.[51]

The scarcity of inheritance cases brought to the religious courts is inextricably linked to the fact that the legal awareness of the Islamic system of inheritance among Indonesian Muslims is still not well developed. According to the survey conducted by R. Otje Salman, in Cirebon only 19 per cent of the Muslim population knew about the Islamic system of inheritance. He also reported that the number of Muslims who preferred to resort to the Islamic system to deal with their problems of inheritance was 41.5 per cent; meanwhile the number of those who preferred the *adat* system was marginally higher, at 41.7 per cent. Although the percentage of the preference for both laws was fairly evenly balanced, their consistency was different. Interestingly perhaps, the consistency of those who preferred the Islamic system was lower than those who preferred the *adat* system: namely, 36.65 per cent in the Islamic system and 73.67 per cent in *adat* law. It can be concluded from these findings that the legal awareness of the Islamic system of inheritance of Muslims in Cirebon in particular is fairly low, and that *adat* law is their preferred alternative to solve problems of inheritance.[52]

Salman rightly states that the preference for *adat* law shown by Indonesian Muslims in cases of inheritance illustrates the conflict between *adat* and Islamic law. Facing the problem of the share between males and females, Indonesian Muslims often preferred the equal share of 1:1, which *adat* law maintains, instead of 2:1, which is insisted upon by the Islamic system. Although Islamic law has plainly offered alternative systems, namely *hibah* and *wāṣiyat,* which the *'ulamā'* recommend as a way to obviate any injustice in apportioning a deceased's estate among the heirs, from a practical point of view, the system of inheritance remains to be practiced but with *adat* law holding pride of place.[53] This demonstrates that the social values of Indonesian Muslims are not conducive to a ready acceptance of the Islamic system of inheritance.

In addition, the paucity of inheritance cases brought to the religious courts may be associated with the fact that the issue of inheritance is related to wealth. When disputes arise in such cases, litigants often give priority to material benefits rather than religious aspects. Yahya Harahap found that having been provided with two systems, a plaintiff often utilized the system which he or she thought could benefit him or her more. Islamic or religious motivation played almost no role in the matter. This tendency, according to him, may be explained by looking at several facts. When *adat* law, which respects matrilineal and patrilineal familial systems, was still applied in the civil courts, that is before 1961, female parties (daughters) tended to bring their cases to the religious courts hoping that they could get at least a half portion of what their brothers received (sons of the deceased, be that father or mother), as the religious courts applied the Islamic system. Had they submitted the cases to the civil courts, they would have been given no portion at all. In contrast, male parties (sons) were inclined to go to the civil courts, hoping that they would be granted the entire estate.[54] When the new *adat* law, which sustains the 1:1 ratio for males and females, was adopted and applied in the civil courts, and a number of the religious courts had given rulings in inheritance cases applying the Islamic system, their attitudes changed. Female parties preferred the civil courts, as they knew that they would be granted an equal share with male parties; meanwhile male parties went to the religious courts expecting that they would be given a larger share than their sisters.[55]

Many scholars might not agree with the conclusions Harahap and Salman drew from their surveys, arguing that the majority of Indonesian Muslims adhere to the system of Islamic inheritance and agree to solve cases involving this in the religious courts.[56] What Lev found may also be not relevant to what both Harahap and Salman concluded. Lev argues that, although at the time the religious courts in Java were disadvantaged in inheritance matters, people from that section of society in which Islam was strong remained loyal to them.[57] However, regardless of the divergent conclusions drawn at that time, inheritance is now indeed considered in the *kompilasi* and the 1989 Act as an area of Islamic family law to which people embroiled in a dispute may resort of their own free will, under which the material benefits to the disputants, if embraced, can be maintained. The Act indeed includes an important phrase limiting the jurisdiction of religious courts over inheritance. The phrase explicitly implies that the claimants to an estate can choose one of the systems to be used in the division of the estate, *adat* or Islamic law, or a general or a religious court.[58] Judges interviewed believed that this rule was certainly a contributory factor in limiting the number of inheritance cases they hear.

Besides this, inconvenience and procedural complexities contribute enormously to the reluctance of Indonesian Muslims to solve their inheritance cases in religious courts. Muslims in Cianjur and Rangkasbitung, for instance, generally tend to apply Islamic law in deciding inheritance cases. As the decisions issued by the courts do not necessarily differ from those made by the *'ulamā'*, in the sense that both apply Islamic law without any effect to other legal acts, many prefer to seek a solution to such cases before the *'ulamā'*. They believe that bringing their cases to the courts might only complicate the cases between the parties concerned. They do understand that conciliation (*perdamaian*) stemming from the maxim *"Al-riḍā sayyid al-aḥkām (conformity or agreement is the highest rule*)," popular among judges in the religious courts as well as the *'ulamā,'* can be attempted in the courts, but the formal procedures often form an insurmountable hurdle to their going to court. Instead, they prefer to go to the village head or religious leaders for an easy, uncomplicated solution to their problems.

What I observed and heard in the room of a female lawyer, who is also the owner of the hotel where I lodged during my fieldwork in Cianjur, clearly illustrates that these factors are relevant. The lawyer, who knew the reason I had come to Cianjur, invited me to her office one night where two persons, a brother and a sister, were already present. It did not take me long to grasp that these two persons were involved in an inheritance case in which they were the plaintiffs and had been found against. I had been invited there to analyze the case and help the lawyer understand the Islamic law of inheritance correctly. I will not discuss the case in detail but, in broad outline, it involved one (second) wife and five children from two wives. Three children, one daughter and two sons, are from the first wife who had died after the husband (the deceased in the case) had died, and the two who appeared in the lawyer's office are from the second wife, who is still alive. Having been proven that a certain part of the estate of the deceased had accrued during his marriage with the first wife, while none was accrued during his marriage with the second, it was only the estate which the deceased had acquired before he got married (bought property) which was inherited by the two children of the second wife. Meanwhile the three children of the first wife were awarded shares of both the property acquired by their father alone and that gained by their father in conjunction with their mother. In this respect, the first wife, the mother of the three children, deserved to have half of the joint property, as well as her share of the inheritance. The distribution of this (her) estate was made in court. This is because she had also died, and her share became an inherited estate which should also be handled by the court.

Receiving less than the two sons of the first wife, the son of the second wife could not accept the decision of the lower court of Cianjur and wanted to take the case to the appellate court, for which he asked the lawyer to help him win the case. During our discussion, the two persons seemed very upset and disappointed. Repeatedly the brother said that what he demanded was to receive the same share as his two half-brothers, arguing that he was of the same sex and social position as his two brothers, being a son of the deceased. In this respect, it is clear that he did not comprehend either the nature of the case or the Islamic law of inheritance. The lawyer said that she could help him if he could provide evidence that the whole estate was acquired by their father before he married the first wife, an assumption which the brother had believed, but he repeatedly questioned why he should do so. The nature of this case is interesting in itself but there are two particular points I want to stress. Even though it is true that they were undoubtedly disappointed with the decision, their uneasiness and anxiety also stemmed from the fact that they no longer had a good relationship with their half-brothers and half-sister by the other mother. The sister said that she felt remorseful about this and was convinced that had they decided not to go to court but to the *'ulamā'* and or local leader or head of village, a better solution might have been achieved and their good relationship might have remained intact. She felt that the formal procedure and the very nature of the court had placed the members of this family in an uneasy situation. However, deeply disappointed by the decision of the religious court, the brother was convinced that the result may have been more propitious had they taken the case to the civil court.

Along with the procedural complexities and the existence of the shared jurisdictions between the religious and general courts, the introduction of new rules of inheritance in the *kompilasi* has had a remarkable influence on the reluctance of Indonesian Muslims to come to the courts. For those who strictly adhere to the Islamic legal views of the established Sunnite schools of Islamic law, the application of such concepts as obligatory bequest and representation of heirs was seen to deviate from the established Islamic legal systems adhered to by the Indonesian Muslims. They refuse to go to the religious courts, which they consider not in keeping with Islamic law. They seemed to be worried that they would too become deviants from the Sunnite system they believed to be the most authoritative Islamic legal system.[59] Many of the *'ulamā'* in West Java, some of whom are former judges of the religious courts, contested the rules and expressed their opposition on various occasions, especially in their speeches at religious gatherings.

III The Compliance of Muslim Society with the *Kompilasi*: The Case of Divorce

So far, we have discussed to what extent the *kompilasi* has been effective in gaining acceptance among Indonesian Muslims as an instrument to administer their legal familial issues. Any measure of its efficacy can be seen not only in its usage in judicial practice in the courts, but also the extent to which it has been able to influence social attitudes to socio-legal activities. In other words, it is important to see to what extent the law functions as a tool of social engineering. In this context, it is worth remembering that the issuing of the *kompilasi* aimed to manage and control the practices for solving marital disputes in the Muslim community, meaning that the solution must be sought before a State institution, namely the religious court, and to restrict the rate of divorce and polygyny in particular in society. Since the extent of the realization of the first aim has been discussed above, we now turn to the second, and examine whether or not the *kompilasi* has decreased the rate of divorce.

Certainly, according to some surveys, after the issuing of the 1974 Marriage Law the percentage of divorces decreased.[60] Looking at official court records, Gavin W. Jones concluded that the application of legal restrictions on divorce in the Marriage Law has played a significant role in the declining rate of marital disruption.[61] In principle, the survey by Cammack supports Jones. Yet he concludes that the decrease does not arise just from the application of the Law; other substantial factors have also contributed to this tendency. He bases his conclusion on the fact that the decrease in the divorce rate occurs only in some regions in which in fact divorce was already rare, and that in the regions where the rate was high before, it is still high. In other words, his research shows that the application of the Marriage Law does not significantly impact on divorce trends on a large scale.[62]

Continuing the trend which had developed since the application of the 1974 Marriage Law, for several years after the issuing of the *kompilasi*, as mentioned before, there was a relative decrease in the divorce rate in several areas. It is reported that, according to the statistical data issued by the Ministry of Religious Affairs in 1992, 1993, and 1994, the number of cases of divorce registered in religious courts declined.[63] After 1994, it increased again. In Bekasi, for instance, it is estimated that in 2004 the number of the divorce cases registered in the religious courts was much higher than that in 2003.[64] The calculation of the number of divorce cases to be tried in a day in the court of South Jakarta shown above also illustrates the increase in the divorce rate. While the number of divorces to be tried by this court on one day in 2000 was only seven plus about the same number of *sub-judice* cases, as such approximately fourteen, the number of divorces heard in 2002 was more than eighteen per day. A survey conducted by the Centre for the Research and the Development of the Ministry of Religious Affairs in 1996 mentioned that in Blitar, East Java, the divorce rate was very high, being one in six marriages.[65] In Malang, in the period January to July in 2004 alone, the religious court registered 2274 cases of divorce. The total number of divorce cases registered in this court in 2004 is estimated to have been higher than that in 2003.[66] The unavoidable inference is that the issuing of the *kompilasi* has not prevented the increase in the divorce rate among Indonesian Muslims.

Indubitably, the kompilasi has placed a number of requirements and set procedures on a petition to divorce. Nonetheless, rather than the requirements and procedures preventing divorces, the problems faced by a couple prompt them more readily to seek a divorce.

There are various factors which contribute to the high rate of divorce in Indonesia. M. Kuchiba and his collaborators, who discuss the trend in divorce among Malay people, including some regions of Malaysia and Indonesia, mention the social immaturity of a couple when they marry, the effect of the kinship system, and the widespread belief that fate plays a role in divorce as major contributors to this situation.67 Gavin W. Jones cites the same factors, although he also emphasizes polygyny and economic problems. The Indonesian Fertility and Mortality (IFM) Survey, focusing on marriage and divorce in Indonesia, cites several factors which are thought to facilitate divorce, including the rights of spouses and their families to children from the marriage, age of the couple when entering into marriage, the marriage present (bride price/dowry), residence after marriage, and the prevailing view of divorce in society.68 Among all these factors cited, my research concludes that the strong belief that fate plays a significant role in divorce and the system of kinship, as well as its effect on the maintenance of the family of divorced people and their children, still has a strong bearing on the practice of divorce in recent times. Importantly, these factors, which I classify as external factors, would not be able to exert any great affect on divorce unless other direct factors existed as well. These include economic incompatibility, unacceptable behavior of one spouse, a poor relationship with parents-in-law, sharing a husband with another wife, and disagreement over location of residence. If the first category refers to a more universal typology as it touches upon social and cultural problems, the second refers to the conditions which arise within the family itself.

Let me discuss these one by one, beginning with a discussion of the internal factors.

The majority of the population who live in the areas in which I conducted my research are poor. It is true that Jakarta enjoys a reputation as a metropolitan city in which there are groups of very affluent people, but in the wake of mass urbanization, this city also has many slum areas in which poor people live.[69] Understandably many couples in Indonesia were divorced merely because they were forced to lead a very bitter economic existence. In Jakarta, for example, there were many marriages which ended in divorce and the main cause is the economic situation, namely, failure of the husband to provide financial support. YS, aged 24, came to the religious court of North Jakarta to petition a divorce from her husband because he neglected his economic duty. It was also for this reason she did not stress her claim that her would-be ex-husband would give her *nafka* (alimony) and *mut'a* (divorce compensation)[70] during her waiting period, although she knew that these were her right. Her decision not to insist that he fulfill his obligations associated with the divorce stemmed from her conviction that he would never comply. Cynically, she asked how she could expect such rights if, when she was still his wife, he had never provided her with *nafka lahir* (financial support). During my attendance at divorce hearings held in the religious court of South Jakarta, I learned that of seven divorce cases initiated by wives, four were petitioned on the grounds of economic problems.

The statistical data issued by the Ministry of Religious Affairs show that many women in Jakarta are indeed forced to divorce because of economic problems. Such cases accounted for 1548 out of 2444 cases in the year 2000. This record is also pertinent to my analysis on the judgments on divorce in the religious courts – for this discussion see again the table on divorce cases in Chapter 6. Thirty-three cases out of fifty-two divorce cases initiated by women were granted because of their husbands' failure to provide financial support. The rest were granted on various grounds, such as continuous dispute, sixteen; acute illness of husbands, including madness or mental aberration, two; and polygyny, one.

Several reasons were usually mentioned by both plaintiffs and witnesses to explain why husbands failed to support their family financially. They included joblessness, negligence, and disappearance/desertion. Among these reasons, the desertion of a husband is the most frequently recorded reason associated with husbands' failure to provide their family with financial support. Twenty-three out of thirty-three divorce cases brought on the grounds of the husband's failure to provide financial support were related to the desertion of a husband who had left the marital home. Although the husband's failure to provide financial support does not necessarily result from his disappearance, but can also be attributed to his being unemployed or purely negligent, almost every case of divorce on the grounds of the failure of the husband to provide financial support was granted in the absence of the husband, thirty-one cases in all; the two other cases were heard in the presence of the husbands. Many husbands are reluctant to come to court to discuss their problems with judges. Ironically, the reluctance of husbands to come to court is beneficial to wives who are sure they want to break with their husbands. The absence of husbands in the court, not to mention their disappearance from their native city, has in fact often made it easier for wives to prove their claims of their husbands' failure to provide financial support before the courts.

Bearing these reasons in mind, what happened in Cianjur is particularly interesting to note here. To ease economic woes, many wives in Cianjur go to Arab countries to work as servants. While they might have imagined that after they had finished their contract in these countries they would have better life in their native region, namely Cianjur, with a nice house and money saved, their wish often did not come true. Not infrequently they found that their husbands had spent most of the money they had sent on their personal needs and remained jobless. Some of them heard that their husbands had played around with other girls and some even found that their husbands had married other girls. Confronted with such irresponsible attitudes on the part of their husbands, many wives who just returned from abroad petitioned for divorce, arguing that they no longer had the patience to stay married to irresponsible (*tidak bertanggung jawab*) or jobless (*pengangguran*) husbands.[71]

A parallel trend is the recent emergence of foreign newcomers in Cianjur. These people usually serve as agents or recruiters of women seeking work in Arab countries. To facilitate their contacts and also to be sure of a warm welcome, they often marry girls from this city. After several years of working as agents in Cianjur, it was not uncommon for them to be moved to another city. This meant that their contact with the wives slackened and finally they simply ignored them. After waiting for several months or even years, these wives came to the courts requesting divorces on the ground of their husbands' failure to provide material and immaterial support (*nafkah lahir dan batin*).[72]

Protracted disputes, which resulted from such causes as mentioned above as disagreement over location of residence, the reprehensible behavior of one spouse, poor relationship with parents- or sisters- and brothers-in-law, and sharing a husband with other girls or wives, also constituted very important reasons to divorce. As has been mentioned in passing, cases of divorces initiated by wives on the grounds of protracted disputes, as illustrated in the judgments in my collection, consisted of a fairly significant number, sixteen out of fifty-three cases. If added to divorce cases initiated by husbands on these same grounds, these numbers would be much more significant. In fact, almost all the thirty-five cases of divorce initiated by husbands were granted on the grounds of protracted dispute, namely thirty-two. The other three cases were granted because of the acute illness of wives, mental or physical.

Sociological and cultural aspects, such as the strong belief that fate plays a hand in divorce, and the type of kinship system in the regions, definitely lent credence to these other reasons.[73] Looking at the conviction that fate plays a role in divorce, people of the regions in which I conducted my research believe that people must be compatible or *cocok,* or be *jodoh,* in order to live together harmoniously. In general, people who think this way are convinced that, if a couple is to be compatible, fate must be involved as compatibility is mystically bestowed. On the basis of these complementary beliefs, both wife and husband should not necessarily feel regretful or guilty if they cannot get along in marriage. This leaves a way open for a couple to seek a divorce without bitter recriminations. They believe that being *jodoh* or being divorced is destiny.[74]

Just to demonstrate the belief that fate is irrefutably involved in divorce and that being incompatible is not a mistake of one of the spouses, it is interesting to record here that in Cianjur and Indramayu, several couples who wished to seek a divorce came to the religious court or to Office of Religious Affairs (KUA) together by motorcycle.[75] The fact that the phrases *sudah tidak jodoh lagi* (no longer compatible) or *jodohnya sudah habis* (the compatibility is over) were often expressed during my conversations with a number of women who petitioned for divorce or were going to be divorced also illustrates their belief in the strong role of fate in the continuation or dissolution of their marriages. It should, nevertheless, be noted that, although for some girls being divorced and then remarrying indicates that they are desirable women which boosts their egos,[76] being divorced is not what they expected.

Significantly, the system of kinship in the regions in which I conducted my research is generally bilateral, and this is also believed to have contributed to the rate of divorce. Relating this kind of system of kinship to ego, Kuchiba concludes that a couple in this bilateral type of kinship system belongs to two families and enjoys a considerable measure of independence. Accordingly, a husband can have a strong sense of belonging to his wife's family if he relies heavily upon his wife's parents. When he divorces, there is no resistance to his returning to his own family. Likewise, the wife when divorced does not have to feel any qualms about returning to her own family. The same can be said about their unmarried children. They are normally members of their parents' families. If their parents separate, the real parent child-relationship does not change and neither does their relationship with their grandparents' families.[77]

The problem is that in this kind of system, husband and or wife often find themselves caught in a conflict of loyalty. When a conflict arises between his wife and his parents, a husband is placed in the dilemma of having to choose the side of his wife or his parents. The reverse is true for a wife when her husband and her family are in conflict. When a spouse prefers to be loyal to his or her parents, divorce is often inevitable.[78] What happened to one female litigant in the South Jakarta court clearly illustrates this. She petitioned for divorce because her husband could not respect her parents, which meant they often complained to her about her husband's attitude. When the wife confronted her husband with this, it inevitably engendered tension, with the husband continuously pestering her about whether she would still prefer to be his wife or to get divorced. Having often been challenged in such a way, she decided to come to the court without her husband's knowledge.[79] While I did not know if she was granted the divorce, I thoroughly understand that she was faced by a conflict of loyalty and, considering that her husband was not an easy man, she decided to take her parents' side.

The problem of bilateral kinship can easily be abstracted from the conditions for divorce (*keadaan perkara*) laid down in the legal judgments of some of the cases in my collection. In cases of divorce on the grounds of protracted dispute, almost all the evidence of the conditions relevant to such divorce cases revealed that one of the spouses, either wife or husband, had left the marital home, if they had one, and returned to his or her parents' house before the divorce was petitioned. When divorce was petitioned on the grounds of economic problems, some conditions in the divorce cases in the copies of judgments often also recorded that, since the husbands had failed to support their families, this duty had been assumed by the wife's birth family. During my attendance at hearings, I noticed that almost all the families, particularly parents, of the wives petitioning for divorce, while asserting that the financial burden of their daughter' family had been thrust upon them, repeatedly questioned the benefit of prolonging the marriage of their daughters whose husbands had no longer assumed the financial responsibility for a certain period. Therefore, under such conditions, wives, who stress that marriage is an economic partnership, tend to end their marriages and consider leading a life alone but with greater reliance on their parents to be a much better option.

Wives (mothers) have no fear of being unable to support the children in their custody. Indeed this is what most of them strive for, as they feel that they have more right to claim custody. Indeed, although the Shāfi'ite legal code gives the mother custody of a daughter until puberty and a son until he is seven, the *kompilasi* raises the ages of the children, whether a daughter or son, to twelve. Basically, although the custody of their children is accorded to their mothers, their fathers are required to contribute to their children's support until the children are adults. In practice, more husbands paid maintenance only during the first few months and some paid no maintenance at all.[80] Wives who petition for divorce usually acknowledge these common practices and understand that they can find themselves in such a predicament. Safe in the knowledge that it is customary practice for the economic burden of supporting the children to fall on the mothers, who can rely on their extended families, the wives are not worried about getting divorced.

Therefore, although the *kompilasi* has set a number of qualifications and procedures for divorce, couples with economic problems, a fraught familial relationship, or with a belief that having been in a rough patch in their marital relationship plus knowing they are able to rely heavily on their parents they are no longer *jodoh*, do not take account of the qualifications and procedures set down in the *kompilasi* as obstacles to divorce. Accordingly the divorce rate remains high. This is clearly because, rather than considering the *kompilasi* an obstacle to divorce, the litigants (particularly plaintiffs) think that the *kompilasi* has provided them with grounds to use or to select in obtaining a divorce. In fact, when petitioning for divorce, plaintiffs, although they almost never explicitly referred to the specific points in either *kompilasi* or *fiqh* books, always stressed the existence of one or more reasons for divorce that are included in the State laws on marriage. In cases in which defendants (husbands) have failed to provide wives with financial support by their negligence or unemployment, wives filing as plaintiffs often not only said that their husbands had failed to maintain them but also assured the court that their husbands had pronounced *ta'līq ṭalāq*, thereby deviating from the marriage agreement pronounced in the *ta'līq ṭalāq* which the *kompilasi* takes as one of grounds for divorce. In divorce cases on the ground of continuous dispute, plaintiffs, be they husbands or wives, often stressed the absence of happiness in their marital life, leading them to conclude that marriage, of which the purpose according to the *kompilasi* is to create a happy life, can no longer be continued.

Consequently, while I noticed that by various methods judges always tried to persuade the plaintiffs to think matters over and try to live harmoniously and withdraw their requests,[81] the efforts of courts to reconcile couples were relatively ineffective. According to research done in 1995 in Indramayu, since 1989, there have been only two couples who have withdrawn their petitions for divorce after they had been encouraged to reconcile. In Cianjur and Rangkasbitung, the attempts by judges to have couples reconcile only worked in approximately one out of a hundred cases.[82] When I was at the court in South Jakarta, I talked to a woman who was dealing with the official papers for withdrawing her petition for divorce. This woman said that the reason she had petitioned for divorce was something which could still be tolerated, namely, her husband's poor relationship with her family. When she petitioned for divorce on these grounds, her husband who admitted he still loved her responded promptly and promised the judges and his wife that he would change his behavior. The wife, who trusted in his promise, withdrew her claim. Despite this, in general judges' efforts at reconciliation in this court have failed to stir the litigants, particularly plaintiffs.[83] Hence, it can be assumed that the motives for divorces among litigants are more effective and attuned to the granting of divorce – and that the procedures set down the *kompilasi* are not strong enough to prevent it.

While all these factors are highly relevant to the continuing high divorce rate, there are other contributory, influential factors. First among them is the attitude of judges in viewing the substance of a marriage. Most judges seemed to stress that the purpose of marriage is to create a happy life and family. Happiness is the core of the marriage. They feel that to maintain a marriage claimed to be broken by one or both party(ies) means condemning them a life of misery. Problems of and complaints made by one or both parties involved in a marriage are taken as symptoms that a marriage is no longer enjoyable and beneficial, and therefore should be terminated. The second cogent factor is that the classical doctrine of divorce in Muslim society is too loose. This factor was clearly revealed in the previous section of this chapter, namely in the discussion of the legal awareness of divorce in society.

So far in the discussion I have quoted details of several cases to support my assertion. However, to demonstrate more clearly that tiny or insignificant problems in marriage, and the belief that fate is involved in divorce, are inter-related factors for divorce petitions, and that reconciliations attempted by the court hardly ever work and consequently judges take divorce for granted, three divorce cases whose hearings I attended in the religious court of South Jakarta in 2003 and of Rangkasbitung in 2005 will be specifically recorded here. Case One, heard in the religious court of South Jakarta, involved a husband who petitioned for divorce because his wife was considered unfair. Present in the court were three judges, a clerk, the husband, aged twenty-six, and the wife, aged twenty-three, who had been married about fourteen months earlier and had one child aged about twenty months. The wife was accompanied by her mother, who entered the courtroom with the couple but was asked to leave during the hearing since she frequently interrupted even though she was requested not to do so.

The story of their meeting and marriage is quite interesting in understanding the later disharmony which blighted their marriage, leading to the husband's petition for divorce. The husband told the court he had become close to his prospective wife when she had frequently consulted him about her relationship with her boyfriend. After several months of friendship, they fell in love and began a sexual relationship from which the wife became pregnant. In the four month of her pregnancy, they were married and their marital life was said to be fine. But after their child was born, a dispute began to brew. It started with a conversation about the wife's love story with her previous boyfriend about which they had always talked about before. In the course of this, the wife, as she said herself, admitted to her husband that it had once nearly become a sexual relationship but was not consummated, as the boyfriend suddenly felt pain in his genital area. The wife also told the court that she had told her husband this because her husband forced her to admit if she had had a sexual relationship with her previous boyfriend.

The effect of the wife's frankness was unexpectedly serious, as the husband, who was sure that his wife had actually had a real sexual relationship with her previous boyfriend, began to hate his wife. As he said to the judges, he felt cheated by his wife, as she had not confessed this before, and added that he would not have married her if he had known it. Because of this and of the loss of his feelings for her, from which he, as he frankly admitted, could no longer have a sexual relationship with his wife, he wanted to divorce her. The wife, who strongly refuted her husband's accusation, repeatedly assured the judges that she had had a pre-marital relationship only with her husband. Although she contested her husband's petition, she, as she said to judges, could do nothing if her husband would not reconsider his intention. To release her bitter feelings she said that she was not his *jodoh*.

Another case, also heard in the religious court of Jakarta Selatan, involved a wife who petitioned for divorce because her husband, who was a public transport driver (*sopir metromini*), was a drug addict and could not support her appropriately. Present in the court were three judges, a clerk, the husband and the wife. The wife, who seemed to be very sure that her petition for divorce would be granted, admitted to having grown tired of her husband's behavior. She felt that she had given her husband enough opportunities to change his bad habits but could no longer stand it. Although the judges assured her that the husband could gradually improve his behavior and that he still loved her, the wife was quite insistent about her petition which they finally granted.

The last case heard in the religious court of Rangkasbitung involved a wife who petitioned for divorce because her husband was disproportionately jealous of everyone approaching and talking to her. Present in the court were three judges, a clerk, the wife and two witnesses, one of whom was asked to leave the courtroom after they had been asked to take the oath. The husband was absent at this second hearing, but present at the first. Observing the performance of the wife, I could understand why he was always worried about losing her. The wife was pretty, attractive, and young, attributes which aroused the husband's worries that another man could easily be attracted to her. As he did not show up for the second hearing, which I attended, I did not know what the husband looked like but was told that he was far older than the wife. The wife understood that jealousy betokened love, but unfortunately, the husband's attitude had harmed her as his jealousy was excessive and expressed in verbal abuse addressed to her, and in his strict imperative that she was not allowed to leave home. Above all, when he was in a jealous rage, he denied his wife appropriate finance.

The problem culminated when the wife found job in a mini-supermarket and was about to begin. The husband, who had left the wife for almost a month but knew of the wife's plan to work via a friend, came to her saying that he would not allow her to work in the supermarket. Furthermore, accompanied by a *jawara*, he also went to the manager of the supermarket warning him to not employ his wife. No longer able to tolerate her husband's attitude, the wife came to the religious court to petition for divorce. After the hearing, I was told by the judges that the husband did not want to divorce her. The wife, as I noticed myself, was so fixed in her intention and said, at the end of the hearing when asked if she had still something to say, that she fully trusted that the judges would treat the case fairly; and that she came to the court to be divorced from her husband by the judges, and did not care what her husband wanted. She also stated that she would prefer to bear whatever stigma people attached to her rather than to go and live with her husband again. Although the case was not yet finalized at the time, as the husband's reaction still needed to be heard, I was informed by the judges that the petition would be granted. Commenting on this case, the chief judge said that when a woman has stated she foregoes all her claims, they as judges require no further evidence to establish that her mind was poisoned with bitter hatred toward her husband.

These cases illustrated that in practice it is quite difficult for judges to prevent the occurrence of divorce. Attempts at reconciling couples in the courts have dwindled into mere procedures or ritual practices which do not contribute much to achieving the stated goal. In my view these cases also demonstrate that both parties, husbands and wives, have employed their own strategies in divorce cases in the courts, an issue that needs further analysis.

Conclusion

The issuing of the *kompilasi* is inextricably related to the fact that, although there were several attempts to ban it, the institution of Islamic justice in Indonesia survived and evolved. Over the course of time, it has even gained more legal standing within the national legal system. The issuing of the Islamic Judicature Act in 1989 was one instance which proved that the *kompilasi* has gained more formal and legal recognition. The Act unified the competence, structure, and legal procedures of the religious courts across Indonesia. More importantly, the Act put an end to the superiority of the civil court over the religious court in terms of executorial force. One article in the Law on Marriage of 1974 required that a religious court submit its decision to a civil court to have it confirmed. The Act abrogated the rule, and from then on no confirmation of the decision of the religious court by the civil court has been needed.

The issuing of the *kompilasi*, a uniform reference for the religious courts, was the outcome of a long struggle waged by Indonesian Muslims to have Islamic law applied in Indonesia. As in other Muslim countries, it constitutes the manifestation of Islamic law at least in part, and therefore represents the last stronghold for the preservation of Islamic identity in Indonesia. The Indonesian Government, which recognizes the stabilizing nature of the Islamic family law covered in the *kompilasi*, moved to support the issuing of the *kompilasi* and ratified it by Presidential Instruction in 1991. Projects to modernize the nation and legal rationalization advocated by the Government itself can be considered the best support in its struggles to meet the demands of Indonesian Muslims to introduce Islamic (family) law into a national legal system through the *kompilasi*.

Examined more closely, the accomplishment of effectuating the application of Islamic law, the issuing of the *kompilasi*, is the culmination of the attempt by a few Muslim scholars who sought to establish a more distinctive Islamic law relevant to Indonesian conditions. Hasbi al-Shiddieqy and Hazairin are considered the founding contributors. Through their particular ideas of an "Indonesian *madhhab*" and a "national *madhhab*," these two champions promoted the concept of creating a specific school of Islamic law in Indonesia. Just when these attempts were about to be disregarded, Munawir Sjadzali, the then Minister of Religious

Affairs, revived them by launching the idea of the re-actualization of Islamic law. Although these protagonists have all done spadework in the making of the *kompilasi,* it was Bustanul Arifin who played an even more important role in the dynamics behind its realization. He served at the time as the Chief of the Islamic Chamber in the Supreme Court dealing with issues passed on from the religious courts. As the person in charge of developing the religious courts. Arifin was bothered by the fact that these courts still lacked a systematic legal procedure and point of reference. Sharing the ideas of the earlier scholars just mentioned, in the period of his leadership of the Chamber, Arifin moved to rectify the discrepancies plaguing the religious courts. Examining the project for the *kompilasi* in more detail, Arifin's role was much more significant than the Act itself, for which he served as head of committee. However, his role was far more significant that this; it was he who proposed the project of the *kompilasi* to the President. Arifin admitted that he was very tentative about the right time for proposing it and why the project needed to be implemented. The idea that Pancasila, the sole ideology of Indonesia, needed to be protected from various perceptions of Islamic law prevalent among Indonesian Muslims, and the crisis in political support experienced by the President just at that time, are thought to have been two matters which turned the tables in favor of the project. What Arifin has said in fact fitted the assumption made by many scholars – that the issuing of the *kompilasi* assumed a political character.

As did Hazairin, al-Shiddieqy, and Syadzali, Arifin realized that the Islamic law applied in the religious courts varied and that classical texts were no longer suitable to the conditions currently prevailing in Indonesia. In his vision of the project, Arifin also intended to include local practices in Indonesia. To accomplish this, he introduced innovative rules which adopted *adat* and tackled gender issues. Though not all these recommendations were incorporated, the *kompilasi* did succeed in introducing such changes as rules governing obligatory bequest and the representation of heirs. However, so far its success seems to be only on paper. In fact it has run the gauntlet of criticism, as many scholars have challenged the issues raised and posed pertinent questions about the Islamic rationale of the rules.

The emergence of the debate on the *kompilasi* is obviously an inevitable outcome of the fact that the initial proposals on certain issues, such as the representation of heirs, were contested, and that the majority of the Indonesian Muslims was and has been until very recently dominated by traditionalist forces. It is true that modernists have emerged as opponents of the traditionalist groups but, ever since they have made their voice heard, it seems that their thoughts on Islamic law and their arguments have not had any significant influence on the latter. Whereas, the modernists' ideas have seemed progressive within their own circles, but unlike their counterparts in other Islamic countries, they, as Lev pointed out in 1970s, have not cooperated with non-Islamic groups in support of family law reforms.[1] Paradoxically, rather than making a significant impact on traditionalist thought, modernist thought itself has grown more conservative. As I have pointed out, those who countered the reforms made in the *kompilasi* did so by introducing their arguments within the strict confines of the Islamic context, arguing that the reforms have to be worked out using methodologies which demonstrate their Islamic roots. When the law on an issue is clearly described in the Islamic classical texts, any reform of it so as to accommodate *adat* practice is considered to deviate from the established Islamic legal doctrine and is therefore continually contested.

It is then clear that the review of the debate on its reforms reveals the employment of an *ad hoc*, incoherent approach to the reforms introduced by its compilers. In the case of inheritance issues, revealed in the application of the representation of heirs and obligatory bequests, the reforms have employed the principle of *maṣlaḥa mursala* and a claim to *ijtihād* (independent legal reasoning) not positively rooted in Islamic values, but negatively based on a lack of conflict with any Qur'ānic injunction. The lack of consistency in methodology can be seen in the law itself. For example, while the provision for the inheritance rights of orphaned grandchildren did meet a particular need, it clashed with the established Islamic classical system of inheritance. Here, regardless of the gender of an orphaned grandchild of the deceased, the collaterals (brothers and sisters) of the deceased could now be deprived of their shares and these shares could be added to his or her share.[2] However, the deceased's own daughter would not be excluded from these same collaterals. The rule of limitation which is confusing and is considered to stand on rather shaky ground in the *kompilasi* is another example of the inconsistent utilization of the methodology to achieve reform.

Having been debated among Muslim scholars as well as Muslim judges, the Indonesian reforms of Islamic family law face a basic problem. Indonesia is a country whose Muslim community has strongly encouraged the use of Islamic sources so that the methodology employed must express an Islamic rationale. Therefore, it seems that what John L. Esposito noted when reviewing the Pakistani and Egyptian reforms also holds true for the case of Indonesia. He said "... if reform is to be truly accepted by the majority of Muslims in each country, and if it is to produce a rule that is both comprehensive and consistently developed, the reforms must be supported by a systematic methodology whose Islamic roots can be demonstrated."[3] Although claimed to be grounded on Qur'ānic texts, both reforms of the representation of heirs and obligatory bequests in the *kompilasi* have failed to employ methodology which could reveal their Islamic character.

Therefore, although needed, the reform cannot ignore the various perspectives of Islamic law, and the consistent employment of an Islamic rationale is lacking, which means the reform will create serious problems. *First,* it raises questions about the Islamic character of the laws. The reforms will be often accused of resulting from a misinterpretation of text and or an interpretation of text which is vehemently made, as merely to meet the norm or the measure designed before and subjectively accepted. The fact that a number of Muslim scholars have accused some reforms made in the *kompilasi* of being merely inspired by *adat* law and ignoring the Islamic character of such a law has been proven to be the case. Although considered to be one of the sources of Islamic law,[4] *adat* or *'urf* cannot in fact easily achieve the status of a fifth basis for the law. Once a clear text has been established about a certain legal question, Muslim scholars will not directly, or even at all, accept *'urf* to legitimize the passage of a certain legal question into Islamic law. *Second,* the upshot is that the *kompilasi* as a whole is viewed as not being representative of the thoughts on Islamic law of any group of Indonesian Muslims. In fact, the two major Indonesian Muslim organizations, NU and the Muhammadiyah, have castigated the *kompilasi* as an immature product. Viewing it from their own perspectives, in accordance with their tendency to adhere to Islamic sources in the tradition of legal deduction, NU finds the *kompilasi* still lacking in *fiqh* orientation, and the Muhammadiyah claims it lacks Qur'ānic rationale. Having felt that their aspirations and perspectives about justice have not been fully heard, feminists have also confronted the rules which embrace gender bias.

A more concrete opposition to the reforms can be seen in the work of religious courts. Although judges have been trained to develop a deeper commitment to State law, enshrined in the *kompilasi,* many continue to adhere to the classical legal doctrines in cases in which the *kompilasi* takes different stance from such texts. In their judgments, they reveal that the legal doctrines expressed in the classical texts still have the upper hand as far as they are concerned. The inevitable consequence of this attitude of a number of judges is the great variety of judgments on issues dealt with in the courts. Ineluctably, uncertainty about legal transactions is unavoidable. In the case of inheritance in which a daughter(s) opposes collaterals, various decisions resorting to different legal references have subsequently been issued, giving the collaterals the right to share with the daughter(s) in some judgments on the basis of the *fiqh* texts, and excluding them altogether and awarding the whole share to the daughter(s) in others, in such an instance on the basis of the reformed rule of the *kompilasi.* Therefore, in some cases such as marriage during pregnancy, in which the founders of the schools of Islamic law had set different laws, judges referring to the *kompilasi* have made quite uniform decisions; in others for which the *kompilasi* has reformed the rules, judges, some of whom refer to the reformed rule and others to the classical doctrines, have ironically handed down various judgments.

Confronted with some other reforms, many judges also still feel free to interpret when reaching a decision on the cases before them. Citing public utility, they have often deviated from the *kompilasi* and looked at *fiqh* texts instead. The cases of *ḥaḍāna* of under-age children provide some of the best examples. As I have pointed out, the *kompilasi* rules that the right to *ḥaḍāna* of under-age children devolves on their mothers. The *kompilasi* makes no mention at all of the qualifications of or limitations on mothers for acquiring this right. Yet when judges have known that a mother had become an apostate and hence considered her religiously deviant, they show no reluctance about deviating from the *kompilasi* and depriving her of this right, transferring it to other parties, such as the father. Besides considering that the *kompilasi* stresses the good of the children, judges can transfer the right of a person to *ḥaḍāna* to other relatives. Judges have referred to the opinion of the majority of the *'ulamā'* that being Muslim is one of the qualifications for person to be a guardian. Rules on *ithbāt nikāh* and the minimum age of marriage for girls and boys are other examples which demonstrate that public utility has often led judges to deviate from the *kompilasi* and turned them again in the direction of the *fiqh* texts for the legal basis of their judgments.

It is therefore very clear that in terms of their preference for their legal doctrines to the provisions in the *kompilasi*, cultural assumptions in which the public interest takes pride of place do seem indeed to have been confined. We have already seen a number of examples in which their decisions were determined by their understanding of local concepts and customs and for which an attempt has been made to find legal support in the *fiqh* books. Faced with cases of petitions such as *ithbāt nikāḥ* and in giving permission for under-aged couples to get married, which if acceded to by the judges could have a positive effect according to local assumptions, but is not allowed according to the *kompilasi*, judges have often looked to the *fiqh* books and followed a distinctive approach, daring to oppose the *kompilasi*. They have considered that it is better for the common good that the rules of the *kompilasi* be set aside in favor of a judgement which is more suitable to achieving a socially useful goal. Prioritizing a local assumption above what is set in the *kompilasi* when solving such cases, however, does not seem to have given the judges satisfaction in terms of their legal reasoning. To support their application of such a distinctive approach, besides weighing whether it will be beneficial, they need to present it in such a way as to demonstrate conformity with the sources of the Islamic law.

One result of this is that, rather than the *kompilasi* assuming a leading position as was intended, classical *fiqh* texts remain the dominant source of reference in the judgments in religious courts. As matter of fact, in their judgments, judges who deviate from the *kompilasi* see no other course open to them than citing the classical legal texts as the basis for their decisions. The dominance of the classical texts in the judgments of the religious courts is also shored up by the strong assumption among judges that the Arabic texts can bestow some more innate legitimacy or justification on the decision they have made. In some cases, judges do in principle agree with the rules in the *kompilasi*, as they take the same line as the *fiqh* books, but, when deciding such cases as divorce by *ta'līq ṭalāq*, divorce initiated by the wife because of her strong aversion to her husband, and cases of "verstek" divorce, whose rules have indeed been covered in the *kompilasi*, the majority of judges still quote the classical doctrines from the *fiqh* books when mentioning relevant articles in the *kompilasi*. It seems that this back-up gives the judges more confidence and security in issuing their decisions.

No less significant is the fact that judges in the religious courts are convinced that the character of the religious court needs to be different from the other courts. With the "religious" title attached to their courts, judges need to demonstrate their "Islamic" identity unequivocally and show that they are "Islamic." They think that one possible, concrete way of dealing with this problem effectively is to explore the relevant Arabic texts in the Qur'ān, Prophetic tradition, and *fiqh* books. As the majority of Indonesian Muslims adhere to Shāfi'īte school of Islamic law, they believe that religious practices should be properly observed, and that the use of Arabic is a practical barometer in assessing the quality of their religious observances. Therefore, Arabic occupies a fundamental position in their religious life, including their judicial activities. Moreover, society at large, particularly *'ulamā'*, also often insists they work in a more 'Islamic' way. For this purpose, as I have pointed out, the word *basmallah* written at the top of a judgment, formerly written in the Romanized script in certain religious courts, is now written in Arabic script, a move which has not been imitated by civil court judges.

Judges' attitudes both to deviating from the *kompilasi* and feeling more confident and justified by citing the classical texts were also buttressed by their assumption that the *kompilasi* is not a fully proper legal text, as it was issued in the form of a Presidential Instruction and not a Statute whose legal enforcement is binding. In this respect, judges do not feel obliged to abide by the *kompilasi* and consider recourse to other sources as permissible.

Another motivation for their behavior is their desire to uphold the tradition and particularity of the religious courts, namely the *fiqh* books. For a very long time now, references in the religious courts have been to the *fiqh* books; a situation which has built up an indissoluble band between the *fiqh* books and this Islamic institution for justice. Although no longer recruited from the local *'ulamā'* and graduates from *pesantren*, where the *fiqh* books are studied and read, judges in the religious courts still have an indelible association with the *fiqh* books. Before they enrolled at the Islamic universities from which most judges are now recruited, the majority of the students had studied in *pesantren*. Furthermore, *fiqh* books are also one of the set-text subjects in the test prospective judges have to pass. Their ability to read and comprehend the *fiqh* books is still measured and only those who are considered capable of reading and comprehending the *fiqh* books are appointed judges in the religious courts. Accordingly, although they agree with the modernization and standardization of Islamic family law in a modern codified form of law as they have now, they are pervaded by a sense that the *fiqh* books should still be an irrevocable part of their environment. Interestingly, they legitimize their practice by ranging themselves behind the concept of *ijtihād* which is creatively given a new meaning and interpretation and can be called supplementary *ijtihād*.

Consequently, there seems to be indisputable evidence that as the legislated text, the *kompilasi* is still considered an 'open' text. Even though, as is also the nature of codes enacted elsewhere, the open character once attributed to the *fiqh* texts is curbed in this form, and change is only possible if it is introduced by legislative amendment,[5] interpretative modification by individual scholars and by the official authors of Islamic law, such as judges, is still envisioned. While the *kompilasi* also carries the implication of replacing the single authorship of the old *fiqh* texts by a plural legislative voice, the authoritative manual opinion ousted by the authoritative code article,[6] the *fiqh* texts, and their legal doctrines, have become so institutionalized in the Indonesian Muslim community it is impossible for this new code to replace it entirely. In short, taking all these obstacles into consideration, judges are inescapably ambivalent towards the *kompilasi*.

This ambivalence towards the *kompilasi* is also unequivocally expressed in society at large. If the ambivalence of the judges is demonstrated both by their persistence in quoting the *fiqh* texts and their preference in some instances for the legal doctrines covered in them, the ambivalent position of society is shown in its attitude that the religious courts deal with purely administrative matters. Interestingly, the prevalence of such an attitude in society has affected the judicial practices of the judges in the religious courts. This appears most frequently in marital matters, such as divorce and marriage. Although the *kompilasi* decrees that divorce is only operative if a husband pronounces the formula of divorce in the court, many couples, particularly in villages, have sought divorce in their own way, in front of *'ulamā'* or at KUA, an institution for religious affairs which until 1974 was the authority for dealing with such cases. They regard their actions as religiously lawful. For the sake of legalization or to obtain formal evidence of what they have undertaken, a number of them have approached the courts afterwards. This is irrevocable evidence that the application of the *kompilasi* has not met its goal of directing society to solve its familial problems in the courts, that is, to obtain a legal guarantee and certainty. As a consequence, dual validity of both marriage and divorce is still accepted by Indonesian Muslims. Expressions of the invalidity of a marriage or divorce are not recognized under State law, but are lawful according to religious doctrine, and therefore still commonly heard.

It can thus be said that although judges in the religious courts have succeeded in establishing their position as State judges, they have still found it hard to apply the rules by which they should formally abide. Realizing that they cannot force society to resort to State law, the judges are often inclined to go along with the present, temporal interests of the seekers of justice in the courts, even though they may be contradictory to rules as interpreted by the State. The fulfilment of numerous requests for the legalization of marriages not conducted according to the rules demonstrates the weakness of the judges in the religious courts. The reason they prioritize public good or utility rather than applying the letter of the law can be logically accepted. Nevertheless, the fact that they have not succeeded in persuading society to marry according to the State law in the first place, that is, in the front of a marriage registrar, a regulation also based on the concept of the public good, suggests that they do not enjoy a strong position in society.

It is an inescapable conclusion that Indonesian Muslims have felt a need to rectify superannuated laws which undermined gender relations and the equal treatment of women and men, and in searching for solutions they have inevitably led themselves towards legal modernization. To achieve this, it was essential to turn to codification, but the authority of classical legal texts seems to be so entrenched among Indonesian Muslims that their position cannot be challenged too vehemently. What Lev has concluded when he states that Islamic modernism in Indonesia has been less inventive and outspoken doctrinally than in the Middle East seems so far to be justified.[7]

Notes

Introduction

1. John L. Esposito, *Women in Muslim Family Law* (New York: Syracuse University Press, 2001), 51-61.
2. Tahir Mahmood, *Personal Law in Islamic Countries* (New Delhi: Academy of Law and Religion, 1987), 216.
3. *Ibid.*, 99.
4. *Ibid.*, 118.
5. Esposito, *Women in Muslim Family Law*, 81.
6. Atho Mudzhar and Khairuddin Nasution, *Hukum Keluarga di Dunia Islam Modern: Studi perbandingan Keberanjakan UU Modern dari Kitab-Kitab Fiqh* (Jakarta: Ciputat Press, 2003), 19-20.
7. Fikret Karcic, "Applying the Shari'a in Modern Societies", *Islamic Studies* 40: 2 (2001), 214.
8. J.N.D. Anderson, "The Tunisian Law of Personal Status", *International and Comparative Law Quarterly* 7 (April 1958), 266.
9. Tanzilur Rahman, *Islamization of Pakistan* (Karachi: Hamdard Academy, 1987), 7.
10. Brinkley Messick, *The Calligraphic State: Textual Domination and History in a Muslim World* (California: University of California Press, 1993), 63.
11. Yahya Harahap, "Informasi Materi Kompilasi Hukum Islam: Mempositifkan Abstraksi Hukum Islam", in Cik Hasan Bisri, *Kompilasi Hukum Islam dan Peradilan Agama dalam Sistem Hukum Nasional* (Jakarta: Logos Wacana Ilmu, 1999).
12. See 'Islam,' in G.H. Bousquet and Joseph Schacht, *C. Snouck Hurgronje: Selected Works* (Leiden: Brill, 1957), 70-71.
13. Daniel S. Lev, *Islamic Courts in Indonesia: A Study in the Political Bases of Legal Institutions* (Berkeley: University of California Press, 1972), 128.
14. *Ibid.*
15. Max Weber, "Charisma and Institutionalization in the Legal System," in Eisenstadt S. N. (ed.), *Max Weber: On Charisma and Institution Building* (Chicago: The University of Chicago Press, 1968), 81-82.
16. Bryan S. Turner, *Weber and Islam; A Critical Study* (London: Routledge and Kegan Paul, 1974), 108-9.
17. *Ibid.*
18. See Bustanul Arifin, "Kompilasi: Fiqh Dalam Bahasa Undang-Undang", *Pesantren* 2,2 (1985): 5-30.
19. Emile Durkheim, *The Division of Labor in Society*, translated by G. Simpson (New York: Free Press, 1933), 211.
20. John R. Bowen, *Islam, Law and Equality in Indonesia: An Anthropology of Public Reasoning* (Cambridge: Cambridge University Press, 2003), 192-197.

I The Indonesian Religious Courts: Institutional and Judicial Developments

1. Wahyu Widiana, "Peradilan Agama di Indonesia: Status, Prospek, Tantangan dan Solusinya", a Paper presented in seminar on *Peradilan Agama di Indonesia (Religious Courts in Indonesia)* held by the Faculty of Shari'a, IAIN Jakarta, in 2001.
2. Interview with the chairman of the religious court of Rangkasbitung, Rangkasbitung, 13 March 2003.
3. For the discussion on the qualifications for chairmen of the religious courts, see Harahap, *Kedudukan dan Kewenangan*, 119.
4. It should be noted that according to the statistical data in 2002, the population of Banten totaled 8,529,799 with 95.89 per cent Muslims, and the small remaining percentage constituting other adherents. This number is shared over five regencies including Tangerang, Cilegon, Serang, Pandeglang, and Lebak or Rangkasbitung. For a further account, see "Bapeda Propinsi Banten dan Badan Pusat Statistik Kabupaten Serang", 2002. The population of Jakarta, which consists of five regencies, Central Jakarta, East Jakarta, South Jakarta, West Jakarta, and East Jakarta, is 7,470,360. See "Data Statistik Tahun 2005: Suku Dinas kependudukan dan Catatan Sipil Kotamdaya", at www.kependudukancapil.go.id.
5. Interview with Syudjai, the vice-chairman of the religious court of Rangkasbitung, Rangkasbitung, 12 March 2003.
6. Indeed a recent survey indicated that the judges of the religious courts admitted to having jobs (*kerja sampingan*) other than being judges. Some are involved in academic activities, such as being a lecturer at universities or in *pesantren*, some others are engaged in quite informal activities like being *imam* or *khatib* at Friday prayers; see Lubis, *Islamic Justice in Transition*, 327.
7. Interview with the chairman of the religious court of Cianjur, Cianjur, 21 March 2003.
8. See also its judgment No. 1006/Pdt.G/1996/ PAJS which records that the case was registered on 30 October 1996 and that it was given its decision on 5 May 1997.
9. Daniel S. Lev, *Islamic Courts in Indonesia*, 112.
10. For a general overview on the coming of Islam to Indonesia, see for example, Azyumardi Azra, *The Transmission of Islamic Reformism to Indonesia: Networks of Middle East and Malay-Indonesian 'Ulama' in the Seventeenth and Eighteenth Centuries*, Ph.D. Dissertation (New York: Columbia University, 1992). See also, Ibrahim Buchari, *Sejarah Masuknya Islam dan Proses Islamisasi di Indonesia* (Jakarta: Publicita, 1971); Peter G. Riddell, "Arab Migrants and Islamization in the Malay World During the Colonial Period", *Indonesian and the Malay World*, 29: 84 (2001), 113-28; and M.C. Ricklefs, *A History of Modern Indonesia since c. 1300* (London: The Macmillan Press, 1993).
11. Harry J. Benda, *The Crescent and the Rising Sun: Indonesian Islam Under the Japanese Occupation, 1942-1945* (Dordrecht: Foris Publications, 1983), 12.
12. For a comprehensive discussion on Islamization in Java, see, M.C. Ricklefs, "Six Centuries of Islamization in Java," in Nehemia Levtzion (ed.), *Conversion to Islam* (New York: Holmes & Meier, 1979), 100-128; C.C. Berg, "Islamisation of Java," *Studia Islamica*, 1 (1953), 111-142.
13. Fauzan Saleh, *Modern Trends in Islamic Theological Discourse in 20th Century Indonesia* (Leiden: Brill, 2001), 24.
14. Clifford Geertz, *The Religion of Java* (Clencoe: Free Press, 1960).
15. See "Islam Practiced in Indonesia", *Indonesia Mediawatch*, 11 January 2002. www.rsi.com.sg/en/programmes/ind_med_wat/2002/11_01.htm.

16. See Z.A. Noeh and A.B. Adnan, *Sejarah Singkat Pengadilan Agama Islam di Indonesia* (Surabaya: Bina Ilmu, 1983), 3.
17. See Z.A. Noeh, "Kepustakaan Jawa sebagai Sumber Sejarah Perkembangan Hukum Islam", in Amrullah Ahmad, *Prospek Hukum Islam dalam kerangka Pembangunan Hukum Nasional di Indonesia: Sebuah Kenangam 65 Tahun Prof. DR. H. Bustanul Arifin, SH,* (Jakarta: PP-IKAHA, 1994).
18. Zuffran Sabrie (ed.), *Peradilan Agama di Indonesia: Sejarah Perkembangan Lembaga dan Proses Pembentukan Undang-Undangnya* (Jakarta: Ditbinbapera of Ministry of Religious Affairs of the Republic of Indonesia, 1999/2000), 1-12; See also Z.A. Noeh, "Kepustakaan Jawa Sebagai Sumber Sejarah Perkembangan Hukum Islam", in Amrullah Ahmad (ed.), *Prospek Hukum Islam dalam Kerangka Pembangunan Hukum Nasional di Indonesia: Sebuah Kenangan 65 Tahun Prof. Dr. Bustanul Arifin, S.H.* (Jakarta: IKAHA, 1994), 106-108.
19. Abdul Halim, *Peradilan Agama dalam Politik Hukum di Indonesia: Dari Otoriter Konservatif Menuju Konfigurasi Demokratis-Responsif* (Jakarta: PT RajaGrafindo Persada, 2000), 37. See also Ricklefs, *A History of Modern Indonesia*, 4.
20. According to *fiqh*, *qāḍī* or *ḥākim* could be appointed in three ways; *taḥkīm*, *tawliya ahl ḥalli wa al-'aqd*, and *tawliya* by an imam. Noeh mentions the appointment of the *qādī* by the Dutch administration in the colonial period as an example of the third form. He maintained that this sort of appointment was considered valid by *'ulamā'*. See Noeh, "Kepustakaan Jawa", 106. For a detailed explanation about *taḥkīm and tawliya*, see Shaykh Zainuddin ibn 'Abd al-Azīz al-Malībārī, *Fatḥ al Mu'īn bi Sharḥ Qurrat al-'Ain* (Reproduction) (Bandung: Al-Ma'arif, 1978), 137.
21. Abdul Halim, *Peradilan Agama dalam Politik Hukum di Indonesia*, 37. See also Noeh, "Kepustakaan Jawa", 108.
22. M. Yahya Harun, *Kerajaan Islam di Nusantara Abad XVI and XVII* (Yogyakarta: Kurnia Kalam Sejahtera, 1994), 25.
23. Sabrie, *Peradilan Agama*, 3. See also Muhammad Hisyam, *Caught Between Three Fires: The Javanese Penghulu Under The Dutch Colonial Administration 1882-1942*, Ph.D. Dissertation (Leiden: Leiden University, 2001), 28
24. In this respect, Hisyam mentions two other courts besides *Peradilan Surambi* in the Mataram Sultanate in the late eighteenth century, namely the *Peradilan Pradata* and the *Peradilan Balemangu*. It was not clear whether the *Peradilan Balemangu* was the *Peradilan Padu* itself or another *Peradilan*. Unfortunately, Hisyam does not describe this *peradilan* in any detail. While the *Peradilan Pradata*, as far as I am concerned, was undoubtedly the *Peradilan* which transformed into the *Peradilan Surambi* in the reign of Sultan Agung and was revived again as *Peradilan Pradata* in the rule of Amangkurat I. See Hisyam, *Caught between Three Fires*, 28. Having revived the *Peradilan Pradata*, as some writers have analyzed, Amangkurat I intended to halt the growing power of the Muslim religious scholars (*'ulamā'*), which he considered as threatening his position. For details on this, see Tresna, *Peradilan di Indonesia dari Abad ke Abad* (Jakarta: Pradnya Paramita, 1978).
25. Jayapattra is an old Javanese inscription. It is a note or a certificate of victory issued to the winner of a lawsuit. For more information on Jayapattra in particular and types of inscriptions in general, see Mason C. Hoadley, "Continuity and Change in Javanese Legal Tradition: The Evidence of the Jayapattra", *Indonesia*, 11 (April 1971), 95-110; for a comparison see M.B. Hooker, *An Introduction to Javanese Law: A Translation of and Commentary on the Agama* (Arizona: The University of Arizona Press, 1981).
26. Hoadley, "Continuity and Change in Javanese Legal Tradition", 107. For the discussion of other examples of the process of assimilation between Islamic law and *adat*, see Christian Pelras, "Religion, Tradition, and the Dynamics of Islamization in South Sulawesi", *Indonesia*, 57 (1993), 133-154. He mentions that in Sulawesi in

some cases Islamic practices were combined with pre-Islam tradition, such as the Islamic ceremony of *'aqīqa*. This ceremony was performed for a newly born child in combination with the traditional practice of placing the child in its cradle for the first time.

27. Hisyam, *Caught between Three Fires*, 54. The inclusion of criminal issues in the jurisdiction of the *Pengadilan Agama* in Priangan occurred when the Mataram Kingdom was on the point of collapse. In this situation, it was impossible for the *Peradilan Pradata* to treat the criminal issues, which fell under its jurisdiction, and hence the Muslim community submitted the issues to the *Pengadilan Agama* in Priangan. For details on this, see Tresna, *Peradilan di Indonesia*, 107.
28. The Islamic Sultanate of Banten was established in 1527. Its glory in political, cultural and economic aspects peaked in the period of 1651-1676, under the leadership of Sultan Ageng Tirtayasa. In 1682, this Sultanate was fully subjected to the authority of Dutch colonial administration. See Harun, *Kerajaan Islam di Nusantara*, 33 and 39.
29. Martin van Bruinessen, "Shari'a Court, Tarekat and Pesantren, Religious Institutions in the Banten Sultanate", *Archipel* 50 (1995): 165-200.
30. The term "independent *'ulamā'* is opposed to that "dependent *'ulamā'*, on the basis of Benda's categorization of the *'ulamā'* in the colonial period. The former refers to those who did not have any relationship with the governmental system and played their role in *pesantren*, while the latter refers to those who had relationship with or were the assistants to the government, such as *penghulu*. See Benda, *The Crescent and the Rising Sun*, 36.
31. *Ibid.*
32. Martin van Bruinessen, "Kitab Kuning: Books in Arabic Script Used in the Pesantren Milieu", *Bijdragen tot de Taal-, Land- en Volkenkunde*, 146 (1990): 226-69.
33. Cik Hasan Bisri (ed.), *Kompilasi Hukum Islam dan peradilan Agama dalam Sistem Hukum Nasional* (Jakarta: Logos Wacana Ilmu, 1999), 26; See also Noeh and Adnan, *Sejarah Singkat*, 31.
34. The complete title was the *Compendium der Voornaamste Mahommedaansche Wetten en Gewoonten Nopens Erfenissen, Huwelijken en Echtscheidingen* (Compendium of the Principal Islamic Laws and Customs of Inheritance, Marriage and Divorce). Hisyam, *Caught between Three Fires*, 50. For the complete text of the compendium, see Van der Chijs, *Nederlandsch Indisch Plakaatboek VI* (1890): 395-407.
35. Hisyam, *Caught between Three Fires*, 50.
36. *Ibid.*
37. *Ibid.*
38. Sabrie, *Peradilan Agama*, 14.
39. This theory generally holds that for the Hindus the applied law was the Hindu law, and for the Christians it was the Christian law, and for those who were Muslims it was the Islamic law. See Noeh and Adnan, *Sejarah Singkat*, 34.
40. *Priesterraad* means priests' courts. These courts were named *priesterraad* on the mistaken perception that the *Penghulu* and *qāḍī* function as priests.
41. Sabrie, *Peradilan Agama*, 12.
42. Noeh and Adnan, *Sejarah Singkat*, 32-33; see also Hisyam, *Caught between Three Fires*, 59.
43. Noeh and Adnan, *Sejarah Singkat*, 41.
44. For detailed information on the relationship between the *penghulu* and *bupati*, see Hisyam, *Caught between Three Fires*, 68.
45. *Ibid.*, 60-62.
46. Lev, *Islamic Court*, 17. It was reported that the leader of this committee was actually R.A. Hoesen Jayadiningrat, but the main actor was Ter Haar, known for his sympathy with *adat;* see Hisyam, *Caught between Three Fires*, 57.

47. Sabrie, *Peradilan Agama*, 15.
48. Amrullah Ahmad, *Prospek Hukum Islam dalam Kerangka Pembangunan Hukum Nasional di Indonesia: Sebuah Kenangan 65 Tahun Prof. Dr. H. Bustanul Arifin*, S.H. (Jakarta: IKAHA, 1994), 6. See also Halim, *Peradilan Agama*, 37; Sabrie, *Peradilan Agama*, 13.
49. Muchtar Zarkasyi (ed.), *Himpunan Peraturan Perundang-Undangan Badan peradilan Agama di Indonesia* (Jakarta: Ministry of Religious Affairs, 1976), 38. See also Zuffran Sabrie, *Peradilan Agama*, 14.
50. Bustanul Arifin, *Pelembagaan Hukum Islam di Indonesia: Akar Sejarah, Hambatan dan Prospeknya* (Jakarta: Gema Insani Press, 1996), 36.
51. See R.P. Notosusanto, *Peradilan Agama Islam di Djawa dan Madura* (Yogyakarta: s.n., 1953), 19. Notosusanto recorded that after the application of *Staatsblaad 1937 No. 116*, conflicts between religious courts and general courts on the competence of both courts often arise. One such example is that a person (A) came to general court admitting that he is one of the heirs of B (mother or father), but another heir rejected that he is not, because he was born out an illegal marriage between his mother or father with B. This matter, thus, relates also to marriage issues, which come under jurisdiction of the religious courts. The issue then should be submitted to the religious courts first to deal with the marriage matters. See also Lev, *Islamic Courts*, 17; Zuffran Sabrie, *Peradilan Agama*, 16; Hooker, *Islamic Law in South-East Asia*, 254.
52. Lev pointed out that the exclusion of inheritance from the jurisdiction of the religious courts had meant a drop in judges' income, and this was assumed to be the major reason why the judges objected with the policy. See Lev, *Islamic Courts in Indonesia*, 19.
53. Hisyam, *Caught between Three Fires*, 200.
54. Halim, *Peradilan Agama*, 38.
55. Sabrie, *Peradilan Agama*, 17.
56. Hazairin, *Hukum Kekeluargaan Nasional* (Jakarta: Tintamas, 1962), 4.
57. For more information about this organization see Hisyam, *Caught between Three Fires*, 201-209.
58. Noeh and Adnan, *Sejarah Singkat*, 40.
59. Sabrie, *Peradilan Agama*, 18.
60. Lev, *Islamic Courts*, 20.
61. M.B. Hooker, *Islamic Law in South-East Asia*, 255.
62. Noeh and Adnan, *Sejarah Singkat*, 38.
63. For a detailed discussion, see Benda, *The Crescent and the Rising Sun*, 103-150.
64. Noeh and Adnan, *Sejarah Singkat*, 45.
65. Benda, *The Crescent and the Rising Sun*, 116.
66. Noeh and Adnan, *Sejarah Singkat*, 49.
67. Lev, *Islamic Court in Indonesia*, 41.
68. The Ministry of Religious Affairs had earlier been an 'Office for Religious (Islamic) Affairs'. As soon as the Japanese surrendered and independence was proclaimed Indonesian Government changed it into Ministry of Religious Affairs on 3 January 1946. See Hooker, *Islamic Law in South-East Asia*, 255.
69. *Ibid.*, 258.
70. Noeh and Adnan, *Sejarah Singkat*, 53; see also Hooker, *Islamic Law in South-East Asia*, 257.
71. Sabrie, *Peradilan Agama*, 24
72. *Ibid.*, 21. It was some nationalists like the late Professor Supomo who attempted to eliminate the religious courts. See Lev, *Islamic Courts*, 64.
73. Noeh and Adnan, *Sejarah Singkat*, 54.
74. Lev, *Islamic Courts*, 65.

75. Sabrie, *Peradilan Agama*, 22.
76. This *Mahkamah* actually had existed since 1946 on the basis of the permission of the Prime Minister of Central Government of Sumatra, in Pematang Siantar at that time. In the wake of the establishment of the United Republic of Indonesia, the officials of the Islamic Religious Department were moved to the centre, namely Ministry of Religious Affairs, and the Prime Minister of the Provisional Government left Aceh. This left the *Mahkamah Syar'iyyah* unmanaged. Besides, the establishment of the United Republic of Indonesia robbed the *Mahkamah Syar'iyyah* of its legal basis. But as the Acehnese could not be easily persuaded to give up the Mahkamah, the Central Government acceded to their requirement by re-establishing *Mahkamah Syar'iyyah*. See Sabrie, *Peradilan Agama*, 25.
77. As mentioned earlier, religious courts in Banjarmasin had been regulated in *Staatsblad 1937 No. 638*, which upheld the same position as the *Staatsblad 1882 No. 152*, connected to *Staatsblad 1937 No. 116 and 610* for Java and Madura.
78. Sabrie, *Peradilan Agama*, 27-28
79. Mark Cammack, "Indonesia's 1989 Religious Judicature Act: Islamization of Indonesia or Indonesianization of Islam", *Indonesia*, 63 (1997), 148.
80. Lev, *Islamic Court*, 90. Lev mentions that the complete jurisdiction of the new religious courts in the outer Islands (Java, Madura and Banjarmasin) included custody and support of children (*ḥaḍāna*), wakaf, *bayt al-māl*, charity, inheritance, and gifts from inherited estates (*hibah*); see also Hooker, *Islamic Law in South-East Asia*, 262. Looking at their competence, Mahadi even found that, in practice, the religious courts outside Java and Madura and Banjarmasin sometimes went beyond the lines of their formal jurisdiction over inheritance. They, as Mahadi reported, often heard cases relating to property, which were not included in their jurisdiction, such as a conflict about who had proprietary rights. See Prof. Mahadi, "Wewenang Pengadilan Agama", *Hukum Nasional* 3: 2 (1970), 17.
81. Lev, *Islamic Courts*, 90.
82. Meanwhile, in order to control the occurrence of marriages by registering them, the marriage registrars were also supposed to note whether or not the marriages to be registered were lawfully concluded. See Wasit Aulawi, "Sejarah Perkembangan Hukum Islam di Indonesia", in Amrullah Ahmad (ed.) *Dimensi Hukum Islam dalam Sistem Hukum Nasional* (Jakarta: Gema Insani press, 1996), 57-58; see also Sidik Sudarsono, *Masalah Administratif dalam Perkawinan Umat Islam Indonesia* (Jakarta: Dara, 1964), 128.
83. See Muchtar Zarkasyi, *Himpunan Peraturan Perundang-Undangan Badan Peradilan Agama di Indonesia*, 118; see also H. Abdurrahman, *Kompilasi Hukum Islam* (Jakarta: Akademika Presindo, 1992), 22.
84. See Law No. 14/1970 on Basic Law of Judicial Authority.
85. Sabrie, *Peradilan Agama*, 29.
86. It is based on the regulation of its application No. 9/1975.
87. See Ministry of Religious Affairs on *Compilation of Islamic Law, Marriage Law No. I/ 1974 and Islamic Judicature Law* of 1989.
88. See Law No. 1/1974 on Marriage. Article 63 states that every decision made by a religious court must be approved by a general court.
89. This was governed in Article 7 of *Staatsblad* No. 610 of 1937 in juxtaposition with Article 15 of *Staatsblad* No. 638 of 1937, which continued to be applied due to the regulation of Article 11 of the Government Regulation No. 45 of 1945.
90. Lubis, *Institutionalization and Unification of the Islamic Courts*, 39.
91. Noeh and Adnan, *Sejarah Singkat*, 85.
92. Islamic Judicature Act No. 7/1989, Article 107.
93. Islamic Judicature Act No. 7/1989, Article 49 (1).
94. Islamic Judicature Act No. 7/1989, Article 6 and 9.

95. It should be noted here that the annulment of only Article 63 (2) is mainly related to the fact that Law No. 1/1974 on marriage as a whole, as said before, is applied to all Indonesian citizens, regardless of their religion. In addition, the legal procedure of marriage indicated in the Act of 1989 has been adopted from what was included in the Law of 1974 on Marriage. Article 49 (2) of Act of 1989 plainly states that the subject of marriage, as mentioned in Point (1) Letter a, is matters that are regulated in or based on the existing and valid Law of Marriage of 1974.
96. Law No. 1/1974 on Marriage, Article 63.
97. Some Muslim scholars identified the religious courts as 'quasi-courts', as in their opinions up until 1989, the religious courts had no formal legal basis; see Halim, *Peradilan Agama*, 144.
98. Abdul Manan, *Hakim Peradilan Agama: Hakim di Mata Hukum, Ulama di Mata Umat* (Jakarta: Penerbit Pustaka Bangsa, 2003), 84.
99. Act, art. 13 (1).
100. See Lev, *Islamic Court*, 110.
101. Interview with Drs. Mas'udi, the Director of the Project, Jakarta, 3 June 2003.
102. Interview with Drs. Mas'udi, the Director of the Project, Jakarta, 3 June 2003.
103. Harahap, "Tujuan Kompilasi Hukum Islam", 88.
104. See Yahya Harahap, "Informasi Materi Kompilasi: Mempositifkan Abstraksi Hukum Islam", in Cik Hasan Bisri, *Kompilasi Hukum Islam dan Peradilan Agama dalam Sistem Hukum Nasional* (Jakarta: Logos, 1999), 149-156.
105. See Harahap, "Tujuan Kompilasi Hukum Islam", 91.
106. Law No. 35/1999 on Basic Regulation of Judicial Authority, article 11.
107. Act No. 7/1989 on Islamic Judicature, Article 5.
108. The "technical juridical" is generally concerned with the juridical procedure and is accomplished by the Supreme Court in several methods, such as publishing a guidebook containing instructions for performing juridical tasks and holding training for the judges in order to improve their ability and skills; Bisri, *Peradilan Islam dalam Tatanan Masyarakat Indonesia*, 157-158.
109. Law No. 35/1999 on Basic Regulation of Judicial Authority, Article 11A (1).
110. Law No. 35/1999 on Basic Regulation of Judicial Authority, Article 11A (2).
111. Halim, *Peradilan Agama*, 158.
112. On this, see Ministry of Religious Affairs, *10 Tahun Undang-Undang Peradilan Agama*, (Jakarta: Chasindo), 1999. This book includes articles focusing on the review of the application of the 'one roof' system to the religious courts.

II The Making of the *Kompilasi Hukum Islam*

1. Nasir Tamara, *Indonesia in the Wake of Islam: 1965-1985* (Malaysia: ISIS, 1986), 1.
2. B.J. Bolland, *The Struggle of Islam in Modern Indonesia* (Leiden: KITLV, 1970); see also Moh. Mahfud MD, *Politik Hukum di Indonesia* (Jakarta: LP3ES, 1998).
3. M. Kamal Hasan, *Muslim Intellectual Responses to New Order Modernization in Indonesia* (Kuala Lumpur: Dewan Bahasa dan Pustaka, 1982), 79. For a fuller account of the history of this party, see Anthony H. Johns, "Indonesia: Islam and Cultural Pluralism", in John L. Esposito (ed.), *Islam in Asia: Religion, Politics, and Society* (New York: Oxford University, 1987), 202-229.
4. June Chandra Sentosa, *Modernization, Utopia, and the Rise of Islamic Radicalism*, PhD Dissertation (Boston: Boston University, 1996), 127.
5. For the direct statement of the Army, see Bolland, *The Struggle of Islam*, 151.
6. Nasir Tamara, "Islam under the New Order: A Political History," *Prisma* (June 1990):11.

7. Hasan, *Muslim Intellectual Response,* 80.
8. Bolland, *The Struggle of Islam,* 27.
9. For a detailed discussion on this issue, see also Tarmizi Taher, "Changing the Image of Islam", *Studia Islamika* 3: 2 (1996), 6-21.
10. The nine parties were Parmusi, PSSI, Perti, NU, PNI, Roman Catholic party, IPKI, Parkindo, and Murba, see Mahfud, *Politik Hukum di Indonesia,* 264.
11. Anthony H. Johns, "Indonesia", 217; see also Bahtiar Effendi, *Islam and the State: The Transformation of Islamic Political Ideas and Practices in Indonesia,* Ph.D. Dissertation, Ohio University, 1994.
12. The first congress held by women in 1928 had stressed that the act of marriage should not be governed by Islamic principles. In 1937, the Dutch (Indies) Government issued a draft, which stipulated that the marriage should be registered and should be monogamous. This draft was cancelled because of objections raised by Islamic political groups. After independence, in 1957, a draft dealing with the matter was introduced. Again, it was confronted by opposition and was then cancelled. See Andree Feillard, *NU vis-à-vis Negara* (Yogyakarta: LKIS, 1999), 190-191.
13. Feillard, *NU vis-à-vis Negara,* 192.
14. For detailed debated points, see Nani Soewondo, "The Indonesian Marriage Law and Its Implementing Regulation", *Archipel* 13 (1977), 284-85; see also Susan Blackburn and Sharon Bessell, "Marriageable Age: Political Debates on Early Marriage in Twentieth-Century Indonesia", *Archipel* 14 (1977), 132-6.
15. See Katz and Katz, "Legislating Social Change in a Developing Country; The New Indonesian Marriage Law Revisited", *American Journal of Comparative Law* 26 (1978), 309, and "The New Indonesian Marriage Law: A Mirror of Indonesia's Political, Cultural, and Legal System", *American Journal of Comparative Law* 23 (1975), 663. See also Effendi, *Islam and the State,* 134.
16. Santosa, *Modernization, Utopia, and the Rise of Islamic Radicalism,* 124.
17. Halim, *Peradilan Agama dalam Politik Hukum Indonesia,* 118.
18. Mahfud, *Politik Hukum Islam,* 10.
19. Faisal Ismail, "Pancasila as the Sole Basis for all Political Parties and for all Mass Organization: An Account of Muslim's Responses," *Studia Islamika* 3: 4 (1996), 3.
20. Effendi, *Islam and the State,* 135-136. For a full discussion on this issue, see Ismail, "Pancasila as the Sole Basis for All Political Parties and for All Mass Organization", 1-92.
21. Aswab Mahasin, "The Santri Middle Class: An Insider's View", in Richard Tanter and Kenneth Young (ed.), *The Politics of Middle Class Indonesia* (Victoria: CSEAS Monash University, 1990), 139-140.
22. See Nurcholish Madjid, "Keharusan Pembaharuan Pemikiran Islam dan Masalah Integrasi Ummat", in Nurcholish Madjid et al, *Pembaharuan Pemikiran Islam* (Jakarta: Islamic Research Center, 1970), 1-12.
23. *Ibid.,* 4-9.
24. Effendi, *Islam and the State,* 305; see also Robert W. Hefner, "Islamization and Democratization in Indonesia", *Islam in an Era of Nation-States* (Honolulu: University of Hawaii Press, 1997), especially part of 'The Quest for the Middle Class, 90-94.
25. Abdurrahman Wahid, "Islam Punya Konsep Kenegaraan?", *Tempo,* 29 December, (1984), 17.
26. Nurcholish Madjid, "Cita-Cita Politik Kita," in Bosco Carvallo and Dasrizal (ed.,), *Aspirasi Umat Islam Indonesia* (Jakarta: Lapenmas, 1983), 7-36.
27. Hasbullah Bakri, "Lima Dalil Indonesia Bisa Disebut Negara Islam Non-Konstitutional", *Panji Masyarakat,* 439 (August 1983), 29-31.
28. Munawir Syadzali, *Islam dan Tatanegara: Ajaran, Sejarah dan Pemikiran* (Jakarta: UI Press, 1990), 11-20; see also Madjid, "Cita-Cita Politik Kita", 10-16.

29. See Soeharto, *My Thoughts, Words, and Deeds*, English Translation by Sumadi, (Jakarta: PT Gatra Lantoro Gung Persada, 1991), 352.
30. On the broad discussion on the relationship between Islam and State marked by tensions and the change of their relationship towards accommodation and harmony see Dody Truna, *Islam and Politics under the New Order Government in Indonesia, 1966-1990*, MA Thesis (Montreal: McGill University, 1992).
31. Effendi classified the growing accommodation of the State toward Islam into four different types; (1) structural; (2) legislative; (3) infra-structural; and (4) cultural. See Effendi, *Islam and the State*, 303.
32. Effendi, *Islam and the State*, 307-308.
33. Hefner, "Islamization and Democratization in Indonesia", 75. See also his book, *Civil Islam: Muslim and Democratization in Indonesia* (Princeton: Princeton University Press, 2000).
34. The New Order Government included the aspect of religious tolerance in the GBHN development steps set out every five years as one of the aspects of its religious development. Minister of Religious Affairs (1978-1983), Alamsyah Ratu Perwiranegara formulated religious tolerance as a "trilogy of tolerance", namely, tolerance of internal religion, tolerance of inter-religious communities, and tolerance between the religious community and the Government. See Masykuri Abdillah, *Responses of Indonesian Muslim Intellectuals to the Concept of Democracy (1966-1993)* (Abera Network: Hamburg, 1997), 45.
35. See Muhammad Hisyam, "The Interaction of Religion and State in Indonesia", in Johan Meuleman, *Islam in the Era of Globalization: Muslim Attitudes towards Modernity and Identity* (Jakarta: INIS, 2001). See also Sabrie, *Peradilan Agama di Indonesia*, 59. On the full account of the debate, see his book, *Peradilan Agama dalam Wadah Negara Pancasila: Dialog Tentang RUUPA* (Jakarta: Logos, 2001).
36. Effendi, *Islam and the State*, 323.
37. Feillard, *NU vis a vis Negara*, 392.
38. Halim, *Peradilan Agama*, 147.
39. Halim, *Peradilan Agama*, 148. See also Effendi, *Islam and the State*, 323.
40. On the revised clauses of the Act, see the previous chapter of this work. For more details, see Sabrie, *Peradilan Agama*, 84-116.
41. For a detailed account on the discussion of these events see Effendi, *Islam and the State*, 309-314 and 324-339.
42. Ismail Saleh, "Eksistensi Hukum Islam dan Sumbangannya terhadap Hukum Nasional", in Zuffran Sabrie, *Peradilan Agama dalam Wadah Negara Pencasila: Dialog tentang RUUPA* (Jakarta: Pustaka Antara, 1990), 132.
43. Michael Feener wrote an extensive article on this issue of the preliminary attempt of the formulation of an Indonesian *Madhhab*. See Michael Feener, "Indonesian Movements for the Creation of a National Madhhab", *Islamic Law and Society*, 9:1 (2002).
44. Hazairin, *Hukum Kekeluargaan Nasional* (Jakarta: Tintamas, 1962), 10.
45. Hazairin, *Indonesia Satu Mesjid* (Jakarta: Bintang Bulan, 1952).
46. Hazairin, *Hukum Islam dan Masyarakat* (Jakarta: Tintamas, 1963), 7-8.
47. See Hazairin, *Hukum Kekeluargaan Nasional*, 14.
48. In this case, John R. Bowen said that, although Hazairin retained the two-one ratio of shares for males and females, developing Hazairin's concept of bilateralism, his successors like Yahya Harahap, a Supreme Court judge, have proposed an equal division of the shares between male and females; see John R. Bowen, "The Qur'an, Justice and Gender: Internal Debates in Indonesian Islamic Jurisprudence," *History of Religions*, 38:1 (1998), 52-78.
49. Hazairin, *Hukum Kewarisan Bilateral*, 15. The use of the term '*uṣbah* with its three classifications namely: *uṣbah binafsihi*; *uṣbah ma'a al ghayr*; and *uṣbah bighayrihi*, Hazairin claimed indicates that it applied unilaterally, in this case, patrilineally, the

aim of which is to preserve the tribal or clan system. See Hazairin, *Hendak Kemana Hukum Islam* (Jakarta: Tintamas, 1960), 13.

50. Hazirin, *Hukum Kewarisan Bilateral*, 16. See also his *Hukum kekeluargaan Nasional*, 4.
51. Hazairin, *Hukum Kewarisan Bilateral*, 16. For a detailed explanation of who are included into each group, see 22-25.
52. Bowen, "Qur'an, Justice and Gender", 69.
53. Hazairin, *Hukum Kewarisan Bilateral*, 26.
54. *Ibid.*, 6. This Qur'anic verse says "and for every one we had accorded heirs for what the parents, relatives and parties that have made contract leave, therefore give them their portions".
55. Hasbi Al-Shiddiqi, *Syari'at Islam Menjawab Tantangan Jaman* (Jakarta: Bulan Bintang, 1966), 43.
56. Hasbi himself mentioned that Egypt, for example, has been attempting to Egyptianize its *fiqh*. See Nourouzzaman Shiddieqy, *Fiqh Indonesia: Penggagas dan Gagasannya* (Yogyakarta: Pustaka Pelajar, 1995), 231. I argue that what Hasbi meant by 'Egyptianize its *fiqh*' is to make a *fiqh* in accordance with new conditions of Egypt.
57. Shiddieqy, *Fiqh Indonesia*, 230-235.
58. Yudian Wahyudi, *Hasbi's Theory of Ijtihād in the Context of Indonesian Fiqh*, MA thesis (Montreal: McGill University, 1993) 38.
59. When discussing the religio-political publications in connection with the debates of the basis of newly independent Indonesia, Boland included a piece of writing by Hasbi on the principles of Islamic Government (Dasar-*Dasar Pemerintahan Islam*), proposed to the Congress of Indonesian Muslims. Here Hasbi discusses various terms from the Qur'ān and Tradition relevant to the Muslim idea of a State in accordance with Islam, and shows that some teachings of Islamic law can be used for the building a modern Islamic nation; see Boland, *The Struggle of Islam*, 81. However, it was to avoid any political manipulation of his ideas, according Yudian Wahyudi, that Hasbi expanded the book and changed the title to *Asas-Asas Hukum Tata Negara Menurut Syari'at Islam* (Principles of the Constitutional Laws According to the *Shari'a*). See Wahyudi, "Hasbi's Theory of *Ijtihad*", 38.
60. In keeping with the opinion that the gate of *ijtihād* is still open, some Muslim scholars had put some stipulations on its use. One of the stipulations was that *ijtihād* in *madhhab* and beyond the boundaries of the *madhhab* can only be carried out collectively and cannot be done individually. See Ibrahim Hosen, *Persoalan Taqlid and Ijtihad* (Jakarta: Yayasan Wakaf Paramadina, 1987), 328.
61. Munawir Sjadzali, *Ijtihad Kemanusiaan* (Jakarta: Yayasan Paramadina, 1997), 50.
62. Bahtiar Effendi, "Islam and the State of Indonesia", *Studia Islamika* 2: 2 (1995), 109.
63. See Iqbal Abdurrauf Saimima, *Polemik Reaktualisasi Ajaran Islam* (Jakarta: Pustaka Panjimas, 1988).
64. Effendi, "Islam and the State of Indonesia", 112.
65. Saimima, *Polemik Reaktualisai Ajaran Islam*, 4.
66. Sabrie (ed.), *Peradilan Agama di Indonesia*, 38; see also Halim, *Peradilan Agama dalam Politik Hukum di Indonesia*, 127.
67. Interview with Bustanul Arifin, Jakarta, 3 April 2003.
68. See H. Abdurrahman, *Kompilasi Hukum Islam* (Jakarta: Akademika Presindo, 1992), 39-41.
69. Interview with Bustanul Arifin, Jakarta, 3 April 2003. See also, *Panjimas*, 502: 27 (May 1986).
70. See Andree Fillard, *NU vis-à-vis Negara*, 389. Their objection to using the term 'codification' may have been because the term was basically used to adopt and formally codify one school of Islamic law or *madhhab* which had been adhered to by a state for long time and was observed by a number of Muslim countries such as Egypt,

Iran, Sudan, and Syria. It was reported that the greatest challenge not to codify any school of Islamic law formally, although also supported by other Muslim groups, was put forward by the Muhammadiyyah. In the seminar on the preparations for the *kompilasi*, held by the Majlis Tarjih of Muhammadiyyah, the head of the committee stated that the purpose of putting together the *kompilasi* was not to apply any one school of Islamic law in Indonesia forcibly, but to find Islamic rules which would be appropriate to the 'size' and the 'form' of Indonesian society. It seemed that the adherents of the Muhammadiyyah were afraid that the Shāfi'ī school of Islamic law, which is widely observed by Indonesian Muslims and adhered to by NU, would be legally applied in Indonesia The Muhammadiyyah itself is not tightly bound to any school of Islamic law but seeks inspiration in the Qur'ān and the Prophetic tradition. See Abdurrahman, *Kompilasi Hukum Islam*, 60-61.

71. See *The New International Webster's Comprehensive Dictionary of the English Language* (Florida: Trident Press International, 1996), 267.
72. *Ibid.*
73. Interview with Bustanul Arifin, Jakarta, 9 April 2003.
74. For a detailed description on this, see *Kompilasi Hukum Islam* (Jakarta: Dirjenbinbaga, Departemen Agama, 2000), 141. See also Abdurrahman, *Kompilasi Hukum Islam*, 39-41.
75. See H. Abdurrahman, *Kompilasi Hukum Islam*, 39-41.
76. It was assumed that the selection of thirteen *fiqh* books, most of which include the ideas of the Shāfi'i school, to be used as references for the religious courts, was influenced by the fact that in that period the Ministry of Religious Affairs and the religious courts were dominated by the traditionalist *'ulamā'* who adhered strictly to Shāfi'ī school. See Muhammad Atho Mudzhar, *Fatwās of The Council of Indonesian 'Ulamā': A Study of Islamic Legal Thought in Indonesia 1975-1988*, PhD Dissertation (Los Angeles: UCLA, 1990), 80.
77. Abdurrahman, *Kompilasi Hukum Islam*, 42.
78. Interview with Bustanul Arifin, Jakarta, 9 April 2003.
79. See PP IKAHA, *Prospek Hukum Islam*, 12.
80. For the detailed information on this, see *Kompilasi Hukum Islam*, 143.
81. For detailed accounts on the legalization of Islamic family law in Morocco and Egypt, see Dawoud S. El Alami, *The Marriage Contract in Islamic Law in the Shari'ah and Personal Status Laws of Egypt and Morocco* (London: Graham & Trotan Ltd., 1992). See also Ziba Mir-Hosseini, *Marriage on Trial, A Study of Islamic Family Law: Iran and Morocco Compared* (London: I.B. Touris & Co Ltd., 1993).
82. The reason why these three countries were chosen instead of others is that two countries, Egypt and Morocco, had adopted Islamic law to be their applied law, and that the other one, Turkey, in contrast had adopted Western codes for its applied law. See Imam Mawardi, "A Socio-Political Backdrop of the Enactment of the *Kompilasi Hukum Islam*", MA Thesis (Montreal: McGill University, 1998), 76.
83. The seminar was widely reported in the mass media. See for example, *Tempo*, 4 February (1989), 76-77.
84. The participants included thirteen professors of Islamic law, forty-six *kiyais* (traditional Muslim leaders), twenty-one jurists, a number of judges of the Supreme Court, and several rectors of IAIN (State Institute for Islamic Studies).
85. See *Kompilasi Hukum Islam*, 171-178.
86. Abdurrahman, *Kompilasi Hukum Islam*, 47-48.
87. Interviews with Amir Syarifuddin and Minhajul Falah, Jakarta, 19 February, 2003.
88. Mark Cammack, "Inching towards Equality: Recent Developments in Indonesian Inheritance Law," WUML (22 November 1999), 4.
89. Ziba Mir-Hosseini, *Marriage on Trial* (London: Tauris, 2000), 10.
90. Talal Asad, *Rethinking about Secularism and Law in Egypt* (Leiden: ISIM, 2001), 9.

91. Mir-Hosseini, *Marriage on Trial*, 10.
92. Max Weber, *On Charisma and Institutional Building*, edited by S.N. Eisenstadt (Chicago: The University of Chicago Press, 1968), 110-111.
93. See Effendi, *Islam and the State*, 305-306.
94. See Annelies Moors, "Debating Women and Islamic Family Law", *ISIM Newsletter*, 11 (2002).
95. Douglas E. Ramage, *Politics in Indonesia: Democracy, Islam, and Ideology of Tolerance* (London: Routledge, 1995).
96. "Halal Haramnya Kebulatan Tekad", *Tempo*, 26 May (1990), 22-28.
97. See John R. Bowen, *Islam, Law, Equality in Indonesia*, 189
98. See Darul Aqsa et al (eds.), *Islam in Indonesia: A Survey of Events and Developments from 1988 to March 1993* (Jakarta: INIS, 1995), 150.
99. Cecep Lukman Yasin, "The 1991 Compilation of Islamic Law: A Socio-Political Study of the Legislation of Islamic Law in the New Order Period", MA Thesis (Leiden: Leiden University, 2000), 46.
100. This term was used by Yahya Harahap, the Supreme Court judge, to refer to the way the *kompilasi* was promulgated. See M. Fadhil Lubis, "The Unification and the Institutionalization of the Islamic Courts in the New Order Era", *Studia Islamika* 2: 1 (1995), 1-51.
101. This statement expresses the idea that the ruler selected in the event of an emergency was to be obeyed. This expression was first popularized when Soekarno was elected President, but a number of Muslim groups did not want him, even though some others supported him. In order that all Muslims would obey him, in 1954 a conference under the leadership of the Minister of Religious Affairs, Kiyai Maskur, was held which proclaimed that Soekarno was '*walyy al-amri al-ḍarūrī bi al-shauka*'. This expression was to define him as a legitimate President who should be fully obeyed. See Andree Feillard, *NU vis a vis Negara, Pencarian Isi Bentuk dan Makna* (Yogyakarta: LKIS, 1999), 47-49.
102. Interview with Bustanul Arifin, Jakarta, August 2003.
103. Quoted from his report speech on the accomplishment of the project of the *Kompilasi*, 33.
104. See Bustanul Arifin, "Fiqh dalam Bahasa Undang-Undang", A Paper presented in a seminar in Surabaya, 8 July 1995.
105. Wahid and Rumadi, *Fiqh Madzhab Negara*, 168.

III Debates on the *Kompilasi Hukum Islam*

1. Leon Buskens, "An Islamic Triangle: Changing Relationship between Shari'a, State Law, and Local Customs", *ISIM Newsletter* 5 (2000), 8.
2. John R. Bowen, "Shari'a, State, and Social Norms in France and Indonesia", *ISIM Papers* (Leiden: ISIM, 2001), 1-24.
3. See, for an example, M.B. Hooker, "The State and Syari'ah in Indonesia 1945-1995", in Timothy Lindsey (ed.), *Indonesia, Law and Society* (Melbourne: the Federation Press, 1998), 107-108.
4. Lucy Carroll, "Orphaned Grandchildren in Islamic Law of Succession", *Islamic Law and Society*, 5 (1998), 410.
5. Rubya Mehdi records that the Pakistani solution, namely inheritance by right, was considered to be the more radical. The traditionalist *'ulamā'* opposed the system on the grounds that it ravages the spirit and the structure of the Islamic law of inheritance. They were, however, in accordance with the opinion that the problem of an orphaned grandchild should be disentangled, and maintained that an obligatory

bequest has a more valid legal base in the scripture. See Rubya Mehdi, *The Islamization of the Law in Pakistan*, 190.

6. See the *Kompilasi*, Art. 185 (1).
7. See judgment of the Appellate General Court No. 195/1950.The same sort of judgment had been also handed down in earlier times by the Raad van Justitie Batavia in December 12, 1932. This was recorded in "Indisch Tijdschrift van het Recht," 150 (1932): 239. For more details on this, see A.B. Loebis, *Pengadilan Negeri Jakarta in Action: Jurisprudensi Hukum Adat Warisan*, (n.p, n.d) 63.
8. See the *Kompilasi*, Art. 185 (2).
9. See the *Kompilasi*, art. 209 (1 & 2).
10. See Hilman Hadikusuma, *Hukum Waris Indonesia Menurut Perundangan, Hukum Adat, Hukum Agama Hindu, Islam* (Bandung: P.T. Citra Adtya Bakti, 1991), and Surjono Soekanto, "Hak Mewarisi Bagi Janda dan Anak / Anak Angkat," *Hukum Nasional*, 23 (1977), 73-96.
11. John R. Bowen, "Qur'an, Justice and Gender: Internal Debates in Indonesian Islamic Jurisprudence", 76.
12. See the *Kompilasi*, Art. 85, 86, 94, 95, 96 and 97.
13. See Ismail Muhammad Syah, *Pencaharian Bersama Suami Istri di Aceh Ditinjau dari Sudut UU Perkawinan Tahun 1974 dan Hukum Islam*, Ph.D. Dissertation (Jakarta: Universitas Indonesia, 1984), 282-283.
14. Lukito, *Pergumulan antara Hukum Islam dan Adat*, 83.
15. See Hilman Hadikusuma, *Hukum Waris Adat* (Bandung: Penerbit Alumni, 1980), 70-71.
16. The share of the father in such a situation is not definitively decided in the Qur'ān, and this leads him to get *`aṣaba* as clarified in *ḥadīth* transmitted by Bukhari and Muslim, stating "give the definite shares to their owners, and the rests are to be granted to the main group of males." The father is thus considered to be the closest heir after the sons and their generation.
17. Cammack, "Inching toward Equality",11.
18. This letter of clarification is always attached in every publication of handbooks of the *Kompilasi* of Islamic Law. The letter was issued by the Supreme Court as 'Surat Edaran No. 2/ 1994 tentang Pengertian Pasal 177 *Kompilasi* Hukum Islam (Circular Letter No. 2/ 1994 on the Perception of Article 177 of the *Kompilasi* of Islamic Law)'. See Ministry of Religious Affairs, *Kompilasi Hukum Islam*, 179.
19. In such a case a wife takes one quarter of the estate and mother takes her one-third of the remaining three-quarters (the residual), which makes one-quarter. These two shares of the mother and the wife take half of the estate and therefore the remainder or residual which is taken by the father is another one-half of the estate.
20. Interview with Ichtiyanto, Jakarta, 7 August 2003. Many judges find the clarification has cast sufficient light on the problem. In essence this acquiescence is attributable to their unfamiliarity with the comprehensive Islamic law of inheritance. They admitted not having agreed with the written rule and were satisfied with the explanation set out in the circular letter.
21. Dawoud Sudqi El Alami, *The Marriage Contract in Islamic Law in the Shari'ah and Personal Status Laws of Egypt and Morocco* (London: Graham & Trotman, 1992).
22. Mehdi, *The Islamization of Law in Pakistan*, 158.
23. See Khairuddin Nasution, *Status Wanita di Asia Tenggara: Studi Terhadap Perundang-Undangan Perkawinan Muslim kontemporer di Indonesia dan Malaysia* (Jakarta: INIS, 2002), 152.
24. See Leon Buskens, "Recent Debates on Family Law Reform in Morocco: Islamic Law as Politics in an Emerging Public Sphere", *Islamic Law and Society*", 10 (2003), 80, and El Alami and Hinchcliffe, *Islamic Marriage and Divorce Laws*, 206.
25. Nasution, *Status Wanita di Asia Tenggara*, 156.

26. See the *Kompilasi*, Arts. 5 & 6.
27. J. Anderson, "The Personal Law of the Druze Community", *The World of Islam*, 2 (1952), 834.
28. Bowen uses this term to attribute the court system as created by the 1989 Act in regard to divorce. He interprets the Act as considering "... State validity and religious validity were entirely separate matters", a position that was, he goes on to state, complicated by the *kompilasi* of 1991. See Bowen, "Shari'a, estate, and Social Norms in France and Indonesia", 10. He also noted that such a position on divorce law reforms makes the Indonesian case similar to that of Syria, Morocco, and Iraq, but different from that of Tunisia, which has declared divorce out of court religiously invalid. *Ibid.*, 11.
29. Art. 15 (1&2) of the *kompilasi.*
30. The reasons for the controversy focus largely on the vagueness of the Qur'ānic verses on the issue which results in two different interpretation, either in favor of or against polygyny. The controversy is sharpened by the historical fact that the Prophet Muhammad was married to a number of women. See Mehdi, *The Islamization of Law in Pakistan*, 160.
31. *Ibid.*, 160.
32. *Ibid.*
33. See A. Layish and R. Shahan, "Nikāh", *Encyclopaedia of Islam*, 178.
34. *Ibid.*, 179.
35. See John L. Esposito, *Women in Muslim Family Law* (New York: Syracuse University Press, 1982), 92.
36. It is also observed that the decline of the practice of polygyny can be attributed betterment in economic conditions and the relative improvement in women's education. See Mehdi, *The Islamization of Law*, 162.
37. On the early Indonesian women's organizations see Cora Vreede-de Stuers, *The Indonesian Woman: Struggle and Achievements* (The Hague: Moutun & Co., 1960), 89-99.
38. See the *Kompilasi*, Arts. 57 & 58.
39. See the *Kompilasi*, Art. 115 & 116.
40. See the *Kompilasi*, Art. 131.
41. See Martin van Bruinessen, "Traditions for the Future: The Reconstruction of Traditionalist Discourse within NU", in Greg Fealy and Greg Barton (eds.), *Nahdlatul Ulama, Traditional Islam and Modernity in Indonesia* (Monash: Monash Asia Institute, 1996), 163.
42. For more detailed information on the foundation of NU see Greg Fealy, "Wahab Chasbullah, Traditionalism and the Political Development of Nahdlatul Ulama", in Fealy and Barton, *Nahdlatul Ulama*, 1-42.
43. Rifyal Ka'bah, *Hukum Islam di Indonesia: Perspektif Muhammadiyah and NU* (Jakarta: Universitas Yarsi, 1999), 231-232.
44. Rifyal Ka'bah, "Fiqh Muhammadiyah Ketinggalan dari NU", *Suara Hidayatullah* (May 2000), 4.
45. *Ibid.*
46. Interview with Irfan Zidny, Jakarta, 7 August 2003.
47. For a good discussion on the methods of these two organizations, see Rifyal Ka'bah, *Hukum Islam di Indonesia: Perspektif Muhammadiyah and NU*, 228-235.
48. Interview with Irfan Zidny, Jakarta, 7 August 2003. For more details on this, see M.B. Hooker, *Indonesian Islam: Social Change through Contemporary Fatāwā* (Honolulu: Allen & Unwin and University of Hawaii Press, 2003), 57-60.
49. Interview with Irfan Zidny, Jakarta, 7 August 2003.

50. Interview with Irfan Zidny, Jakarta, 7 August 2003. For the details on the Sunnīte views on the issue, see Sharqāwī's *Ḥāshiya 'alā al-Taḥrīr*, 2 (Cairo: Dar Iḥyā al-Kutub al-'Arabiyya), 237-238.
51. See Hooker, *Indonesian Islam*, 53.
52. Interview with Ichtiyanto, Jakarta, 7 August 2003. Statistics released by the Jakarta Civil Registration Office show that from April 1985 to July 1986 there were 239 cases of inter-religious marriages involving 112 Muslim men and 127 Muslim women. See Muhammad Atho Mudzhar, *Islam and Islamic Law in Indonesia: A Socio-Historical Approach* (Jakarta: The Centre for Research and Development of the Ministry of Religious Affairs, 2003), 113.
53. Interview with Ichtiyanto, Jakarta, 7 August 2003, and Ma'rifat Imam, August 2003.
54. Interview with Ichtiyanto, Jakarta, 7 August 2003. His accusation is very much related to the case of inter-religious marriage particularly involving a Muslim man and a non-Muslim woman, which is permitted by Shāfi'ī.
55. Harahap, "Informasi Materi Kompilasi Hukum Islam," 64-65.
56. See Munawir Sjadzali, *Islam: Realitas Baru dan Orientasi Masa Depan Bangsa* (Jakarta: Universitas Indonesia, 1993). For the discussion of the opposition and its arguments, see Saimima, *Polemik Reaktualisasi Ajaran Islam*, 1-146. See also Ahmad Husnan, *Keputusan Al-Qur'an di Gugat* (Bangil: Yayasan al-Muslimun, 1991).
57. See M. Yahya Harahap, "Praktek Hukum Waris tidak Pantas Membuat Generalisasi", in Saimima, *Polemik Reaktualisasi Ajaran Islam*, 124-148.
58. For details on the debate, see El-Yasa Abu Bakr, *Ahli Waris Sepertalian Darah: Kajian Perbandingan Terhadap Penalaran Hazairin dan Penalaran Fiqh Madhhab* (Jakarta: INIS, 1998), 53-65.
59. Ismuha, "Masalah Dzawil Arham dan Ahli Waris Pengganti dalam Hukum Kewarisan Hukum Islam di Indonesia", in *Laporan Seminar Hukum Waris Islam* (Depag: Ditbinbapera, 1982), 75.
60. On this point Michael Feener noted that many have misunderstood the concept of bilateralism developed by Hazairin, thinking that Hazairin wanted to apply the ratio of 1:1 to male and female. I have found that what Feener said is true, as I personally know that a friend dealing with the issue understood that Hazairin developed the system of 1:1 for male and female. See Feener, "Indonesian Movements for the Creation of a National Madhhab", 111.
61. Following the example of Egyptian reforms, Syria by the Law of Personal Status, 1953 (Article 267), Morocco by the Moroccan Code of Personal Status, 1958, (Articles 266-269), Tunisia by the Tunisian Code of Personal Status, 1956, (Articles 91-92), Jordan by the Personal Status (Provisional) Act No. 61/1967, (Articles 180-181), Algeria by the Algerian Law No. 84-11/1984 (under the heading "Tanzeel, Articles 167-172) and Kuwait by the Act No. 51/ 1984 (Articles 227 and 291) have utilized 'obligatory bequests', opting for various methods of application. See John. L. Esposito, 155.
62. See Mehdi, *The Islamization of Law in Pakistan*, 190-192.
63. Interview with Prof. Amir Syarifuddin, Jakarta, February 2003. Syarifuddin mentioned that he was involved in making an additional clause which regulates the limitation of the share of the representative heirs. When the committee agreed to apply the concept of the representation of heirs and to include it in one Article in the *kompilasi*, he confronted them and demonstrated some examples of cases which show disparities. One of them is a case which meant that an aunt would receive a smaller share than her nephew. Comprehending what he described and what he argued, the committee reached an agreement about making an additional rule limiting the share of the representative heirs. Therefore, the clause which regulates the limitation of the share of the representative of heirs was purposefully added to neutralize the occurrence of injustice. It seems clear that Syarifuddin was initially opposed to

the application of the system of representation of heirs; see Roihan Rasyid, "Pengganti Ahli Waris dan Wasiat Wajibah", in Cik Hasan Bisri, *Kompilasi Hukum Islam dan Peradilan Agama dalam Sistem Hukum Nasional* (Jakarta: Logos Wacana Ilmu, 1999), 93.

64. Interview with Drs. Minhajul Falah, Jakarta, February 2003.
65. See Thoha Abdurrahman, "Tinjauan terhadap Hukum Kewarisan KHI di Indonesia" (Yogyakarta: Sekretariat IAIN Sunan Kalijaga, 1992), 8-9; see also Minhajul Falah, "Perbandingan Hukum Kewarisan antara KHI dan Fiqh Mazhab Empat dalam Ketentuan Ahli Waris Beserta Bahagiannya" (Jakarta: Fakultas Syariah IAIN, Jakarta, 1993), 78.
66. For the original text of the *ḥadīth*, see Shahih al-Bukhārī, chapter *al-farā'iḍ*, no. 6239. Compare with Sunan al-Tirmidh, *al-farā'iḍ*, no. 2019, Abū Daūd, *al-farā'iḍ*, no. 2504, and Ibn Mājah, *al-farā'iḍ*, no. 2712.
67. *Ibid.*
68. Interview with Ichtiyanto, Jakarta, 7 August 2003.
69. Interview with Minhajul Falah, Jakarta, 19 February 2003.
70. See Rasyid, "Pengganti Ahli Waris dan Wasiat Wajiba", 96.
71. See Yahya Harahap, "Informasi Materi *Kompilasi* Hukum Islam: Mempositifkan Abstarksi Hukum Islam", in Bisri, *Kompilasi Hukum Islam*, 67.
72. Abdul Aziz Mohammed Zaid, *The Islamic Law of Bequest* (London: Scorpion Publishing Ltd., 1986), 11-13.
73. N.J. Coulson, *Succession in the Muslim Family Law* (Cambridge: The University Press, 1971), 146.
74. John L. Esposito, *Women in Muslim Family Law*, 88. See also Tahir Mahmoud, *Personal Law in Islamic Countries* (New Delhi: Academy of Law and Religion, 1987), 46-47, 136-137,162-163.
75. Lukito, *Pergumulan antara Hukum Islam dan Adat di Indonesia*, 97.
76. Dadan Muttaqin, *Peradilan Agama dan Kompilasi Hukum Islam dalam Tata Hukum Indonesia* (Yogyakarta: UII Press, 1999).
77. Interview with Ali Yafie, a former chairman of the Council of the Indonesian *'Ulamā'* (Majlis 'Ulamā' Indonesia or MUI), February 2003.
78. For details about his ideas on Islamic law reforms, see his books, *PembaharuanPemikiran dalam Hukum Islam* (Padang; Angkasa Raya, 1990); *Permasalahan dalam Pelaksanaan Farai'd* (Padang: IAIN IB Press, 1999); and *Meretas Kebekuan Ijtihad: Isu-Isue Penting Hukum Islam Kontemporer di Indonesia* (Jakarta: Ciputat Press, 2002).
79. Interview with Prof. Amir Syarifudin, Jakarta, February 2003.
80. See Yahya Harahap, "Informasi Materi *Kompilasi* Hukum Islam: Memfositifkan Abstarksi Hukum Islam", in Bisri, *Kompilasi Hukum Islam*, 58.
81. Interview with judges Yustimar and Nur (female) of the religious courts of South and East Jakarta respectively, 23 and 30 January 2003.
82. Interview with Prof. Amir Syarifuddin, Jakarta, 19 February 2003, and Bustanul Arifin, Jakarta, May 2003.
83. Gender discourse was publicly propagated in Indonesia in the 1980s, but only penetrated religious issues in the 1990s. The discourse arrived in Indonesia with the spread of the books written by such feminists as Amina Wadoud Muhsin, Fetima Mernissi, and Zaffrullah Khan. The publication of articles by other feminists such as Rif'at Hassan, Ivonne Haddad, and the journal of 'Ulumul Qur'an' (now no longer published) have also contributed greatly to the introduction of gender discourse in Indonesia. A group of Indonesian women including Wardah Hafidz and Lies Marcoes, who are specialized in gender studies, have since then successfully inspired the rise of groups paying attention to gender issues in Indonesia.

84. This United Nations "CEDAW" introduced in 18 December 1979 has been ratified by Indonesia into UU No. 7/1984.
85. See research reports on "Pembakuan Peran dalam Kebijakan-Kebijakan di Indonesia" (Jakarta: LBH-APIK, 2003); "Sejarah UU Perkawinan dan Pembakuan Perempuan dalam UU No. 1 Tahun 1974 tentang Perkawinan" (Jakarta: LBH-APIK, 2003).
86. See Mesraini, "Gender dan KHI: Studi Kritis atas KHI dalam Perspektif Gender", MA Thesis (Jakarta: IAIN Jakarta, 2001), 160-161, and Musdah Mulia, *Pandangan Islam tentang Poligami* (Jakarta: Lembaga Kajian Agama & Gender, 1999).
87. See, for instance, Inayah Rohmaniyah, "Poligami dalam Perundang-Undangan di Indonesia", *Musawa* 1,1 (March 2002): 101.
88. *Ibid.*, 101.
89. *Ibid.*, 102.
90. See Mesraini, "Gender dan KHI," 184. See also Nuryamin Aini, "Penggunaan Jasa Pengacara dalam Kasus Perceraian: Studi Kasus di Pengadilan Agama Jakarta Selatan", *Ahkam*, 10:4 (2002), 135-152. One of the feminist activists from the Center for Women Studies of IAIN of Jakarta spoke up intensely to change the use of the different terms of divorce for both men and women and make them the same term: '*cerai* or *talak*'.
91. See Mesraini, "Gender dan KHI", 148.
92. See the *Kompilasi*, Art. 129 & 132
93. See Aini, "Penggunaan Jasa dalam Kasus Perceraian", 135-152.
94. Interview with K.H. Irfan Zidny, 7 August 2003.
95. See the *Kompilasi*, Art. 229. It is reported that the inclusion of this provision was initially to compensate Munawir Sjadzali, whose proposal for equating the shares of males and females was not incorporated in the *kompilasi*, and was therefore put at the end the chapter on inheritance. However, in order to utilize it universally for the all three chapters of the *kompilasi*, the drafters decided to put it as a final provision at the end of a whole chapter. Interview with Bustanul Arifin, 3 August 2003.
96. This institution is headed by Taufik Kamil, the Director General of Guidance for Muslim Community and Pilgrimage Facilitation and is supervised by three prominent Muslim scholars of Islamic law, namely, Prof. Dr H. Said Agil Husin Al-Munawar (the Ministry of Religious Affairs), KH. Sahal Mahfud (the general chief of the MUI), and Prof. Dr H.Faisal Ismail, MA (the General Secretary of the Ministry of Religious Affairs). This institution is completed by a number of well-known Muslim scholars of Islamic law, such as Prof. Dr Bustanul Arifin, SH, Prof. Dr Abdul Gani Abdullah, SH, Dr Ichtiyanto SA, SH, APU who have the position of acknowledged experts. This information is taken from the Resolution of the Minister of Religious Affairs No. 416, 27 September 2002 about the election of the members of the institution for studying and developing Islamic law.
97. See "*Kompilasi* Hukum Islam akan Ditingkatkan Jadi UU (The *Kompilasi* Would be Upgraded into Law)", *Gatra*, September 19 (2002), 1.
98. In line with the goal of the seminar, which was to analyze the rules covered in the *Kompilasi*, the major heading of the seminar was defined as 'Debat Kritik terhadap *Kompilasi* Hukum Islam (Critical Debates on the Compilation of Islamic Law').
99. Based on the notes I took during the seminar. For clear points on the issue, see the *Kompilasi*, Art. 19, 20 & 21.
100. See the *Kompilasi*, Art. 79 and 80 (1, 2 & 3).
101. See the *Kompilasi*, Art. 172.
102. See the *Kompilasi*, Art. 83 and 84.
103. See also Kantor Menteri Agama Pemberdayaan Perempuan & PSW IAIN Jakarta, "Laporan Studi Kebijakan dalam Rangka Penyajian dan Perbaikan Undang-Undang Perkawinan" (Jakarta, Kantor Menteri Agama Pemberdayaan Perempuan & PSW IAIN Jakarta, 2000).

104. Interview with Dr. Musdah Mulia, MA. See also a report of JIL interview with her, "*Kompilasi* Hukum Islam Sangat Konservatif", *Jaringan Islam Liberal*, September 2003, 1-5.
105. See "RUU Terapan Peradilan Agama Digodok", *Kompas*, Oktober 2003, 2. I confirmed her use of the word 'barbaric' by letter. She said that the word 'barbaric' is so vulgar and strong that she intentionally chose to shock the conservative *'ulamā'* and make them realize that such a very disgusting rule certainly needs to be changed.
106. www.thcjakartapost.com, 29 April 2005.
107. www.hukumonline.com, 2 November 2004.
108. See "Ministry Proposes 'Progressive, Controversial Revision of Islamic Law," www.tgmmt.org.ucanews.htm, 29 April, 2005.
109. See 'Surat Pimpinan MUI' No. B-414/MUI/X/2004, 12 October 2004.
110. See "Surat Menag RI", No. MA/ 271/2004.
111. See "Surat Menag RI", No. MA/ 274/2004.
112. See "Menteri Agama Larang Diskusikan Draft Hukum Islam", *Tempointeraktif*, 19 October 2004, and "Menteri Agama Bekukan Draft *Kompilasi* Hukum Islam", *Tempointeraktif*, 26 October 2004.
113. Rifyal Ka'bah, "*Kompilasi* Hukum Islam Tandingan/ The Legal Counter Draft of the *kompilasi*", a paper presented in the seminar held by the University of Yarsi, Jakarta, on 29 March 2004.
114. See "Poligami, Masalah Krusial dalam Revisi Undang-Undang Perkawinan", www.hukumonline.com, 2 November 2004.
115. See Huzaemah Tahido Yanggo, *Kontroversi Revisi Kompilasi Hukum Islam* (Jakarta: Adelina, 2005).
116. *Ibid.*, 8.
117. Interview with Prof. Huzaemah Tahido, Jakarta, 12 March 2005.
118. See "Hizbut Tahrir: Menggugat Draft *Kompilasi* Hukum 'Inkar Syariat'", *Buletin Dakwah Islam*, 226 (2004). See also "Kerancuan Metodologi Draft Kompilais Hukum Islam", *Hidayatullah*, 15 (2004).
119. Http:/swaramuslim.net.
120. See "Konspirasi Hukum Peradilan Agama", www.kammimipa.com, 29 April 2005.
121. On these issues of other countries, see articles by Leon Buskens, Dorothea Schulz, and Anna Wurth in, *Islamic Law and Society*, 10: 1 (2003). See also their abstracts in the introduction of the publication by Annelies Moors, "Public Debates on family Law Reform: Participations, Positions, and Styles of Argumentation in the 1990s", *Islamic Law and Society*, 10: 1 (2003).

IV Between the *Kompilasi* and the *Fiqh* Texts

1. For examples of the judgments of the other courts than Islamic where the phrase is used, see Herman Sihombing, *Hukum Adat dalam Keputusan Pengadilan Negeri di Sumatera Barat* (Bandung: Penerbit Alumni, 1975).
2. M. Yahya Harahap, *Kedudukan, Kewenangan, dan Acara Peradilan Agama (UU No. 7-Th 1989)* (Jakarta: Pustaka Kartini, 1997), 347.
3. This structure of the judgment is in line with one of the recommended models to follow. For detailed explanation about the models of the structure of the judgment, *Ibid.*, 351-359.
4. *Ibid.*, 339.
5. Yahya Harahap, *Kedudukan Kewenangan*, 341.
6. See the judgment of the religious Court in Kediri No. 261/ 1976, and the judgment of the religious Court in Denpasar, No. 46/ 1976 on such cases. For more detailed

information about these judgments see *Putusan/Penetapan Pengadilan Agama/Mahkama Syar'iyyah Seluruh Indonesia Setelah Berlakunya UU No. 1/ 1974 Tentang Perkawinan* (Jakarta: Ditjen Bimas Islam Departemen Agama, 1977); see also *Himpunan Putusan/Penetapan Pengadilan Agama* (Jakarta: Proyek Pembinaan Badan Peradilan Agama Departemen Agama, 1979-1980).

7. *Ibid.* The judgments collected in these books are abundantly supported by the quotation of Islamic doctrines from the Qur'ān, *ḥadīth*, and *fiqh* books.
8. Zuffran Sabrie (ed.), *Laporan Hasil-Hasil Monitoring dan Evaluasi (Penelitian) Pelaksanaan Undang-Undang Peradilan Agama dan Kompilasi Hukum Islam*, research report (Jakarta: Ditbinbapera Departemen Agama, 2001), 14.
9. *Ibid.*, 15.
10. Nuryamin Aini, "Budaya Hukum: Melintas Batas Formalisme-Yuridis", *Era Hukum* 3 (2003).
11. The complete title of this *fiqh* book is *Mu'īn al-Ḥukkām 'alā Qadāyā wa al-Aḥkām*, 2 vols. The author's complete name is Ibrāhīm ibn Ḥasan ibn 'Abd al-Rāfī (d. 733/ 1332).
12. Cf. Nuryamin Aini, "Budaya Hukum: Melintas Batas Formalisme-Yuridis", *Era Hukum*, 3 (2003), 4-7.
13. Irfan Zidny has even stated that the *fiqh* book by Sayyid Uthmān is the best *fiqh* book among those on the topic of methods of Islamic legal reasoning. He states that he always refers to this *fiqh* book. Furthermore, he was prepared to state that this *fiqh* book would become his reference in a speech on methods of legal deduction of Islamic law in Asia to be held in Malaysia. Interview with Irfan Zidny, Jakarta, 7 August 2003.
14. See G.F. Pijper, *Fragmenta Islamica, Studien over Het Islamisme in Nederlandsch-Indie* (Leiden: E.J. Brill, 1934), 84; see also Nico Kaptein, "Sayyid Uthman on Documentary Evidence", in *Bijdragen tot de Taal-, Land En Volkenkunde*, 153 (1997), 99. Zaini Ahmad Noeh recorded that the book was indeed one of the references of the *Raad Agama*. See H. Zaini Ahmad Noeh, "Pembacaan Sighat Taklik Talak Sesudah Akad Nikah", *Mimbar Hukum*, 30: 8 (1997), 69. See also Husni Rahim, *Sistem Otoritas dan Administrasi Islam: Studi tentang Pejabat Agama Masa Kesultanan dan Kolonial di Palembang* (Jakarta: PT Logos Wacana Ilmu, 1998), 242-246.
15. See Husni Rahim, *Sistem Otoritas dan Administrasi Islam*, 242-246.
16. Interview with Ali Yafi and Huzemah Tahido, Jakarta, 2003. Rahim also mentioned that although the book gained great acceptance among the *penghulus* of Palembang, among the *'ulamā'* it was not popular. Rahim, *Sistem Otoritas dan Administrasi Islam*, 246.
17. Only a few of the judges among my respondents knew this book. Most know it only by name, and have never read it.
18. Judge Daud Ali of the religious court of East Jakarta knew the book and had read it. He said that the book is useful, but preferred to use other books as references.
19. See Pijper, *Studien over de Geschiedenis*, 84. For a further account on the opinion of Sayyid Uthmān about the issue and his preference for the Nawāwi's *Minhāj al-Ṭālibīn*, see Sayyid Uthmān, *Al-Qawānin al-Shari 'iyya*, 64.
20. Rahim, *Sistem Otoritas dan Administrasi Islam*, 245.
21. Interview with Ali Yafie, Jakarta, February 2003 and with K.H. Irfan Zidny, Jakarta, August 2003. For abundant information about the biography and the works of Sayyid Uthmān, see Azyumardi Azra, *Jaringan Lokal dan Global Islam Nusantara*, (Jakarta: Penerbit Mizan, 2002), 137-164. For further discussion on Sayyid Uthmān and his *fiqh* book *al-Qawānīn*, see Nico Kapten, "Sayyid Uthmān on Documentary Evidence", 85-102; cf. Snouck Hurgronje, 'Sajjid Uthman's Gidds voor de Priesterraden', *Verspeide Geshriften*, Vol. 4-1, 285-303, (Bonn/Leipzig: Kurt Schroeder).

22. For the discussion about *Penghulu* (Penghoeloe), see Hisyam, *Caught Between Three Fires*.
23. See Ditbinbapera, *Alasan Syar'i Penerapan Kompilasi Hukum Islam*, 1-133.
24. Interview with Hidayatullah, Jakarta, March 2003.
25. For its Arabic quotation, see Appendix no. 1.
26. For its Arabic quotation, see Appendix no. 2.
27. The Ministry of Religious Affairs once issued a pocket book which compiles the opinions of the earlier *'ulamā'* complete with the names of the *fiqh* books often cited as the legal consideration of the judgments. This publication was to make it easier for judges to find the correct reference to be used for their judgments. The pocket-sized book is entitled *Kompilasi Hukum Acara dan Materi Peradilan Agama* (Compilation of Legal Procedure and Substantive Laws for Religious Courts).
28. The privileged position of Wahbah Zuhaylī's *al-Fiqh al-Islāmiyy wa Adillatuhu* among Indonesian Muslim scholars can be seen in Satria Effendi's preference for the book in his analytical works on judgments of the religious courts regularly published in the Directorate of Religious Affairs' journal, *Mimbar Hukum*. It was noted that he referred most frequently to this book. See Atho Mudzhar, "Peranan Analisis Yurisprudensi dalam pengembangan Pemikiran Hukum Islam", in Jaenal Arifin dkk, *Prof. Dr. H. Satria Effendi: Problematika Hukum Keluarga Islam Kontemporer* (Jakarta: Prenada Muda, 2004), xi.
29. For the sake of certainty, I checked it and found that it was displayed on page 302 of the second volume. Although he did not identify and specify names of the *fiqh* text and the pages where the judges were not consistent when mentioning them, Nuryamin found that this was also the case within the judges of the religious court in South Jakarta. See Nuryamin, "Budaya Hukum", 9.
30. The fact that the judges often relied on their memory when citing Arabic texts is seen also in other judgments on polygamy identified as No: Pdt.p/2001/PA.Tsm where they cited the verse of the Qur'ān that reads *fankihū mā ṭāba lakum min al-nisā'mathnā wathulātha wa rubā'a* and wrote a wrong verse number for this, i.e. al-Nisā': 31, while it is actually recorded in al-Nisā': 3, and on the qualifications of custodian as will be discussed next. However, this mistake could have happened in the hands of the clerk who retyped the judgment, but who then did not try to check it again and thus also relied on his memory.
31. See Judgment No. 341/1976.
32. See S. Pompe and J.M. Otto, "Some Comments on Recent Developments in the Indonesian Marriage Law with Particular Respect to the Rights of Women", *Verfassung und Rech Ubersee*, 4 (1990), 415; cf. Cammack who reported that since the application of the Law of Marriage some judges appear to be wary of their judgments being overturned by the Supreme Court on cassation and that is why they are inclined towards the Marriage Law. Mark Cammack, "Islamic Law in Indonesia's New Order", *International and Comparative Law Quarterly*, 38 (1989), 53.
33. It should be noted that while the Hanāfite, Hanbalite, and Mālikite schools put the mother's father in the third rank after the mother's mother, the Shāfi'īte school specifies the father as the appropriate person to have custody after the maternal grandmother. The *kompilasi* follows the Shāfi'īte opinion and therefore places the father in the third rank, the first being the mother, the second the maternal grandmother, and thirdly the father.
34. The judgment recorded that it was displayed on page 94.
35. For its Arabic quotation, see Appendix no. 8.
36. For its Arabic quotation, see Appendix no. 9.
37. For its Arabic quotation, see Appendix no. 10.
38. See Art. 156 of the *kompilasi*.

39. In 1977 the religious court of Medan also deviated from the Law of Marriage and decided to give the right of *ḥaḍāna* of the children to their father because the mother was considered to have re-converted to the Christianity after three years as a Muslim. As the legal considerations for its decision, the court mentioned the legal doctrine which states '... there is no right of *ḥaḍāna* for the mother who is religiously deviant'. After mentioning its translation into Indonesian, they emphasized the fact that the parents of the father and all the rest of his family were Muslims, while the family of the mother were non-Muslims. Still, in Medan, the same case had occurred in 1986 and the court gave the same judgment. See Judgment No. PA. b/8/PTS/144/1986.
40. Art. 156 (b) of the *kompilasi.*
41. Satria Effendi, "Analisis Fiqh Terhadap Yurisprudensi Tentang Perceraian: Hak Hadhanah Akibat Perceraian Sebagai Fokus", *Mimbar Hukum,* 21: 6 (1995).
42. There is basically another opinion embraced by Ibn Qāsim, some Hanāfite and Hanbalite adherents, and Muhammad Abū Zahroh, which holds that a guardian must not always be Muslim, particularly when the children are still under age. See Muhammad Abū Zahrah, *Al-Aḥwāl al-Shahṣiyya.* In terms of the under-age period, the majority of earlier *'ulamā'* mention that it starts from the delivery of the baby until he or she attains the age of seven years.
43. Interview with the chairman of the religious court of East Jakarta, Jakarta, 9 February 2003.
44. For its Arabic quotation, see Appendix no. 11.
45. Art. 7 (2) of the Marriage Law.
46. The deviation from this rule was often also made by officials of the Offices of Religious Affairs, *Kantor Urusan Agama,* (KUA). Interestingly, this was done by manipulating the correct age of the would-be groom or bride so that they could enter marital life despite being under the formal ages required in the *kompilasi.* The officials often ignore the known fact that the age of the bride or the groom written in the identity card was not the correct one, but take one upgraded they had obtained from the district office (*kelurahan*).
47. For its quotation, see Appendix no. 12.
48. For its Arabic quotation, see Appendix no. 13.
49. For its Arabic quotation, see Appendix no. 24.
50. Rosen Lawrence, *The Anthropology of Justice: Law as Culture in Islamic Society* (Cambridge: Cambridge University Press, 1989), 46.
51. Interview with Judge A. Lukman of the religious court of Bogor, 7 February 2003.
52. Interview with Judge Daud Ali of the religious Court of East Jakarta, 10 February 2003.
53. Interview with Judge A. Lukman of the religious court of Bogor, 7 February 2003.
54. Interview with Judge M. Yusuf of the religious court of Cianjur, 20 March 2003
55. Interview with Judge Abdul Rasyid of the religious court of Cibinong, 28 February 2003.
56. Interview with Judge M. Yusuf, a male judge of the religious court of Cianjur, Cianjur, 20 March 2003.
57. Interview with Deden Syarifuddin of the religious court of Cibinong, 29 February 2003.
58. Interview with Judge M. Yusuf of the religious court of Cianjur, 20 March 2003.
59. Interview with Judge Rohimah of the religious court of Tasikmalaya, 18 March 2003.
60. The text of the case and its decisions can be also seen in *Mimbar Hukum* 30:7 (1997), 122-151.
61. See Cammack, "Inching towards Equality", 14-15, and Bowen, *Islam, Law and Equality in Indonesia,* 197-198.

62. So the lower court had not decided the case following the traditional doctrine and had not granted the brother the share with the daughter of the deceased as understood by Cammack. See Cammack, "Inching toward Equality", 15
63. Noel J. Coulson, *History of Islamic Law* (Edinburgh: Edinburgh University Press, 1971), 66. It should be noted here that the interpretation by the Sunnites of the word *walad* as referring to only male only happens in this verse, as they interpret the word *walad* appearing in other verses as including both male and female.
64. I mean the word *walad* as generally interpreted in the Qur'ān as male and female and not as translated in the Arabic dictionary which refers to only a male child.
65. See, for an example, Alizar Jas, "Pengertian Kata Walad dalam Surah al-Nisa Ayat 176", *Mimbar Hukum*, 40 (1998).
66. See Baidlawi, "Ketentuan Hak Waris Saudara dalam Konteks Hukum Islam", and Rahmat Syafe'i, "Kajian Terhadap Putusan Mahkamah Agung tentang Kewarisan Saudara dengan Anak Perempuan", *Mimbar Hukum*, 44 (1999). Their understanding is concluded on the fact that on this issue Ibn 'Abbās dealt only with the case in which a sister (aunt) and a daughter were involved and did not discuss a case in which a daughter is left behind with a brother (her uncle). In the Tafsīr of Ibn Kathīr, the view of Ibn 'Abbās on the issue is described as follows: Ibn Jarīr and his colleagues reported that Ibn 'Abbās and Ibn Zubayr said that if a deceased left behind him a daughter and a sister, the sister receives no share (for its Arabic quotation, see Appendix no. 18). See Ibn Kathīr, *Tafsīr Ibn Kathīr* (Beirut: Dār al-Fikr, 1986). The writers also added that none should interpret the word *walad* in Verse 176 as embracing males only. They argue that the word *walad* in Verse 176 refers absolutely to both male and female, but the verse is not to be interpreted in a deviant (*mukhālafa*) way that is, the verse is not to be interpreted as to rule that in the existence of children, collaterals are totally excluded. In other words, this verse only describes the right of inheritance of collaterals when the deceased leaves no children (*kalāla*). Should the deceased leave children, the right of inheritance of collaterals is to be ruled in the Prophetic sayings which state "... give certain shares to the defined heirs and the remaining is the right of the male groups" (transmitted from Ibn 'Abbās) (for its Arabic quotation see Appendix no. 19), and which states "... for the daughters is a half and for a daughter of a son is the portion that makes two-thirds of the shares and the residue is for the sister" (transmitted from Ibn Mas'ūd). For the discussion on this, cf. Bowen, *Islam, Law and Equality in Indonesia*, 197.
67. Even though the writers also claimed that granting the daughter a full share was also a deviation, as no text said so. They claim that should a sister exist but be excluded, the daughter is not to be granted a full share but only half. *Ibid.*
68. See Cammack, "Inching toward Equality", 15.
69. Interview with Wahyu Widiana, March, 2005, Jakarta, and Bustanul Arifin, 2003, Jakarta.
70. All the judgments texts on the case can be also seen in *Mimbar Hukum*, 24: 7 (1996), 128-152.
71. See H. Zain Badjeber, "Analysis Yurisprudensi tentang Perkara Kewarisan: Analisa Acara", *Mimbar Hukum*, 30: 8 (1997), 120-121.
72. Interviews with judges of religious courts of Bogor, Cianjur, Rangkasbitung, 2003.
73. Zain Badjeber, "Analysis Yurisprudensi: Analisis Acara dan Penerapan Hukum", *Mimbar Hukum*", 24: 7 (1996) 120-121.
74. *Ibid.*, 123.
75. Interview with Judge Budi Purwatiningsih of the religious court in Bogor, Bogor, 13 February 2003.
76. See, for examples, Nawāwī's *Minhāj al-Ṭālibīn*, vol. III, 205-210, Ibn Ḥajar's *Tuḥfah al-Muḥtāj*, vol. IV, 117-130, Al-Bājūr's *Ḥāshiya Kifāyat al-Akhyār*, vol. II, 263-266, and Dimyāṭī's *I'ānat al-Ṭālibīn*, col. IV, 132-142.

77. Art. 116 (h) of the *Kompilasi*.
78. H.A. Mukti Arto, SH, *Praktek Perkara Perdata pada Pengadilan Agama* (Yogyakarta: Pustaka Pelajar, 1996).
79. See Fachruddin, "Murtad Sebagai Alasan Perceraian dan Impelementasinya di Pengadilan Agama", *Mimbar Hukum*, 39: 9 (1998), 12-18. Fachruddin also commented that if the stress is placed on the clause of 'resulting in disharmony', the couple should request the divorce on the basis for the reasons for divorce enumerated in point (f) and then the judges should base their judgments on the existence of disputes and arguments between the couple. Should this be done, the apostasy itself is not considered to be affecting the marital relationship at all.
80. The refusal of the judges to hear and try the renunciation of Islam case had produced a quite dramatic and unusual decision even earlier. Pijper recorded that once the court of Demak refused to hear the case of divorce initiated by an apostate woman, arguing that the court was not competent to solve the case brought by a non-Muslim person(s), see Pijper, *Fragmenta Islamica*, 92.
81. See Judgment No. 34/pdt.G/2004/PA.Rks. For more or less the same cases, see Judgment of Rangkasbitung No. 135/Pdt.G/2004/PA.Rks, and Cianjur Judgment No. 326/Pdt.G/2004/PA.Cjr. The Cianjur judgment even cited the Qur'ānic verse of al-Baqara, 221, as its source.
82. See Pijper, *Fragmenta Islamica*, 79-94. See also Rahim, *Sistem Otoritas dan Administrasi Islam*, 246-248.
83. See *Himpunan Putusan Pengadilan Agama Setelah Berlakunya Undang-Undang Perkawinan;* see also Lubis, *Islamic Justice in Transition*, 334.

V The *Kompilasi* and the Need for Religious Legitimacy

1. See *Pelita*, 8 January, 1992.
2. See Fajrul Falaakh, "Peradilan Agama dan Perubahan Tata Hukum Indonesia", in Drs. Dadan Muttaqien, M.Hum (eds.), *Peradilan Agama dan Kompilasi Hukum Islam dalam Tata Hukum Indonesia* (Yogyakarta: UII Press, 1993).
3. Interview with Bustanul Arifin, Jakarta, 12 April 2003.
4. See "Kompilasi Hukum Islam Lahir Karena Kebutuhan Mendesak", *Kompas*, (14 December 1992), 6.
5. Sabrie, *Peradilan Agama*, 183.
6. See *Keputusan Departemen Agama*, 22 July 1991.
7. Noted from his speech at the seminar.
8. See, for instance, judgement of the religious court of Bogor No. 167/Pdt.G/2002/PA. BGR.
9. Interview with Judge Daud Ali of the religious court of East Jakarta, Jakarta, 10 February 2003.
10. See Nurchozin, "Kitab Kuning: Peranan dan Masalahnya di Peradilan Agama", *Mimbar Hukum*, 3:2 (1991).
11. For the discussion on this subject, see Zamakhsyari Dhofier, *The Pesantren Tradition: The Role of the Kyai in the Maintenance of Traditional Islam in Java* (Arizona: Arizona State University, 1999); also his *Tradition and Change in Indonesian Islamic Education* (Jakarta: Office of Religious Research and Development of the Ministry of Religious Affairs, 1995), 126-127.
12. For the discussion of the subjects of the test, see Lubis, "Islamic Justice in Transition", 280.
13. Interview with Zuffran Sabrie, Jakarta, 12 March 2003.

14. See Nurchozin, "Kitab Kuning: Peranan dan Masalahnya di Pengadilan Agama", 59-70. The recruitment of judges in the period of Dutch occupation and the early period of independence was quite simple, but the mastering of the *fiqh* book was the main qualification and was therefore tested. For further information about the recruitment of judges in the period of Dutch occupation, see Hisyam, *Caught between Three Fires*, 42-46.
15. This is also related to the fact that some applicants graduating from either the faculty of law or Islamic law had no *pesantren* backgrounds, as they graduated from state senior high schools like *Madrasah Aliyah Negeri and Sekolah Menengah Atas Negeri*, where the reading of *fiqh* books is not studied.
16. A number of young judges admitted to have been asked to read *Fiqh al-Sunnah* in the selection test to become judges.
17. Interview with Zuffran Sabrie, Jakarta, 6 February 2005. There are ironically some Muslim scholars who think the *Fiqh al-Sunna* is poor quality. "It is a shame that the-would-be judge is considered to be capable or competent of reading *fiqh* books with the *Fiqh al-Sunna* as the standard," one of the Muslim scholars employed in the Indonesian Council of *'Ulamā'* said. Interview in Jakarta, 12 March 2003.
18. That the Arabic of some of the Muslim judges is poor is a fact. The chairman of the religious court of Cianjur, for an example, frankly recounted that the Arabic comprehension of more than three judges left a great deal to be desired. The ability to understand Arabic among the rest varies. Interview in Cianjur, April 2003.
19. See Abdul Gani, "Fakultas Syari'ah: Fungsi, Tugas dan Keluarannya (Faculty of Islamic Law: Role, Task, and its Graduates)", *Mimbar Hukum*, 1:4 (1993).
20. Interview with Zuffran Sabrie, Jakarta, 3 May 2003.
21. See The Islamic Judicature Act of 1989, Art. 13 (g).
22. Interview with Huzaemah Tahido, Jakarta, 11 March 2003.
23. Interview with judge Daud Ali of the religious court of Jakarta, 10 February 2003.
24. See H.L.A. Hart, *The Concept of Law* (Oxford, 1961), 101, and his "Positivism and the Separation of Law and Morals", *Legal Review*, (1958), 71. See also Thomas Morawetz, *The Philosophy of Law: An Introduction* (New York: Macmillan Publishing Co. Inc., 1980).
25. See Imran Ahsan Khan Nyazee, *Theories of Islamic Law: The Methodology of Ijtihād* (Kuala Lumpur: The Other Press, 2002), 298.
26. Lawrence M. Friedmann, "Legal Culture and Social Development", *Law and Society Review*, 4 (1969).
27. See Prof. Dr Bagir Manan, "Pengembangan Sistem Hukum Nasional Dalam Rangka Memantapkan Negara Kesatuan RI Sebagai Negara Hukum", *Mimbar Hukum* 56, (2002), 8.
28. As told by a number of judges of the religious courts of Bogor, Rangkasbitung and Tasikmalaya.
29. Noted from his speech on 27 August, 2003.
30. See, for examples, judgement No. 326/Pdt.G/2004/PA.Cjr, judgement No. 397/Pdt.G/2004/PA.Cjr, and judgement No. 416/Pdt.G/2004/PA.Cjr.
31. Interview with judges of the court of Cianjur, February 2005. Concerning the significance of the Arabic language and its supreme importance as the religious language of Muslims, see Anwar G. Chenje, *The Arabic Language: Its Role in History* (Minneapolis: University of Minnesota Press, 1969), 3-25.
32. Martin van Bruinessen, "Pesantren and Kitab Kuning: Change and Continuity in a Tradition of Religious Learning", in Wolfgang Marschall (ed.), *Texts from the Islands: Oral and Written Traditions of Indonesia and the Malay World* (Berne: The University of Berne, 1994), 124-125.
33. Interview with Wahyu Widiana, Jakarta, 4 March 2005.

34. Interview with one litigant of the religious court of South Jakarta, Jakarta, 23 January 2003.
35. Interview with judge Yustimar of the religious court of South Jakarta, February 2003.
36. For its Arabic quotation, see Appendix no. 5. Arabic statements other than the one cited above are also often referred to by the judges. They read as follows: 'If the love of the wife for her husband has certainly disappeared, her petition for divorce can ultimately be approved in the court' (*Ghāyat al-Murām* by Shaykh al-Majdī) (see Appendix no. 6), and "If the love of the wife for her husband has certainly vanished, their mediators can make a decision on divorce without the approval of either wife or husband" (*Risālat al-Shiqāq*, 22) (see appendix no. 7). See the judgement of the religious court of Rangksbitung No. 144/Pdt. G/ 2002/ PA Rks, and of Cianjur No. 364/Pdt.G/2004/PA.Cjr.
37. See Gerard Wiegers, "Language and Identity: Pluralism and the Use of non-Arabic Language in the Muslim West", in Jan Platvoet and Karel van Der Toorn (eds.), *Pluralism and Identity: Studies in Ritual Behavior* (Leiden: E.J. Brill, 1995), 304.
38. *Ibid.*, 305.
39. In regard with the proposed theories of how Islam spread into the Archipelago, it is stated that to prove the theory that Islam was brought into Indonesia directly by Arab people who were Shāfi'īte adherents is correct, historians (the defenders of the theory) turn to the fact that Indonesian Muslims have long adhered to the Shāfi'īte school and used Arabic in their ritual religious practices. See Suwedi Montana, *Pengenalan Awal Bahasa Arab Sebagai Indikator Pembawa Agama Islam di Indonesia* (Jakarta: Pusat Penelitian Arkeologi Nasional Departemen Pendidikan dan Kebudayaan, 1995).
40. Francis Robinson, "Technology and Religious Change: Islam and Impact of Print", *Modern Asian Studies*, 27: 1 (1993), 246.
41. Cf. Muhammad Qasim Zaman, *The 'Ulamā' in Contemporary Islam: Custodian of Change* (Princeton: Princeton University Press, 2002). I am grateful to Michael Feener for his information about this book.
42. Lev, *Religious court*, 240.
43. *Ibid.*, 237.
44. *Ibid.*, 233.
45. Rifyal Ka'bah, "Fiqh Muhammadiyyah Ketinggalan dari NU", 1-8. See also I.D. Nugraha, "Gender Issue Overshadows Muhammadiyah Congress," *The Jakarta Post* (5 July 2005), 1. Such a phenomenon can be seen in the fact that feminists in Muslim circles come mostly from NU adherents and hardly any from Muhammadiyah members. See John R. Bowen, *Islam, Law and Equality in Indonesia*, 227.
46. Interviews with Judge Daud Ali of the religious court of East Jakarta, February 2003, and Judge M. Yusuf of the religious court of Cianjur, 20 March 2003.
47. The importance attached to religious symbols in the thinking of Indonesian Muslims may be also illustrated by the earlier court letters of the Islamic Sultanates of Melaka and Aceh in which the writers, be they judges or the clerks, always inserted Qur'ānic verses and Sufi terminology, especially in the Preamble and the section of compliments, even though they were writing to a foreign non-Muslim leader. See Ahmat Adam, "Islamic Elements in the Art of Malay Traditional Court Letter Writing", an unpublished paper presented at the 35th *International Congress of Asian and North African Studies*, Budapest, Hungary, 7-12 July 1997.
48. For its Arabic quotation, see Appendix no. 14.
49. For its Arabic quotation, see Appendix no. 15.
50. For its Arabic quotation, see Appendix no. 16.
51. For its Arabic quotation, see Appendix no. 17.

52. Interview with judges of the religious courts of East Jakarta and South Jakarta, 23 January and 10 February 2003.
53. See, for example, the judgment of the religious court of Tasikmalaya No. 1537/ Pdt.G/2002/PA.Tsm and the judgment of the religious court of Cianjur No. 379/ Pdt.G/2004/PA.Cjr. For their Arabic quotations, see Appendix no. 3 and 4.
54. Interview with the chairman of the religious court in Tasikmalaya, Tasikmalaya, 18 March 2003. Actually, since it is still recommended that the legal procedure of the trial in the religious courts be sourced from the HIR, they can cite the article in the HIR which deals with it. I found a few judgments mentioned the HIR as the legal basis for such a case.
55. Interview with judge Ikhwan of the religious court of South Jakarta, April 2003.
56. Chapter 1 on general provision, UU No. 14/1970.
57. See Harahap, *Kedudukan Kewenangan dan Acara Peradilan Agama*, 44.
58. Sjadzali, *Ijithad Kemanusiaan*, 50. See also Hosen, *Persoalan Taqlid dan Ijtihad*, 328.
59. Imran Ahsan Khan Nyazee, *Theories of Islamic Law: The Methodology of Ijtihād* (Kuala Lumpur: The Other Press, 2002), 186-187.

VI Judges, '*Ulamā*', and the State: Legal Practices of Society

1. Lubis, *Islamic Justice in Transition*, 289.
2. Interview with judge Adib of the religious court in Bogor, Bogor, 7 February 2003.
3. Cf. Lubis, *Islamic Justice in Transition*, 307-308.
4. Interviews with judges of the religious courts of Cianjur, Rangkasbitung, Tasikmalaya, and Bogor.
5. Manan, *Hakim di Mata Hukum*, 30.
6. Interview with Zufran Sabrie, Jakarta, 25 January 2005.
7. It is reported that at a conference in 1996, the Indonesian Council of '*Ulamā*' (MUI) of Aceh discussed cases of divorce declared out of court or without the authorization of the court and the legal effects of these, particularly on the period when the *iddah* (waiting period) begins. The Council discussed the issue because it learned that such divorces are still practiced in some sections of society. See Al Yasa Abubakar, "Ihwal Perceraian di Indonesia: Perkembangan Pemikiran dari Undang-Undang Perkawinan sampai *Kompilasi* Hukum Islam", *Mimbar Hukum*, 44 (1999).
8. Hisako Nakamura, *Divorce in Java* (Yogyakarta: Gadjah Mada University Press, 1983).
9. Interview with Zufran Sabrie, Jakarta, 25 January 2005.
10. Based on my personal interviews with a number of litigants in the religious court of Cianjur, 20-22 March 2003.
11. A number of litigants in Cianjur, particularly those living miles away from the court, complained about the costs they incurred arranging a divorce in the court. While they agreed with the standard charge applied in the court, they saw the cost of transportation as a burden. Two respondents admitted to having spent 50,000 rupiahs on transportation for one session and twice as much if they brought one witness. The cost of transportation would increase if other parties failed to show up and the judges gave them another opportunity to appear on another occasion in the session of the same process where they also had to be present. Personal interviews, 20 March 2003.
12. Such practices were also common among rural Muslim people of Nglegok, East Java. See Badan Penelitian dan Pengembangan Agama, "Pengkajian Tentang Pandangan Masyarakat terhadap Perkawinan, Perceraian dan Poligami: Studi Kasus di

Kecamatan Nglegok" (Jakarta: Badan Penelitian dan Pengembangan Agama Departemen Agama, 1995), 27.

13. Cf. Cik Hasan Bisri, "Dimensi Sosial Budaya dalam Pelaksanaan Kekuasaan Badan Peradilan Agama", *Mimbar Hukum*, 49 (2000), 32-33.
14. Interview with the vice-chairman of the religious court of Cianjur, Cianjur, 20 March 2003.
15. Interview with Drs. Sutarjo, Warung Gunung, Rangkasbitung, 4 February 2005.
16. Interview with Drs. Muhyidin, Warung Gunung, Rangkasbitung, 4 February 2005.
17. Interview with *Ibu* Amah, Rangkasbitung, 5 February 2005.
18. Drs. Choirul Fuad Yusuf dan Drs. Mohammad Rosyid Fauzi, *Laporan Kajian Proyektif Ketatalaksanaan di Lingkungan Departemen Agama tentang Survei Potensi Fisik dan Sosial Kantor Urusan Agama (KUA)* (Jakarta: Departemen Agama RI Badan Litbang Agama dan Diklat Keagamaan, 2001).
19. Interview with Anwar of the religious court of Rangkasbitung, Rangkasbitung, 13 March 2003.
20. In this region the presence of *jawara* is very common. For preliminary information about this group, see Sartono Kartodirdjo, *Pemberontakan Petani Banten 1888* (Jakarta: Pustaka Jaya, 1984). For further information, see M.A. Tihami, "Kepemimpinan Kyai dan Jawara di Banten", Thesis, University of Indonesia, 1992; Mohamad Hudaeri, "Tasbih dan Golok", *Istiqra*, 2: 1 (2003), 57-87.
21. It is reported that besides the fact that many *jawara* have assumed important positions in the political and social realms, this group has no difficulty in sponsoring a person to an important position in the government system. The appointment of Joko Arismunandar as the governor of the province of Banten was said to be attributable to his agreement to enter into an engagement with Ratu Atut Chosiah, the daughter of a charismatic *jawara*. His engagement to her prompted *jawara* to lend this couple their support and also led them to influence society in general to rally behind them. See Hudaeri, "Tasbih dan Golok", 70.
22. Interview with vice-chairman of the religious court of Rangkasbitung, Rangkasbitung, 2 February 2005.
23. Interview with judges of the religious court of Rangkasbitung, Rangkasbitung, 3 February 2005.
24. Interview with Judge Abdul Gani, Rangkasbitung, 4 February 2005.
25. It should be noted that the certificates of divorce are made in quadruplicate, each with a different color and those given to both husband and wife are the red copy (for the husband) and the yellow copy (for the wife). One of the other two is kept in the court, the other one is sent to the relevant KUA.
26. Interview with Muhammad Anwar of the court of Rangkasbitung, Rangkasbitung, 13 March 2003.
27. Interview with the vice-chairman of the religious Court of Cianjur, Cianjur, 20 March, 2003.
28. Such cases had also occurred in a number of courts. In Garut, where Judge Isak had worked earlier as a judge, more than three cases had been identified within his period of employment there. One which he mentioned to me was readily identified by the court, as the name of the clerk on the certificate was written as the undersigned who, at the time the certificate was issued, no longer worked in the court of Garut but had been transferred to another court. The acknowledgment of the invalidity of the certificate was revealed when the holder of the certificate (a husband) told one of officials of the court that he was given a certificate of divorce, even though he had never been summoned to or appeared in the court, and showed it to the judge. The official who began to doubt the authenticity of the certificate took it to the court; with other officials and judges, he checked it and found that it was fraudulent as it included the name of the clerk who had been transferred years before the

certificate was issued. It also carried an unrecorded registration number. It is suspected that the falsification of the name of the clerk was the work of a certain KUA official who knew the name of the clerk of the court of Garut, but did not realize that he had been moved to another court. Interview with Judge Isak and Judge Asep Imaddudin, February 2005. In the court of Subang, more cases had been come to light and a number of KUA officials of Subang had been accused of illegal practices and had been reprimanded. Interview with Judge Abdul Gani, the vice-chairman of the court of Rangkasbitung, who had served before as a judge in Subang, Rangkasbitung, February 2005.

29. Interview with AD and ML, the religious court of South Jakarta, 22 January 2005.
30. These judges' position can be seen in, for an example, Judgment No. 144/Pdt.G/2002/PA.Rks on a case of divorce where the wife as plaintiff said that her husband had divorced her almost two years ago. They did not, for example, stress the period when the wife had to begin her *iddah*.
31. Michael G. Peletz, *Islamic Modern: Religious Courts and Cultural Politics in Malaysia* (Princeton: Princeton University Press, 2000), 156.
32. In this regard, several questions or remarks made by Bowen may be worthy citing here. Is the KHI's definition that divorce is an action which must occur in the court merely for the purpose of State law? If so, how can it be considered as Islamic law? Is it Islamic law because it is the result of an *ijmā*? See Bowen, "Sharī'a, State and Social Norms in France and Indonesia", 11.
33. Mark Cammack, "Indonesia's 1989 Religious Judicature Act: Islamization of Indonesia or Indonesianization of Islam", *Indonesia* 63 (1997), 162-165.
34. M.B. Hooker, *Indonesian Islam: Social Change through Contemporary Fatawa* (Honolulu: Allen & Unwin, 2002), 151.
35. *Ibid.*, 151.
36. See also, "Kawin Siri Karena Kompilasi Kurang Tersosialisasi", *Kompas*, 22 January 2002.
37. The cost is variable. While the amount of money to be submitted to the Government Treasury is around 3,000 rupiahs, the whole cost required differs from one district to another ranging from 80,000 rupiahs to 105,000 rupiahs, or about 8 to 10 Euros. This amount will increase if the marriage is to be concluded in the bride's house and not on the KUA premises, which means that the couple invites the KUA registrar to come to the house (*nikah bedolan*).
38. Interview with Drs. Sutarjo, Rangkasbitung, 4 February 2005. Research on the physical and social potential of KUA also revealed that, in villages like Pandeglang and Situbondo, arbitrary marriages (*nikah di bawah tangan*) are still entered into for these reasons. See Arsyad, *Survei Potensi Fisik and Sosial Kantor Urusan Agama*, 23.
39. Because they are poor, they often do not think of sending their children to school where the children's birth certificates, for which they would have to produce their own marriage certificate, will be needed.
40. Ministry of Religious Affairs, *Himpunan Data Statistik Perkara di Lingkungan Peradilan Agama Seluruh Indonesia Tahun 2000* (Jakarta: Departemen Agama RI, 2002), 246-247.
41. Tim Penulis Rahima (ed.), "Studi Praktek Polygamy dan Perceraian di Cinere, Jakarta Selatan", (Jakarta: Rahima, 2003).
42. Kustini, *Pengkajian tentang Pandangan Masyarakat terhadap Perkawinan, Perceraian dan Poligami* (Jakarta: Litbang Departemen Agama, 1995).
43. Arsyad and Fauzi, "Survei Potensi Fisik dan Sosial KUA", 17.
44. Interview with Drs. Sutarjo, Rangkasbitung, 4 February 2005.
45. Interview with ZB, a female teacher at Government Primary School (Sekolah Dasar Negeri /SDN) of Warung Gunung, Rangkasbitung, 3 February 2005.

46. As illustrated in the judgment of the religious court of Tasikmalaya No. 4/Pdt.p/2001/PA.Tsm.
47. Interview with Anwar of the religious court of Rangkasbitung, 13 March 2003.
48. Interview with Judge Yusuf of the religious court of Cianjur, Cianjur, 20 March 2003. The principle reads *al-muslimūn 'alā shurūṭihim*.
49. See the judgment of the religious court of South Jakarta No. 19/Pdt.P/1997/PAJS.
50. Interview with Judges Effendi and Anwar, 5 February 2005. Unfortunately they failed to find the judgments so that I could not copy them.
51. *Himpunan Data Statistik Perkara di Lingkungan PA Seluruh Indonesia Th 2000* (Jakarta: Ditbinbapera Depag, 2002).
52. R. Otje Salman, *Kesadaran Hukum Masyarakat terhadap Hukum Waris* (Bandung: Alumni, 1993); see also Rofiqul Umam "Hendak Kemana Hukum Waris Islam (Whither the Islamic Law of Inheritance)", *Pelita* (21 August 1992), 4.
53. *Ibid.*
54. In the matrilineal system, children have no rights to the estate of their deceased parents. Meanwhile, in the patrilineal system, only male children have right to the estate. See Harahap, "Praktek Hukum Waris Tidak Pantas Membuat Generalisasi", 128-132.
55. See Harahap, "Praktek Hukum Waris Tidak Pantas Membuat Generalisasi" 133.
56. Saimima, *Polemik Reaktualisasi*, 140-165.
57. Lev, *Islamic Court*, 20-21.
58. See Art. 49. The principle that the claimants to an estate be given a choice of the law governing distribution of property has its ground on the historical debate about the extent to which Islamic laws had replaced *adat* in matters of inheritance. See Cammack, "Indonesia's 1989 Religious Judicature Act", 157.
59. Interview with Deden, the clerk of the religious court of Cibinong, Cibinong, 17 February 2003. See also Ministry of Religious Affairs, *Monitoring dan Evaluasi Pelaksanaan Undang-Undang Peradilan Agama dan Kompilasi Hukum Islam* (Jakarta: Ditbinbapera, 2001), 58.
60. See Gavin W. Jones, *Marriage and Divorce in Islamic Southeast Asia*, (Kuala Lumpur: Oxford University Press, 1994), 259; June S. Katz & Ronald S. Katz, "Legislating Social Change in a Developing Country: The New Indonesian Marriage Law Revisited", *Journal of Comparative Law*, 309 (1978), 310; and Gavin W. Jones, Yahya Asari & Tuti Djuartika, "Divorce in West Java", *Journal of Comparative Family Studies*, 35 (1995), 395.
61. Jones, *Marriage and Divorce in Islamic Southeast Asia*, 246-248.
62. See Mark Cammack, "An Empirical Assessment of Divorce Law Reform in Indonesia", *Studia Islamika*, 4: 4 (1997), 104.
63. See also Bisri, "Dimensi Sosial Budaya", 29-30.
64. See "Percerain di Bekasi Karena Soal Sepele", *Kompas*, Thursday, 24 April 2003.
65. Balitbang, "Pengkajian Tentang Pandangan Masyarakat terhadap Perkawinan, Perceraian dan Poligami", 23.
66. See "Di Malang 10 Kasus Gugatan Cerai Dalam Sehari", *Tempointeraktif*, 18 August, 2004.
67. M. Kuchiba, Y. Tsubouchi, N. Maede, *Three Malay Village: A Sociology of Paddy Growers in West Malaysia* (Honolulu: University Press of Hawaii, 1979), 33-34.
68. Yasmine Al-Hadar, *Perkawinan dan Perceraian di Indonesia: Sebuah Studi antar Kebudayaan* (Jakarta: Lembaga Demografi Fakultas Ekonomi Universitas Indonesia, 1977), 65.
69. T. Ashakul, *Regional and Provincial Urban and Population Projections*, Background Report 2-2, National Urban Development Policy Framework (Bangkok: Thailand Development Research Institute, 1990).

70. It must be noted that the *kompilasi* states that wives have the right to *mut'a* property after divorce if they are not responsible for the reason for divorce or if they are divorced without fault. See the *kompilasi*, Art. 149.
71. Noted from hearings of divorce cases in the court of Cianjur, February 2005. But while what they stated in court was to some extent true, many wives' petitions for divorce were also motivated by the fact that they had already found other men to marry. Judges told me that one of them frankly said that she wanted to marry an Arab man and had invited him to come to Indonesia to arrange the marriage. Interview with judges of the court of Cianjur, February 2005.
72. Interview with NN, one of litigants in the court of Cianjur, February 2005. I witnessed two cases of this and was informed that there were quite a few such marriages in the city.
73. Since the average age of both girls and boys at marriage has increased, this is no longer relevant to the remaining high rate of divorce in Indonesia, particularly in my research areas. In fact, the judgments on divorce in my collection in which the identities of the couple are displayed indicated that their average age at marriage is 20.
74. Jones, *Marriage and Divorce in Islamic South-East Asia*, 224.
75. Interview with judges in the religious court of Cianjur, 20 March 2003. See also Syuhada Abduh and Mursyid Ali (eds.), "Pengkajian tentang Pandangan Masyarakat terhadap Perkawinan, Perceraian dan Poligami: Studi Kasus di Desa Rancahan dan Gabus Wetan Kabupaten Indramayu Jawa Barat", (Jakarta: Puslitbang Kehidupan Beragama, Departemen Agama, 1994-1995), 1-20.
76. See Jones, *Marriage and Divorce in Islamic South-East Asia*, 229. Judge Abdul Gani narrated that in Subang, where he earlier served as a judge, divorce and remarriage are easy and normal practices for girls. He even described marriage, divorce, and remarriage as a home industry and consequently a means to acquire property, as girls when married are entitled to be accorded certain property by their prospect husbands. Hence, the more frequently a girl marries the more property she acquires. Interview with Judge Abdul Gani, Rangkasbitung, 5 February 2005.
77. Kuchiba, *Three Malay Villages*, 41.
78. See Yasmine al-Hadar, *Perkawinan dan Perceraian di Indonesia*, 67.
79. Interview with Yulia, South Jakarta, April 2003.
80. This usually happens to divorcées whose ex-husbands are not civil servants. Wives whose husbands are civil servants employed by the Government are more fortunate. They can claim the rights for their children's financial support from their fathers under the provision that the agreed amount of financial support for their children can be directly deducted from the monthly salaries of their husbands. See also Puslitbang Departemen Agama, "Pandangan Masyarakat Terhadap Perkawinan, Perceraian dan Poligami", (Jakarta: Puslitbang Departemen Agama, 1995), 28-29.
81. Jokingly, one judge in Cianjur asked a woman, who had petitioned for divorce on the grounds of the absence of her husband for one year and his neglect of his financial responsibility, whether she would not regret if after her petition had been granted the husband came home with a nice car. By putting this question the judge was trying to make her rethink her decision, but the woman answered spontaneously that she would never regret it, even though the husband were to offer her such a car plus a bag full of money.
82. Interviews with the judges of the religious courts of Cianjur and Rangkasbitung, 2003, and confirmed through further interviews in 2005.
83. Interview with the clerk of the religious court of South Jakarta, February 2003.

Conclusion

1. Lev, *Islamic Court*, 233.
2. Look at the example above in which the deceased leaves a daughter, a daughter of a son and sister and which grants the daughter and the daughter of a son each half, while the sister gets nothing. Meanwhile according to classical Islamic system of inheritance, half goes to the daughter and one-sixth to the daughter of a son, and the remaining one-third goes to sister.
3. Esposito, *Women in Muslim Family Law*, 101.
4. See Haim Gerber, *Islamic Law and Culture* (Leiden: E.J. Brill, 1999), 105.
5. See Messick, *The Calligraphic State*, 69-70.
6. *Ibid.*, 71.
7. Lev, *Islamic Court*, 226.

Appendices

1. مـن علـق طلاقـا بصـفة وقـع بوجودهـا عمـلا بمقتضـى اللفـظ

Man 'allaqa ṭalāqan bi ṣifatin waqa'a biwujūdihā 'amalan bimuqtaḍā al-lafẓ (Sharqāwi 'alā al-Taḥrīr).

2. واذا صـدر تعليـق الطـلاق بصـفة مـن مكلـف و وجـدت تلـك الصـفة فـى غـير تكليـف فـان الطـلاق المعلـق بهـا يقـع

Wa idhā ṣadara ta'līq al-ṭalāq bi ṣifatin min mukallafin wa wujidat tilka al-ṣifat fī ghayr taklīfin fa inna al-ṭalāq al-mu'allaq bihā yaqa? (Bājūrī's Ḥāshiya Kifāyat al-Akhyār, 153).

3. و القضـاء علـى غائـب عـن البلـد او المجلـس لتعـزز جـائز ان كـان لمـدع حجـة مقبولـة

Wa al-qaḍā 'alā ghā'ibin 'an al-balad aw al-majlis li ta'azzuzin jā'izun in kāna li mudda'in ḥujjatun maqbūlatun (Ibn Ḥajar's Tuḥfat al-Muḥtāj, Vol. 10, 164).

4. مـن دعـي الـي حـاكم مـن حكـام المسـلمين فلـم تجـب فهـو ظـالم لا حـق لـه

Man du'iya ilā ḥākimin min ḥukkām al-muslimīn falam tujab fahuwa żālimun la ḥaqqa lahu ('Ulūm al-Qur'ān, 405).

5. اذا اشـتدت رغبـة الزوجـة عـن زوجهـا طلـق عليهـا القاضـي طلقـة

Idhā ishtaddat raghbat al-zawjat 'an zawjihā ṭallaqa 'alaihā al-qāḍī ṭalqatan (Al-Anṣārī's Minhāj al-Tullāb, Vol. IV, 346).

6. اذا اشـتد عـدم رغبـة الزوجـة لزوجهـا طلـق عليـه القاضـي طلقـة

Idhā istadda 'adam raghbat al-zawjat li zawjihā ṭallaqa 'alaihi al-qāḍī ṭalqatan'

7. اذا اشـتد عـدم رغبـة الزوجـة لزوجهـا يجـوز لحكمـه و لحكمهـا ان يـو الطـلاق من غير رضـاهما قعـا

Idhā istadda ʻadam raghbat al-zawjati li zawjihā yajūzu liḥakamihi wa liḥakamihā an yūqiʻā al-ṭalāq min ghayri riḍāhumā (Risālat al-Shiqāq, 22.)

8. وشـرائط الحضـانة سـبعة: العقـل والحريـة والـدين والعفـة بلـد الممـيز والخلـع مـن الـزوج فـان اختلـع والاءمانـة والإقامـة فـي شـقطت حضـانتها شـرط منهـا اى السـبعة فـي ' ألأم

Wa sharāʼiṭ al-ḥaḍāna sabʻatun: al-ʻaql, wa al-ḥuriyyat, wa al-dīn, wa al-ʻiffah, wa al-ʻamānah, wa al-ʻiqāmat fi balad al-mumayyiz, wa al-khuluʼ min al- zawj, fa in ikhtallaʼ sharṭun minhā ay al-sabʻatu fi al- ʻumm saqa-ṭat haḍānatuhā (Dimsaqi's Kifāyat al-Akhyār, Vol. II, 152.)

9. والعفـة والأمانـة فـلا حضـانة لفاسـق تركـه الصـلاة

Al-ʻiffatu wal-ʻamānatu fa lā ḥaḍānata li fāsiqin ta rakahu al-ṣalāt (Bājūrī's Ḥāshiya Kifāyat al-Akhyār, Vol. II, 198).

10. فـلا حضـانة لفاسـقة والفاسـقة لا تلـي

Fa lā ḥaḍānata li fāsiqatin wa al-fāsiqātu la talī (Bājūrī's Ḥāshiya Kifāyat al-Akhyār, Vol. III, 203).

11. وفـي الـدعوي بالنكـاح علـي إمـراة ذكـر صـحته وشـروطه فـي وشاهدى عدل و رضـاها نحوولـي

Wa fī al-daʻwā bi al-nikāḥ ʻalā imraʼatin dhikru ṣiḥḥatihī wa shurūṭihi fī naḥwa waliyyin wa shāḥīday ʻudūlin wa riḍāha (Baʼalawī's Bughyat al-Mustarshidīn).

12. و تصـدق المـراة بـي دعـوى البلـوغ بحيـض

Wa taṣaddaqa al-marʼatu fī daʻwā al-bulūgh biḥayḍin (Dimyaṭī's Iʼānat al-Ṭālibin, Vol. II, 3145).

13. و يجـوز لوالـي الصـبي ان يزوجـه اذا راى فـي ذالـك اي لمصـلحة العفـة والخدمـة

Wa yajūzu liwāliyy al-ṣabiyy an yuzawwijahu idhā rāʻa fī dhālika ay limaṣlaḥat al-iffaḥ aw al-khidmah (Al-Muhadhdhab, Vol. II, 40.)

14. وأوفوا بالعهد إن كان العهدمسئولا

Wa 'aufū bi al-'ahdi inna kāna al-ahda mas'ūla (al-Isrā': 34).

15. ويجب للمعتدة الرجعية السكنى والنفقة والكسوة

Wa yajibu li al-mu'taddah al-raj'iyyah al-suknā, wa al-nafaqa, wa al-kiswa (al-Bājūrī's Ḥāshiya Kifāyat al-Akhyār, Vol. III, 203).

16. مقدرة من النكاح ونفقة العدة

Wa nafaqat al-'iddat muqaddaratun min al-nikāḥ (Nawawī's Minhāj al-Ṭālibīn, 116).

17. منها الرجعية فلها النفقة والسكنى بالاجماع

Minhā al-raj'iyyat fa lahā al-nafaqah wa al-suknā bi al-´ijmā? (Dimsāqī's Kifāyat al-Akhyār, Vol. II, 132).

18. فانكحواماطاب لكم من النساء مثنى وثلاث وربع فان خفتم
الاتعدلوا فواحدة

Fankiḥū mā ṭāba lakum min al-nisā' mathnā wa thulātha, fa in khiftum allā ta'dilu fa wāḥidatan.

19. وقدنقل ابن جرير و غيره عن ابن عباس و ابن الزبير انهما
كان يقولان في الميت ترك بنة و اخة انه لا شيئ للاخت

Wa qad naqala ibn Jarīr wa ghairuhu 'an Ibn Abbās wa Ibn al-Zubayr annahumā kāna yaqūlāni fi al-mayyit taraka bintan wa ukhtan innahu la shay li al-'ukht

20. ألحقوا الفرائض باهلها فما بقي فهوا لأولى رجل ذكر

Al-ḥiqū al-farā'iḍa biahlihā famā baqiya fahuwa li awlā rajulin dhakarin

21. لإبنته النصف ولإبنة الإبن بينهم تكملة لثلثين وما
الأب و الأم بقي فلى الأخت من

li ibnatihi al-niṣf wa li ibnati al-'ibn baynahum takmilatan lithuluthayni wa mā baqiya fali al-ukht min al-'abb wa al-'umm

22. حدثنا أدم حدثنا أبو هزيل بن سرحبيل قال سئل أبو موسى
عن بنت وابنة إبن وأخت فقال للبنت النصف وللأخت

النصف وأت ابن مسعود فسيتابعني فسئل ابن مسعود وأخبر بقول أبى موسى فقال لقد ضللت إذا وما أنا من المهتدين أقضى فيها بما قضى النبى صلى الله عليه وسلم للابنت النصف و لإبنت إبن السدس تكملة الثلثين وما بقي فلى الأخت فأتينا أبا موسى فأخبرناه بقول إبن مسعود فقال لا تسألونى مادام هذا الخبر فيكم

Ḥaddathanā 'Ādam ḥadathanā Abū Qays sami'tu Huzayl bin Sarahbīl qāla su'ila abū Mūsa `an bintin wabnati ibnin wa ukhtin fa qāla li al-binti al-niṣf wa li al-ukhti al-niṣf wa `ti ibna Mas'ūd fa sayutābi'unī fa su `ila ibnu Mas'ūd wa ukhbira bi qawli abī Mūsa fa qāla laqad ḍalaltu idhan wa ma `anā min al-muhtadīn aqḍī fīhā bimā qaḍā al-Nabiyy ṣalla Allahu `alaihi wa sallama lil ibnati al-niṣf wa libnati ibnin al-sudus takmilata al-thuluthayni wa mā baqiya fa li al ukhti fa `ataynā `abā Mūsa fa akhbarnāhu bi qawli ibn Mas'ūd faqāla la tas`alūnī mā dāma hādhā al-khabar fīkum (Saḥīḥ al-Bukhārī, chapter *al-farā`iḍ*, no. 6239).

23. أبغض الحلال عند الله هوا الطلاق

Abghaḍ al-ḥalāl 'inda Allāh huwa al-ṭalāq

24. درء المفاسد مقدم على جلب المصالح

Dar'u al-mafāsid muqaddamun 'alā jalb al-maṣāliḥ

P U T U S A N

NOMOR : 397/Pdt.G/2004/PA.Cjr

بِسْمِ اللهِ الرَّحْمنِ الرَّحِيْمِ

DEMI KEADILAN BERDASARKAN KETUHANAN YANG MAHA ESA

Pengadilan Agama Cianjur yang memeriksa dan mengadili perkara perdata tertentu pada tingkat pertama, telah menjatuhkan putusan sebagaimana tersebut di bawah ini dalam perkara "Cerai Gugat" antara :---

EHA SALSIAH binti H. OMAN RUKMANA, umur 41 Tahun, agama Islam, pekerjaan Ibu Rumah Tangga, tempat tinggal Kampung Jero Rt. 02/03 Desa Maleber Kecamatan Karang Tengah, Kabupaten Cianjur. Selanjutnya disebut **"PENGGUGAT"** ;----------------------

BERLAWANAN DENGAN

LUKI ABU BAKAR S. bin EFENDI, umur 45 Tahun, agama Islam, pekerjaan Wiraswasta, tempat tinggal Kp. Kalibunder Rt. 02/07 Desa Maleber Kecamatan Karang Tengah, Kabupaten Cianjur. Selanjutnya disebut **"TERGUGAT"** ;--

Pengadilan Agama tersebut ;--

Telah membaca dan mempelajari berkas perkara ;----------------------------------

Telah mendengar keterangan Penggugat dan saksi keluarganya di persidangan ;-

TENTANG DUDUKNYA PERKARA

Menimbang, bahwa Penggugat dengan surat Gugatannya tertanggal 26 Oktober 2004 yang terdaftar di Kepaniteraan Pengadilan Agama Cianjur dengan Register

5

a. Tafsir al-Munir, surat al-Baqarah 232;------------------------

Artinya: "jangan enggan engkau untuk menikahkan putrinya kepada calon suaminya, apabila mereka saling menyukai dalam keadaan (ma'ruf) baik, yang dimaksud dengan ma'ruf adalah sikap mental yang baik dari hukum syara, susila, kesopanan dan adat istiadat".------------------

Rasulullah saw. dari Aisah ra.:------------------------------

Artinya: "Apabila seorang perempuan menikah tanpa ijin walinya, nikahnya batal. Jika si suami telah menggaulinya maka dia berhak menerima mahal sekedar menghalalkan farjinya. Apabila walinya enggan atau menolak menikahkannya maka sulton (Hakim) lah yang menjadi wali bagi perempuan yang tidak memiliki wali".------------------------

Menimbang, bahwa berdasarkan hal-hal dan bukti-bukti serta pertimbangan tersebut di atas, maka permohonan pemohon dipandang telah memenuhi syarat-syarat permohonannya maka permohonan pemohon dapat dikabulkan;------------------------------------

Mengingat, segala peraturan perundang-undangan yang berlaku serta hukum syara' yang berkaitan dengan perkara ini;-----------

MENGADILI

MENETAPKAH:

1. Mengabulkan permohonan Pemohon;------------------------------
2. Menetapkan bahwa orang tua Pemohon (HUSNOHO) selaku wali nikah adalah wali adlol;--------------------------------------
3. Membebankan pemohon untuk membayar biaya perkara;-----------

Demikian Penetapan Pengadilan Agama Tasikmalaya Dijatuhkan pada hari Selasa, 26 Juni 2001 M. bertepatan dengan 4 Rabi'ul Tsani 1422 H. oleh Kami DRS. MEMET MOCH. SOLEH,SH. sebagai Hakim Ketua Majelis, DRS. ODING SUPANDI,SH. dan DRS. ENTUR

- Bahwa alasan Pemohon dengan dukungan bukti P-3 dan keterangan salah seorang saksinya meskipun keterangannya secara de auditu sedangkan Termohon menolak namun penolakan nya atau bantahannya itu tidak dibuktikan, maka sudah dianggap cukup terbukti alasan Pemohon teresebut ; -- --------------------
- Bahwa dengan terbuktinya dalil permohonan Pemohon sehingga dianggap telah beralasan secara hukum dan telah sesuai berdasakan pasal 116 huruf (g) Kompilasi Hukum Islam ; ----
- Bahwa Majelis Hakim memperhatikan Alqur'an Surat Albaqarah ayat 221 :

ولا تنكحوا المشركت حتى تؤ منّ , ولآ مة مؤ منة خيرمن المشركة ولوا عجبتكم

" Dan janganlah kamu nikahi wanita-wanita musyrik, sebelum mereka beriman. wanita musyrik walaupun dia menarik hatimu sesungguhnya wanita budak yang mu'min lebih baik dari wanita musyrik " ; ---
- memperhatikan dalil dari Kitab Mada hariyatul Jauzaini Juz I halaman 83, terjemahannya sebagai berikut : " Isiam memilih lembaga Thalak/cerai ketika rumah tangga sudah dianggap goncang serta sudah dianggap tidak bermanfaat lagi nasihat/perdamaian dan hubungan suami istri telah hampa, sebab meneruskan perkawinan berarti menghukum salah satu suami istri dengan penjara yang berkepanjangan, ini adalah aniaya yang bertentangan dengan keadilan "
- bahwa secara eks officio, karena perjalanan rumah tangga Tergugat dengan Penggugat sudah cukup lama, maka oleh Majelis diharuskan Pemohon Konpensi / Tergugat Rekonpensi untuk menghargai jasa-jasa Termohon Konpensi / Penggugat Rekonpensi sebagaimana akan dituangkan dalam amar putusan ; ---

Menimbang, bahwa berdasarkan pertimbangan-pertimbangan tersebut diatas, alasan perceraian yang diajukan Pemohon dapat diterima untuk dikabulkan sesuai ketentuan pasal 39 ayat (2) Undang Undang Nomor 1 Tahun 1974 jo pasal 70 ayat (1) Undang Undang Nomor 7 Tahun 1989 ; --

Dalam Rekonpensi :

Menimbang, bahwa Pemohon Konpensi menjadi Tergugat Rekonpensi dan Termohon Konpensi menjadi Penggugat Rekonpensi ; --

Menimbang, bahwa gugatan Penggugat tersebut termasuk dalam tugas dan wewenang

Menimbang, bahwa dari keterangan tiga orang saksi tersebut telah terungkap fakta-fakta dalam rumah tangga Penggugat dan Tergugat, bahwa benar Penggugat dan Tergugat telah berpisah selama lebih dari dua tahun yang disebabkan karena sering terjadi perselisihan dan pertengkaran. Bahwa pertengkaran itu sendiri terjadi karena Tergugat tidak mau bekerja/mencari nafkah, dan mempunyai kebiasaan buruk yaitu sering main judi dan minum minuman keras, bahkan akhirnya Tergugat telah menikah lagi dengan perempuan lain, dan menceraikan Penggugat secara di bawah tangan; --

Menimbang, bahwa berdasarkan fakta-fakta tersebut Pengadilan menilai bahwa rumah tangga Penggugat dengan Tergugat sudah sulit untuk dirukunkan, oleh karena itu maka harus dinyatakan bahwa gugatan Penggugat telah memenuhi salah satu alternatif alasan perceraian sebagaimana maksud pasal 19 (f) Peraturan Pemerintah Nomor 9 Tahun 1975 jo. pasal 116 (f) Kompilasi Hukum Islam di Indonesia; --

Menimbang, bahwa oleh karena gugatan Penggugat tidak ternyata melawan hukum dan telah terbukti, sementara Tergugat tidak datang menghadap di persidangan,maka berdasarkan pasal 125 HIR, gugatan Penggugat beralasan untuk dikabulkan dengan verstek; ----------------------

Menimbang, bahwa Majelis Hakim sependapat dengan ahli Hukum Islam sebagaimana tercantum dalam kitab *Ghayat al-Muram Li Syaikh al-Majdi* yang menyatakan : ---

اذا اشتد عدم رغبة الزوجة لزوجها طلق عليه القاضي طلقة

Artinya : "Apabila seorang isteri sudah sangat tidak senang kepada suaminya, maka Hakim dapat menjatuhkan talak satu suaminya". ------------

Menimbang, bahwa perkara ini termasuk dalam lingkup sengketa perkawinan, maka berdasarkan pasal 89 ayat (1) Undang-Undang Nomor 7 Tahun 1989, seluruh biaya perkara dibebankan kepada Penggugat; --------------------------

Mengingat, hukum syara' dan segala peraturan

P U T U S A N

NOMOR:2368/Pdt.G/1999/PA.Tsm.

BISMILLAAHIR ROHMANIR ROHIM

DEMI KEADILAN BERDASARKAN KETUHANAN YANG MAHA ESA

Pengadilan Agama Tasikmalaya yang mengadili perkara perdata dalam tingkat pertama dalam persidangan majlis telah menjatuhkan putusan sebagai berikut dalam perkara antara :---

ENGKAS KUSNANDAR BIN ENANG, Umur 47 tahun, Pekerjaan Wiraswasta Agama Islam, Pendidikan SMP, tempat tinggal di Kp. Cipanaga Rt.04/06 Desa Cikukulu Kec. Karangnunggal Kab. Tasikmalaya, yang selanjutnya disebut --------------------"PEMOHON"------------------------

L A W A N :

ROHAYATI BINTI TAHU, Umur 40 tahun, Agama Islam, Pendidikan SD, Pekerjaan Ibu rumah tangga, tempat tinggal di Kp.Cipanaga Rt.04/06 Desa Cikukulu Kec.Karangnunggal Kab. Tasikmalaya yang selanjutnya disebut -----------------"TERMOHON"-------------------------

Pengadilan Agama tersebut;------------------------------------

Telah mempelajari berkas perkara yang bersangkutan;----------

Telah mendengar keterangan Pemohon dan Termohon dan saksi-saksi;---

TENTANG DUDUKNYA PERKARA:

Menimbang, bahwa Pemohon dengan surat permohonannya tanggal 4 Nopember 1999 yang terdaftar dalam Register perkara nomor: 2368/Pdt.G/1999/PA.Tsm mengajukan hal hal sebagai berikut;--

Bahwa Pemohon telah menikah kepada Termohon pada tanggal 11 Pebruari 1991 dihadapan pejabat Kantor Urusan Agama Kecamatan Cihideung Kab.Tasikmalaya, sebagaimana dalam kutipan Akta nikah nomor: 497/36/II/1991;---------------------------

Bahwa setelah menikah Pemohon dengan Termohon pernah merasakan kehidupan berumah tangga yang bahagia, sehingga telah dikarunia satu orang anak;---------------------------------

Bahwa akan tetapi kebahagiaan itu tidak berlangsung lama, karena sejak bulan Agustur 1999 rumah tangga antara Pemohon dan Termohon mulai goyah dikarenakan antara Pemohon dan Termohon sering terjadi perselisihan yang sulit didamaikan sehingga antara Pemohon dan Termohon telah berpisah rumah selama 1 bulan lamanya;--------------------------------------

Bahwa sebab terjadinya perselisihan tersebut disebabkan Termohon suka kasar atau berbicara suka lancang dan Termohon sering mengancam Pemohon, mau membunuh Pemohon, dan pernah meludahi muka dan nampar Pemohon,----------------------------

Bahwa untuk mempertahankan keutuhan rumah tangga sudah ditempuh baik melalui kedua belah pihak, orang tua maupun pihak lain, akan tetapi usaha tersebut tidak berhasil;-------------

Bahwa keutuhan rumah tangga Pemohon dengan Termohon sudah tidak dapat dipertahankan lagi dan tidak ada harapan untuk bersatu lagi sehingga perceraian ditempuh merupakan jalan dari semua pilihan yang ada;---------------------------------

Bahwa berdasarkan hal tersebvt diatas,maka Pemohon memohon agar Pengadilan Agama Tasikmalaya menjatuhkan putusan sebagai berikut;--

PRIMER

1.Mengabulkan permohonan Pemohon ;--------------------------

2.Menetakan mengijinkan kepada Pemohon untuk ikror menjatuhkan thalak satu terhadap Termohon;-------------------------

3.Menetapkan biaya perkara menurut hukum;--------------------

SUBSIDER

Apabila Pengadilan Agama berpendapat lain dalam peradilan yang baik mohon keputusan yang seadil-adilnya;

Menimbang bahwa majelis hakim telah berusaha mendamaikan kedua belah pihak yang berperkara akan tetapi usaha tersebut tidak berhasil.

Menimbang maka dibacakanlah Permohonan pemohon yang isinya tetap dipertahankan oleh Pemohon.

h. Pendapat ahli hukum islam yang terdapat dalam kitab Syarqowi alat Tahrir juz II halaman 308 yang berbunyi :

ومن علق طلاقا بصفة وقع بوجودها عملا بمقتضى اللفظ

Artinya : Barang siapa yang menggantungkan thalak dengan sesuatu sifat, maka jatuhlah thalaq itu dengan adanya sifat tersebut menurut dhohirnya ucapannya;---

Menimbang, bahwa tergugat telah membayar iwadl sebesar Rp. 1.000,- (seribu rupiah);----------------------------------

Menimbang, bahwa berdasarkan pertimbangan - pertimbangan tersebut diatas dan telah terbukti kebenarannya serta gugatan penggugat telah memenuhi syarat-syarat gugatan dan tidak melawan hukum, maka gugatan tersebut perlu dikabulkan;---

Menimbang, bahwa biaya perkara yang timbul dalam perkara ini dibebankan kepada Penggugat sesuai dengan pasal 89 ayat (1) Undang - undang No. 7 tahun 1989 ;-----------

Mengingat, segala peraturan perundang - undangan yang berlaku serta hukum syara' yang berkaitan dengan perkara ini;---

<u>M E N G A D I L I</u>

Memutuskan:

1. Menyatakan bahwa Tergugat telah dipanggil dengan patut untuk menghadap di persidangan tidak hadir ;-------------
2. Menetapkan syarat-syarat ta'lik talak telah terpenuhi;--
3. Mengabulkan Gugatan Penggugat dengan Verstek ;----------
4. Menjatuhkan tolak satu khul'i Tergugat (ASEP BUDIYANA bin DAYAT) kepada Penggugat (EUTIK NURHAYATI binti ZENAL MUTTAQIN), dengan iwadl Rp. 1.000,-;-------------------
4. Menghukum Penggugat untuk membayar seluruh biaya perkara sebesar Rp. 148.000,- (seratus empat puluh delapan ribu rupiah);---

Demikianlah Putusan pengadilan Agama Tasikmalaya dijatuhkan pada hari ini kamis tanggal Kamis tanggal 21 Nopember 2002 M. bertepatan dengan tanggal 16 Ramadhan 1423 H. oleh Kami Drs. ODING SOPANDI, SH. sebagai Ketua Majelis, Drs. ENTUR MASTUR, SH. dan Drs. ABCO DJAELANI masing - masing sebagai hakim Anggota, Putusan mana pada hari itu juga dibacakan dalam sidang yang terbuka untuk umum oleh Majelis tersebut yang dihadiri oleh ENDANG PIPIN, SH., Sebagai Panitera Pengganti serta kuasa Penggugat tanpa hadirnya Tergugat;---

Menimbang, bahwa untuk mempersingkat uraian putusan ini, maka segala sesuatu yang terdapat dalamberita acara persidangan dianggap masuk dalam bagian yang tidak terpisahkan dalam putusan ini ;-----------------------------------

TENTANG HUKUMNYA :

Menimbang, bahwa maksud dan tujuan Gugatan Penggugat adalah sebagaimana tersebut di atas ;------------------------

Menimbang, bahwa Tergugat telah dipanggil oleh Pengadilan Agama Tasikmalaya dengan sah dan patut tetapi tergugat tidak pernah datang dan tidak datangnya itu tidak beralasan yang dibenarkan oleh hukum, berdasarkan pasal 27 Peraturan Pemerintah Nomor 9 tahun 1975, maka harus dinyatakan tergugat tidak hadir;-----------------------------------

Menimbang, bahwa berdasarkan keterangan Penggugat juga bukti P-1 terbukti bahwa antara Penggugat dengan Tergugat telah terikat oleh perkawinan yang syah ;-----------------

Menimbang, bahwa berdasarkan keterangan Penggugat dengan dikuatkan oleh dua orang saksi yang masing - masing dibawah sumpahnya, telah terbukti bahwa tergugat telah pergi meninggalkan penggugat yang lamanya sampai sekarang kurang lebih 3 tahun dan selama itu pula tergugat tidak memberi nafkah kepada penggugat, dengan demikian harus dinyatakan tergugat telah melanggar ta'lik talak poin 1, 2, dan point 4, maka alasan perceraian sebagaimana dimaksud dalam pasal 46 jo. pasal 116 huruf (g) Kompilasi Hukum Islam telah cukup terpenuhi, serta sesuai dengan dalil sebagai berikut;--

a. Pendapat ahli Hukum Islam yang terdapat dalam kitab Tuhfah Juz 10 halaman 164 yang berbunyi ;---------------

والقضاء على غائب عن البلد او المجلس لتوار او تعزز جائز ان كان لمدع حجة مقبولة

Artinya : Mengadili terhadap orang yang tidak ada ditempat tinggalnya karena bersembunyi atau membangkang, hal itu boleh asal bagi Penggugat mempunyai alasan yang dapat diterima ;--------------------

Responses of 122 Respondents on a Number of Reformed Rules in KHI

No	*Issues/Cases*	*In number and percentage*		*Descriptions/ Reasons*
		Agreed	*Disagreed*	
1	*Riddah*/apostasy as a ground for divorce	101(82.8%)	21(17.2%)	Most of those who agreed did not stipulate the emergence of disharmony as specified in the *kompilasi*. So, apostasy alone can become an absolute ground for divorce
2	Representation of heirs	80(65.6%)	42(34.4%)	50 of those agreed found that additional clause limiting the portion of the representative is fair rule. The remaining 30 did not want limitation. Those who did not agree preferred to apply the system of wasiat wajiba to the problem of orphaned grandchildren.
3	*Wasiat Wajiba* to adoption	92(75.4%)	30(24.6%)	Those who did not agree found that the rule is too hasty in giving the adopting parties shares of inheritance. They tend to suggest that the *kompilasi* recommend the adopting parties make testament (wasiat).
4	Daughter(s) versus Collaterals	71(58.2%)	42(34.4%)	9 of the respondents did not comprehend the rule. They did not give their comments on the issue (7.4%). Those who did not agree based their opinion on their interpretation on Ibn Abbas' saying that daughter does not cover brother of the deceased (uncle(s) of the daughter) but only sister of the deceased (aunt(s) of the daughter).
5	Joint property	122(100%)	0	The fact that all the respondents agreed with the rule is due to: 1. the issue is related to living parties, and the rule has not been dealt with by either in the *fiqh* or in the Qur'an, 2. the issue is rightly related to the notion of right equality between spouses which has been the subject of legal reformation.

The References of Judgments on Most Frequently Debated Issues

No	*Issues/ Cases*	*To KHI*	*To Fiqh Texts*	*To KHI and Fiqh Texts*
1	6 judgments on cases of *riddah/* apostasy within marriage	-	2	4
2	4 judgments on cases of representation of heirs	1	2	1
3	3 judgments on cases of daughter(s) versus collateral(s).	1	2	

PRESIDEN
REPUBLIK INDONESIA
INSTRUKSI PRESIDEN REPUBLIK INDONESIA
NOMOR 1 TAHUN 1991
PRESIDEN REPUBLIK INDONESIA

Menimbang:

a. Bahwa Alim Ulama Indonesia dalam lokakarya yang diadakan di Jakarta pada tanggal 2 sampai dengan 5 Pebruari 1988 telah menerima baik tiga rancangan buku Kompilasi Hukum Islam, yaitu Buku 1 tentang Hukum Perkawinanm, Buku II tentang Hukum Kewarisan, dan Buku III tentang Hukum Perwakafan.
b. bahwa Kompilasi Hukum Islam tersebut dalam huruf a oleh Instansi Pemerintah dan oleh masyarakat yang memerlukannya dapat dipergunakan sebagai pedoman dalam menyelesaikan masalah-masalah di bidang tersebut.
c. Bahwa oleh karena itu Kompilasi Hukum Islam tersebut dalam huruf a perlu disebarluaskan.

Mengingat: pasal 4 ayat (1) Undang-Undang Dasar 1945.

MENGINSTRUKSIKAN

Kepada : Menteri Agama

Untuk

PERTAMA: Menyebarluaskan Kompilasi Hukum Islam yang terdiri dari:

a. Buku I tentang Hukum Perkawinan
b. Buku II tentang Hukum Kewarisan
c. Buku III tentang Hukum Perwakafan

Sebagai telah diterima dalam Lokakarya di Jakarta pada tanggal 2 sampai dengan 5 Pebruari 1988, untuk digunakan oleh masyarakat yang memerlukannya.

KEDUA: Melakasanakan Instruksi ini dengan sebaik-baiknya dan dengan penuh tanggung jawab.

Dikeluarkan di Jakarta
Pada tanggal 10 Juni 1991

PRESIDEN REPUBLIK INDONESIA
ttd

SOEHARTO

Salinan sesuai dengan aslinya
SEKRETARIAT KABINET RI
Kepala Biro Hukum dan Perundang-undangan
ttd
BAMBANG KESOWO, SH,LLM.

KEPUTUSAN MENTERI AGAMA REPUBLIK INDONESIA NOMOR: 154 TAHUN 1991 TENTANG PELAKSANAAN INSTRUKSI PRESIDEN REPUBLIK INDONESIA NOMOR 1 TAHUN 1991 TANGGAL 10 JUNI 1991 MENTERI AGAMA REPUBLIK INDONESIA

Menimbang :

a. bahwa Instruksi Presiden Republik Indonesia Nomor 1 Tahun 1991 tanggal 10 Juni 1991, memerintahkan kepada Menteri Agama untuk menyebarluaskan Kompilasi Hukum Islam untuk digunakan oleh Instansi Pemerintah dan oleh masyarakat yang memerlukannya.
b. bahwa penyebarluasan Kompilasi Hukum Islam tersebut perlu dilaksanakan dengan sebaik-baiknya dan penuh tanggung jawab.
c. bahwa oleh karena itu perlu dikeluarkan Keputusan Menteri Agama Republik Indonesia tentang Pelaksanaan Instruksi Presiden Republik Indonesia Nomor 1 Tahun 1991 tanggal 10 Juni 1991.

Mengingat :

1. Pasal 4 (1) dan Pasal 17 Undang-Undang Dasar 1945.
2. Keputusan Presiden Republik Indonesia Nomor 44 Tahun 1974 tentang Pokok-Pokok Organisasi Departemen.
3. Keputusan Presiden Republik Indonesia Nomor 15 Tahun 1984 Tentang Susunan Organisai Departemen dengan segala perubahan terakhir Nomor 4 Tahun 1990.
4. Keputusan Menteri Agama Republik Indonesia Nomor 18 Tahun 1975 tentang Susunan Organisasi dan Tata Kerja Departemen Agama yang telah dirubah dan disempurnakan terakhir dengan Keputusan Menteri Agama Republik Indonesia Nomor 75 Tahun 1984.

MEMUTUSKAN

Menetapkan :	KEPUTUSAN MENTERI AGAMA REPUBLIK INDONESIA TENTANG PELAKSANAAN INSTRUKSI PRESIDEN REPUBLIK INDONESIA NOMOR 1 TAHUN 1991 TANGGAL 10 JUNI 1991.
Pertama :	Seluruh Instansi Departemen Agama dan Instansi Pemerintah lainnya yang terkait agar menyebarluaskan Kompilasi Hukum Islam di bidang Hukum Perkawinan, Kewarisan dan Perwakafan sebagaimana dimaskud dalam diktum Pertama Instruksi Presiden Republik Indonesia Nomor 1 Tahun 1991 untuk digunakan oleh Instansi Pemerintahan dan masyarakat yang memerlukannya dalam menyelesaikan masalah-masalah di bidang tersebut.
Kedua :	Seluruh lingkungan Instansi tersebut dalam diktum pertama dalam menyelesaikan masalah-masalah di bidang Hukum Perkwinan, Kewarisan dan Perwakafan sedapat mungkin menerapkan Kompilasi Hukum Islam tersebut di samping Peraturan Perundang-undangan lainnya.
Ketiga :	Direktur Jenderal pembinaan Kelembagaan Agama Islam dan Direktur Jenderal Bimbingan Masyarakat dan Urusan Haji mengkoordinasikan pelaksanaan Keputusan Menteri Agama Republik Indonesia ini dalam bidang tugasnya masing-masing.
Keempat :	Keputusan ini mulai berlaku sejak ditetapkan.

Ditetapkan di Jakarta
Pada tanggal 22 Juli 1991
MENTERI AGAMA
TTD
H. MUNAWIR SJADZALI

PRESIDENT OF THE REPUBLIC OF INDONESIA
INSTRUCTION OF PRESIDENT OF THE REPUBLIC OF INDONESIA
NUMBER 1 / 1991
PRESIDENT OF THE REPUBLIC OF INDONESIA

Considering :

a. that in the national seminar held in Jakarta from 2 to 5 February 1988 the Ulama of Indonesia have well accepted three drafts of the Compilation of Islamic Law, that consist of book one concerning marriage law, book two concerning inheritance law and book three concerning endowment law.
b. that the Compilation of Islamic Law mentioned in point a can be used as a reference by governmental institutions and by society governed by it in resolving the issues mentioned.
c. that the Compilation of Islamic Law mentioned at point a must be disseminated.

Based upon: Article 4 point (1) State Constitution 1945.

INSTRUCTS

To: Minister of Religious Affairs

to

FIRST: Disseminate the Compilation of Islamic Law which consists of:

a. Book I on Marriage Law
b. Book II on Inheritance Law
c. Book III on Endowment Law

As it has been approved within the national seminar held in Jakarta from 2 to 5 February 1988, in order that it is used (as a reference) by the governmental institutions and society governed by it.

SECOND: Realize the Instruction with his best and highest responsibility.

Issued in Jakarta on 10 June 1991
PRESIDENT OF REPUBLIC OF INDONESIA
Signed

SOEHARTO

The copy appears as its original
STATE SECRETARIAT OF RI
THE HEAD OF BUREAU OF LAW AND STATUTES
ttd
BAMBANG KESOWO, SH,LLM.

DECREE OF THE MINISTER OF RELIGIOUS AFFAIRS THE REPUBLIC OF INDONESIA NUMBER: 154 YEAR 1991 ON THE REALIZATION OF THE INSTRUCTION OF PRESIDENT OF THE REPUBLIC OF INDONESIA NUMBER 1 YEAR 1991 DATED 10 JUNE 1991 MINISTER OF RELIGIOUS AFFAIRS OF THE REPUBLIC OF INDONESIA

Considering :

a. that the Instruction of President of the Republic of Indonesia Number 1 Year 1991 on 10 June 1991, instructs the Minister of Religious Affairs to disseminate the Compilation of Islamic Law in order to be used by the governmental institutions and society concerned.

b. that the dissemination of the Compilation of Islamic Law must be realized (by the Minister of Religious Affairs) with his best and highest responsibility.

c. that based on the above, a Decree of the Minister of Religious Affairs on the Realization of the Instruction of the President of the Republic of Indonesia Number 1/1991 dated 10 June 1991 needs to be issued.

Based upon :

1. Article 4 (1) and Article 17 of State Constitution 1945.
2. the Decree of the President of the Republic of Indonesia Number 44 /1974 on the Principles of the Department Organizations.
3. the Decree of the President of the Republic of Indonesia Number 15/ 1984 on the Structures of the Department Organizations with its complete final amendments Number 4/ 1990.
4. the Decree of the Minister of Religious Affairs of the Republic of Indonesia Number 18/ 1975 on the Structures of Organizations and the Working Procedures of the Department of Religious Affairs which was amended by the Decree of the Minister of Religious Affairs of the Republic of Indonesia Number 75 / 1984.

DECIDES

To issue : A DECREE OF THE MINISTER OF RELIGIOUS AFFAIRS OF THE REPUBLIC OF INDONESIA ON THE REALIZATION OF THE INSTRUCTION OF THE PRESIDENT OF THE REPUBLIC OF NDONESIA NUMBER 1 YEAR 1991 DATED 10 JUNE 1991.

First : All the institutions of the Ministry of Religious Affairs and other governmental institutions are to disseminate the Compilation of Islamic Law on laws of marriage, inheritance and endowment as indicated from the first dictum of the Instruction of the President of the Republic of Indonesia Number 1/1991 in order that it be used as a reference by the governmental institutions and society concerned when resolving issues mentioned.

Second : All the domains of the institutions mentioned in the first dictum when resolving issues of marriage, inheritance and endowment must apply, besides the other regulations, the Compilation of Islamic Law mentioned to the greatest possible extent.

Third : The Director General of the Development of Religious Institutions and the Director General of the Supervision of Society and Hajj Affairs must coordinate in the realization of this Decree of the Minister of Religious Affairs based on their specialized tasks.

Forth : This Decree has legal effect beginning on its date of issuance.

Issued in Jakarta
Dated 22 July 1991
MINISTER OF RELIGIOUS AFFAIRS
SIGNED
H. MUNAWIR SJADZALI

Bibliography

Abdillah, Masykuri (1997), *Responses of Indonesian Muslim Intellectuals to the Concept of Democracy (1966-1993)*. Hamburg: Abera Network.

Abduh, Syuhada and Ali, Mursyid (eds.) (1995), "Pengkajian tentang Pandangan Masyarakat terhadap Perkawinan, Perceraian dan Poligami: Studi Kasus di Desa Rancahan dan Gabus Wetan Kabupaten Indramayu Jawa Barat", *Research Report*. Jakarta: Puslitbang Kehidupan Beragama, Departemen Agama.

Abdurrahman (1992), *Kompilasi Hukum Islam*. Jakarta: Akademika Presindo.

Abdurrahman, Thoha (1992), "Tinjauan terhadap Hukum Kewarisan KHI di Indonesia". Yogyakarta: Sekretariat IAIN Sunan Kalijaga.

Abubakar, El-Yasa (1998), *Ahli Waris Sepertalian Darah: Kajian Perbandingan Terhadap Penalaran Hazairin dan Penalaran Fiqh Madhhab*. Jakarta: INIS.

Abubakar, El-Yasa (1999), "Ihwal Perceraian di Indonesia: Perkembangan Pemikiran dari Undang-Undang Perkawinan sampai Kompilasi Hukum Islam", *Mimbar Hukum*, 44.

Adam, Ahmat (1997), "Islamic Elements in the Art of Malay Traditional Court Letter Writing", unpublished paper presented at the 35th International Congress of Asian and North African Studies, Budapest, Hungary, 7-12 July.

Ahmad, Amrullah (1994), *Prospek Hukum Islam dalam Kerangka Pembangunan Hukum Nasional di Indonesia: Sebuah Kenangan 65 Tahun Prof. Dr. H. Bustanul Arifin, S.H.* Jakarta: IKAHA.

Aini, Nuryamin (2002), "Penggunaan Jasa Pengacara dalam Kasus Perceraian", *Ahkam*, 10: 4, Faculty of Shari'a, UIN, Jakarta.

Aini, Nuryamin (2003), "Budaya Hukum: Melintas Batas Formalisme-Yuridis", *Era Hukum* 3.

Al-Hadar, Yasmine (1977), *Perkawinan dan Perceraian di Indonesia: Sebuah Studi antar Kebudayaan*. Jakarta: Lembaga Demografi Fakultas Ekonomi Universitas Indonesia.

Alizar, Jas (1998), "Pengertian Kata Walad dalam Surah al-Nisa Ayat 176", *Mimbar Hukum*, 40.

Al-Malibari, Shaykh Zainuddin ibn 'Abd al-Aziz (1978), *Fatḥ al Mu'īn bi Sharḥ Qurrat al-'Ayn*, (Reproduction). Bandung: Al-Ma'arif.

Al-Shiddieqy, Hasbi (1966), *Syari'at Islam Menjawab Tantangan Jaman*. Jakarta: Bulan Bintang.

Anderson, J.N.D. (1952), "The Personal Law of the Druze Community", *The World of Islam*, 2, 834.

Anderson, J.N.D. (1958), "The Tunisian Law of Personal Status", *International and Comparative Law Quarterly*, 7.

APIK (2003), "Pembakuan Peran dalam Kebijakan-Kebijakan di Indonesia". Jakarta: LBH-APIK.

Arifin, Bustanul (1995), "Fiqh dalam Bahasa Undang-Undang". Paper presented in a seminar in Surabaya, 8 July.

Arifin, Bustanul (1996), *Pelembagaan Hukum Islam di Indonesia: Akar Sejarah, Hambatan dan Prospeknya*. Jakarta: Gema Insani Press.

Arto, Mukti Arto (1996), *Praktek Perkara Perdata pada Pengadilan Agama*. Yogyakarta: Pustaka Pelajar.

Asad, Talal (2001), *Rethinking about Secularism and Law in Egypt*. Leiden: ISIM Papers.

Ashakul, T. (1990), *Regional and Provincial Urban and Population Projections*, Background Report 2-2, National Urban Development Policy Framework. Bangkok: Thailand Development Research Institute.

Aulawi, Wasit (1996), "Sejarah Perkembangan Hukum Islam di Indonesia", in Amrullah Ahmad (ed.) *Dimensi Hukum Islam dalam Sistem Hukum Nasional*. Jakarta: Gema Insani press.

Azra, Azyumardi (1992), *The Transmission of Islamic Reformism to Indonesia: Networks of Middle East and Malay-Indonesian 'Ulama'in the Seventeenth and Eighteenth Centuries*. Ph.D. Dissertation. New York: Columbia University.

Azra, Azyumardi (2002), *Jaringan Lokal dan Global Islam Nusantara*, Jakarta: Penerbit Mizan.

Badan Penelitian dan Pengembangan Agama (1995), "Pengkajian Tentang Pandangan Masyarakat terhadap Perkawinan, Perceraian dan Poligami: Studi Kasus di Kecamatan Nglegok", research report. Jakarta: Badan Penelitian dan Pengembangan Agama Departemen Agama.

Badjeber, Zain (1996), "Analisis Acara dan Penerapan Hukum", *Mimbar Hukum*, 24: 7.

Badjeber, Zain (1997), "Analysis Yurisprudensi tentang Perkara Kewarisan: Analisa Acara", *Mimbar Hukum*, 30: 8.

Baidlawi and Rahmat Syafe'i (1999), "Ketentuan Hak Waris Saudara dalam Konteks Hukum Islam: Kajian Terhadap Putusan Mahkamah Agung tentang Kewarisan Saudara dengan Anak Perempuan", *Mimbar Hukum*, 44.

Bisri, Cik Hasan (ed.) (1999), *Kompilasi Hukum Islam dan peradilan Agama dalam Sistem Hukum Nasional*. Jakarta: Logos Wacana Ilmu.

Bisri, Cik Hasan (ed.) (2000), "Dimensi Sosial Budaya dalam Pelaksanaan Kekuasaan Badan Peradilan Agama", *Mimbar Hukum*, 49: 3.

Benda, Harry J. (1983), *The Crescent and the Rising Sun: Indonesian Islam Under the Japanese Occupation, 1942-1945*. Dordrecht: Foris Publications.

Berg, C.C. (1953), "Islamisation of Java", *Studia Islamica*, 1.

Blackburn, Susan and Bessel, Sharon (1977), "Marriageable Age: Political Debates on Early Marriage in Twentieth-Century Indonesia", *Archipel*, 14, 132-136.

Bolland, B.J. (1970), *The Struggle of Islam in Modern Indonesia*. Leiden: KITLV.

Bowen, John R. (1998), "The Qur'an, Justice and Gender: Internal Debates in Indonesian Islamic Jurisprudence", *History of Religions*, 38:1, 52-78.

Bowen, John R. (1998), "You May Not Give It Away: How Social Norms Shape Islamic Law in Contemporary Indonesian Jurisprudence," *Islamic Law and Society* 5, 3: 382-408.

Bowen, John R. (2001), "Shari'a, State, and Social Norms in France and Indonesia", *ISIM Lectures*. Leiden: ISIM, 1-24.

Bowen, John R. (2003), *Islam, Law, Equality in Indonesia*. Cambridge: Cambridge University Press.

Buchari, Ibrahim (1971), *Sejarah Masuknya Islam dan Proses Islamisasi di Indonesia*. Jakarta: Publicita.

Buletin Dakwah Islam (2004), "Hizbut Tahrir: Menggugat Draft Kompilasi Hukum Inkar Syariat", *Buletin Dakwah Islam*, 226.

Buskens, Leon (2000), "An Islamic Triangle: Changing Relationship between *Shari'a*, State Law, and Local Customs", *ISIM Newsletter* 5.

Buskens, Leon (2003), "Recent Debates on Family Law Reform in Morocco: Islamic Law as Politics in an Emerging Public Sphere", *Islamic Law and Society*, 10: 1.

Cammack, Mark (1989), "Islamic Law in Indonesia's New Order", *International and Comparative Law Quarterly*, 38.

Cammack, Mark (1997), "An Empirical Assessment of Divorce Law Reform in Indonesia", *Studia Islamika*, 4: 4.

Cammack, Mark (1997), "Indonesia's 1989 Religious Judicature Act: Islamization of Indonesia or Indonesianization of Islam", *Indonesia*, 63.

Cammack, Mark (1999), "Inching towards Equality: Recent Developments in Indonesian Inheritance Law", *WUML Dossier* (22 November).

Carroll, Lucy (1998), "Orphaned Grandchildren in Islamic Law of Succession", *Islamic Law and Society*, 5: 1.

Coulson, N.J. (1971), *Succession in the Muslim Family Law*. Cambridge: The University Press.

Coulson, N.J. (1971), *History of Islamic Law*. Edinburgh: Edinburgh University Press.

De Stuers, Cora Vreede (1960), *The Indonesian Woman: Struggle and Achievements*. The Hague: Moutun & Co.

Departemen Agama (1977), *Putusan/Penetapan Pengadilan Agama/Mahkama Syar'iyyah Seluruh Indonesia Setelah Berlakunya UU No. 1/1974 Tentang Perkawinan*. Jakarta: Ditjen Bimas Islam Departemen Agama.

Departemen Agama (1980), *Himpunan Putusan/Penetapan Pengadilan Agama*. Jakarta: Proyek Pembinaan Badan Peradilan Agama Departemen Agama.

Departemen Agama (1992), *Compilation of Islamic Law, Marriage Law No. I/1974 and Islamic Judicature Law* of 1989. Jakarta: DEPAG.

Departemen Agama (1999), *10 Tahun Undang-Undang Peradilan Agama*. Jakarta: Chasindo.

Departemen Agama (2000), *Inpres R.I Nomor I/1991 Kompilasi Hukum Islam di Indonesia*. Jakarta: Dirjenbinbaga, Department Agama.

Departemen Agama (2001), *Laporan Hasil-Hasil Monitoring dan Evaluasi (Penelitian) Pelaksanaan Undang-Undang Peradilan Agama dan Kompilasi Hukum Islam*, Research Report. Jakarta: Ditbinbapera Departemen Agama.

Departemen Agama (2001), *Monitoring dan Evaluasi Pelaksanaan Undang-Undang Peradilan Agama dan Kompilasi Hukum Islam*. Jakarta: Ditbinbapera.

Departemen Agama (2002), *Himpunan Data Statistik Perkara di Lingkungan Peradilan Agama Seluruh Indonesia Tahun 2000*. Jakarta: Departemen Agama RI.

Durkheim, Emile (1993), *The Division of Labor in Society*, translated by G. Simpson. New York: Free Press.

Effendi, Bahtiar (1994), *Islam and the State: The Transformation of Islamic Political Ideas and Practices in Indonesia*, Ph.D. Dissertation. Ohio: Ohio University.

Effendi, Bahtiar (1995), "Islam and the State of Indonesia", *Studia Islamika*, 2: 2.

Effendi, Satria (1995), "Analisis Fiqh Terhadap Yurisprudensi Tentang Perceraian: Hak Hadhanah Akibat Perceraian Sebagai Fokus", *Mimbar Hukum*, 21: 6.

El Alami, Dawoud S. (1992), *The Marriage Contract in Islamic Law in the Shari'ah and Personal Status Laws of Egypt and Morocco*. London: Graham & Trotan Ltd.

Esposito, John L. (1982), *Women in Muslim Family Law*. New York: Syracuse University Press.

Esposito, John L. (2001), *Women in Muslim Family Law*. New York: Syracuse University Press.

Fachruddin (1998), "Murtad Sebagai Alasan Perceraian dan Impelementasinya di Pengadilan Agama", *Mimbar Hukum*, 39: 9.

Falaakh, Fajrul (1993), "Peradilan Agama dan Perubahan Tata Hukum Indonesia", in Drs. Dadan Muttaqien, M.Hum (eds.), *Peradilan Agama dan Kompilasi Hukum Islam dalam Tata Hukum Indonesia*. Yogyakarta: UII Press.

Falah, Minhajul (1983), "Perbandingan Hukum Kewarisan antara KHI dan Fiqh Mazhab Empat dalam Ketentuan Ahli Waris Beserta Bahagiannya", Faculty of Shari'a, IAIN, Jakarta.

Fealy, Greg (1996), "Wahab Chasbullah, Traditionalism and the Political Development of Nahdlatul Ulama", in Greg Fealy and Greg Barton, *Nahdlatul Ulama, Traditional Islam and Modernity in Indonesia*. Australia: Monash University.

Feener, Michael (2002), "Indonesian Movements for the Creation of a National Madhhab", *Islamic Law and Society* 9:1.

Feillard, Andree (1999), *NU vis a vis Negara, Pencarian Isi Bentuk dan Makna*. Yogyakarta: LKIS.

Gani, Abdul (1993), "Fakultas Syari'ah: Fungsi, Tugas dan Keluarannya (Faculty of Islamic Law: Role, Task, and its Graduates)", *Mimbar Hukum*, 1:4.

Gatra (2002), "Kompilasi Hukum Islam akan Ditingkatkan Jadi UU (The Compilation Would be Upgraded into Law)", *Gatra*, (19 September).

Geertz, Clifford (1960), *The Religion of Java*. Clencoe: Free Press.

Gerber, Haim (1999), *Islamic Law and Culture*, Leiden: E.J. Brill.

Hadikusuma, Hilman (1980), *Hukum Waris Adat*. Bandung: Penerbit Alumni.

Hadikusuma, Hilman (1991), *Hukum Waris Indonesia Menurut Perundangan, Hukum Adat, Hukum Agama Hindu, Islam*. Bandung: P.T. Citra Adtya Bakti.

Halim, Abdul (2000), *Peradilan Agama dalam Politik Hukum di Indonesia: Dari Otoriter Konservatif Menuju Konfigurasi Demokratis-Responsif*. Jakarta: PT RajaGrafindo Persada.

Harahap, M. Yahya (1988), "Praktek Hukum Waris tidak Pantas Membuat Generalisasi", in Saimima, *Polemik Reaktualisasi Ajaran Islam* 1997, *Kedudukan, Kewenangan, dan Acara Peradilan Agama (UU No. 7-Th 1989)*. Jakarta: Pustaka Kartini.

Harahap, M. Yahya (1999), "Informasi Materi Kompilasi Hukum Islam: Memfositifkan Abstarksi Hukum Islam", in Cik Hasan Bisri, *Kompilasi Hukum Islam dan Peradilan Agama dalam Sistem Hukum Nasional*, Jakarta: Logos Wacana Ilmu.

Hart, H.L.A. (1958), "Positivism and the Separation of Law and Morals", *Legal Review*.

Hart, H.L.A. (1961), *Concept of Law*. Oxford: Oxford University Press.

Harun, M. Yahya (1994), *Kerajaan Islam di Nusantara Abad XVI and XVII*. Yogyakarta: Kurnia Kalam Sejahtera.

Hasan, M. Kamal (1982), *Muslim Intellectual Responses to New Order Modernization in Indonesia*. Kuala Lumpur: Dewan Bahasa dan Pustaka.

Hasbullah Bakri (1983), "Lima Dalil Indonesia Bisa Disebut Negara Islam Non-Konstitutional", *Panji Masyarakat*, 439 (August), 29-31.

Hazairin (1952), *Indonesia Satu Mesjid*. Jakarta: Bintang Bulan.

Hazairin (1960), *Hendak Kemana Hukum Islam*. Jakarta: Tintamas.

Hazairin (1962), *Hukum Kekeluargaan Nasional*. Jakarta: Tintamas.

Hazairin (1963), *Hukum Islam dan Masyarakat*. Jakarta: Tintamas.

Hefner, Robert W. (1997), "Islamization and Democratization in Indonesia", *Islam in an Era of Nation-States*. Honolulu: University of Hawaii Press.

Hefner, Robert W. (2000), *Civil Islam: Muslim and Democratization in Indonesia*. Princeton: Princeton University Press.

Hidayatullah (2004), "Kerancuan Metodologi Draft Kompilais Hukum Islam", *Hidayatullah*, 15.

Hisyam, Muhammad (2001), "The Interaction of Religion and State in Indonesia", in Johan Meuleman, (ed.)., *Islam in the Era of Globalization: Muslim Attitudes Towards Modernity and Identity*. Jakarta: INIS.

Hisyam, Muhammad (2001), *Caught Between Three Fires: The Javanese Penghulu Under The Dutch Colonial Administration 1882-1942*, Ph.D. Dissertation. Leiden: Leiden University.

Hoadley, Mason C. (1971), "Continuity and Change in Javanese Legal Tradition: The Evidence of the Jayapattra", *Indonesia*, 11.

Hooker, M.B. (1981), *An Introduction to Javanese Law: A Translation of and Commentary on the Agama*. Arizona: The University of Arizona Press.

Hooker, M.B. (1998), "The State and Syari'ah in Indonesia 1945-1995", in Timothy Lindsey, *Indonesia, Law and Society*. Melbourne: The Federation Press, 107-108.

Hooker, M.B. (2002), *Indonesian Islam: Social Change through Contemporary Fatawa*. Honolulu: Allen & Unwin.

Hosen, Ibrahim (1987), *Persoalan Taqlid and Ijtihad*. Jakarta: Yayasan Wakaf Paramadina.

Hosseini, Ziba Mir (1993), *Marriage on Trial, A Study of Islamic Family Law: Iran and Morocco Compared.* London: I.B. Touris & Co Ltd.

Hudaeri, Mohamad (2003), "Tasbih dan Golok", *Istiqra,* 2: 1.

Hukum Online (2004), "Poligami, Masalah Krusial dalam Revisi Undang-Undang perkawinan", *www.hukumonline.com,* (2 November).

Hurgronje, Snouck, 'Sajjid Uthman's Gidds voor de Priesterraden', *Verspreide Geschriften,* 4-1. Bonn/Leipzig: Kurt Schroeder.

Husnan, Ahmad (1991), *Keputusan Al-Qur'an Digugat.* Bangil: Penerbit Yayasan al-Muslimun.

Indonesian Mediawatch (2002), "Islam Practiced in Indonesia", *Indonesia Mediawatch,* (11 January).

Ismail, Faisal (1996), "Pancasila as the Sole Basis for all Political Parties and for all Mass Organization: An Account of Muslim's Responses", *Studia Islamika,* 3: 4, 3.

Jaringan Islam Liberal (2003), "Kompilasi Hukum Islam Sangat Konservatif", *Jaringan Islam Liberal* (September).

John, Anthony H. (1987), "Indonesia: Islam and Cultural Pluralism", in John L. Esposito (ed.), *Islam in Asia: Religion, Politics, and Society.* New York: Oxford University Press.

Jones, Gavin W. (1994), *Marriage and Divorce in Islamic Southeast Asia* (Kuala Lumpur: Oxford University Press.

Jones, Gavin W., Asari, Yahya and Djuartika, Tuti (1995), "Divorce in West Java", *Journal of Comparative Family Studies,* 35.

Ka'bah, Rifyal (1999), *Hukum Islam di Indonesia: Perspektif Muhammadiyyah and NU.* Jakarta: Universitas Yarsi.

Ka'bah, Rifyal (2000), "Fiqh Muhammadiyyah Ketinggalan dari NU", *Suara Hidayatullah,* May, 1-8.

Ka'bah, Rifyal (2004), "Kompilasi Hukum Islam Tandingan/ The Legal Counter Draft of the Compilation of Islamic Law", a paper presented in the seminar held by the University of Yarsi, Jakarta, on 29 March.

Kammi (2005), "Konspirasi Hukum Peradilan Agama", *www.kammimipa.com,* (29 April).

Kantor Menteri Pemberdayaan Perempuan & PSW IAIN Jakarta (2000), "Laporan Studi Kebijakan dalam Rangka Penyajian dan Perbaikan Undang-Undang Perkawinan", Jakarta, Kantor Menteri Pemberdayaan Perempuan & PSW IAIN Jakarta.

Kaptein, Nico (1997), "Sayyid Uthman on Documentary Evidence", in *Bijdragen tot de Taal-, Land En Volkenkunde,* 153.

Karcic, Fikret (2001), "Applying the Shari'a in Modern Societies", in *Islamic Studies,* 40: 2.

Katz, June S. and Katz, Ronald S. (1975), "The New Indonesian Marriage Law: A Mirror of Indonesia's Political, Cultural and Legal System", *American Journal of Comparative Law,* 23.

Katz, June S. and Katz, Ronald S. (1978), "Legislating Social Change in a Developing Country: The New Indonesian Marriage Law Revisited", *Journal of Comparative Law,* 309.

Kelib, Abdullah (1993), *Peradilan Agama dan Kompilasi Hukum Islam dalam Tata Hukum Indonesia,* Yogyakarta: UII Press.

Kompas (2002), "Kawin Siri Karena Kompilasi kurang Tersosialisasi", *Kompas,* (22 January).

Kompas (2003), "Percerain di Bekasi Karena Soal Sepele", *Kompas,* Thursday, (24 April).

Kompas (2003), "RUU Terapan Peradilan Agama Digodok", *Kompas,* October.

Kompas (2004), "Di Malang 10 Kasus Gugatan Cerai Dalam Sehari", *Tempointeraktif,* (18 August).

Kuchiba, M., Tsubouchi, Y. and Maede, N. (1979), *Three Malay Villages: A Sociology of Paddy Growers in West Malaysia.* Honolulu: University Press of Hawaii.

Kustini (1995), *Pengkajian tentang Pandangan Masyarakat terhadap Perkawinan, Perceraian dan Poligami.* Jakarta: Department of Religious Affairs, Puslitbang.

Lawrence, Friedman (1969), "Legal Culture and Social Development", *Law and Society Review*, 4.

LBH APIK (2003), "Sejarah UU Perkawinan dan Pembakuan Perempuan dalam UU No. 1 Tahun 1974 tentang Perkawinan". Jakarta: LBH-APIK.

Lev, Daniel S. (1972), *Islamic Courts in Indonesia: A Study in the Political Bases of Legal Institution*. Berkeley: University of California Press.

Loebis, A.B. (n.d.), *Pengadilan Negeri Jakarta in Action: Jurisprudensi Hukum Adat Warisan*. Jakarta: n.p.

Lubis, M. Fadhil (1995), "The Unification and the Institutionalization of the Islamic Courts in the New Order Era", *Studia Islamika*, 2: 1, 1-51.

Lubis, M. Fadhil (1995), *Islamic Justice in Transition: A Socio-Legal Study of The Agama Court Judges in Indonesia*. Ph.D. Dissertation. Los Angeles: UCLA.

Madjid, Nurcholish (1970), "Keharusan Pembaharuan Pemikiran Islam dan Masalah Integrasi Ummat", in Nurcholish Madjid et.al *Pembaharuan Pemikiran Islam*. Jakarta: Islamic Research Center, 1-12.

Madjid, Nurcholish (1983), "Cita-Cita Politik Kita," in Bosco Carvallo and Dasrizal (ed.,), *Aspirasi Umat Islam Indonesia*. Jakarta: Lapenmas, 7-36.

Mahadi (1970), "Wewenang Pengadilan Agama" in *Hukum Nasional*, 3: 2.

Mahasin, Aswab (1990), "The Santri Middle Class: An Insider's View", in Richard Tanter and Kenneth Young (ed.), *The Politics of Middle Class Indonesia*. Victoria: CSEAS Monash University.

Mahfud, Moh., M.D. (1998), *Politik Hukum di Indonesia*. Jakarta: LP3ES.

Mahmood, Tahir (1972), *Family Law Reforms in the Moslem World*. New Delhi: The Indian Institute.

Mahmood, Tahir (1987), *Personal Law in Islamic Countries*. New Delhi: Academy of Law and Religion.

Majelis Ulama Indonesia (2004), 'Surat Pimpinan MUI' No. B-414/MUI/X/2004, (12 October).

Manan, Abdul (1992), "Pengembangan Sistem Hukum Nasional Dalam Rangka Memantapkan Negara Kesatuan RI Sebagai Negara Hukum", *Mimbar Hukum* 56.

Manan, Abdul (2003), *Hakim Peradilan Agama: Hakim di Mata Hukum, Ulama di Mata Umat*. Jakarta: Penerbit Pustaka Bangsa.

Mawardi, Ahmad Imam (1998), "A Socio-Political Backdrop of the Enactment of the *Kompilasi Hukum Islam*", MA Thesis. Montreal: McGill University.

Mawardi, Ahmad Imam (2003), "The Political Backdrop of the Enactment of the Compilation of Islamic Laws in Indonesia," in Arskal Salim and Azyumardi Azra (eds.), *Shari'a and Politics in Modern Indonesia*, 125-47.

Menteri Agama (2004), 'Surat Menag RI", No. MA/ 271/ 2004.

Menteri Agama (2004), "Surat Menag RI", No. MA/ 274/ 2004.

Mesraini (2001), "Gender dan KHI: Studi Kritis atas KHI dalam Perspektif Gender", MA Thesis, Jakarta, IAIN Jakarta.

Messick, Brinkley (1993), *The Calligraphic State: Textual Domination and History in a Muslim World*. California: University of California Press.

Moors, Annelies (2003), "Public Debates on Family Law Reform: Participations, Positions, and Styles of Argumentation in the 1990s", *Islamic Law and Society*, 10:1.

Morawetz, Thomas (1980), *The Philosophy of Law: An Introduction*. New York: Macmillan Publishing Co. Inc.

Mudzhar, Atho, M. (1990), *Fatwas of The Council of Indonesian 'Ulama: A Study of Islamic Legal Thought in Indonesia 1975-1988*, Ph.D. Dissertation. Los Angeles: UCLA.

Mudzhar, Atho, M. (2003), *Islam and Islamic Law in Indonesia: A Socio-Historical Approach*. Jakarta: Religious Research and Development and Training.

Mudzhar, Atho, M. (2004), "Peranan Analisis Yurisprudensi dalam pengembangan Pemikiran Hukum Islam", in Jaenal Araifin dkk, *Prof. Dr. H. Satria Effendi: Problematika Hukum Keluarga Islam Kontemporer.* Jakarta: Prenada Muda.

Mudzhar, Atho, and Nasution, Khairuddin (2003), *Hukum Keluarga di Dunia Islam Modern: Studi perbandingan Keberanjakan UU Modern dari Kitab-Kitab Fiqh.* Jakarta: Ciputat Press.

Mulia, Musdah (1999), *Pandangan Islam tentang Poligami*, Jakarta: Lembaga Kajian Agama & Gender.

Nakamura, Hisako (1983), *Divorce in Java* Yogyakarta: Gadjah Mada University Press.

Nasution, Khairuddin (2002), *Status Wanita di Asia Tenggara: Studi Terhadap Perundang-Undangan Perkawinan Muslim kontemporer di Indonesia dan Malaysia.* Jakarta: INIS.

Noeh, Zaini Ahmad (1980), *Sebuah Perspektif Sejarah Lembaga Islam di Indonesia.* Bandung: PT. Al-Ma'arif.

Noeh, Zaini Ahmad (1994), "Kepustakaan Jawa Sebagai Sumber Sejarah Perkembangan Hukum Islam", in Amrullah Ahmad (ed.), *Prospek Hukum Islam dalam Kerangka Pembangunan Hukum Nasional di Indonesia: Sebuah Kenangan 65 Tahun Prof. Dr. Bustanul Arifin, S.H.* Jakarta: IKAHA.

Noeh, Zaini Ahmad (1997), "Pembacaan Sighat Taklik Talak Sesudah Akad Nikah", *Mimbar Hukum*, 30: 8.

Noeh, Z.A., and Adnan, A. B. (1983), *Sejarah Singkat Pengadilan Agama Islam di Indonesia.* Surabaya: Bina Ilmu.

Notosusanto, R.P. (1953), *Peradilan Agama Islam di Djawa dan Madura.* Yogyakarta: s.n.

Nyazee, Imran Ahsan Khan (2002), *Theories of Islamic Law: The Methodology of Ijtihād.* Kuala Lumpur: The Other Press.

Peletz, Michael G. (2000), *Islamic Modern: Religious Courts and Cultural Politics in Malaysia.* Princeton: Princeton University Press.

Pelras, Christian (1993), "Religion, Tradition, and the Dynamics of Islamization in South Sulawesi", *Indonesia*, 57.

Pijper, G.F. (1934), *Fragmenta Islamica, Studien over Het Islamisme in Nederlandsch-Indie.* Leiden: E.J. Brill.

Pompe S, and Otto J.M. (1990), "Some Comments on Recent Developments in the Indonesian Marriage Law with Particular Respect to the Rights of Women", *Verfassung und Rech Ubersee*, 4.

Rahim, Husni (1998), *Sistem Otoritas dan Administrasi Islam: Studi tentang Pejabat Agama Masa Kesultanan dan Kolonial di Palembang.* Jakarta: PT Logos Wacana Ilmu.

Rahima (2003), "Study Praktek Polygamy dan Perceraian di Cinere, Jakarta Selatan", research report. Jakarta: Rahima.

Rahman, Tanzilur (1987), *Islamization of Pakistan.* Karachi: Hamdard Academy.

Ramage, Douglas E. (1995), *Politics in Indonesia: Democracy, Islam, and Ideology of Tolerance.* London: Routledge.

Rasyid, Roihan (1992), "Pengganti Ahli Waris dan Wasiat Wajibah", in Cik Hasan Bisri, *Kompilasi Hukum Islam.*

Ricklefs, M.C. (1979), "Six Centuries of Islamization in Java," in Nehemia Levtzion (ed.), *Conversion to Islam.* New York: Holmes & Meier.

Ricklefs, M.C. (1993), *A History of Modern Indonesia since c. 1300.* London: The Macmillan Press.

Riddell, Peter G. (2001), "Arab Migrants and Islamization in the Malay World during the Colonial Period", *Indonesian and the Malay World*, 29: 84.

Rohmaniyah, Inayah (2002), "Poligami dalam Perundang-Undangan di Indonesia", *Musawa*, I: 1 (March).

Rosen Lawrence (1989), *The Anthropology of Justice: Law as Culture in Islamic Society.* Cambridge: Cambridge University Press.

Sabrie, Zuffran (ed.) (2000), *Peradilan Agama di Indonesia: Sejarah Perkembangan Lembaga dan Proses Pembentukan Undang-Undangnya.* Jakarta: Ditbinbapera of the Department of Religious Affairs of the Republic of Indonesia.

Sabrie, Zuffran (ed.) (2001), *Peradilan Agama dalam Wadah Negara Pancasila: Dialog Tentang RUUPA.* Jakarta: Logos.

Saimina, Iqbal Abdurrauf (1988), *Polemik Reaktualisasi Ajaran Islam.* Jakarta: Pustaka Panjimas.

Saleh, Fauzan (2001), *Modern Trends in Islamic Theological Discourse in 20th Century Indonesia.* Leiden: Brill.

Saleh, Ismail (1990), "Eksistensi Hukum Islam dan Sumbangannya terhadap Hukum Nasional", in Zuffran Sabrie, *Peradilan Agama dalam Wadah Negara Pencasila: Dialog tentang RUUPA.* Jakarta: Pustaka Antara.

Salman, R. Otje (1993), *Kesadaran Hukum Masyarakat terhadap Hukum Waris.* Bandung: Alumni.

Sentosa, June Chadra (1996), *Modernization, Utopia, and the Rise of Islamic Radicalism,* Ph.D. Dissertation. Boston: Boston University.

Shaham, A. Layish R., "Nikah", *Encyclopaedia of Islam,* 178.

Shiddieqy, Nourouzzaman (1995), *Fiqh Indonesia: Penggagas dan Gagasannya.* Yogyakarta: Pustaka Pelajar.

Sihombing, Herman (1975), *Hukum Adat dalam Keputusan Pengadilan Negeri di Sumatera Barat.* Bandung: Penerbit Alumni.

Sjadzali, Munawir (1990), *Islam dan Tatanegara: Ajaran, Sejarah dan Pemikiran.* Jakarta: UI Press.

Sjadzali, Munawir (1993), *Islam: Realitas Baru dan Orientasi Masa Depan Bangsa.* Jakarta: Universitas Indonesia.

Sjadzali, Munawir (1997), *Ijtihad Kemanusiaan.* Jakarta: Yayasan Paramadina.

Soeharto (1990), *My Thoughts, Words, and Deeds,* English Translation by Sumadi. Jakarta: PT Gatra Lantoro Gung Persada.

Soekanto, Surjono (1977), "Hak Mewarisi Bagi Janda dan Anak / Anak Angkat," *Hukum Nasional,* 23, 73-96.

Soewondo, Nani (1977), "The Indonesian Marriage Law and Its Implementing Regulation", *Archipel,* 13, 284-285.

Sudarsono, Sidik (1964), *Masalah Administratif dalam Perkawinan Umat Islam Indonesia* Jakarta: Dara.

Syah, Ismail Muhammad (1984), "Pencaharian Bersama Suami Istri di Aceh Ditinjau dari Sudut UU Perkawinan Tahun 1974 dan Hukum Islam". A Doctoral Dissertation. Jakarta, 282-283.

Syarifuddin, Amir (1990), *PembaharuanPemikiran dalam Hukum Islam,* Padang: Angkasa Raya.

Syarifuddin, Amir (1999), *Permasalahan dalam pelaksanaan Farai'd,* Padang: IAIN IB Press.

Syarifuddin, Amir (2002), *Meretas Kebekuan Ijtihad: Isu-Isue Penting Hukum Islam Kontemporer di Indonesia.* Jakarta: Ciputat Press.

Taher, Tarmizi (1996), "Changing the Image of Islam", *Studia Islamika,* 3: 2, 6-21.

Tahido, Huzaemah (2001), *Fiqh Perempuan Kontemporer.* Jakarta: Al-Mawardi Prima.

Tamara, Nasir (1986), *Indonesia in the Wake of Islam: 1965-1985.* Malaysia: ISIS.

Tamara, Nasir (1990), "Islam under the New Order: A Political History," *Prisma,* June.

Tempo Interaktif (2004), "Menteri Agama Bekukan Draft Kompilasi Hukum Islam", *Tempointeraktif,* (26 October).

Tempo Interaktif (2004), "Menteri Agama Larang Diskusikan Draft Hukum Islam", *Tempointeraktif*, (19 October).

Tempo, "Halal Haramnya Kebulatan Tekad", *Tempo*, 26 May 1990.

Tihami, M.A. (1992), "Kepemimpinan Kyai dan Jawara di Banten", MA. Thesis, Jakarta: University of Indonesia.

Tresna (1978), *Peradilan di Indonesia dari Abad ke Abad*. Jakarta: Pradnya Paramita.

Truna, Dody (1992), *Islam and Politics under the New Order Government in Indonesia, 1966-1990*, MA Thesis. Montreal: McGill University.

Turner, Bryan S. (1974), *Weber and Islam: Critical Study*. London: Routledge and Kegan Paul.

Umam, Rofiqul, "Hendak Kemana Hukum Waris Islam (Whither the Islamic Law of Inheritance)", *Pelita*, (21 August 1992).

Van Bruinessen, Martin (1990), "Kitab Kuning: Books in Arabic Script Used in the Pesantren Milieu", *Bijdragen tot de Taal-, Land- en Volkenkunde*, 146.

Van Bruinessen, Martin (1994), "Pesantren and Kitab Kuning: Change and Continuity in a Tradition of Religious Learning", in Wolfgang Marschall (ed.), *Texts From the Islands: Oral and Written Traditions of Indonesia and the Malay World*. Berne: The University of Berne.

Van Bruinessen, Martin (1995), "Shari'a Court, Tarekat and Pesantren, Religious Institutions in the Banten Sultanate", *Archipel* 50.

Van Bruinessen, Martin (1996), "Traditions for the Future: The Reconstruction of Traditionalist Discourse within NU", in Greg Fealy and Greg Barton, *Nahdlatul Ulama, Traditional Islam and Modernity in Indonesia*.

Van der Chijs (1890), *Nederlandsch Indisch Plakaatboek VI*,

Wahid, Abdurrahman (1984), "Islam Punya Konsep Kenegaraan?", *Tempo*, 29 December, 17.

Wahyudi, Yudian (1993), *Hasbi's Theory of Ijtihād in the Context of Indonesian Fiqh*, MA thesis. Montreal: McGill University.

Weber, Max (1968), "Charisma and Institutionalization in the Legal System," in Eisenstads S.N. (ed.), *Max Weber: On Charisma and Institution Building*. Chicago: The University of Chicago Press.

Weber, Max (1967), *Max Weber on Law in Economy and Society*. New York: Simon and Schuster.

Widiana, Wahyu (2000), "Peradilan Agama di Indonesia: Status, Prospek, Tantangan dan Solusinya", paper presented in seminar on *Peradilan Agama di Indonesia (Islamic justice in Indonesia)* held by the Faculty of Shari'a, IAIN Jakarta, in 2001.

Wiegers, Gerard (1995), "Language and Identity: Pluralism and the Use of non-Arabic Language in the Muslim West", in Jan Platvoet and Karel van Der Toorn, *Pluralism and Identity: Studies in Ritual Behaviour*. Leiden: E.J. Brill.

Yanggo, Huzaemah Tahido (2005), *Kontroversi Revisi Kompilasi Hukum Islam*. Jakarta: Adelina.

Yusuf, Choirul Fuad, and Fauzi (2001), Mohammad Rosyid, *Laporan Kajian Proyektif Ketatalaksanaan di Lingkungan Departemen Agama tentang Survei Potensi Fisik dan Sosial Kantor Urusan Agama (KUA)*. Jakarta: Departemen Agama RI Badan Litbang Agama dan Diklat Keagamaan.

Zaid, Abdul Aziz Mohammed (1986), *The Islamic Law of Bequest*. London: Scorpion Publishing Ltd.

Zarkasy, Muchtar (1992), *Himpunan Peraturan Perundang-Undangan Badan Peradilan Agama di Indonesia*. Jakarta: Departemen Agama.

Zarkasyi, Muchtar (ed.) (1976), *Himpunan Peraturan Perundang-Undangan Badan peradilan Agama di Indonesia*. Jakarta: Department of Religious Affairs.

Zuhri, Saifuddin (1979), *Sejarah Kebangkitan Islam dan Perkembangannya di Indonesia*. Bandung: Al-Ma'arif.

Index

ICAS PUBLICATIONS SERIES

Monographs

Marleen Dieleman
The Rhythm of Strategy. A Corporate Biography of the Salim Group of Indonesia
Monographs 1
2007 (ISBN 978 90 5356 033 4)

Sam Wong
Exploring 'Unseen' Social Capital in Community Participation. Everyday Lives of Poor Mainland Chinese Migrants in Hong Kong
Monographs 2
2007 (ISBN 978 90 5356 034 1)

Diah Ariani Arimbi
Reading Contemporary Indonesian Muslim Women Writers. Representation, Identity and Religion of Muslim Women in Indonesian Fiction
Monographs 3
2009 (ISBN 978 90 8964 089 5)

Edited Volumes

Sebastian Bersick, Wim Stokhof and Paul van der Velde (eds.)
Multiregionalism and Multilateralism. Asian-European Relations in a Global Context
Edited Volumes 1
2006 (ISBN 978 90 5356 929 0)

Khun Eng Kuah-Pearce (ed.)
Chinese Women and the Cyberspace
Edited Volumes 2
2008 (ISBN 978 90 5356 751 7)

Milan J. Titus and Paul P.M. Burgers (eds.)
Rural Livelihoods, Resources and Coping with Crisis in Indonesia. A Comparative Study
Edited Volumes 3
2008 (ISBN 978 90 8964 055 0)

Marianne Hulsbosch, Elizabeth Bedford and Martha Chaiklin (eds.)
Asian Material Culture
Edited Volumes 4
2009 (ISBN 978 90 8964 090 1)

Hans Hägerdal (ed.)
Responding to the West. Essays on Colonial Domination and Asian Agency
Edited Volumes 5
2009 (ISBN 978 90 8964 093 2)

Derek Heng and Syed Muhd Khairudin Aljunied (eds.)
Reframing Singapore. Memory – Identity – Trans-Regionalism
Edited Volumes 6
2009 (ISBN 978 90 8964 094 9)

Friederike Assandri and Dora Martins (eds.)
From Early Tang Court Debates to China's Peaceful Rise
Edited Volumes 7
2009 (ISBN 978 90 5356 795 1)

Erich Kolig, Vivienne SM. Angeles and Sam Wong (eds.)
Identity in Crossroad Civilisations. Ethnicity, Nationalism and Globalism in Asia
Edited Volumes 8
2009 (ISBN 978 90 8964 127 4)

Khun Eng Kuah-Pearce and Gilles Guiheux (eds.)
Social Movements in China and Hong Kong. The Expansion of Protest Space
Edited Volumes 9
2009 (ISBN 978 90 8964 131 1)

Huhua Cao (ed.)
Ethnic Minorities and Regional Development in Asia. Reality and Challenges
Edited Volumes 10
2009 (ISBN 978 90 8964 091 8)